North Carolina

MAY 20th 1775
N C
APRIL 12th 1776

WESTHOLME STATE MILITARY HISTORY SERIES

North Carolina

A Military History

The Twelfth State of the Union

John R. Maass and Mark L. Bradley

WESTHOLME
Yardley

All images are from the Library of Congress, except where noted.

Westholme Publishing, LLC
904 Edgewood Road
Yardley, Pennsylvania 19067
Visit our Web site at www.westholmepublishing.com

ISBN: 978-1-59416-323-4
Also available as an eBook

Printed in the United States of America

To Robert M. Calhoon and Don Higginbotham

Contents

Maps

Introduction

As one of the first colonies explored and established in North America, what we now call North Carolina boasts a military history that goes back over four hundred years. From the expeditions of Spanish conquistadors in the mid-sixteenth century to English attempts to establish coastal outposts in the 1590s, the new land saw a variety of military actions since its earliest exploration, including conflicts with Native Americans, the expansion of European dynastic wars to the New World, and the race to secure ready access to slaves, riches, and other resources.

Establishment as an English (and later British) colony by the mid-seventeenth century did not bring perpetual peace to Carolinians. In addition to continued clashes with Indians over trade and land encroachment, several political disputes led to internal violent rebellions within the colony that undermined the stability and prosperity of North Carolina. Moreover, the colony's chronic inability to provide for its own defense made it a haven for pirates, leading to several naval operations to eradicate these maritime criminals.

For North Carolina, the American Revolution proved to be a painful experience. The new state was the scene of several key battles and campaigns during the war years, bringing devastation to many of its farms and communities. Moreover, hostilities between Patriots supporting independence and Loyalists who retained their allegiance to the British king were particularly violent and retributive, creating a bitter divide that lasted years. In the early nineteenth century, Carolinians also participated in the War of 1812 and the Mexican War, albeit in limited roles.

During the American Civil War, North Carolina played a pivotal role. As part of the Confederate States of America, the Tar Heel State was the scene of several important battles, including New Bern, Plymouth, Fort Fisher, and Bentonville. Moreover, in 1865, one of the two main armies of the Confederacy surrendered to Union forces at the Bennett Place near Durham Station, effectively ending the conflict. North Carolina provided key Rebel leaders such as Braxton Bragg, William D. Pender, and Stephen D. Ramseur, plus 125,000 Confederate soldiers to fight for Southern independence, as well as 3,321 white federal soldiers and 5,032 US Colored Troops who fought to preserve the Union and end slavery. In the postwar years, the state had to endure a military occupation during Reconstruction, but by the end of the nineteenth century, Carolinians once again served in the US Army during the Spanish-American War.[1]

The twentieth century saw two tragic world wars, conflicts on a massive scale, pitting the forces of dictators and tyrants against western democracies and parliamentary states. North Carolina contributed to the war efforts of both conflicts by its men and women in uniform and with several major military camps and bases within its borders, including Fort Bragg and Camp Lejeune. Finally, Tar Heels served in great numbers during the Cold War—particularly in Korea and Vietnam—and in current conflicts of the War on Terror.

This volume of Westholme's State Military History Series will provide readers with a comprehensive overview of North Carolina's long and storied martial past, recounting wars from the colonial period to the present, and relating the heroism and sacrifices of its citizens and soldiers over the past four centuries.

1. The Early Colonial Period

INITIAL EXPLORATIONS

The first attempts by European powers to occupy what is today the state of North Carolina were primarily military operations. The early history of the Tar Heel State shows it was claimed and occupied by two empires attempting to gain an advantage over their enemies during periods of conflict, although modern students, casual readers, and visitors to historic sites in the eastern United States often learn that colonies along the Atlantic coastline of North America were settled by those seeking religious freedom or commercial gain. By establishing military outposts along the Carolina coast in the sixteenth century, however, Spain and England sought to solidify their competing claims to territory in the New World, and to set up bases from which to attack their Old World rivals during periods of warfare, often undeclared.

Although material wealth was certainly a factor for the Spanish and the English, their efforts to inhabit North Carolina permanently came out of geopolitical pressures and the hostilities they created. Despite their competing interests in America, both powers failed for the same reasons in their attempts to set up distant military posts in North Carolina. Logistical difficulties, war with each other in European waters, and armed opposition of local Native Americans meant that by the first few years of the 1600s, neither England nor Spain had a single soldier or sailor within North Carolina.

THE SPANISH IN THE CAROLINAS

The early involvement of Spain in the exploration, exploitation, and settlement of the New World is most notable for the first successful voyage of Christopher Columbus to what became known in Europe as the West Indies in 1492. Columbus was merely the first of many Europeans during the next two centuries to explore that part of the New World eventually called North America. Spain first established small outposts, and later colonies, in the Caribbean Sea and on the Spanish Main (the northern coast of South America), but in the first half of the sixteenth century, a number of Iberian

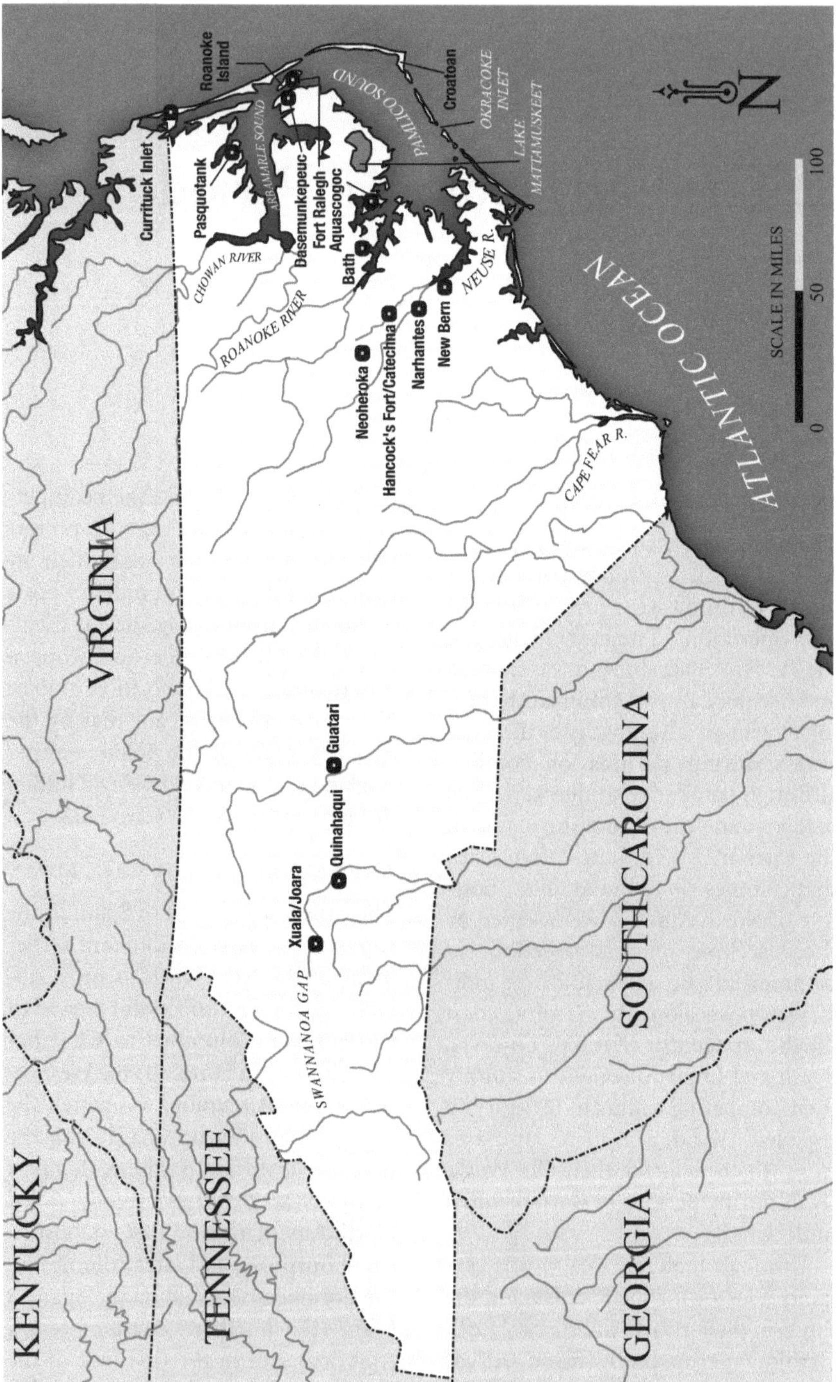
KENTUCKY
VIRGINIA
TENNESSEE
SOUTH CAROLINA
GEORGIA
ATLANTIC OCEAN
Currituck Inlet
Roanoke Island
Pasquotank
ALBAMARLE SOUND
Dasemunkepeuc
Fort Ralegh
Aquascogoc
PAMLICO SOUND
Croatoan
OKRACOKE INLET
LAKE MATTAMUSKEET
CHOWAN RIVER
ROANOKE RIVER
Bath
Neoheroka
Hancock's Fort/Catechna
Narhantes
New Bern
NEUSE R.
CAPE FEAR R.
Guatari
Quinahaqui
Xuala/Joara
SWANNANOA GAP
SCALE IN MILES
0
50
100
N

explorers reconnoitered North America's Atlantic and Gulf coasts. Among these adventurers were many well-known historical figures. Juan Ponce de Leon, conqueror of Puerto Rico, traveled in 1513 through the southern wilderness of what the Spanish called Florida, seeking an elixir for aging—as well as wealth and Indian slaves. The first documented instance of a European encountering the coastline of the modern Carolinas was in 1524, when the Florentine seafarer Giovanni da Verrazano, in the service of King Francis I of France, made two brief landfalls near present-day Cape Lookout. In the early 1500s, Francisco Gordillo and Pedro de Quejo began a voyage from the island of Española (Hispaniola) and sailed along the North American coast as far north as Delaware Bay. Quejo described part of the coast as having barrier islands, high sand dunes, and numerous pine trees, a possible early reference to North Carolina's distinctive shoreline.[1] Quejo's party also explored land around the mouth of the South Santee River, what they called the Rio Jordan, in what is now South Carolina.[2]

In 1526, sugar planter Lucas Vasquez de Ayllon, licensed by the Spanish King Charles V, commanded a seafaring expedition from Santo Domingo along the Atlantic coastline, where the men and women of the group attempted to plant a colony at Sapelo Sound in modern Georgia.[3] Ayllon built the town of San Miguel de Guadalupe, but the nascent settlement failed within three months when Ayllon died and his group faced disease, lack of food, desertions, slave revolts, Indian attacks, and inadequate support from Spanish authorities in the Caribbean. In addition to explorers and colonizers, by the early 1500s, Spanish slave traders encountered indigenous people along the North American coast, while shipwrecked vessels provided the setting for interactions with Indians as well.[4]

These voyages of reconnaissance were more than early surveys of the American shores and attempts to search for riches and slaves. The Spanish were also intent on establishing several military outposts on the North American coast to serve as fortified naval bases from which they could attack marauding French privateers and pirates, who in the early sixteenth century began to trade with the natives and attack Spanish ships in the Caribbean. Philip II, king of Spain from 1556 to 1598, also sought to establish colonies to thwart potential French settlements, evangelize the Indians, and protect Spain's valuable new possessions in the West Indies.[5] An attempted French fortified settlement in the early 1560s at Port Royal Sound, though short lived, alerted Spanish authorities to the danger posed by their European rivals in the New World.[6]

Spaniards did not limit their missions of discovery to the American coast. Even before Philip ascended the throne, Spanish adventurers had begun their explorations into the interior of what became the southeastern United States. The first to travel by foot throughout this region was the conquistador Hernando de Soto, a man of extensive experience in the Americas. He had been granted a license (*asiento*) to conquer and colonize La Florida, which the Spanish considered to be all of North America as it was then

Hernando de Soto.

known, and to exploit the reputed wealth in the form of gold and silver of these unknown lands. Indicative of the military nature of the expedition, de Soto received an appointment as governor and captain-general of La Florida, as well as governor of Cuba.[7] Coming ashore near Tampa Bay in March 1539, with an army of six hundred soldiers, dozens of slaves, several priests, and perhaps a few women, de Soto led his well-armed column north on what was to be an epic, four-thousand mile journey that ended in 1543 at the mouth of the Mississippi River. Part of the expedition's route took the Spaniards from South Carolina into the western part of North Carolina in 1540, as de Soto followed ancient Indian trails upstream along the Wateree and Catawba Rivers. Based on his experience in Peru, where rich silver mines were located in the mountains, de Soto turned west from what is now the area around Hickory and headed for the Blue Ridge in search of riches. After spending two days at the Indian town he called Xuala, located several miles from modern Morganton, the Spanish host continued across the mountains (probably at Swannanoa Gap), then traveled through most of the modern states of the American South. Finding few riches but encountering numerous native enemies and difficult terrain, de Soto finally died of fever on the banks of the Mississippi before the desperate survivors of his command were able to leave the mighty river's delta and sail for Mexico in 1543.[8]

De Soto failed to discover any wealth, aside from caches of inferior quality river pearls he and his men came across as they explored the dense forests and numerous waterways of the American South, and his expedition did not establish any permanent settlements or military posts there. Nevertheless, his wilderness excursions encouraged other men in Spanish service to establish a presence along the Atlantic coast, with an eye toward thwarting French designs, capturing slaves to labor on Caribbean sugar plantations, and protecting their other lucrative New World possessions. The Spanish maintained that the southeastern lands of North America were their exclusive possession, by right of their explorations earlier in the sixteenth century. They also buttressed their claim based on an episode in 1566, in which a forlorn group of shipwrecked Spanish sailors planted a cross in the name of their emperor on the Carolina coast near Currituck Inlet on the Outer Banks, although no settlement or fort was established there.[9] As was customary among all European powers of the day, claiming ownership of a newly discovered land had to be substantiated by actually occupying it in order to realize any such pretentions to possession. With this in mind, Spanish royal authorities sought to establish a presence along the American shores with the foundation of St. Augustine as a military post in 1565 on the Atlantic coast of what is now northern Florida.[10]

Having erected their fortified base at St. Augustine, the Spanish moved quickly to expand their control of North American territory. By the late 1550s, French pirates had become a serious danger to Spanish shipping in the sea lanes of the western Atlantic and had cut Spain's vital revenues from the New World in half through their incessant attacks. As a result, it became imperative for the Spanish to establish another base north of St. Augustine, protect the valuable silver fleets, support Spain's claim to Florida, and provide succor to the numerous Spanish shipwrecks on the American coast.[11] Under the command of Pedro Menendez de Aviles, an experienced privateer and captain-general of Spain's Indies fleet, the Spanish planted several outposts on the Atlantic coast, including Santa Elena, established in April 1566 near the site of an earlier French establishment at the harbor in Port Royal Sound. This small outpost, on present-day Parris Island, South Carolina, including Forts San Salvador and San Felipe, was to be the Spanish capital in North America, although it was permanently abandoned ten years later.[12]

Soon after landing at Santa Elena, Menendez decided to reconnoiter the interior of the country, establish several outposts there among the native peoples, and search for a secure overland route to the Spanish-controlled silver mines at Zacatecas, Mexico, which in his geographical ignorance he believed to be relatively close. The expedition would shore up Spanish claims to the unknown territory and establish amiable relations with native peoples along the way, with hopes of converting them to Roman Catholicism as well.[13] No doubt he hoped that friendly relations with the local indigenous societies would also lead to the discovery of gold, silver, jewels, or other riches that the Spanish could exploit. Menendez also organized the mission to relieve the logistical problems of having too many men in the new and precarious coastal settlement, and because the overcrowded garrison had just endured a mutiny. Thus, he ordered his subordinate, Captain Juan Pardo, an infantry officer who had arrived at Santa Elena in July 1566 with a force of 250 men, to prepare an expedition to explore the wilderness and claim it for the Spanish Crown. Pardo had earlier led a two-month exploration along the modern Georgia/South Carolina border and therefore had experience commanding this type of reconnaissance. The captain led 125 soldiers on foot from the Carolina coast on December 1, 1566, following several rivers north into the uncharted territory.[14]

Early the following month, Pardo's force reached the village of Joara. This was the ancient seat of a Mississippian chiefdom and an extensive trade center, located on Upper Creek, a tributary of the Catawba River in the Blue Ridge foothills. It was also the same town de Soto called Xuala (near mod-

The French Broad River at the Swannanoa.

ern Morganton, North Carolina) when he had been there two decades earlier, situated in "a rich land . . . of mountain ridges and flat tracks of arable land, good for all the crops of the world," according to one Spaniard. Pardo distributed gifts to Indian leaders in a diplomatic effort to maintain a cordial relationship with the local people. The soldiers built a small defensive post, called Fort San Juan, which included four or five structures and was likely surrounded by a wooden palisade. This fort, as one historian has concluded, was "the earliest European settlement in the interior of the present-day United States" and was intended to be a permanent Spanish outpost. Seeing snow in the mountains, the Spanish commander decided to forego further exploration to the west that winter. Rather, Pardo left thirty men there, under the command of Sergeant Hernando Moyano de Morales, with "their munitions of powder, matchcord, balls, and maize to eat." The soldiers were armed with crossbows and harquebuses, heavy matchlock guns. Pardo led the rest of his men east and reached the Indian town called Quinahaqui, close to what is now the Piedmont town of Catawba. At this point he received word that Santa Elena was under the threat of a seaborne French attack. He marched directly there with all but four of his soldiers and a missionary, and reached the coast in early March 1567.[15]

Sometime after Pardo departed the fort at Joara, Sergeant Moyano and twenty soldiers traveled with a party of the village's warriors in the early spring through rugged mountains to attack hostile Chiscas Indians at a fortified town called Maniateque in southwestern Virginia, near Saltville. Some evidence shows that after the successful attack, the Spanish sergeant received payment in gold from his indigenous allies. After their return, Moyano made a preemptive strike with a dozen or so soldiers to assist a local chief against threatening native towns in eastern Tennessee, where the soldiers burned villages and crops, having crossed the Blue Ridge Mountains at Swannanoa Gap, and descended along the French Broad River.[16] The Spanish moved farther west to the Chiaha region and built a small palisade fort there, near the fortified native capital of Olamico, in the upper Tennessee River Valley. Soon, Moyano was met by his commander, Captain Pardo, who had received word in September that the sergeant's tramontane foray had met with trouble and hurriedly marched to his relief with a force of approximately one hundred men.

From Olamico, where hostile Muskogean-speaking Indians remained nearby, the Spanish soldiers established a second stronghold named Fort San Pablo, but they fought no additional engagements with local natives while in Chiaha.[17] Pardo considered further expeditions from this point on the western side of the Appalachians, but fearing native attacks, he began a movement back across the Blue Ridge in good order. The column reached Joara on November 6, and three weeks later, on November 24, Pardo left an ensign and thirty men at the fort while he proceeded to the coast with the rest of his weary soldiers. In mid-December, the Spanish built Fort Santiago, with log and earth bastions, tall towers, and wooden palisades at Guatari near today's Trading Ford on the Yadkin River. Along the rivers of the Carolina Piedmont, several smaller defensive posts, dependent on the Indians for food and other necessities, were established at the same time among the native villages. Leaving small details of soldiers at all of these posts, in early January, Pardo continued his trek to the coast and arrived back at Santa Elena on March 2, 1568.[18]

At some point after Pardo had departed Joara, for reasons still unknown, the native people attacked Fort San Juan and killed all the Spanish garrison except one soldier, Juan de Badejoz, who managed to flee to Santa Elena, walking and hiding from hostile natives for thirty days as he followed the Catawba and Wateree Rivers south. Evidence shows that Fort San Juan was burned, although it is not clear whether this occurred at the time the Spanish were there or afterward. As would be the case at the English settlements at Roanoke and Jamestown, perhaps the Spanish soldiers wore out their welcome with excessive demands for food, or indiscretions with native

Princess Xualla presenting a necklace of pearls to Hernando de Soto, at Cofachiqui.

women.[19] Word reached Santa Elena by May 1568 that Indians had attacked and destroyed all the forts in the distant foothills and mountains, including the recently constructed Fort Santiago on the Yadkin and the remote outpost in Chiaha.[20] Eventually, even Santa Elena was abandoned and burned by the Spanish under pressure from hostile Indian neighbors, and in the following decades, almost all visible traces of the Spanish presence in the Carolinas disappeared.

ROANOKE

As Spanish efforts to establish a permanent military presence in the Carolinas eventually met with failure, English attempts to do the same were just beginning. England came late to the contest for colonies in the Western Hemisphere, long after the Spanish, French, and Portuguese had laid claim to the most valuable islands and coastlines of the Caribbean and South America. Nevertheless, Crown officials, military leaders, and London businessmen recognized the need to found a permanent establishment in

Sir Walter Ralegh, engraving by Simon van de Passe.

the New World in the late 1500s. The basis for the English claim to North America rested on the voyages of John Cabot, a Genoese maritime explorer financed by Bristol merchants who hoped to find a new trade route to the Far East. In 1497, Cabot had explored the eastern coast of Canada,[21] sailing under a charter from the English king, Henry VII. It is uncertain exactly where he explored in North America, but it was most likely north of Cape Cod. Additionally, by the last few decades of the fifteenth century, English fishing vessels were active off Newfoundland.[22]

For much of the sixteenth century, the focus of English colonization was not the New World but closer to home in Ireland.[23] Many English nobles—including Walter Ralegh (also spelled Raleigh)—had vast tracts of land there and sought to populate the island with English settlers at the expense of the native Irish. By the last quarter of the century, however, English interest in America had increased. Spain had already established a major presence in the New World and had reaped immense economic benefits from its efforts to exploit the Americas. This new wealth did not escape the notice of the English upper classes, and soon England and Spain were commercial and political adversaries, locked in a rivalry accentuated by profound religious differences. Spain's commercial success in the New World, and its political dominance in Europe, posed a serious threat to England's autonomy, if not its very existence.[24] However, Queen Elizabeth I ruled a weak country in the second half of the sixteenth century, one not in a position to challenge Spain directly, even in America. England's grip on Ireland was limited and tenuous at best, while neighboring Scotland was still a separate kingdom, under the influence of the French, with whom England did not have an amicable relationship. Elizabeth tried to maintain a careful cordiality with Spain, but the Spanish dominance and bellicosity in the Netherlands, directed against Protestants there, threatened England's own geopolitical safety. The accounts of abuses and violence (some of which were undoubtedly exaggerated) perpetrated by Philip's powerful armies just across the English Channel alarmed Elizabeth for the safety of her own land and people. Would England be next to suffer attacks by Spain's powerful fleet and armies? As historian Karen O. Kupperman has noted, England tried to "maneuver between the superpowers, France and Spain," attempting to avoid conflict in what was the Cold War of the sixteenth century, particularly in terms of religious conflict. By the early 1570s, the English queen allowed her subjects to volunteer for military service in the Low Countries against the Spanish in the wars of religion, and a few years later, Englishmen took a more active, if not totally overt, way of combating the Spanish enemy.[25]

Prior to the reign of Henry VIII of England (r. 1509–1547), relations between the Spanish and the English had been harmonious, due in part to their mutual enmity toward France. With Henry's contentious divorce of his Spanish wife Catherine of Aragon and his feud with the Roman Catholic Church over his marital controversy, good will between the two kingdoms began to wane. After the death of Henry, and his son Edward VI in 1553, the diplomatic situation seemed to improve somewhat on the accession to the English throne of Queen Mary, the Catholic daughter of Catherine of Aragon. Mary's marriage in 1554 to Philip II of Spain, son of Emperor Charles V, worried rather than placated her Protestant opponents, especially when Charles abdicated in 1556, making Mary's new husband the king of Spain. Mary's death two years later brought Elizabeth I, an unwavering Protestant, to the English throne, where she reigned forty-four years, during most of which time she was without foreign allies. She was an ardent foe of the Spanish, who supported the claim of her archrival Mary Stuart ("Queen of Scots") to rule England. After becoming Elizabeth's prisoner in 1586 following her deposition in Scotland by Protestant nobles, the Roman Catholic Mary suffered execution in February 1587, a shocking event that brought on outright war between Spain and England and eventually led to the attack on the British Isles by the Spanish Armada in 1588.[26]

By the 1570s it had become clear to Queen Elizabeth, many of her advisers, and a number of enterprising English sea captains that Spain could be weakened short of a full-scale war in Europe and in the waters of the English Channel. Rather, the English began to attack Spanish shipping and colonial possessions in the New World, but instead of state-based warfare on the high seas and the American coast, Elizabeth allowed the practice of privateering, wherein ships privately owned and outfitted but authorized by her government attacked and captured enemy vessels and their cargoes. In 1577, Elizabeth read a document titled "A discourse how Her Majesty may annoy the King of Spaine by fitting out a fleet of shippes of war under pretence of Letters of Patent, to discover and inhabit strange places." This proposal, written by Sir Humphrey Gilbert, allowed English vessels to attack Spanish ships and colonial possessions without involving the queen directly, and let the cash-strapped monarch avoid a costly naval buildup. It was, instead, closer to a private understanding between Elizabeth and the many nautical adventurers who sailed west and south from the British Isles to get rich at the expense of the wealthy Spanish. She approved the proposal, which in effect gave the daring English "sea dogs" a virtual license to raid Spain's New World possessions and capture its ships at sea. The queen also got a share of the profits these sea raiders accumulated on their voyages.[27]

While lucrative for English crews, attacking Spanish ships laden with gold and silver mined in Peru, Mexico, and Cuba on their way from colonial seaports back to Spain could have only a limited effectiveness if poorly supported by the home government. Several of Elizabeth's advisers, most notably her court favorite, Walter Ralegh, realized that in order to challenge Spanish power more effectively, England had to build its own colonies and bases in the New World, to allow for attacks on the Spanish fishing and treasure fleets in the western Atlantic and Caribbean Sea. From the 1560s, Spanish treasure ships gathered at Havana, then sailed in the summer for home, frequently navigating through the Florida Strait or the Bahama Channel and floating up the Gulf Stream, sometimes as far north as the waters off Kill Devil Hills on the Outer Banks before turning east to cross the North Atlantic. From this need for permanent military outposts in the New World from which to raid, capture, and disrupt Spanish shipping emerged the impetus for the establishment of a colony at Roanoke in what became North Carolina.[28]

With a six-year charter, Queen Elizabeth authorized Sir Humphrey Gilbert in 1578 to explore the North American coast and establish colonies there in the "heathen and barbarous lands" not already claimed or occupied by any "Christian Prince or people."[29] This was a wise choice, as Gilbert had served in the Netherlands against the Spanish and in Ireland putting down several native rebellions, for which he was knighted. He was a strong advocate of using terror to subjugate the indigenous Irish during the process of colonization and developed a notoriety for doing so by his "astonishing ruthlessness" in an age when such practices were common. After a few unsuccessful attempts at transatlantic expeditions, Gilbert set sail for Newfoundland in June 1583, with a small fleet and the financial backing of several wealthy Bristol merchants. In August he made landfall on the rocky North American coast in Newfoundland, but due to the inhospitable nature of the territory, he abandoned his efforts at colonization there and sailed for home. Gilbert's flagship sank in a violent storm off the Azores on the return voyage, and he perished in the disaster.[30]

Undeterred by this calamity, Ralegh, Gilbert's ambitious younger half-brother, assumed Gilbert's interest in the charter and obtained additional financial backers. The staunchly Protestant Ralegh was a well-known courtier, soldier, and businessman in Elizabethan England, and for many years a favorite of the queen. In 1584, he received a new charter in his own right and, though barred by Elizabeth from personally sailing, launched an exploratory expedition of two ships commanded by Captains Philip Amadas and Arthur Barlowe, assisted by Simon Fernandez, a Portuguese-born pilot living in England who had previous experience navigating American waters. The ships left from Plymouth, England, in late April 1584, followed Columbus's original route west from the Canary Islands, and reached the Carolina coast on July 13, at what they called Port Ferdinando, opposite the south end of Roanoke Island inside the Outer Banks. The location looked promising for staging raids on Spanish convoys from a secure, permanent base. The island was concealed within the barrier islands of the coast and was largely immune to a direct attack by sea, especially by large Spanish warships, whose deep drafts would prevent them from nearing it. This spot would also allow smaller English vessels to remain active in American waters all year, without the need to return to home ports in the British Isles for refitting.[31] Moreover, Amadas and Barlowe found the island to be a "most pleasant and fertile ground," populated by friendly indigenous people.[32]

The natives the English encountered were part of three major groups inhabiting the Outer Banks and shallow sounds in the later sixteenth century: the Secotans, Weapemeocs, and Chowanocs, all Algonquian-speaking peoples. The Chowanocs lived on the western side of the Chowan River, while on the eastern side of the river were the Weapemeocs, who occupied the land down to the north shore of Albemarle Sound. Between Albemarle Sound and the Pamlico River to the south was the home of the Secotans, led by the chief Wingina. His brother, Granganimeo, was the local ruler on Roanoke Island and the first tribal leader to meet Amadas and Barlowe shortly after their arrival. South of the area these three main groups occupied were hostile Indians, who were unaffiliated politically with the Secotans, Weapemeocs, and Chowanocs. These included the Pamlicos, the Neuse, and the Coree, all Iroquoian speakers. Perhaps as many as seven thousand native peoples of the Algonquian and Iroquoian language and cultural groups lived in this coastal region in the late sixteenth century.[33]

The inhabitants of Roanoke Island were frequently at odds with neighboring Indians, especially those on the southern shores of Pamlico Sound. In fact, shortly before the arrival of the English ships, the Secotans and Pamlicos had fought a brief war in which Wingina had been severely wounded, making him unable to travel to meet the Europeans on the Outer Banks when they came ashore. As the English would soon discover, Indian warfare was somewhat limited in scale, wherein the warriors used bows and arrows, clubs, and wooden swords.[34] Thomas Hariot, who accompanied the 1585 Gilbert expedition, published "A Brief and True Report" of the new land he observed and included some details on Indian warfare. The native people had "no edged tools or weapons of iron or steel" and did not know how to manufacture them. The "only weapons they possess are bows made of witch hazel, arrows made of reeds, and flat-edged wooden truncheons, which are about a yard long." Hariot also described the warrior's "armour made of sticks wickered together with thread, and they carry shields made of bark." In terms of tactics, "their manner of making war against each other is by a surprise attack, either in the dawn of day or by moonlight, by ambush, or by some such subtle trick. Set battles are very rare. When they do take place, it is always in the forests, where the natives may defend themselves by leaping behind a tree after they have shot their arrows."[35] While the initial interaction with the Indians of Roanoke was peaceful, hostility came to characterize the relationship between Englishmen and some of the native peoples soon enough.

Barlowe's men explored the area from Roanoke Island, where they were invited by the local native peoples to establish a temporary camp near their village during a six-week stay, though they still did not meet the wounded chief Wingina. The Englishmen and Indians traded food, hides, pearls, metalware, and other goods despite the language barrier, although the English never let their guard down and remained wary of the Secotans. The natives were impressed by the strangers' metal knives, axes, and hatchets, and "would have given anything for swords," according to Barlowe, who also noted that the Indians trembled in fear when the Englishmen discharged their firearms. The Indian leader Granganimeo, with whom the Englishmen first interacted, attempted to get the soldiers to attack the Roanoke Indians' enemy at a palisaded village called Pomeiooc east of modern Lake Mattamuskeet. Barlowe declined to become involved in the rivalry against these Neiosioke people, whom the Roanoke Islanders described as warlike and aggressive. Still friendly with the Secotans, the English persuaded two local tribesmen, Manteo and Wanchese, to return to London with them. The Indians planned to learn all they could of English power while there, hoping to better understand how to use their new white allies against their local enemies. As it turned out, Manteo, a Croatoan, remained friendly to the English after his return to Virginia the following year, but Wanchese did not befriend them and remained true to his Roanoke people and their chief, Wingina.[36] Not all was peaceful for the men of Ralegh's reconnaissance, however. Although the details are obscure, it seems that while exploring the north coast of Albemarle Sound, a detachment of soldiers under the command of Amadas fought a sharp skirmish with native warriors in which several Englishmen were killed. The survivors had to return to Roanoke in haste, where they rejoined Barlowe and the rest of the expedition. The enemy warriors were not Secotans of Roanoke Island, with whom the English newcomers remained on good terms.[37]

It should be remembered that Ralegh's first mission was for the most part a military expedition, not primarily an effort at colonization or trade, although the prospect for immediate financial gain was never far from the thoughts of the planners or officers of the voyage. Ralegh consulted a military expert during the planning stages, possibly Sir Roger Williams, a veteran of the sixteenth century wars on the European continent. Ralegh was advised to employ a strong force of about eight hundred soldiers, some of whom would build a large fort inside of which the town would be located. The expedition would need an engineer and, perhaps most importantly, a general in overall command, as well as lesser military officers. Armorers and specialists in fortification would be useful as well, although a suggested plan for defensive works was more elaborate than could reasonably be constructed in America. Other advisers Ralegh consulted warned him that the men should be held in strict order, firmly disciplined, so as not to alienate the natives, and that soldiers would be needed to guard the primary camp or station from Indians and the Spanish.[38]

The new settlement Ralegh envisioned was intended to be a base for attacking Spanish shipping and a haven for repairing and resupplying English raiding ships.[39] Yet despite the important military and strategic implications of Ralegh's efforts to establish a post on the American coast, Queen Elizabeth contributed few funds, no ships, and only a small supply of gunpowder to the effort. "Essentially the venture was to be a private one, with the Queen's authority and blessing but little material help," wrote noted historian of Roanoke David B. Quinn.[40] However, the success of the initial scouting mission in summer 1584 led to more resources being made available to Ralegh to further his efforts at establishing an English presence in what was then known as Virginia, a huge area encompassing all of modern North Carolina. Under Ralegh's overall direction, the next voyage was led by his ambitious cousin, Sir Richard Grenville, an experienced soldier fighting Turks in Hungary and formerly the sheriff of Cornwall, where he battled the power of the Catholic aristocracy for the queen. Grenville left England in April 1585, with seven well-armed ships, given the ongoing hostilities with Spain. As this was to be another military expedition, Grenville's command included three hundred soldiers and skilled auxiliaries,[41] most armed with pistols and a cavalier or a pike. The men also brought bows and arrows on board, some armor, and wooden shields to ward off primitive

A Chief of Roanoke, Theodor de Bry, engraver.

Indian weapons. Grenville's pilot was Simon Fernandez, who had been on the previous year's expedition. Philip Amadas, the colony's admiral, sailed with the fleet as well. Also joining the expedition was Ralph Lane, a contentious soldier and courtier who had until recently been serving as sheriff of County Kerry in Ireland. Lane was to act as the colony's governor once the expedition landed in Virginia to establish a military base.[42]

During the voyage, a violent storm scattered the ships off Portugal, and one of the smaller vessels was lost. The fleet's armed flagship, the queen's own *Tyger*, landed at Puerto Rico, where crew members built another ship over the course of two weeks. On the journey north toward Virginia, the ships engaged in privateering in the West Indies, during which time one of them, *Lyon*, become separated from the rest of the fleet. Despite these setbacks, in late June 1585, the remaining vessels of Grenville's fleet arrived at

Wococon (modern Portsmouth Island) on the Outer Banks, where they found some of the other scattered ships already at anchor. The lighter boats sailed into the sound by late July and established an outpost on the northern end of Roanoke Island. Here they finally encountered Wingina, who invited the English to live nearby—and away from rival native peoples. Grenville and his pilots, however, found the site ill suited for larger ships. The same sandbars that prevented Spanish galleons from approaching near the island also forced the larger English ships to anchor off the banks in the open sea, which exposed them to stormy weather and enemy forces. Despite Grenville's concerns, Governor Lane ordered the construction of a defensive work, which he named Fort Ralegh, as well as other necessary buildings to support the settlement. Calling it "the newe forte in Verginia," Lane knew that some fortification was necessary on the initial landing site, even if the Englishmen later chose a more suitable location for their privateering base.[43]

Although no contemporary plans, drawings, or illustrations exist for the new defensive structure, it is known from written descriptions and modern archaeology that Fort Ralegh was a conventional design, which included several strong points at the corners. The earthen fort mounted several cannons as well, but it is unknown if the fort had a palisade or was simply fenced. Ralegh's advisers in England had recommended a fort large enough to surround all the houses and to include an open square. It was to be five sided and protected by a palisade of vertically emplaced logs—a plan similar to the fort erected at Jamestown some twenty years later. Instead Lane's men built the fort with perhaps one structure within it and several houses outside the defenses. Archaeological evidence suggests the fort was largely completed by September 1585, and it appears the fort was constructed in a diamond shape, with bastions projecting from three sides, enclosing approximately fifty square feet. The walls were six-feet high from the inside, with a firing step along them in the interior. It should be recalled that this small fort at the northern tip of Roanoke Island was intended to protect the Englishmen from a seaborne attack launched by Spaniards, not to defend the channels or the ships anchored nearby. It was simply too small for that and lacked adequate long-range artillery to repel enemy warships.[44]

As work on the island's defenses proceeded, *Tyger* lost most of the supplies and food on board when its pilot ran the ship aground in shallow water. This setback forced the expedition leaders to limit their stay on the Carolina coast and temporarily revise their plans to make Roanoke a major privateering haven. Instead, Lane stayed with a small force of one hundred men to search nearby for a better site with a proper harbor while Grenville and his ships returned to England with the rest of the soldiers because of the inadequate supplies on hand. The Englishmen also elected to send one of their smaller ships back to England immediately to advise Ralegh in London of the pressing need for resupply and that Grenville would soon return.

Given the lack of remaining supplies available, Lane's men would have to forage for provisions or obtain them from the indigenous people on the mainland—an uncertain prospect, to be sure. Grenville planned to send supplies back to the colony by Easter of the following year.[45]

One incident illustrates the increasingly strained relationship between the English explorers and the local Indians—and the quick resort to violence by the Europeans commanded by Lane. Prior to Grenville's departure for England in August 1585, he, Lane, and a large party of soldiers explored the mainland on the western side of Pamlico Sound. They were searching for a better site for their settlement, or perhaps for a second location for an outpost once Englishmen arrived in greater numbers later that year. The troops went to the village of Pomeioc, a palisaded town "compassed abowt with poles starcke faste in the grownd," then traveled by water up the Pungo River to a Secotan village called Aquascogoc, south of Lake Mattamuskeet, where they were not particularly welcomed. The next day they discovered that a silver cup or chalice was missing from one of their boats. Grenville ordered a small party under Captain Amadas to obtain the missing cup, assumed to be stolen by an Indian, but after Amadas demanded its return from the natives, none of the Secotans produced it. He burned Aquascogoc and its surrounding cornfields in retaliation, a massive overreaction that contributed to the increasingly strained relations between Europeans and indigenous peoples surrounding Roanoke. Given the perilous situation the English were in with regard to supplies, it was a foolish decision.[46]

Once the repairs to *Tyger* were completed, Grenville sailed back to England in late August. On this return voyage, he had captured a large Spanish prize in the Atlantic, further encouraging privateering for the English, especially among those who had backed the mission financially.[47]

Once Grenville's ships disappeared from view over the eastern horizon, the remaining men on Roanoke Island were almost totally dependent on the Indians for food. Provisions must have been obtained from local native groups well disposed to the English, since the Europeans had arrived at Roanoke too late in 1585 to plant their own crops. Lane and his men, however, were largely distrustful of the native peoples, perhaps from their experience in Ireland, where the indigenous Irish were regarded as crude barbarians whom the more civilized English eyed warily. As tensions rose, Lane became increasingly violent toward the neighboring Indians, who resented the Europeans' persistent demands for food and feared the deadly Old World diseases the newcomers had brought with them. Lane also became something of a tyrant to his own troops, enforcing discipline in a strict and overbearing fashion. The Englishmen appear to have stayed on Roanoke Island over the winter, although Lane sent a small party to explore and map the Chesapeake region to the north, where he planned to establish a permanent privateering base the next year. When spring came, Lane explored to the west, on Albemarle

Sound, where his encounters with the native populations went poorly.[48]

Predictably, matters between Englishmen and nearby Indians turned violent, primarily with those natives located on the mainland directly west of the island, led by Wingina, whose seat of power was the village of Dasemunkepeuc. Wingina's people had benefited from their proximity to the Englishmen at Roanoke Island since Barlowe's initial exploratory mission in 1584, given the trade goods they were willing to exchange. No doubt due to pressure the European colonists put on Wingina's people for sustenance, Lane's heavy-handed approach to relations with the native groups, diseases associated with the whites' arrival, and Grenville's overreaction to the missing silver chalice, the Roanoke Indians turned hostile toward the European soldiers on the island and, with Wingina's active lead, decided to attack the newcomers.[49] The chief "arrived at the conclusion that his people's problems stemmed from contact with the English," a historian has succinctly noted. Wingina informed Lane that a large group of allied Indians were meeting at a council led by Menatonon, a Chowanoc chief whose people lived inland on the western shores of Albemarle Sound. Their purpose, Wingina told the English commander, was to decide their future relationship with the Europeans on Roanoke, the implication being that Menatonon and other native leaders secretly planned to destroy the island settlement and fort by a sudden attack. Although in a double cross Wingina secretly sent word to Menatonon's council that Lane was coming to disrupt the summit, Lane and his armed men were able to surprise the gathered Indians, capture Menatonon, and take his son, Skiko, hostage. Menatonon informed Lane that the meeting of Indian allies had been Wingina's doing, not his. The leader of the Chowanocs also told Lane that farther inland were several mines where Indians obtained what sounded to the English commander like gold or copper. Intrigued by these reports, Lane decided to launch a waterborne expedition up the Moratuc (Roanoke) River with forty volunteers, Manteo, a few native guides, and the expectation that his men would be supplied along the way by local villages. In reality, Wingina had sent word to the Moratucs that Lane's mission was to kill the natives and destroy their towns, which resulted in the alarmed Indians removing themselves and their supplies from Lane's route. The Englishmen quickly deduced that Wingina and Menatonon had tricked them into making a western exploration in hopes of their ruin by starvation and exposure.[50]

While the English soldiers continued their expedition in boats, at one point they were attacked by Indians shooting arrows at them from shore. Lane's men fired back with their smoothbore firearms, then landed and searched for the enemy but found no one nearby. Lane later wrote that "the Savages forthwith quitted the shoare, and betooke themselves to flight: wee landed, and having faire and easily followed for a smal time after them, who had wooded themselves we know not where." Although his men suffered no casualties, the sudden attack gave Lane pause, and with dwindling supplies and little prospect of obtaining more, he elected to return to Roanoke Island the next day. The men had so little food by then that they were reduced to eating sassafras leaves, some fish stolen from the weirs of local Indians, and their own dogs. Lane's force reached Roanoke Island the day after Easter, hungry and exhausted, and with no sign of the arrival of Grenville's relief ships, which were expected at any time.[51]

Lane's return must have startled Wingina, who probably did not expect the soldiers to survive their hunt for the western mines. The Roanoke chief decided to abandon the island with his people without planting any crops there, an obvious danger to the prospects of the struggling English colony, as Lane well knew. Later the Indians broke their fish weirs and stopped providing any food to the English settlement, which forced Lane to scatter his hungry men into small groups to live off the land. "At that time wee had no weares for fish, neither coulde our men skill of the making of them, neither had wee one graine of Corne for seede to put into the ground," Lane later reported. Meanwhile, Wingina prepared an attack on the Roanoke settlement and sought the help of other sympathetic Indian tribes in his plan, which included the capture and execution of Lane and all other English officers, as well as the destruction of the buildings and fortification on the island.[52]

Prior to the Indian attack, however, Lane learned of Wingina's scheme. Wingina had moved a large number of his men to Roanoke, ostensibly for a council with the English, but fighting soon broke out in the woods near Fort Ralegh. Only a few casualties resulted, and the following day, June 1, Lane and two dozen soldiers pursued the Indians to the mainland, where Wingina and his warriors had relocated. Using a ruse to approach Wingina's camp, the English attacked once they were in the chief's presence, shouting "Christ is our victory." In the skirmish, Wingina was shot by an English musketeer and fell to the ground. While Lane's men fought and captured other Indians nearby, the wounded Wingina suddenly jumped to his feet and sprinted for the woods. As he fled for safety, one of Lane's Irish servants shot Wingina again with a heavy, large-caliber firearm called a petronel, a weapon fired with its butt resting against the chest. Through the smoke, other soldiers chased the injured chief into the woods, one of whom managed to reach him and sever his head, which he presented to Lane as a trophy. The brief melee now over, the English soldiers returned by boat to Roanoke, still on guard for further attacks.[53]

Although Wingina's plans to attack Roanoke had been thwarted, the dearth of provisions remained a critical problem for Lane's famished command. No relief ships had come to Roanoke by Easter—in fact, none had even sailed by then—but Ralegh had been working on resupply arrangements in summer 1585, even before Grenville's *Tyger* and the other ships of the storm-scattered fleet arrived near Roanoke. Just before the relief fleet's departure, however, the queen redirected it to Newfoundland to warn unsuspecting English ship captains there of the outbreak of hostilities with

Spain.[54] Instead, the colony received no succor until early June 1586, in the form of a fleet of English ships commanded by Sir Francis Drake, a noted privateer well favored by Queen Elizabeth. Drake had been attacking Spanish ports and ships in the West Indies, Florida, and the Spanish Main for a year with more than twenty ships under his command. He may have hoped to use Roanoke as a base for supplies and refitting, unaware of how little the colony could offer his fleet. During his voyage of the previous year, he had attacked the Spanish outpost at St. Augustine, looted the town and fort, and brought several captured cannons to Roanoke, intended for the island's fortifications. Initially, Lane and Drake discussed a plan for the famous sea raider to reinforce and leave supplies for the Roanoke garrison, including several small boats. In the end, however, Lane and his council of advisers decided to abandon the embattled Roanoke settlement because of the "weakness of our company," the perpetual supply problems they faced, and the failure of Grenville's promised relief ships to appear. Drake consented to take the weary soldiers on board for the return voyage to England.[55]

Lane's men hastily prepared for departure and sailed as soon as possible with Drake's fleet in such eagerness that they left behind three of their men, who were away from the settlement. Manteo also embarked with Lane and his soldiers, his second voyage to England. A few days later, a small supply ship dispatched by Ralegh finally arrived at Roanoke, but after finding no signs of any Englishmen in the area, it returned home. Even more disappointing to the colony's backers in England, Grenville and three fully loaded supply ships, along with several hundred men, appeared off the Outer Banks about one month after Lane had abandoned the outpost at Roanoke. Illustrative of how firmly tied to privateering the attempts at establishing the English position at Roanoke were, Grenville's arrival on the Carolina coastline was delayed by his decision to attack Spanish shipping on his way to relieve the settlement, as well as the late start his fleet made from England. War against the Spanish was tied to profit for Ralegh, Grenville, and their investors back home, not colonization of the New World. Once into the sound with his smaller ships, Grenville searched around the island, and apparently on the mainland as well, but saw no sign of Lane's men. He managed to capture three Indians, who probably told him of Lane's departure. At that point, Grenville decided to leave fifteen men on the island to maintain the fort, along with four cannons and supplies for one year, under the command of a "Master Coffin." Given the small size of this detachment, he must not have thought there was much of a threat from local Indians or the Spanish. Grenville's ships remained only briefly on the coast before putting out to sea, bound for England.[56]

If not fortunate in their efforts to establish a military outpost from which to harass the Spanish in American waters, the English were at least persistent. Despite the hardships endured by the members of the first expeditions, the presence of unfriendly indigenous people, the lack of profits realized from these ventures, and the enormous lo-

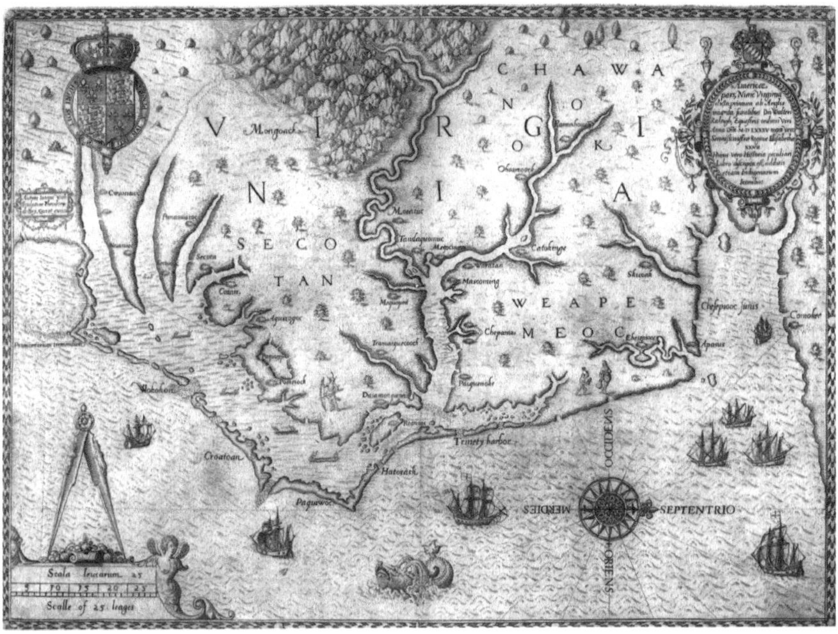

Map of Roanoke Colony.

gistical difficulties of outfitting and sustaining a far-flung enterprise on the American coast, a third attempt at establishing a settlement in America took shape in 1587. Spearheaded by John White of London, a painter of nature and mapmaker who had accompanied the first 1585 Roanoke expedition, this was to be an expedition not primarily of a military nature but one designed to establish a permanent commercial establishment at or near Chesapeake Bay. The settlement would be organized as a corporation and include families who were to establish farms there. White was to be the colony's governor, with twelve assistants designated to serve as a board of directors once they reached Virginia. The expedition would also take with it Manteo, still in England, who sought to return to America with White.[57]

The new colonists, or planters, as they were called, left Plymouth on May 8, 1587, and once again, the ship captains decided to engage in privateering along the route to Virginia, which delayed the expedition's arrival in the New World, much to White's displeasure. They finally arrived at the Outer Banks in July and soon disembarked at Roanoke. The fleet stayed with the settlers at Roanoke until late August, but rather than move on to the intended destination of Chesapeake Bay, the captains decided to leave the colonists at the island so the ships could return to privateering before foul weather precluded it. Stuck on the island now, the settlers found that while the fort on the north end of the island was in general disrepair, the nearby houses and buildings constructed earlier were still erect. They were able to restore and occupy them quickly, which improved their prospects and morale—at least for several days.[58]

Soon the colonists understood, with the help of Manteo, that the local native people were largely unfriendly. Once the new settlers had explored Roanoke Island, they realized that the fifteen men Grenville had left behind the previous year were not to be found. In fact, they learned that this detachment had been attacked by Indians with arrows and clubs, led by Wanchese. They fought a one-hour skirmish, during which the Indians set several buildings on fire, killed one Englishman, and wounded several others. One later colonist recorded that thirty of

> the men of Secota, Aquascogoc, and Dasamongueponke . . . conveied themselves secretly behind the trees, neere the houses, where our men carelesly lived . . . two of those Savages appeared . . . calling to them by friendly signes. . . . Wherefore two of the chiefest of our Englishmen, went gladly to them: but whilest one of those Savages traitorously embraced one of our men, the other with his sword of wood, which he had secretly hidden under his mantell, stroke him on the head, and slewe him . . . the other Englishman . . . fled to his companie, whome the Savages pursued with their bowes, and arrowes, so fast, that the Englishmen were forced to take the house, wherein all their victuall and weapons were: but the Savages foorthwith set the same on fire, by meanes whereof, our men were forced to take up such weapons as came first to hand, and without order to runne foorth among the Savages, with whome they skirmished above an howre . . . another of our men was shotte into the mouth with an arrowe, whereof he died: . . . The place where they fought, was of great advantage to the Savages, by meanes of the thicke trees, behinde which the Savages through their nimblenes, defended themselves, and so offended our men with their arrowes, that our men being some of them hurt, retire fighting to the water side, where their boate lay, with which they fled . . . whither, as yet we knowe not.[59]

The Englishmen were never seen again. As if to add emphasis to the news of the soldiers' fate, soon after the settlers' arrival at Roanoke, one of their number, George Howe, was killed with arrows by Roanoke Indians while fishing for crabs in shallow water two miles from the fort and his body subsequently mutilated. The attacking Indians were neither seen nor caught and rapidly returned to the mainland in canoes. To the new arrivals on the island, the attack seemed unprovoked, but perhaps the violence was in revenge for something perpetrated earlier by the soldiers Grenville had left behind.[60]

Knowledge of the fate of Grenville's men, along with Howe's death, led White to decide to attack the Indians in retaliation. Guided by Manteo, White and a group of twenty-five men attacked the mainland village of Dasemunkepeuc on the morning of August 9, convinced that the hostile Indians had come from this town. White's command managed to catch the Indians off guard as they rushed into the village. Unfortunately, as Manteo helped White discover, the Indians there were not those who had killed

Howe but friendly Croatoans who had temporarily occupied an abandoned village to gather up food left behind by Secotans. At least one friendly native was killed during the confused dawn attack before White's party realized the mistake.

By mid-August, the fleet that had brought White and his colonists to Roanoke was ready to sail home for England, determined to capture Spanish ships and treasure in the Atlantic on the way. No doubt with the knowledge that previous attempts to establish a permanent outpost at Roanoke were hampered by a dire lack of provisions and other stores, the colonists begged John White to return to England with the ships in order to make sure fresh supplies would come soon. At first reluctant to leave the settlers, including his daughter and son-in-law, he eventually agreed. White arrived back in England in November 1587 and immediately began to organize a resupply effort.[61]

The story of the colonists left behind at Roanoke is a familiar one and has become known as the mystery of the "Lost Colony," since they were not heard from again or located after the English returned to Roanoke. White tried repeatedly to put together ships and money to attempt a relief expedition to Virginia. The Spanish, however, precluded any such expedition by their massive maritime threat against England in 1588, when they assembled a huge armada to attack the British Isles and conquer Elizabeth's realm. Compared to this substantial menace, the few hundred colonists across the Atlantic clinging to a precarious toehold along the Carolina shore were insignificant. In August, the English defeated Philip II's armada in the channel, all but eliminating the possibility of an invasion, but Elizabeth was wary of Spanish designs against her realm the next year as well and refused to allow any ships to sail for Roanoke.[62]

While Spain concentrated on attacking England in summer 1588 with its powerful fleet, Spanish military leaders also sought to locate and destroy the Roanoke settlement, of which they had heard rumors and reports for years. That same summer, officials at St. Augustine dispatched a ship to find the English coastal base to the north. This scouting vessel managed to locate the small harbor at Port Ferdinando and other evidence of the English settlement but did not attack it. Once the ship returned and its captain reported his observations, the St. Augustine authorities apparently concluded that the Roanoke base was too weak to be a significant threat to Spanish fleets in the western Atlantic and sent no expedition to eliminate the English colony.[63]

Meanwhile, John White had to wait until 1590 before he could arrange a return to the island settlement. He managed to sail on ships captained by men more interested in capturing Spanish prizes on the high seas than helping the faraway colony—yet another instance of the influence of privateering on English voyages to the Outer Banks, the only way to make the trips profitable. White finally reached Roanoke in August but found only the word "CROATOAN" carved on a wooden post at the fort, a prearranged code word to indicate that the colonists had decided to relocate there. All of the colonists' houses had been pulled down, but what remained was an enclosed palisade of tree trunks and a few outer works, "very Fort-like." Several cannons lay about the ruins of the settlement, and other items were discovered scattered on the ground, including four guns and some lead and shot. But White found no evidence of an attack against the settlement from either the Spanish or nearby Indians. A fierce storm forced the explorers to return to the ships after spending only a few hours on land looking for signs of the settlers and persuaded the sailors to leave the coast and head east into the Atlantic. White could not get the captains to go to Croatoan and was never able to search again for the colonists, although he maintained hope that they had survived somewhere in the wilderness of North Carolina, perhaps with an Indian community.[64] The English abandoned all further efforts to settle on or near Roanoke Island after the mysterious disappearance of White's colony, but in the first decade of the seventeenth century, they renewed their efforts to establish a New World presence, this time in the Chesapeake Bay region, in 1607 at a place they named Jamestown.

Once Jamestown became a viable English colony, the unsuccessful attempts to plant a privateering base and a settlement in the Outer Banks were forgotten. Ralegh had more-pressing concerns than Roanoke, as did other investors in the project. By the 1590s, Roanoke was seen in England as a commercial failure and a military disappointment. The area around Roanoke offered a poor harbor from which to attack Spanish shipping and for resupplying privateers. Even the Spanish came to conclude that Roanoke was "inhospitable" and that English plans to maintain a base there was "Idle talk." Poor relations with several of the surrounding Indian groups also made the establishment of a post in North Carolina difficult, as did the daunting transatlantic logistical challenges.[65] As one recent historian of Roanoke has written, "Ralegh's Roanoke ventures failed because those native people in the region . . . who initially welcomed the newcomers, decided to withdraw their support and assistance."[66] Once John White and his companions left the shores of the Outer Banks after their unsuccessful attempt to locate the "lost" colonists, coastal North Carolina no longer factored into the military plans of seventeenth-century England.

2. A Spirit of Disobedience: Rebellions, Indian Wars, and Pirates

After John White's expedition failed to locate the missing English settlers of Roanoke Island in 1590, the colony eventually known as North Carolina remained largely unsettled until the second half of the seventeenth century. Although the English devoted significant resources to the settlement at Jamestown starting in 1607, investors and adventurers in London had little further interest in the Outer Banks and the sounds of the Carolina coast. Not until the 1650s did whites begin to move south from the plantations along Virginia's Tidewater rivers and the Chesapeake Bay, and these migrants were often members of society's bottom rung who moved south to find better situations. Others came from the West Indies, New England, Switzerland, and Germany for land and better opportunities. Their small farms and settlements often put them at odds with the indigenous people who already lived on the coastal plain of North Carolina. Moreover, the colony's isolated location, distance from imperial authorities, and lawless atmosphere seems to have incubated a rebelliousness among the white inhabitants there, leading to several domestic disturbances and revolts. These tumults were about the power to control the colony and its financial resources, and they created an unstable political and economic environment for several decades. They also demonstrated the colony's inability or unwillingness to raise soldiers, money, and provisions to quell internal dissent or for defense against Indian attacks.[1]

THE PROVINCE OF CAROLINA

The Virginia Company, a group of English investors and entrepreneurs looking for wealth and a sea passage to the riches of the Orient, founded Jamestown in 1607 on the lower James River. This colony—the first permanent English settlement in the New World—suffered numerous setbacks and hardships during its first half century of existence, including disease, starvation, internal dissent, and devastating Indian attacks. By the 1650s, however, the outlook for the colony's success began to brighten. The white population began to increase as new immigrants arrived from England, and the colony's chronic sustenance and health problems improved. Jamestown's increasing population led to a demand for arable land, as growing numbers of indentured servants fulfilled their contracts without dying first and looked to establish themselves on small farms. Tensions arose over time as good land became harder to come by, since wealthy planters had acquired much of it—especially along the rivers and streams of the Tidewater—leaving disgruntled small farmers with poorer acreage to cultivate.

In order to find better prospects, as early as 1655, newly free settlers in Virginia's Tidewater area began to move south through the almost impenetrable Great Dismal Swamp to Albemarle Sound. Since this remote region was far from government authorities in London, difficult to reach from Jamestown, and free from taxation, many debtors, runaways, and outlaws sought refuge in the Albemarle area. This was the first significant settlement of the region since the Roanoke colony had been abandoned at the end of the sixteenth century, and it soon gained a notorious reputation. Referred to by colonial Virginia Gov. Thomas Culpeper as "the Sinke of America, the Refuge of our Renegadoes,"[2] even the colony's own charter deemed it a land "only inhabited by some barbarous people, who have no knowledge of Almighty God."[3]

After the restoration of Charles II to the English throne in 1660, the English king richly rewarded several of his subjects who had remained loyal to him during his nine-year exile. He made a huge land grant in 1663 to eight of them, who were known as the lords proprietors, and called the land "the Province of Carolina," an area that extended from Virginia south to what is now northern Florida, and west to the Pacific Ocean. During the 1600s, most of the early settlement of this huge territory was on Albemarle Sound's north shore, and in modern South Carolina.

The proprietors hoped to make money from their land grant by selling parcels to European immigrants seeking land in the New World, and from extractive commercial ventures. Initially these wealthy rulers, none of whom ever moved to Carolina, intended to set up a feudal system of government, but that proved impossible to establish given the great distance from London to the colonial settlements, which were small and dispersed over a large area. Moreover, the cagey settlers were unwilling to abide by any such arrangement. Rather, the colony's proprietors installed a governor for the small Albemarle Sound settlements, a council to advise him, and an assembly elected by local landowners to act as a legislature. Recognizing the danger these colonies faced from European and native threats, the colony's charter of 1663 granted the proprietors the right "to erect, raise and build within the said province and places aforesaid, or any part or parts thereof, such and so many forts, fortresses, castles, cities, boroughs, towns, villages and other fortifications whatsoever, and the same or any of them to fortify and furnish with ordinance, powder, shot, armory, and all other weapons, ammunition, habilements of war, both offensive and defensive, as shall be thought fit and convenient for the safety and welfare of the said province and places, or any part thereof."[4]

Additionally, the charter allowed inhabitants of the nascent settlements to "levy, muster and train all sorts of men, of what condition or whereso-ever born, in the said province for the time being, and to make war and pursue the enemies aforesaid, as well by sea as by land, yea, even without the limits of the said province, and by God's assistance to vanquish and take them, and being taken to put them to death by the law of war, or to save them at their pleasure." In prescient forethought, the king also gave the lords leave to crush internal dissent, "in case of rebellion, tumult or sedition, (if any should happen,) which God forbid, either upon the land within the province aforesaid, or upon the main sea." The proprietors obtained "full power and authority, to exercise martial law against mutinous and seditious persons of those parts, such as shall refuse to submit themselves to their government, or shall refuse to serve in the wars, or shall fly to the enemy, or forsake their colours or ensigns, or be loyterers or straglers, or otherwise howsoever offending against law, custom or discipline military."[5]

Despite the proprietors' establishment of a government for the new colony—at least on paper—the people who inhabited the land were difficult to rule and generally displeased with their rulers. Most settlers resented attempts to govern them, refused to cooperate with governors appointed by the proprietors, and were so spread out across the Albemarle region as to make effective government unworkable.[6] Moreover, restrictions on their tobacco trade in the form of Navigation Acts and associated taxes on commerce beginning in 1670 increased colonial antipathy toward the proprietary government and its representatives in Carolina. Shortly thereafter, the province's struggling planters suffered from years of poor harvests due to hurricanes, floods, and droughts, and sporadic conflicts with nearby Chowanoc Indians added to the colonists' unease. Unable to pay the required quitrents to the proprietors, the colonists seethed with anger at the unsympathetic English lords, who refused to help mitigate their distress.[7]

CULPEPER'S REBELLION

In April 1672, Peter Carteret, the colony's acting governor and distant cousin of proprietor Sir George Carteret, sailed to England to present the colonists' many grievances and hardships to the proprietors in London. Before departing, he appointed John Jenkins as acting governor in his absence. Carteret did not return to Carolina, so Jenkins remained the colony's executive, even after his commission to do so expired in fall 1674. Jenkins paid little attention to tax collection, no doubt to the settlers' great satisfaction and his own popularity. One year later, a new assembly formed, which was dominated by settlers of the "proprietary faction," those who had arrived after the granting of the charter in 1663. This "party" elected as its speaker Thomas Eastchurch, an ambitious man and the surveyor of the colony, who had Jenkins arrested for "several misdemeanours." Jenkins's association with the "anti-proprietary faction" no doubt explains why Eastchurch seized him, at least in part, and then assumed the role of governor himself (though not the title).[8]

In early 1676, Jenkins's supporters obtained his release from custody by force, and for some time both he and Eastchurch tried to rule the province. Eastchurch and Thomas Miller, another partisan of the proprietary faction who had come to Carolina by 1673, fervently opposed Jenkins. Although Miller was briefly jailed for treason, he traveled to Virginia and soon joined Eastchurch on a voyage to England to report the political turbulence in the Albemarle colony to the proprietors and to secure official appointments in Carolina. After giving their testimony, the lords appointed Eastchurch as governor and Miller as customs collector and secretary of the colony. Meanwhile, back in Albemarle, Jenkins and his supporters dissolved the colony's assembly and took power, ruling until July 1677, at which time they reluctantly surrendered their powers to Miller, who arrived in Carolina that month. Eastchurch, however, did not sail with Miller back to the Albemarle settlements after the two stopped in the West Indies, so the latter appointed himself president of the council (de facto governor) on his arrival in Carolina, in addition to his tax-collecting responsibilities. Having failed to prevent his landing with a threatening mob, Miller's opponents contested his right to govern, as he had not been properly appointed to the post—a position later confirmed by the proprietors. Often moving about the colony with an armed guard of minions who were rumored to be "fugitives from Bacon's Rebellion" of 1676 in Virginia, Miller arrested some of his adversaries, fined them, and tampered with legislative elections to bolster his dubious gubernatorial claims. He threatened to hang his opponents, and evidence shows that just prior to the outbreak of Culpeper's Rebellion, the acting governor ordered all Carolinians to turn in their arms to him. Miller also held court sessions guarded by sympathetic members of the militia, a clear threat to Carolina settlers and their liberties. As one of the proprietors later wrote, Miller "did many extravagant things," which "startled and disaffected the people towards him." His high-handedness directed at Jenkins's supporters and the colonists' general discontent set the stage for North Carolina's first uprising, known as Culpeper's Rebellion, in December 1677.[9]

Centered mostly in what is now Pasquotank County,[10] the "great Tumult & Rebellion"[11] began on December 1, 1677, sparked by Miller's arrest of several of his opponents, including George Durant, a well-known leader of the antiproprietary party, and Zachariah Gillam, a New England sea captain trading tobacco in the colony with his brig *Carolina.*[12] Gillam had brought crates of weapons in his ship's holds, allegedly for the colonists' use against threatening Indians, but actually for use against the proprietary government. The sea captain's arrest and the confinement of his crew led an armed party of about forty rebels to capture and imprison Miller and several of his adherents after they released Durant and Gillam from confinement. "With force of arms," including "swords, guns, and pistolls,"

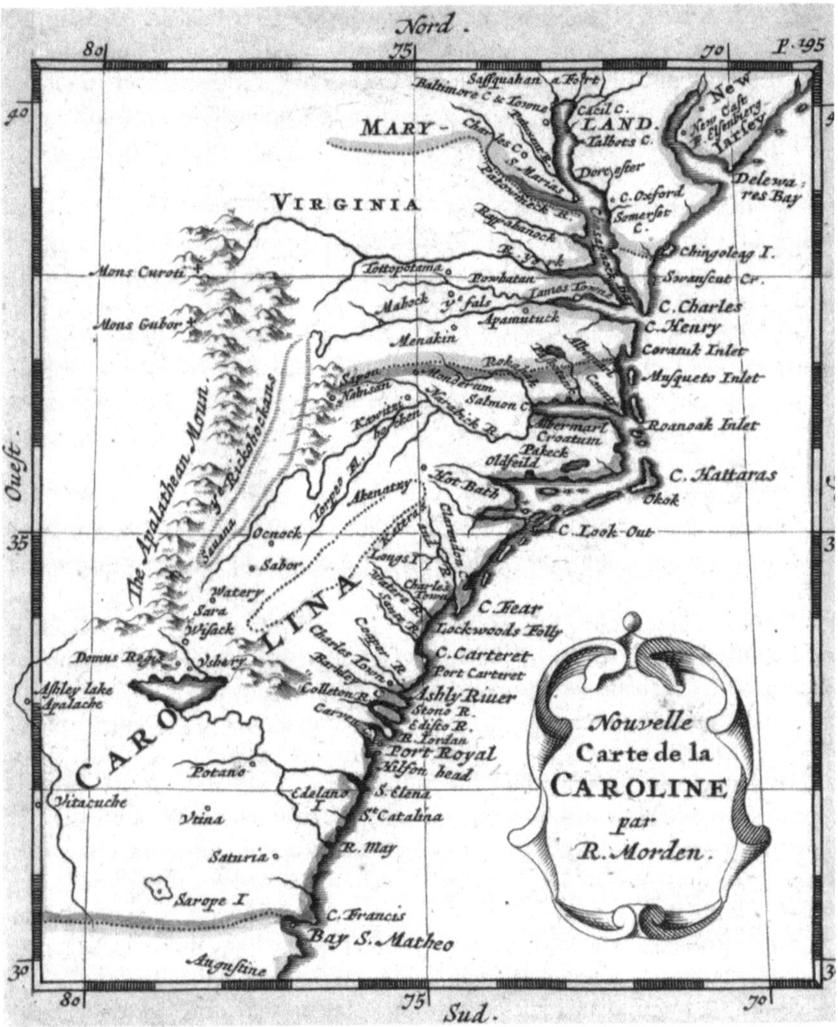

Nouvelle carte de la Caroline, 1688.

the insurgents rushed the house in which Miller was staying and seized public records there and at other nearby buildings. The rebel leaders then went on board Gillam's ship, at anchor off Pasquotank, and obtained from him "fresh new" cutlasses "for themselves and many of the rest of their gang," according to Miller. Durant quickly became one of the revolt's key leaders, along with former customs collector Valentine Bird and John Culpeper, who had recently moved to Albemarle from Charles Town and had something of a checkered reputation.[13]

A few days later, armed insurgents moved west into the Chowan district "where the like disturbance was begun and more violently agitated by . . . Culpeper." The rebels seized the "Marshall of the County" and all of his official records, and with an armed escort brought the official back to confinement in Pasquotank. After two weeks, rebels removed Miller and the other prisoners to Durant's house at the southern tip of the Perquimans district, secured by "a guard of 60 to 70 men in arms," who isolated the prisoners from the community and each other.[14] Valentine Bird led an expedition of several insurgents to Miller's home to locate more of his official papers and, once found, returned to Durant's house. After the revolt's leaders perused the documents, they publicly accused Miller of "blasphemy, treason, and other crimes" and "clapt [him] in irons." The rebels also threw the county's stocks and pillory into the river, a symbolic blow to Miller's authority.[15] Several days later, a party of armed men from the Currituck district arrived, bringing with them Henry Hudson, a deputy tax collector, as their prisoner. Some angry rebels even called for the summary executions of Miller and his deputies.[16]

By no means did all of the Albemarle inhabitants favor the rebellion. A 1679 "Representation concerning the rebellion in Albemarle County," sent to the proprietors in London possibly for use in Culpeper's later trial, stated "the Principalls and Heads of this Rebellion were not only prompted thereunto by ambition and envy" but also "personall and particular crimes they knew themselves guilty of and accountable for whenever a Governor should come." The petitioners singled out certain leaders of the revolt, including "Captain Zackery Gilham who supplied them with many fire armes and other weapons of War," and Culpeper, "a person that never is in his element but whilst fishing in troubled waters."[17] Some proprietary supporters also feared that the unrest would lead slaves, servants, and poor whites to use the rebellion as a means of abolishing the colony's social order, much as Bacon's Rebellion of 1676 threatened to do in neighboring Virginia.[18]

At this point, perhaps in an effort to cast a semblance of legality onto their proceedings, the insurgents formed a parliament, which elected John Jenkins "Generalissome" and Thomas Cullen legislative speaker. The unofficial assembly—a "mocke Govermt by force of men in Armes," according to one of Miller's supporters—also formed a court to try the proprietary officials then in custody.[19] Miller reported that he was brought in irons before a "rabble" jury, of which Durant was the attorney general and Culpeper "their Chief Councillour and scribe." During the trial, the rebel leaders received a proclamation from Governor Eastchurch, who had finally arrived in Virginia ("at the very nick of tyme," wrote Miller), demanding those in revolt lay down their arms, free Miller and others held captive, and resume the lawfully appointed government. Although the trial was halted, Jenkins and other leaders ignored the governor, refused to make public the proclamation, and ordered an armed force to move to the northern border of the Albemarle colony to prevent Eastchurch from entering the fractious province.[20] Consequently, Eastchurch applied to Virginia's Gov. William Berkeley to help put down the Carolina revolt, but Eastchurch died of a fever several weeks later, and his entreaty was neglected. Unlike Bacon's Rebellion in Virginia the preceding year, English authorities sent no troops to quell the Albemarle unrest, most likely because Carolina was a proprietary colony, and the violence was contained to what many in London considered a remote backwater.[21] Jenkins assumed the leadership of the colony again until the end of 1678, while Culpeper served as customs collector. John Harvey, an Albemarle planter without connection to the revolt, received a temporary appointment as governor from the proprietors in 1679. By the next year "a de jure government was functioning throughout the colony," although Harvey died in January and was succeeded (once again) by the former rebel John Jenkins.[22]

After two years of close confinement "in a logghouse 10 or 11 foote square purposely built for him" and "kept from all access of friends or humane converse,"[23] Thomas Miller finally escaped from the Albemarle colony in late 1679 and returned to England, where he aired his grievances to the proprietors and English customs officials. Culpeper, then in England to present the insurgents' case to high officials, was consequently arrested for his role in the turmoil in Carolina. After an investigation by the Lords of Trade and Plantations and the Commissioners of Customs, Culpeper went on trial for high treason in November 1680 by the King's Bench in London. He was represented by none other than Lord Shaftesbury, one of the proprietors, who obtained Culpeper's acquittal on the basis that there was no legal government in place in Albemarle at the time of the disturbances, and thus his client could not have committed treason. Shaftesbury and his fellow lords apparently wished to minimize the reports of riots in the Albemarle colony, so that their property and charter were not taken from them by the king, and thus they favored setting Culpeper free.[24] Zachariah Gillam was also arrested in London but freed because of lack of evidence against him. Miller never returned to America, and authorities jailed him for embezzlement while a customs officer in England. He died behind bars about 1685.

GIBBS'S REBELLION, 1690

The political turbulence in the Carolina colony's northern district did not end with Miller's departure from America. In 1682 or 1683, Seth Sothel, a new proprietor, arrived in Albemarle from England to begin his tenure as the colony's governor. After a disastrous tenure marked by graft, fraud, and other abuses of office, in 1689 the Albemarle assembly found Sothel guilty of crimes while governor and exiled him for one year. The same year, to govern the colony, the proprietors replaced him with Phillip Ludwell, an Englishman residing in Virginia who had been secretary of state, commander of the militia, and a member of the House of Burgesses. Although Sothel tried to regain power in 1690 he failed, and Ludwell retained his executive position, hoping to bring order to the Carolina settlements, which had seen years of raucous internal dissent. Prior to Ludwell's arrival in Carolina, however, John Gibbs had assumed the role of colonial governor upon Sothel's removal. Gibbs was a wealthy planter related to proprietor Christopher Monck, the Duke of Albemarle, and as a high-ranking member of Albemarle society he felt entitled to the gubernatorial reward based on his previous appointment as cacique, or local political boss, under the colony's constitution. Ludwell's arrival in the colony with a genuine commission from the proprietors in England did not persuade the obstinate Gibbs to quit the post, setting up a conflict known as Gibbs's Rebellion. Publicly, Gibbs called Ludwell a "rascal, impostor, and usurper" and declared he would fight to keep his position as governor. To demonstrate his authority, Gibbs led a group of armed men to the precinct court at Pasquotank and broke up the proceedings on the basis that the court had no commission from him to conduct its business. Rebels seized two court officials and forcibly removed them to Virginia, where Gibbs owned a plantation. This seems to have been the end of any conflict associated with his showdown with Ludwell, who was soon confirmed in his title by the proprietors in London.[25]

CARY'S REBELLION, 1711

North Carolina's turbulence in the seventeenth century was characterized by limited violence and predominantly internal issues. The beginning of the following century saw another disturbance, this one with a religious background to it, known as Cary's Rebellion. By the 1690s, the Albemarle region was home to a growing Quaker population. John Archdale of Buckinghamshire, England, a recently converted Quaker who had purchased the proprietary rights of John Berkeley, became governor in 1694, while other members of the Society of Friends also assumed political power. Five years later, native Carolinian Henderson Walker became the Albemarle region's governor after Archdale returned to England.

As a firm Anglican, Walker managed to have the colony's assembly pass a vestry act to make the Church of England Albemarle's official church, to be financially supported by taxes paid by Anglicans and Quakers alike. This measure was hugely unpopular with the Quakers, as was the controversy within Carolina upon the ascension of Queen Anne to the English throne in 1702. In the past, Quaker officeholders were not required to swear allegiance to a new monarch (and thus violate a religious tenet) but were allowed to affirm their loyalty instead. Walker's administration refused to allow this accommodation, and thus conscientious Friends were unable to serve in the government—including the assembly. Thomas Cary, an Englishman and stepson of a proprietor, became governor in 1705; he too opposed Quaker power in Albemarle, and required the test oath from them as well. Attorney and Assemblyman John Porter traveled to London on behalf of the Carolina Friends to seek redress from the queen's officials and returned with orders to remove Cary from the governorship. Cary, in Charles Town at the time, had appointed Virginia-born attorney William Glover as his official

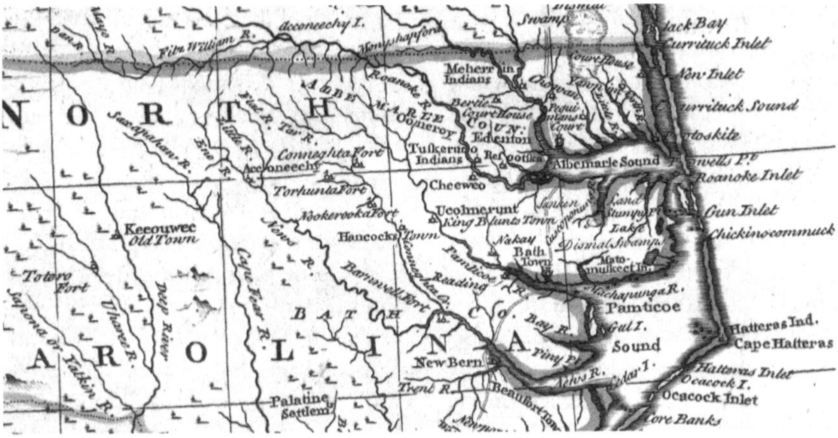

A new & accurate map of the provinces of North & South Carolina, Georgia (detail), 1752.

representative, and soon Glover's adherents bitterly opposed Porter's Quaker faction. In 1708, Glover's opponents forced him to flee to Virginia, and Cary returned to govern until 1711, this time attempting to include Quakers within the government.[26]

Tensions in the northern area of Carolina increased in December 1710, when Edward Hyde, a distant relative of the queen, arrived via Williamsburg to assume the governorship. Thomas Cary, John Porter, and men of the Quaker faction called into question Hyde's commission, while Hyde became closely identified with the Anglicans of the colony, particularly those in the Chowan district.[27] Cary and his supporters disputed Hyde's calling of a new assembly as well and opposed its enactments. The colony degenerated into political chaos as two different assemblies met simultaneously, each claiming the other was illegitimate. Matters came to a head when Hyde and the assembly dominated by his supporters nullified all laws passed by Cary's administration and enacted harsh laws against libel, sedition, and officeholding by Quakers—measures even some of Hyde's supporters felt were too severe.[28] Hyde's adherents arrested Cary and Porter for high crimes and misdemeanors, primarily related to the Cary administration's failure to collect proper quitrents from Carolina settlers. The two escaped captivity in May 1711, and Cary raced to his home in newly established Bath County south of Albemarle Sound to collect men and arms. "The differences in the Government of North Carolina are grown to such a highth as to engage the inhabitants there to take up arms against one another," reported Virginia's lieutenant governor, Alexander Spotswood.[29]

Hyde gathered his own force on Salmon Creek in presentday Bertie County and led over one hundred men across the Albemarle Sound into Bath County to capture Cary and break up his forces on the Pamlico River. Cary had fewer men with him, but after fleeing his home on Hyde's approach, they fortified a new location, probably at Archbell Point near Bath Town, the defenses of which included several cannons. Realizing the strength of the position Cary's men occupied, Hyde withdrew his force from the area on June 1.[30] Fortune seemed to favor Cary's small command, for at this point a merchant ship captained by Richard Roach arrived in Albemarle Sound with weapons and munitions for the anti-Hyde rebels.[31] Cary's men used some of the newly acquired heavy guns to arm several small ships and prepared to attack Hyde's position, which was at the Chowan River home of wealthy merchant Thomas Pollock, a Scotsman and one of Hyde's chief supporters. In the meantime, Hyde recognized that his own force was outnumbered and lacked the firepower Cary had just obtained from Roach's ship. So the beleaguered Hyde sent a messenger to Virginia to seek help from Governor Spotswood, an experienced military veteran. The Carolina governor called for any troops Virginia could spare and also requested the dispatch of marines then stationed on boats off the Virginia shore to "strike a greater Terrer in the people." Spotswood, perhaps with his martial blood up at the news of insurrection in the colony to the south, promised to send a marine detachment and a small force of colonial militia from the frontier to Hyde's rescue.[32] Spotswood also sent a stern letter to Cary on June 21 in which he warned him to "consider what severe penaltys are due to the author of a commotion which may fairly come under the denomination of a Rebellion."[33]

While Hyde sought help from Virginia, Cary and his followers were not idle. Approaching Pollock's house by the shore with their armed vessels, Cary's men attacked on June 30, firing on the dwelling and attempting to land a group of men nearby. Hyde's men unexpectedly fired back from cover, and soon the startled landing party returned to the ships, which sailed away under fire. For reasons still unknown, Cary's force came ashore several miles down the sound and retired to the woods—leaving only three men to guard their ships. Hyde's pursuing men caught up to the boats, boarded them, and captured the guards, all of their weapons, and their munitions. Cary's rebels returned to Bath County to regroup, but when word reached them of the impending arrival of English marines (although not the Virginia militia), their support began to wane. The marines arrived in the Albemarle region in late July, the rebellion collapsed, and Cary, Porter, and several of his lieutenants prudently fled to Virginia. Eventually, Cary was captured and sent to England for trial, but like John Culpeper, he was not convicted of treason. Released from prison, he made his way back to Carolina, where he faded into obscurity.[34]

INDIAN CONFLICTS

The rebellions of Culpeper, Gibbs, and Cary were conflicts of internal dissent, in which Carolinians objected to heavy-handed government, taxes, rents, or religious discrimination or struggled to consolidate political power. Early Carolinians also encountered another type of internal threat during the seventeenth and early eighteenth centuries, that from the colony's indigenous inhabitants. The Roanoke Island settlers of the 1580s had also battled their native neighbors, as detailed above. For much of the seventeenth century, too few Europeans lived in the Albemarle region to foment hostilities with Indians there. In the second half of the century, however, this demographic situation began to change, as more planters moved into the northern part of the Carolina colony, while others attempted to settle the Cape Fear area farther south. In their hunger for land, white settlers pushed west to, and across, the Chowan River, where they encroached on the territory of the Meherrin and Chowan Indians. Similarly, Indians encountered settlers intruding upon their land on both branches of the upper Cape Fear River. Moreover, disease among the native peoples south of Pamlico Sound decimated Indian communities there and left a huge swath of "unoccupied" land ripe for new settlers to claim. Pressure on Indian groups from Europeans seeking good land was a familiar dynamic in early America and predictably resulted in violent conflict.[35]

In the 1660s, English settlers from the island colony of Barbados made several attempts to settle on the lower Cape Fear River, in what was then called Clarendon County, named for the Earl of Clarendon, proprietor Edward Hyde. Their initial forays were unsuccessful, but by 1666, the Barbadians and settlers from New England had established themselves in the region. Like the Roanoke Island settlers decades before, these Englishmen found themselves short of supplies, dependent upon their native neighbors (whose tribal name is unknown today), and soon in conflict with them. It may also be that the colonists engaged in capturing and selling native people into slavery in the West Indies. In the Clarendon County War, the Indians forced the colonists to abandon their Cape Fear settlements by 1667.

To the north, friction between white settlers expanding to the west of the Chowan River led to a two-year bloody clash with the Chowanoc Indians, who eventually suffered defeat in 1677 at the hands of Albemarle colonists who had been strengthened by the timely arrival of arms in a trading vessel. Over the next several decades, relations between the Carolinians and various native peoples continued to sour over land issues, slave trading, unfair trading practices, and a host of other small misunderstandings that, when compounded over time, engendered resentments and hostilities. North Carolina went to war with the Core Indians, a small native group related to the Tuscarora along the lower Neuse River, in 1704. These Indians were forced to relocate as a result of the limited fighting, which angered their Tuscarora neighbors. In 1707, one Carolinian reported that the settlers on the Pamlico complained that "they expected ye Indians every day to come and cutt their throat[s]." By 1711, the eastern part of the Carolina colony was a tinderbox ready to be ignited, particularly along the Neuse and Pamlico Rivers.[36]

The most powerful people of Piedmont North Carolina through the first quarter of the eighteenth century were the Tuscarora Indians, who lived to the west and south of the nascent colonial settlements. They were a powerful but not united people of about eight thousand individuals. Native towns were the key political units, and the Tuscaroras were sometimes divided among themselves. Also divided were the Carolinians, factionalized by region, political allegiance, and conflicting personalities among their leaders, as seen in the recent Cary's Rebellion. These divisions played a significant role in what came to be called the Tuscarora War, which devastated part of the colony before South Carolina forces defeated the indigenous foe.[37]

War broke out in Bath County soon after the founding of New Bern and establishment of plantations around what is now Pollocksville, settled in 1710 by Swiss and German immigrants under the leadership of Baron Christoph von Graffenried, a friend to several of the proprietors. The Neuse River town was situated on the site of a Tuscarora village called Chattooka, the residents of which had been pushed off the land by European settlers. When Graffenried and Surveyor General John Lawson traveled up the Neuse River in early September 1711 with two black slaves to explore a possible riverine route to Virginia and to scout new lands for exploitation, hostile Tuscaroras of the lower towns captured them and quickly executed Lawson at the village of Catechna (near modern Grifton) on Contentnea Creek. Led by King Hancock, these Tuscarora Indians of the lower towns allied with several other native coastal peoples who had been similarly displaced by encroaching white settlers and suffered from predatory slave traders. Hancock gathered about five hundred well-armed warriors at Catechna in mid-September and was poised to attack the European encroachers. The upper town Tuscaroras, however, refused to join the native coalition and remained neutral throughout the conflict because of their proximity to Virginia and the Albemarle settlements, which they feared. Nevertheless, given the distracting tumult of Cary's Rebellion that summer and the Indians' secretive preparations for war, when the Indians began their attacks against the white settlers on September 22, the well-organized assault was a surprise.[38]

The native attacks began in the morning along the Neuse, Trent, and Pamlico Rivers in the Bath region, "without any previous Declaration of War, or show of Discontent," according to Virginia Gov. Alexander Spotswood.[39] The colonists were unprepared for the hostilities, having few men available to defend the scattered settlements, little arms and munitions, and no substantial defensive works to shelter noncombatants. Approximately 250 well-armed warriors of the Tuscarora, Machapunga, Coree, Pamlico, and Bear River tribes attacked unsuspecting whites in a coordinated assault, and within hours over one hundred settlers were killed, with many more wounded and captured. Spotswood reported that at sunrise, Indian warriors "began a barbrous massacre, on the inhabitants of the Frontier plantations, killing without distinction of age or sex about sixty English, and upwards of that number of Swiss and Palatines, besides a great many left dangerously wounded." Some of the dead were horribly mangled, and torture seems to have been common. The warriors carried clubs and firearms, and in many cases they were better armed than the settlers they attacked.[40] The raiders burned houses, barns, and crops; ran off cattle; and avoided large towns to concentrate on small settlements and isolated plantations. Some Carolinians escaped to Bath, New Bern, and the Brice plantation, situated along the Trent River. After three days of slaughter, the Indians withdrew to their villages, taking about twenty-five prisoners, mostly women and children, and left a scene of death and destruction that depopulated large swaths of territory.[41]

Because the Tuscaroras in the northern part of the colony did not enter the war, the Albemarle region suffered no attacks. Gov. Edward Hyde, upon hearing reports of the violence and the accompanying atrocities, sent off urgent pleas for assistance to his counterparts in Virginia and South Carolina and began to assemble armed companies to defend the colony from further Indian depredations, although most of the Albemarle region's Quakers refused to muster. The ongoing political divisions resulting from Cary's Rebellion made it difficult for desperate colonial authorities in North Carolina to react to the situation effectively, and the divided assembly did little to assist in the colony's defense.[42] Spotswood observed of Hyde's difficulties that the "spirit of disobedience to which they have been long accustomed still prevails so much that he can hardly persuade them to unite for their common safety."[43]

The initial military response to the Tuscarora attack by North Carolina was feeble. In October, the president of the provincial Executive Council, Thomas Pollock, managed to collect about 150 men in the Chowan district to attempt an attack on hostile Tuscarora forces to the south of Albemarle Sound. Pollock marched south with his men to Bath and joined with additional soldiers from the Neuse River under Captain William Brice, a planter with something of a sordid past. Brice led his company of fifty men up the Neuse to occupy an abandoned Indian town, but the rest of Pollock's troops at Bath refused to march west against the Indians. After being ambushed by three hundred Tuscarora warriors near Catechna, Brice retreated to his own devastated plantation on the Trent River.[44]

Virginia's governor reacted to the outbreak of war by sending militia to the border of the Albemarle district to ensure that northern Tuscaroras did not enter the war. He also sent a small supply of powder, clothing, and blankets to assist the Carolinians and stopped trade between his colony and Indian groups to the south, although he refused to allow his colony's militia to march into North Carolina.[45] Governor Hyde received more substantial assistance from South Carolina. In early November, that colony agreed to provide money and a force of about seven hundred friendly Catawba and Yamasee Indians led by white officers, and several dozen colonial troops under Irish-born Colonel John Barnwell, to march into North Carolina and attack the Tuscarora warriors and their allies. Many of Barnwell's troops joined him with the expectation that any enemies they captured could be sold as slaves for their own profit. Barnwell's men reached the Neuse River in January 1712 but were not joined by any North Carolina soldiers as he had expected. Moreover, desertions reduced his own force to four hundred effectives.[46] Undaunted by North Carolina's lack of support for his expedition and encouraged by the prospect of enslaving the Tuscaroras and their allies, Barnwell's force on January 30 attacked the important Tuscarora village of Narhantes by the Neuse River, thirty miles from New Bern. Barnwell's command overwhelmed the Tuscaroras in an hour-long battle in which fifty-two Tuscaroras died, including ten women who had fought the Carolinians at close quarters with bows and arrows. Barnwell's Indians looted the town before they burned it, and once satisfied with their booty, many of them deserted.[47]

After destroying Narhantes, Barnwell moved his dwindling force north to Bath Town, burning and plundering other Tuscarora villages and strongholds on the way. At one point his column received a spirited Indian attack while crossing the Pamlico River, which his men managed to fight off. After being joined by sixty-seven poorly armed North Carolinians near Bath, Barnwell's force totaled approximately 250 men, most of whom were allied Yamasee Indians. Late in February, he moved his soldiers about fifty miles west to the Tuscarora fort at Catechna, which the whites called Hancock's Town. This fort was deserted, but Barnwell learned that one hundred thirty well-armed warriors were in strong defenses called Hancock's Fort several miles away, a significant log fort with four round bastions, an earthen trench, and abatis.[48]

Barnwell's initial attack on March 5 against the stout fort failed, after which his small force began a siege of the Indian position. The Carolinians constructed a small log work of their own near Hancock's Fort that allowed them to fire on the Indians and threaten their water supply as well. The Tuscarora warriors countered this move by bringing several white captives inside their defenses, where they began to torture them within earshot of Barnwell's camp. They killed one prisoner before Barnwell agreed to negotiate a truce, in which the Indians released several prisoners and promised to return twenty-two more after Barnwell withdrew to the east after his unsuccessful five-day campaign.[49]

The South Carolina commander expected the Indians to meet him March 19 at Batchelours Creek near New Bern to deliver the hostages and discuss peace terms.[50] When the Tuscaroras failed to appear on the scheduled date, Barnwell launched a second attempt in April to destroy the native fort near Hancock's Town, this time taking along artillery. After constructing their own stockade a few miles away (named after their commander), Barnwell's force of 153 whites and 128 Indians deployed their cannons and dug siege lines to compel the Tuscaroras to come to terms on April 17, although they had not managed to breach the enemy fort's walls after ten days of operations. Though Barnwell's command had suffered few casualties, it was weakened by a lack of supplies, which was probably his main reason for consenting to a truce rather than continuing attempts to reduce the fort. The Tuscaroras released their captives, destroyed part of the fort at Hancock's Town, and agreed to cease construction of additional fortifications. They also agreed to surrender King Hancock and several other Indian notables, although he had already escaped to Virginia before their capitulation. Despite these concessions, it was clear to at least some Carolinians that Barnwell's expedition failed to defeat the Tuscaroras; Governor Hyde and others lambasted him for not finishing off the enemy. Slighted, Barnwell and his remaining men left for South Carolina, taking some Indians as slaves as they left Tuscarora territory. This action, in native eyes, betrayed the terms of the truce and led them to plan further hostilities.[51]

Renewed warfare in summer 1712 was once more devastating to the white inhabitants of central North Carolina, and some residents began to leave the beleaguered colony altogether. Few Carolinians volunteered for military duty to defend the colony, and Virginia sent no troops at all, primarily because North Carolina authorities refused to feed them. Moreover, the colony's response to the attacks was weakened by the refusal of Quakers to support the war and a yellow fever outbreak that summer, which took the life of Governor Hyde. Once again, South Carolina provided the necessary soldiers and supplies for operations against the Tuscaroras.[52]

In December 1712, a force of thirty-three white soldiers and about nine hundred Indians under Colonel James Moore marched from South Carolina to Bath Town, and eventually to the Albemarle region, to gather supplies and additional volunteers. Once outfitted, the refurbished army marched back to the Neuse River. Moore, a South Carolina native of the Goose Creek area, led his men through heavy snow and cold temperatures to the lower Tuscarora towns in early March. He aimed for Neoheroka, the Tuscaroras' main stronghold west of Fort Hancock near present-day Snow Hill.[53]

The Indians' elaborate log fort at Neoheroka included roofed bastions, underground bunkers, and a hidden trench leading to their water source. Undeterred by these formidable defenses and reinforced by additional munitions from Virginia, Colonel Moore initiated a classic siege with approach trenches, supported by three batteries, to reduce the fort. After exploding a large charge of gunpowder under a section of the fort's wall on March 20, the Carolinians and allied Indians attacked, beginning a bloody, three-day battle that ended with the fort in ruins and the Tuscaroras defeated. The fighting killed approximately 350 Tuscarora warriors (many of them burned to death), with 392 taken prisoner, all of whom were enslaved by their captors. Moore wrote that it was "as hard a battle as was ever fought against Indians." As one recent historian has written, "this was an enormous casualty count for any native society, and it devastated the southern Tuscaroras," essentially ending their ability to resist the Carolinians' offensive threats. Twenty-two of Moore's white soldiers and thirty-five of his Indians were also killed in the operations at Neoheroka. Although most of the northern Tuscaroras remained in North Carolina after the war, the defeat at Neoheroka led Indians of the southern towns to migrate to northern New York among the Five Nations Confederacy, also known as the Iroquois.[54]

After the victory at Neoheroka, Moore's force—reduced by many Indians leaving for home and numerous Carolina deserters—engaged in smaller operations against enemy bands of Coree and Machapunga warriors allied with the Tuscarora. These hostile natives launched sporadic but deadly hit-and-run raids against isolated settlers and plantations from the swamps between Roanoke Island and the Machapunga River, at the headwaters of Pamlico Sound. As Thomas Pollock reported in November 1713, "some scattered parties of our enemies do still distress us out of their swamps and lurking-places, killing many of our people."[55] Moore's forces could not subdue all of the elusive Indians, nor could they prevent their depredations. Rather, North Carolina authorities settled a peace treaty with the remaining Tuscaroras, Corees, and Machapungas in February 1715, by which these Indians received a land reservation in today's Hyde County. Other than a limited role in the Yamasee and Cheraw Wars (1715–1718) in South Carolina, this was the last major Indian conflict to involve North Carolina directly until the French and Indian War (1754–1763).[56] The Tuscarora War left the colony in desperate condition from the destruction of plantations, the disruption of trade, and significant public debt. The devastation and killing came close to wiping out all white settlements below Pamlico Sound, and but for South Carolina's military support and the neutrality of the northern Tuscaroras, the Indians probably would have succeeded in doing so. Instead, as a recent historian has concluded, "the collapse of the Tuscarora in 1713 removed the major obstacle to European expansion in North Carolina. The sixty-year period that whites spent clinging to the eastern sounds was then followed by a sixty-year dash to the Appalachians and beyond."[57]

PIRATES ON THE COAST

Many historians of North Carolina have dubbed the last decade of the seventeenth century and the first two of the eighteenth century as "the Golden Age of Piracy," given the prevalence of brigands prowling the colony's coast and using its ports, banks, and inlets for refuge. Piracy in North American and Caribbean waters was a major concern for merchants, ship captains, seamen, and English authorities for much of the early colonial period, particularly in coastal North Carolina. While pirates did not engage in state-sanctioned military actions per se, their eradication did in fact call for a military response in the early 1700s. Only with the death in 1718 of Blackbeard—perhaps America's most famous pirate—did this troublesome period in the colony's maritime history end.[58]

Even as early as the 1680s, North Carolina had earned a reputation as a refuge for pirates, some of whom shared their ill-gotten booty with colonial officials to avoid interference with their illicit endeavors. As the foremost historian of Carolina piracy has written, the colony's "isolated backwaters provided a perfect haven for the vagabond pirates, and equally appealing were the weak authority of proprietary officials, the sparse settlement, and the relative poverty of the colony."[59] Indeed, pirates and privateers (state-licensed commerce raiders) often enjoyed the support of the common people because smuggled goods were cheaper and more plentiful than those coming into the colony laden with legal duties. North Carolina's geography was well suited to shelter pirates' ships and to conceal their operations, as the seaboard offered a "unique combination of a dangerous outer coast, shoaly sounds, winding creeks, and vast tidal marshes that provided refuges for pirates and smugglers."[60]

Stede Bonnet.

Eventually, complaints from irate merchants whose goods were seized by pirates and the loss of customs revenues from legal trading led English and colonial authorities to institute a campaign to suppress piracy in the West Indies and the coast of North America. One of their prime targets was Stede Bonnet, known at the time as the "Gentleman Pirate." Bonnet was a respectable plantation owner on Barbados and a former militia major who inexplicably turned to piracy in 1717. He used the waterways of Cape Fear to hide and repair his ships between attacks on shipping and coastal towns, and it was here that he was located by Colonel William Rhett of South Carolina, under orders from that colony's governor to capture pirates and destroy their vessels. On September 26, 1718, Rhett and his command of 130 men attacked Bonnet's forty-five outlaws. After a bloody battle of several hours, the Carolinians captured the notorious pirate and thirty-six of his crew, although eighteen of Rhett's men died in the fierce engagement. Taken to Charles Town, all but three of the pirates were executed by colonial officials, but Bonnet escaped. Soon retaken, he was executed by hanging on December 10, reportedly while "clutching a bouquet of wilted flowers."[61]

Colonial America's most infamous pirate was Edward Teach, sometimes called Thack, better known as Blackbeard. He was born in England and became a pirate in American waters at the end of Queen Anne's War in 1713, initially operating from the port of New Providence in the Bahamas, sail-

Blackbeard.

ing *Queen Anne's Revenge* as early as 1710, until British authorities drove him to seek a new lair. In North Carolina, Teach used Bath as his home port by 1718. From there he staged his voyages of piracy on his new eight-gun sloop, *Adventure,* against English, colonial, and foreign ships.[62] The colony's governor, Charles Eden, was thought by Teach to be less than vigorous in his pursuit of pirates, and other North Carolina merchants and officials seemed willing to engage in illicit trade with maritime outlaws.[63] Blackbeard's relationships with some North Carolina officials at Bath was one of collusion when it came to dividing prizes and spreading bribes around, so that it finally fell to Governor Spotswood of Virginia to rid the Carolina coast of Blackbeard's menace, which he saw as "rescueing the Trade of North Carolina from the Insults of Pyrates."[64]

Spotswood launched a combined land and sea operation under Captain Ellis Brand to attack Blackbeard at Ocracoke Inlet, where the pirate was rumored to be establishing a new base at an inlet called Thatch's Hole. Lieutenant Robert Maynard commanded the seaborne part of the expedition and sailed on *Jane,* aboard which he reached Ocracoke on November 21, 1718, along with *Ranger* and the expedition's land force. In the subsequent brief battle the next day on board *Jane* and *Adventure,* Blackbeard was killed by a sword blow from behind, along with ten of his men, while twelve of Maynard's men died in the fight and twenty-two were wounded. Spotswood described the battle from reports he received after the fight:

> I thought it necessary to put a Stop to ye further Progress of the Robberys, and for that purpose, having prevailed with our Assembly to give considerable Rewards for the Apprehending and destroying of these and other Pirates I hired two Sloops, furnished them w'th Pilotts from Carolina, concerted w'th the Capt's of his Maj'ty's Ships of this Station the proper Measures for extirpating that Gang of Pyrates. These Sloops, fitted with Men and Officers from the King's Ships, Came up with Tach at Oecceh inlett on ye 22nd Nov'r last, and after an obstinate Resistance, wherein Tach, w'th nine of his men, were killed, and nine more made prisoners, and took his Sloop, w'ch was mounted w'th 8 Guns, and in all other respects fitted rather for piracy than Trade.

Maynard cut off Teach's head and strung it from *Adventure*'s bowsprit before he sailed back to Virginia two weeks later. Authorities in Virginia displayed the skull of the decapitated pirate near the capital as a warning to others bent toward piracy. The pirates' "golden age" was in effect at an end.[65]

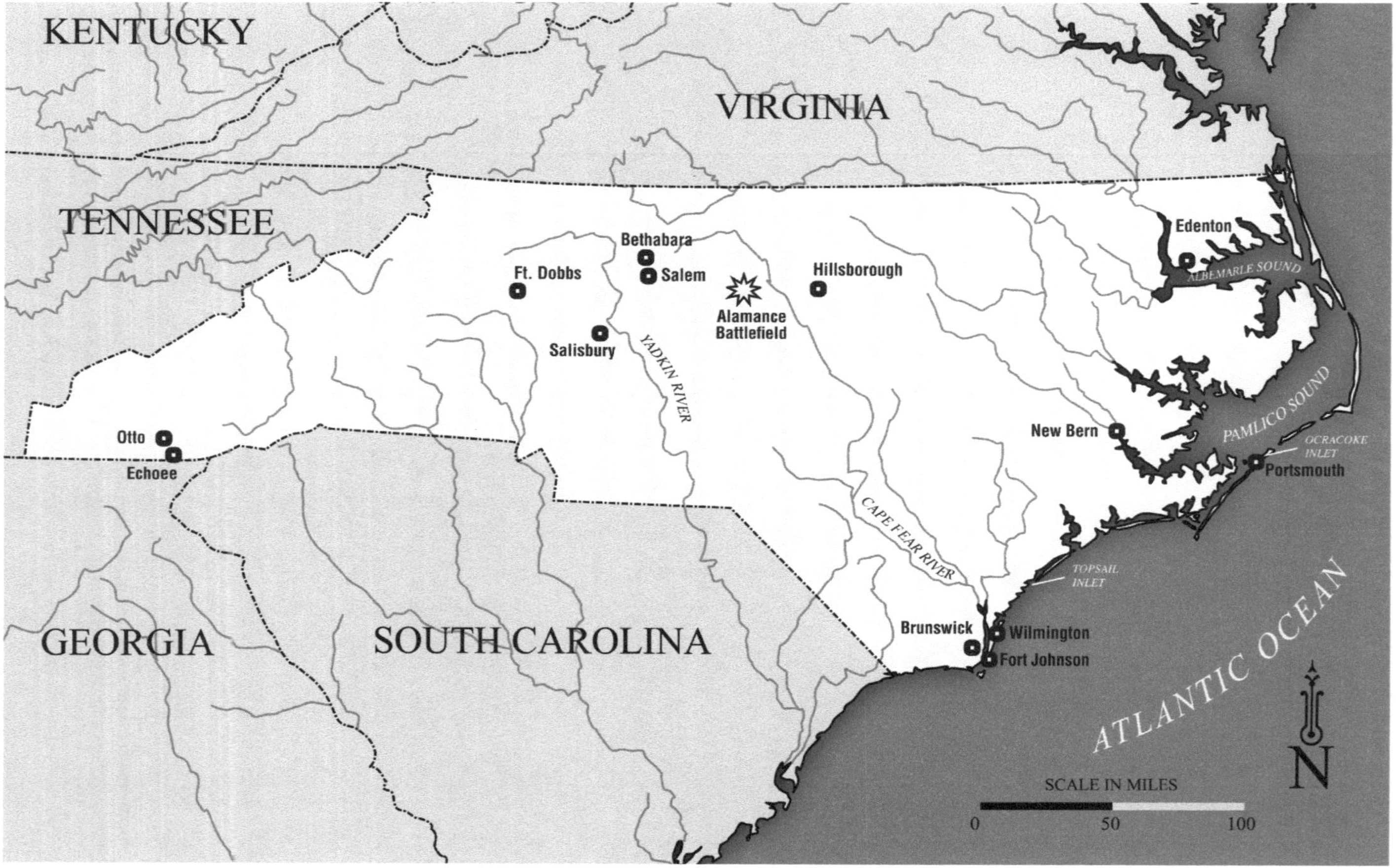
KENTUCKY
VIRGINIA
TENNESSEE
GEORGIA
SOUTH CAROLINA
ATLANTIC OCEAN
Edenton
ALBEMARLE SOUND
Bethabara
Salem
Ft. Dobbs
Hillsborough
Alamance Battlefield
Salisbury
YADKIN RIVER
PAMLICO SOUND
OCRACOKE INLET
Portsmouth
New Bern
Otto
Echoee
CAPE FEAR RIVER
TOPSAIL INLET
Brunswick
Wilmington
Fort Johnson
SCALE IN MILES
0
50
100
N

3. Wars of Empire

EARLY IMPERIAL CONFLICTS

In 1729, the British Crown took over the administration and government of colonial North Carolina, having purchased the shares of seven of the eight proprietors.[1] For Carolinians, the absence of the proprietary government meant little in their daily lives, although from that point until the beginning of the American Revolution, there was more stability in the office of governor than during the tumultuous proprietary years. The new royal government also became more closely connected with British imperial concerns and now "had a much closer relationship to the King and Privy Council and to various British administrative agencies."[2] Moreover, as time went on, London authorities increasingly exercised the royal prerogative in matters affecting the colony, which was often resented and resisted by North Carolinians. This opposition created a growing antagonism between royal governors appointed by the Crown and the inhabitants' representatives in the lower house of the colonial assembly.[3]

During North Carolina's period of royal government, the colony became enmeshed in Britain's conflicts with France and Spain. Although the province was poor and (at least until the 1750s) sparsely populated, the king and his ministers called on the colony to contribute soldiers and money for campaigns in North America and the Caribbean during times of war. From the early 1740s until 1763, North Carolina participated in several military campaigns, faced invasions, and reacted to British demands for assistance in its imperial struggles. Danger of invasion from Spanish-held Florida worried Carolina officials, particularly before Georgia was settled as a buffer colony in 1733. So did the threat of Indian attacks from the west, often encouraged by the French and Spanish in the backcountry. The colony's ports were vulnerable to seaborne attack from European powers as well. Not until the end of the French and Indian War in 1763 did these military concerns abate, although the threat from Native Americans remained.[4]

North Carolina first got a taste of imperial warfare in the War of the Spanish Succession. This conflict was known in the American provinces as Queen Anne's War, a struggle in which England battled France and Spain primarily in Europe from 1702-1713. During that time, enemy warships periodically raided the undefended North Carolina coast, where colonial authorities went to considerable expense "in establishing a force to repel them." With little or no assistance from London to defend the province, Carolinians were "open and exposed to every invasion, being an easy prey to their merciless and insulting Enemys the French and Spaniards," reported a British customs official. The turbulent political situation within the colony that culminated in Cary's Rebellion further weakened North Carolina's ability to respond to enemy incursions, as did the destructive Tuscarora War.[5]

Over two decades later, the conflict between the British and Spanish known in America as the War of Jenkins' Ear began in October 1739 over maritime trade issues in the Atlantic, including an incident at sea in which Spanish sailors sliced off the ear of an English captain named Jenkins. Britain's war aim was to cripple Spanish trade on the high seas and the Caribbean and to capture territory in America, the West Indies, and the Spanish Main (as Spain's South American mainland possessions were then called). To bolster his naval strength, King George II authorized American colonial governors to "issue forth, and grant commissions . . . for arming and fitting our private Ships of War, for the apprehending, seizing and taking the Ships, Vessels, and Goods belonging to the King of Spain, His Vassals, and Subjects." This, of course, was a license for privateers to attack enemy ships at their pleasure.[6]

On a grander scale, in 1741, Vice Admiral Edward Vernon received the command of a joint land and sea expedition against the fortified Spanish port of Cartagena, on the coast of modern Colombia. To support this ambitious campaign, the British military establishment called on the American colonies to raise an unusually large regiment of 3,373 officers and men to join over eight thousand troops at Jamaica before being transported to Cartagena to attack the city and its formidable defenses.[7] Each North American colony was to raise at least one company of soldiers, except South Carolina and Georgia, which were threatened by Spanish forces at nearby St. Augustine. This was the first conflict in which North Carolina raised troops to serve alongside British regulars. The American regiment's commander was Colonel William Gooch, the lieutenant governor of Virginia and a former British officer in the 16th Regiment of Foot. His new command, designated the 43rd Foot, was divided into four battalions, each of which included one of North Carolina's four companies of one hundred men, armed and equipped by the British Crown. As a recent historian has described the American colonial troops, these men were "a mixed bag of farmers, tradesmen, craftsmen, laborers, debtors, militiamen, ex-convicts, the destitute, and the unemployed, each with his own reason for joining." Nevertheless, recruiting was brisk. In

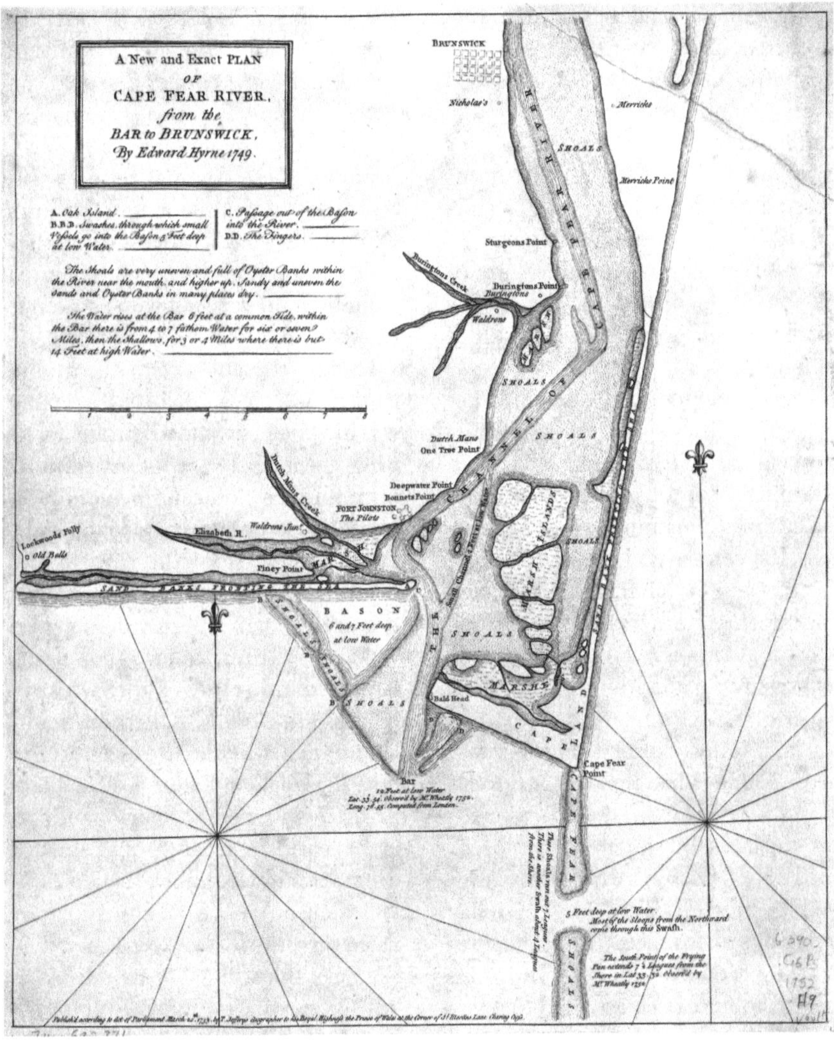

A new and exact plan of Cape Fear River, from the bar to Brunswick, 1753.

fact, the colony's governor, Gabriel Johnston, reported that "in those Northern Parts of the Colony adjoining to Virginia we have got 3 Companies of 100 men each tho some few deserted since they began to send them on board the Transports at Cape Fear." He also observed that the colony could "have easily have raised 200 more if it had been possible to negotiate the Bills of Exchange in this part of the Continent; but as that was impracticable, we were obliged to rest satisfyed with four Companies." Soldiers in Gooch's regiment were to be uniformed in unlaced red coats with green cuffs and facings, although how many of the men were clothed according to these regulations is unknown. The Crown provided muskets and accoutrements for the companies as well. Before sailing for the West Indies, the regiment numbered about 3,600 men, with recruiting no doubt stimulated by expectation of land grants and the "lure of lute on the Spanish Main," though few of these men ever saw a farthing of plunder.[8]

The regiment's thirty-six companies began to reach Jamaica in transport ships in early December 1740, North Carolina's men having sailed from Edenton and Wilmington in November (the colony was too poor to hire the transports). Gooch's men arrived earlier than anticipated by British army logisticians, who had done little to prepare for the American soldiers. Most of Gooch's regiment remained on their leaky, crowded ships because army planners had sent no tents to Jamaica for their use. The "unseasoned" provincials soon sickened, and dozens died of poor rations, exposure, scurvy, and tropical diseases. The men "lay dying like rotten sheep," one soldier remarked. Moreover, the colonial troops appear to have been assigned to onerous tasks as Vernon's forces proceeded to Cartagena because most of the British officers regarded the American recruits as poor soldiers fit mainly for menial work. The expedition finally arrived near Cartagena in late February 1741. During the offensive against the port city, only a few of Gooch's men saw action on shore, as all but a few hundred of the colonial soldiers had been previously assigned to serve aboard Vernon's men-of-war to replace the many sailors lost to disease.[9] In April 1741, for example, 2,203 men of the American regiment served on British ships, while only 527 remained aboard the regiment's transports. Many of these colonial soldiers suffered harsh treatment and beatings from British naval officers while they toiled at their naval tasks, separated from their officers and with no avenue of recourse.[10]

During the attempt to storm and capture Cartagena, British leadership was incompetent, and a detrimental rivalry ensued between the expedition's army and navy officers, including Admiral Vernon. Most of the soldiers suffered terribly from the climate and diseases, and the army's attacks against the well-designed Spanish defenses were disastrous, once they were launched in April 1741 after weeks of delays.[11] In early May, Vernon finally abandoned the disastrous efforts to take the port, and after a subsequent unsuccessful operation at Santiago, Cuba, the provincial troops returned to Jamaica in December. By that time, 485 men of Gooch's command were listed on returns as sick, 851 served on the navy ships, and 119 were listed as "fit for duty." Two hundred fourteen had died during the previous month alone. Despite these devastating losses, in March 1742, British leaders ordered the American regiment to accompany an attack on the Spanish city of Porto Bello, Panama; this effort also ended in failure that summer. By October that year, the American regiment numbered only 17 officers and 130 men fit for duty, along with 200 men drafted into another regiment and 268 soldiers on the sick rolls. Later that month, the regiment was finally disbanded and the survivors shipped home, including one transport vessel to North Carolina carrying the Cape Fear company raised in 1740. Only twenty-five soldiers remained from this group, and records do not indicate that any more troops returned to North Carolina. Gooch's soldiers had "undergone a good deal of hazard, and hardships, during their service in this part of the world," wrote a senior British officer in 1742, an understatement given the shockingly high losses suffered by the men and officers of the American regiment.[12]

Admiral Vernon's debacle at Cartagena did not end the conflict between Spain and Great Britain. By 1740, the War of Jenkins' Ear was overshadowed by and became part of the War of the Austrian Succession, a predominantly European conflict that pitted Austria and Great Britain against Prussia, Spain, France, Bavaria, and Saxony over dynastic issues until the Treaty of Aix-la-Chapelle in 1748. During this time, French and Spanish ships raided the North Carolina coast, capturing ships and plundering towns as part of what American colonists called King George's War. In 1745, "for the better securing of the Inhabitants of [the Cape Fear River] from any Insult and Invasion," the North Carolina Assembly authorized the construction of Fort Johnston (at today's Southport), named in honor of Gov. Gabriel Johnston, although construction did not begin until 1748. The assembly had "Reason to fear that such Parts of this Province which are situated most commodious for Shipping to enter may be invaded by the Enemy," and the "Entrance of Cape Fear River, from its known Depth of Water and other Conveniences for Navigation, may tempt them to such an Enterprize, while it remains in so naked and defenceless a Condition as it now is." The legislature required that the fort "shall be large enough to contain at least Twenty Four Cannon, with Barracks and other Conveniences for Soldiers," but by the time the war ended, the work was incomplete.[13]

The latter few years of the struggle with Spain were ones in which the colony's "trade is so distressed, Our Ships Plundered in our Harbours & our Coasts Insulted by a Cruel & Vigilent Enemy," according to Governor Johnston,[14] probably referring to events of 1747. "Several small Sloops & Barcalonjos came creeping along the shore from St Augustine full of armed men," he reported to the Board of Trade in London a few years later, "mostly Mulattoes & Negroes, their small Draught of water secured them from the attacks of the only [British] ship of war then on this station." These Spanish raiders "landed at Ocacock Core sound, Bear Inlet, and Cape Fear, where they killed several of his Majesty's subjects, burned some ships and several small Vessels, carried off some Negroes, and slaughtered a Vast number of Black Cattle and Hogs." Johnston complained that "these Practices were continued all the summer 1747 and enraged the People to the highest degree, they exclaimed that there was no safety for them without Forts." He reminded the board that "as there was no money in the Treasury Forts could not be erected without an immediate Emission of Publick Bills," by which he meant paper currency issued within the colony. Knowing that London officials generally disapproved of colonial paper emissions, Johnston explained that he tried "to do it in such a manner that his Majesties service, and the Country in General, will be greater gainers by it." Thus, Johnston required that "Four Forts should be built, two large Ones, one at Ocacock the other at Cape Fear, and two smaller, One at Core sound, the other at Bear Inlet," and that the amount of paper money be strictly limited. "His Majesty has gained four Forts," the governor assured the Board, "one of them . . . at Cape Fear already finished [Fort Johnston], and the rest going about."[15]

In 1747, Spanish ships attacked and looted the small town of Beaufort on Core Sound, but the most significant event of King George's War in North Carolina was the September 1748 Spanish naval attack on Brunswick, a deep water port founded in 1725 along the lower Cape Fear River south of Wilmington. On September 3, two Spanish privateers sailed into the river under false English colors, passed Fort Johnston undetected, and anchored three miles below Brunswick, on the river's right bank. As detailed in a newspaper report, the Spaniards "landed about 60 men, who march'd by Land to the Town; immediately on their coming to Town the sloops fired at it, which made all the Inhabitants run away." The privateers then spent several days looting the town and capturing several small vessels at the port, which they intended to take with them, along with plundered valuables.[16]

Although initially scattered, Brunswick's residents were quick to regroup and plot a counterattack. Port Collector William Dry III gathered a group of sixty armed men, "one third Negroes," at nearby Orton Plantation. Dry led the small force to the port town and attacked the plundering Spanish in the town and on the wharfs, taking them by surprise. One of the Spanish ships fired "Partridge Shot very briskly" at Dry's men, but the Carolinians routed the Spanish on shore, some of whom tried to escape in a brig at the end of the wharf while others jumped into the water to escape. Most of the Spanish raiders surrendered, while Dry's men shot the Spaniards who tried to flee: "many were slain in the Bushes," one report noted. Soon the town's defenders managed to set fire to one of the Spanish sloops with a well-placed shot from their small cannon on land. While Dry had his men rescue some of the surviving privateers in the water, the "Negroes, now like mad Devils, shot many swimming, in spight of all Orders to the contrary." The other enemy ship still fired on the town, but after unsuccessfully trying to get Dry to release the captives, the Spanish captain sailed off. The Carolinians lost only a handful of men defending the town but sustained approximately £1,000 sterling in property damages.[17]

NORTH CAROLINA AND THE SEVEN YEARS' WAR, 1754–1763

A few years after the conclusion of King George's War in the colonies, the largest imperial war to date ignited in the American backcountry over frontier land claims. The Seven Years' War was a global conflict involving Great Britain, its colonies, and Prussia against France, Spain, Russia, Austria, and (in America) their Indian allies, in which the British emerged triumphant in 1763. The North American phase of this war is known as the French and Indian War, which started in 1754 in the wilderness of western Pennsylvania over the control of the Ohio River Valley, a region claimed by France, Great Britain, and Native Americans. Most of the American campaigns in this nine-year struggle took place in Canada, northern New York, and western Pennsylvania and included the more famous battles associated with the war: Fort Duquesne, Fort Ticonderoga, Fort William Henry, the siege of Louisbourg, and Quebec. Contrary to popular belief and much of the war's historiography, Britain's southern colonies were also involved in the conflict, including North Carolina. While the colony had limited resources and a widely dispersed and contentious population, and was not the scene of any major military campaigns during the imperial contest, the French and Indian War nonetheless had a significant impact on North Carolina.[18]

While the Seven Years' War did not begin in Europe until 1756, in America the conflict began two years earlier. In 1753, London officials asked North Carolina's acting governor, Executive Council President Matthew Rowan, to watch the colony's frontiers for French and Indian threats. Rowan was also expected to call the assembly into session in order to authorize and finance preparations for war in cooperation with other colonies "in case of any invasion." The following year, the assembly voted to provide assistance to Virginia for that province's efforts to secure the Forks of the Ohio, a strategic location at the site of modern Pittsburgh on land claimed by the Old Dominion, Pennsylvania, and the French. The Carolina lawmakers authorized £12,000 in paper currency to raise and equip one regiment of 750 provincial soldiers for service in the Ohio Country. Rowan appointed Scottish-born Colonel James Innes, a veteran of the 1741 Cartagena campaign and a member of the colony's council, to command the regiment and lead it to Virginia. North Carolina's ongoing financial problems impeded the efforts to get the new regiment properly organized and ready to march. Even before the soldiers marched off from the colony, Rowan had to reduce its strength to 450 recruits due to a lack of available arms, uniforms, and provisions. Logistical problems continued for Innes's command as the men marched toward Winchester, in the Shenandoah Valley. Merchants and suppliers in Virginia refused to accept paper currency issued by North Carolina's assembly, so Innes was unable to purchase provisions for the men as they moved north. The regiment was instead obliged to drive cattle and hogs with them to slaughter as needed, or to trade them for supplies.[19]

Innes's regiment was an unimpressive collection of men—"neither disciplined nor armed," observed South Carolina Gov. James Glenn—and by the time the unit reached Winchester, desertion and illness had reduced its strength and morale. One company of the regiment from western North Carolina mutinied at Staunton, Virginia, over pay as they marched north in the Shenandoah Valley and could not be persuaded to go farther. At Winchester, the Carolinians discovered that Virginia Gov. Robert Dinwiddie had not arranged for provisions or ammunition for them, as he expected them to be supplied from their own province. Meanwhile, a combined force of Virginia provincials under Lieutenant Colonel George Washington and a British independent company from South Carolina ignominiously surrendered to French troops and their Indian allies on July 4, 1754, at Fort Necessity, a small wilderness outpost in Pennsylvania, about sixty miles from Fort Duquesne, at the Forks of the Ohio. The weary North Carolinians did not arrive on the frontier in time to see any action against the enemy or assist Washington. With little expectation of support from Virginia and desertions increasing, Innes had to disband the regiment on August 11 and send the remainder of his ragged soldiers home.[20]

Following the fiasco of the colony's attempt to contribute troops for Virginia's relief in 1754, the following year North Carolina recruited a company of one hundred men to serve under Captain Edward Brice Dobbs (nephew of the colony's new royal governor, Arthur Dobbs, and a commissioned British army officer). These recruits were uniformed in blue wool coats with red cuffs and facings, and armed with large-caliber Dutch muskets, steel bayonets, and belly boxes for their cartridges. In spring 1755, Dobbs's company sailed up the Potomac to Alexandria in preparation for a major summer campaign, and from this port the captain marched the men to Fort Cumberland, a post along the Potomac in western Maryland. Here they joined the troops of General Edward Braddock, the senior British army commander in America, whose mixed force of army regulars and provincials prepared to blaze a wilderness trail to the Ohio and capture the strategic French post of Fort Duquesne.[21]

Once they joined Braddock's gathering army in late May, Dobbs's company—now reduced to seventy-two men due to desertions—was attached to the brigade of Colonel Thomas Dunbar, a British regular officer. Braddock set out for Fort Duquesne soon thereafter with his entire force, but after the expedition's progress suffered delays by the army's excessive baggage and the difficult mountainous terrain, the general divided his command in two. A strong contingent of troops unburdened of equipment, wagons, and artillery led by Braddock proceeded more quickly toward the Ohio River, while Dunbar followed with the remaining troops in their wake. Braddock's lead element was almost completely wiped out by French colonial troops and hundreds of enemy Indians a few miles short of Fort Duquesne on July 9. The North Carolinians, as part of Dunbar's rear element, were not involved in the disaster, saw no fighting, and retreated with their brigade and Braddock's survivors to Fort Cumberland by July 17. Once safe at the fort, many of the Carolinians began to desert, especially after Dunbar took his British redcoats back to Philadelphia in August, leaving the frontier of Virginia and Pennsylvania open to enemy attacks.[22]

The following year, North Carolina once again provided a small contingent of troops to strengthen British forces in a northern campaign. At the urging of Governor Dobbs, the colony managed to put four companies of provincials on foot commanded by Captain Dobbs to participate in operations in 1756. Few records exist regarding the North Carolina troops in the northern theater that year, but Governor Dobbs did report that he "sent over 4 Companies under the Command of my son" to New York and appointed him major since he also had a commission in the British regulars. These troops traveled by ship to New York City, then up the Hudson River to Albany by May. The Carolinians subsequently served along the Mohawk River at German Flatts, supporting the British logistical efforts to supply Fort Oswego, until it was captured by French forces under General Louis-Joseph de Montcalm on August 14.[23] By summer, however, the colony could no longer maintain and pay the troops in upstate New York because of logistical and financial constraints. Senior British army officers attempted to enlist the remaining Carolinians in regular army battalions en masse, and while some of the men joined the 60th (Royal American) Regiment of Foot, most of the soldiers refused and were discharged.[24]

The British had won few victories in America by that point, but their handling of the war changed markedly in 1757 when William Pitt became the secretary of state for the Southern Department and assumed responsibility for the Crown's war efforts. He acted vigorously to increase colonial involvement in the North American military campaigns, primarily by treating them as imperial partners and offering to reimburse the colonies' expenses in providing troops and supplies. Pitt urged Governor Dobbs to "use all your influence" with the assembly to obtain men and money for the coming year. He also asked North Carolina "to raise with the utmost Expedition as large a number of Provincial Forces as may be for the Service of the ensuing campaign," beyond what was required for local defense. Pitt retained General John Campbell, Lord Loudoun, as military commander in America, and the general met with the southern colonial governors in Philadelphia to plan strategy in March 1757. Loudoun asked Governor Dobbs to have North Carolina furnish four companies of soldiers, half of whom were to serve one year in South Carolina in anticipation of possible hostilities with the Cherokees on the western frontier.[25]

In 1757, the North Carolina Assembly voted to provide £5,300 for military use and required that its provincial companies serve up to six months in South Carolina, although it later compromised by allowing Dobbs to deploy the soldiers in any colony he saw fit.[26] In the end, the Indian threat to South Carolina was not dangerous enough to warrant Dobbs's sending his newly raised companies to the frontier.[27] Dobbs instead sent the troops to garrison coastal forts, and one company went to Pennsylvania. The colony also raised and maintained two companies of rangers in the backcountry to guard against "any incursions of the Indians." At the end of the year, Dobbs was able to report to Pitt that "we are still free from any Incursions of the Indians in this province, having kept 2 Companies on the Western Frontier, but must now remove one of them to secure our Forts and Batteries on the Sea Coast."[28]

In 1758, British and American authorities launched several campaigns against the French and Indians in North America, including a final effort to capture Fort Duquesne. Brigadier General John Forbes, a veteran of the War of the Austrian Succession and the Scottish Jacobite Rising of 1745, commanded the British and colonial effort to march from Carlisle, Pennsylvania, across the Allegheny Mountains to the Forks of the Ohio with a force of approximately seven thousand men. Although the advance element of Forbes's column was bloodied in a September skirmish with French and Indians operating from Duquesne, the general immediately marched toward the fort in November upon receipt of intelligence that the French had recently evacuated the position. The British force reached its objective on November 25 and found the fort had been hastily abandoned and burned by the enemy.[29]

At the urging of Secretary Pitt and Governor Dobbs,[30] the North Carolina Assembly voted to provide support for Forbes's campaign when it met in late April. The colony agreed to raise three hundred troops under Major Hugh Waddell for Forbes's operations in Pennsylvania and authorized £7,000 to support these soldiers until they reached the British army's camp in Pennsylvania. One company marched north from the Carolina frontier up the Great Wagon Road while two others went by ship to Alexandria, then marched overland to rendezvous with Forbes. Much like the difficulties encountered in 1754, Waddell's men were in "absolute want of everything," including muskets, tents, and uniforms. By July 20, the two companies that had traveled through Alexandria mustered only ninety-six men, having lost about one hundred soldiers from desertion, and their progress marching to Forbes's army was slow. One officer of the 60th Regiment said the Carolinians were "in a pitiable condition, and lack health, uniforms, and everything. I have never seen such misery. I believe they are good only for eating our provisions and guarding a fort."[31]

Once at the army's main camp, the Carolina troops fell under the command of George Washington, along with the other provincial companies from Virginia, Pennsylvania, Maryland, and Delaware. On the march to Fort Duquesne, Waddell's men served as rangers for the army and provided valuable intelligence to General Forbes as the troops marched west through the dense forests of Pennsylvania. While posted at the newly erected Fort Ligonier on Loyalhanna Creek (forty-five miles from Fort Duquesne) in October, they helped fight off a three-hour Indian attack. Three North Carolina provincials were killed during the fighting. After reaching the abandoned Fort Duquesne with Washington's brigade in late November, the Carolina companies received their discharge at the fort and marched overland for home under Waddell's command.[32]

While North Carolina encountered difficulty raising, arming, and equipping quality soldiers to serve in its provincial companies throughout the war because of the colony's straitened finances and recalcitrant populace, for Governor Dobbs, the colonial assembly also proved to be a hindrance to effective military mobilization. After 1754, the North Carolina Assembly became parsimonious with its funds to support the British war efforts and confrontational with Dobbs over matters related to the royal prerogative, which the touchy governor was invariably quick to defend. Having previously authorized the large regiment of 750 men in 1754 along with £12,000 to provide for them, by late 1757, the assembly only allowed three companies of fifty men each.[33] As noted above, the colony had placed three hundred men under Waddell to serve in Pennsylvania with Forbes in 1758. However, in the second assembly session that year, the legislators refused to provide more men or money for prosecuting the war, primarily because of ongoing political conflicts with Dobbs and the delegates' claims of limited resources.[34] At the assembly's session of May 1759 at New Bern, the legislature again failed to provide any aid for the war, citing the governor's infringement of its own rights of financial appropriations and his vehement opposition to the appointment of the legislature's own agent to London. The contentious session prompted a frustrated Dobbs to write to the Board of Trade, "I hope we shall soon have peace, and then his Majesty will have no great demands upon this Province."[35]

In addition to providing a limited number of men and funds for the war's northern military campaigns, North Carolina sought to provide for the colony's defense on its seacoast and western frontier. The assembly authorized renovations on Fort Johnston near Brunswick, which Dobbs described as "one small square fort with 4. little bastions and a Fosse, the ramparts and Parapets of a Sandy earth faced with upright pines which were all rotten, in which they had only 6. or 7. small ship iron guns all honeycombed, 3. or 4. of which were 2. pounders and the rest 4. pounders and no garrison but 2. or 3. men to keep the fort and this was all the safety in the Province to defend the most navigable river in the Province, the river of Cape Fear."

Conjectural view of Fort Dobbs reconstructed on original site. (*Courtesy Scott Douglas, Fort Dobbs State Historic Site*)

Construction also began on smaller coastal batteries at Ocracoke Inlet, Portsmouth, and Topsail Inlet. The governor petitioned London officials several times to construct a battery at Point Lookout as well, but it was never constructed. In recognition of the threat from the Cherokees, in 1755 the colony authorized construction of a fort to serve as a base for one of the western companies of rangers and for the protection of frontier settlers in distant Rowan County. Construction of the hewn-log fort was completed in 1756 and it was named Fort Dobbs, standing on one of the "Forks of the Yadkin" along Sherrill's Path, near modern Statesville. Although no contemporary drawing or plan of the fort has been discovered, observers described the structure in 1756 as

> A good and Substantial Building of the Dimentions following (that is to say) The Oblong Square fifty three feet by forty, the opposite Angles Twenty four feet and Twenty-two, In height Twenty four and a half feet as by the Plan annexed Appears, The Thickness of the Walls which are made of Oak Logs regularly Diminished from sixteen Inches to Six, it contains three floors and there may be discharged from each floor at one and the same time about one hundred Muskets the same is beautifully scituated in the fork of Fourth Creek a Branch of the Yadkin River.

This fort was the only defensive structure built by the colony on the frontier during the French and Indian War, although many settlers fortified their own homesteads once the conflict with the Cherokees erupted, and the small Moravian settlement of Bethabara was stockaded as well.[36]

Isolated attacks and sporadic violence by Cherokee raiding parties in North Carolina and Virginia in 1759 steadily transformed by the next year into a full-scale conflict known as the Cherokee War. The Cherokee Nation, located in the far western reaches of the Carolinas and in what is now eastern Tennessee and northern Georgia, was one of the most powerful native groups in the American South. By the mid-1750s, they had become increasingly alienated from the English colonies because of encroaching white settlements in their traditional homeland. French emissaries to the Cherokees often fanned the flames of their resentment and anxiety. The Cherokees had long been allied with the British, but in 1758, white militiamen attacked and killed a small party of Cherokees traveling through southwestern Virginia after the Indians had slaughtered some stolen cattle. This violent incident enraged the Cherokees and sparked numerous retaliatory raids in the Carolina backcountry starting in 1759.[37] Indian war parties struck farms and towns, including Salisbury, which forced hundreds of settlers to flee their homes, move east, and cross the Yadkin River for safety. Alarms spread all over the frontier, particularly after a group of Cherokees returning from Forbes's expedition killed a dozen settlers in the upper Yadkin River Valley in late April 1759.[38]

South Carolina's frontier was also hard hit by violence, which prompted the colony's governor, William Lyttelton, to plan a fall military expedition against the Cherokees and request assistance from Virginia and North Carolina. Governor Dobbs responded promptly to the call for aid after he received Lyttelton's urgent message on October 1. He summoned the colonial council to meet, ordered county militia officers to place their men in readiness for anticipated service on the frontier, and commissioned Hugh Waddell as colonel of militia, with orders to mobilize the militia regiments in the western counties of Anson, Rowan, and Orange. Dobbs directed Waddell to cooperate with Lyttelton's campaign or with Virginia forces moving into Cherokee territory from the north. He also sent Lyttelton "a Supply of Barrils of Gunpowder and 4000 weight of Bullets[,] Swan Shot and Lead, & 1500 Flints," all that was in his power to do until the colony's assembly met in Wilmington at the end of November.[39] When the assembly did convene, it voted £5,000 for the campaign, along with £2,900 for the completion of Fort Johnston. Getting troops to serve in the field was another matter. Waddell had difficulty with the backcountry militia forces under his command, particularly since the majority of the embodied troops refused to serve outside North Carolina's borders. None of Waddell's forces served with Lyttelton, whose bloodless campaign in western South Carolina ended in late December with hostage taking and an agreement to ensure the Cherokees halted their frontier depredations.[40]

Despite Lyttelton's treaty with the Cherokees, violence again erupted in North Carolina's western counties in winter and spring 1760, concentrated along the Catawba, Yadkin, and Broad Rivers. A group of over sixty Cherokees attacked Fort Dobbs on the night of February 27, but they were defeated outside the defensive walls. The garrison suffered two men wounded, but a boy outside the fort was killed. Waddell described the incident and his company's counterattack to Governor Dobbs:

> We had not marched 300 yds from the fort when we were attacked by at least 60 or 70 Indians. . . . We recd the Indian's fire: When I perceived they had almost all fired, I ordered my party to fire which We did not further than 12 Steps each loaded with a Bullet and 7 Buck shot, they had nothing to cover them as they were advancing either to tomahawk or make us prisoners . . . the Indians were soon repulsed with I am sure a considerable Loss, from what I myself saw as well as those I can confide in they cou'd not have less that 10 or 12 killed and wounded.[41]

Companies of rangers patrolled the frontier while settlers erected log blockhouses and stockades scattered from Smiths River (in today's Rockingham County) to the Holston River in Tennessee. Hundreds of families fled to the protection of the new Moravian settlements east of the Yadkin, as Cherokees attacked farms as far east as modern Mayodan.[42]

With the backcountry engulfed in violence, Governor Dobbs called the assembly to meet in April at New Bern to raise troops and money for the colony's defense and to assist the main British war effort, now led by Major General Jeffrey Amherst. In an unusually divisive session, Dobbs and the lower house battled over various political issues, the colony's court system, military aid, and money. In the end, the governor rejected the assembly's military bill as "crude and undigested," encumbered by extraneous riders, and useless. Thus at a time when the frontier was a scene of death and destruction and a renewed campaign against the Cherokees was getting underway in South Carolina, the assembly and the governor found no way to compromise to allow a military aid measure to pass.[43]

Arthur Dobbs was nothing if not persistent, and in another attempt to convince legislators to defend the colony and attack the Cherokees, he called for an assembly session for June 1760, to see if "the spreading flames of war will induce them to give a supply and raise Men without Clogs or Delay now [that] the storm approaches." Dobbs implored the assembly to provide for the province's defense and support the spring campaign against the Cherokees, which included hundreds of British regulars led by Colonel Archibald Montgomery, supported by Virginia and South Carolina. In light of the violence raging in the backcountry, North Carolina's lower house agreed to provide £12,000 and three hundred men in four companies which could serve outside the colony.[44] This support was too late to be of assistance, however, as Montgomery and his force of redcoats, rangers, and provincials suffered a defeat after Cherokees ambushed the British column on June 27 along the Little Tennessee River, near modern Otto, North Carolina. The redcoats lost seventeen men killed, and sixty-six were wounded in the mountainous terrain well suited to Cherokee tactics. Montgomery marched his bloodied force back to Charleston and departed for New York with most of the regulars.[45]

At the assembly's next session in November 1760, Dobbs rejected a proposal to raise five hundred soldiers and £16,494 for defense against the Cherokees and to help neighboring colonies. General Amherst hoped the colony's inhabitants would not be "backward in Exerting themselves to their utmost," but the governor again found the bill to have too many unrelated riders attached. Dobbs called the legislature to meet again in March 1761, although he had little hope that the members could be prevailed upon to provide meaningful military assistance.[46] In the meantime, the war in the northern theater had ended with British victories at Quebec in 1759 and Montreal the following year. General Amherst began to transfer troops from Canada to the West Indies and the southern mainland colonies, including a force of regulars under Lieutenant Colonel James Grant that arrived in South Carolina in January for service against the Cherokees. Grant initiated his campaign from Fort Ninety-Six in May, expecting Virginia and North Carolina to send their own troops to the frontier in support of his operations.[47]

In Wilmington, assemblymen gathered at the end of March to debate providing support for Grant's upcoming expedition. After condemning Dobbs for rejecting their aid bill during the previous session, they allowed for five hundred men to be raised for the new campaign, supported by £20,000 in paper currency, to which Dobbs reluctantly assented. Grant's column marched from Fort Prince George, in South Carolina's far backcountry, to the Cherokee's Middle Settlements in western North Carolina in June, and after defeating an enemy force in the mountains near Echoee, his troops destroyed Cherokee towns, crops, and granaries in their homeland. Grant's victorious column returned to Fort Prince George by July 9, and the defeated Cherokees asked for peace the next month.[48]

In North Carolina, Governor Dobbs ordered his colony's troops to move to Fort Dobbs on the frontier, under

Blue Ridge Mountains, western North Carolina.

Colonel Waddell's command. These men were to cooperate with a Virginia regiment under Colonel William Byrd III to attack and destroy the Cherokee's tramontane Overhill Towns, in Tennessee. Byrd's successor, Lieutenant Colonel Adam Stephen, sent an urgent request to Waddell in September asking that he immediately send the North Carolina troops to Long Island on the Holston River, even in separate detachments if necessary. Waddell replied that his men were inadequately armed and accoutered but managed to march over four hundred men from Bethabara across the Blue Ridge to Long Island on the Holston River (presentday Kingsport, Tennessee) by the end of October. By this time, the hostilities had for the most part ended, and the Overhill Cherokees signed a peace treaty with Virginia on November 20. No longer needed on the frontier, Waddell and his provincials marched away from the Holston River on December 1, ending all military action for North Carolina troops for the war. Although Dobbs, Amherst, and officials in London still called for support from the colony in 1762, the assembly declined to offer any further assistance, citing its "present Impoverished Circumstances." Most likely with the Indians defeated in the backcountry and no further threats from the French, Carolinians saw no need to pay for additional military assistance to the Crown. Dobbs did provide a small garrison for the coastal forts with the approval of his council and raised some additional troops with discretionary funds, but for the most part the Seven Years' War was over for North Carolina.[49]

With the exception of 1754, during which North Carolina attempted to provide a large regiment of provincials for service on the Ohio, the colony offered modest assistance to the imperial war efforts, even while its borders were under attack from hostile Cherokees. The assembly had issued £72,000 in proclamation money beginning in 1754, and £30,776 in interest-bearing treasury notes, great sums for a poor colony. Dobbs's letters to Pitt, Loudoun, and the Board of Trade show his frustration with the colonial assembly for their parsimony and—in his eyes—obstructionism. After eight years of political battles with the colony's lower house, Dobbs recognized a new atmosphere in North Carolina, at least that which was represented in the colonial assembly. In a letter to General Amherst in 1762, he made an ominous prediction. "It will be necessary," he wrote the British commander, "to have some British Force to Keep Down the rising Spirit of Independency."[50]

4. The Regulator Movement and the Battle of Alamance, 1771

BACKCOUNTRY TURMOIL

Historians of the so-called War of the Regulation in North Carolina have interpreted this colonial backcountry protest movement in a variety of ways. For much of the nineteenth century and afterward, many scholars regarded the conflict as the opening skirmish in the American Revolution. William Edward Fitch's 1905 book *Some Neglected History of North Carolina* is an example, in that Fitch styled the conflict's culminating 1771 Battle of Alamance as "the First Battle of the American Revolution."[1] Likewise, a granite monument erected in 1880 at the Alamance battlefield reads: "First Battle of the Revolution Here was Fought the Battle of Alamance. May, 16, 1771. Between the British and the Regulators."[2]

While historian Roger Ekirch is correct that "the Regulation is in fact one of the few events in the state's early history that has aroused any significant level of historiographical debate," serious scholars today do not consider the regulator movement and the Battle of Alamance to be the catalyst to the American Revolution.[3] Instead, as a prominent student of North Carolina history concludes, the controversy that led to the military violence "was a local problem which required a local solution. No theory of government was involved and therefore the War of the Regulation which culminated in the Battle of Alamance must be regarded as one of the preliminary thrusts before the Revolution while the people and the colonial officers were trying to adjust the demands of the masses to the requirements of the government."[4] Despite the proximity of the regulator hostilities to the outbreak of the Revolutionary War, a direct link between the two conflicts cannot be made.

Although most modern historians would agree that the regulator uprising in North Carolina was the "largest agrarian rebellion before Independence had taken place,"[5] they have reached different conclusions about the causes of the upheavals from the mid-1760s to the struggle's end in 1771. Some students of the period find that the Regulation was a "protest against aristocratic domination of government" and the "most articulate, comprehensive, and violent of these protests."[6] Others conclude that it was "not attempted as a revolution" but was instead "a peasants' rising, a popular upheaval."[7] The movement has also been interpreted as a "sectional controversy," one between eastern elites and poor backcountry settlers. "The Regulator movement must . . . be viewed as one of a series of clashes between east and west," writes noted historian William S. Powell.[8] Still others examine the protest movement through the lens of class conflict, religious affiliation and fervor, and social structures.[9]

Those who considered themselves regulators were for the most part from Piedmont and western frontier counties, whose "main aims were to combat corruption among local officials and to increase participation of farmers in the political system."[10] Without a clear leader of the faction, Herman Husband of Orange County was its primary thinker, writer, and public figure. Regulators opposed the local "courthouse rings," made up of abusive and dishonest men appointed by the governor or his representatives to key positions within underrepresented counties, particularly Rowan, Anson, Orange, and Granville. Additional factors leading to the rural unrest included high taxes and fees, insecure land titles, and the scarcity of money in the backcountry. The regulators "pursued legal and extralegal means to put a stop to practices by local officials that they considered extortionate."[11] Beginning in 1764, they tried to redress their complaints by presenting petitions to colonial officials, meeting with local officeholders and men of influence, and filing lawsuits. Then they moved to refusing to pay taxes, repossessing seized property, and breaking up court proceedings in their frustration to be heard. As early as 1765, angry backcountry men even took up arms against surveyors and rent collectors and attempted to disrupt court sessions. Only when their legal attempts at reform failed did they turn to large-scale violence. Although it is misleading to call a movement with only one pitched battle a war, the protests of the regulators did provoke a significant military reaction from colonial officials leading to a violent engagement near Alamance Creek, the executions of some of the movements' participants, and the subsequent relocation of many protesters.[12]

After years of failing to gain redress for their grievances or any meaningful reforms from the assembly (in which they were underrepresented), the regulators of Orange County and surrounding areas turned to violence in early fall 1770. Their target was Edmund Fanning, the county's powerful clerk of the Superior Court, who was responsible for collecting court fees. He was widely known and despised for abusing his power, converting public funds to his own use, and overcharging poor farmers at court. Two years earlier, Fanning had reported that Orange County had become "the very nest and bosom of rioting and rebellion," with people there conspiring to "refuse the payment of Taxes and to prevent the execution of Law, threatening death and immediate destruction to myself and others."[13] In September 1770, a mob attacked and abused Fanning in Hillsborough, the county seat of Orange, and disturbed the court proceedings there as well. It was a disorderly scene, reported in the *Virginia Gazette*:

A very large number of those people, headed by men of considerable property, appeared in Hillsborough, armed with clubs, whips, loaded at the ends with lead or iron (a stroke from which would level the strongest man) and many other offensive weapons, and at once beset the courthouse. The first object of their revenge was Mr. John Williams, a Gentleman of the law, who they assaulted as he was entering the court; him they cruelly abused with many and violent blows with their loaded whips on the head, and different parts of his body, until he by a great good fortune made his escape, and took shelter in a neighbouring store. They then entered the courthouse, and immediately fixed their attention on Colonel Fanning, as the next object of their merciless cruelty; he expected his fate, and had retired to the Judge's seat, as the highest part of the courthouse, from which he might make the greatest defence against these bloodthirsty and cruel savages; but, poor Gentleman, vain were all his efforts, for after behaving with the most heroic courage he fell a sacrifice to numbers, and suffered a cruelty the richest language can but faintly paint. They seized him by the neck, dragged him down the steps, his head striking violently on every step, carried him to the door, and forcing him out, dragged him on the ground over stones and brickbats, struck him with their whips and clubs, kicked him, spit and spurned at him, and treated him with every possible mark of contempt and cruelty; until at length, by a violent effort of strength and activity, he rescued himself from their merciless claws, and took shelter in a house.

The regulators followed Fanning and continued to beat him, then accosted the judge, Richard Henderson, and "told him his turn was next." The judge prudently escaped town the next day, which prompted the mob to destroy Fanning's house and its contents, including his china, books, papers, and money. Rioters "entered his cellars, and after satiating and gorging their more than savage stomachs with his liquors stove and threw in the streets the remainder." Next, "to shew their opinion of courts of justice they took from his chains a negro that had been executed some time, and placed him at the lawyer's bar, and filled the Judge's seat with human excrement, in derision and contempt of the characters that fill those respectable places." The paper concluded that "all civil government in Orange County is relaxed, the courts of justice totally stopped, and every thing reduced to the power and controul of a set of men who call them selves regulators; but are in fact no other than a desperate and cruel banditti actuated by principles that no laws can restrain, no honour or conscience bind."[14] With these tumults, the regulator movement had escalated into violence and insurrection, what Gov. William Tryon deemed an "alarm to the security and wellbeing of the Civil rights of the Inhabitants of this Province."[15]

The North Carolina Assembly reacted to this violence with alarm, especially in light of rumors that insurgents planned to march on New Bern to release Herman Husband from jail, where he had been kept after his expulsion from the assembly, to "lay the town in ashes."[16] On January 15, 1771, fearful lawmakers passed "*An Act for Preventing Tumultuous and Riotous Assemblies, and for the More Speedy and Effectually Punishing the Rioters, and for Restoring and Preserving the Public Peace of This Province,*" more commonly known as the Johnston Riot Act. This law (introduced by Onslow County Assemblyman Samuel Johnston) was meant to quell "many seditious riots and tumults . . . in divers parts of this Province to the Disturbance of the Public Peace, the Obstruction of the Courts of Justice, and tending to subvert the Constitution," which were "continued and fomented by persons dissatisfied with his Majesty's Government." The act stipulated that if ten or more people unlawfully assembled "to the disturbance of the public peace" and failed to disperse after being commanded to do so by legal authorities within one hour, the rioters would be "adjudged Felons and shall suffer Death as in Case of Felony." Disturbing court proceedings and attacking court officials "riotously and tumultuously" fell under the death penalty as well, an obvious reaction to the Hillsborough riots the previous fall. The colonial militia was responsible for enforcing this new law and soon had the opportunity to do so in the spring.[17]

In January 1771, Tryon began planning to quell the rebellion if the regulators continued to riot. Tryon was a former officer in the British 1st Regiment of Foot Guards and veteran of the Seven Years' War, in which he had served briefly in Europe, and thus had experience in conducting military operations. He had arrived in North Carolina in October 1764 to assume the position of colonial governor two years after the death of Gabriel Johnston. Although Tryon was initially sympathetic to some of the regulators' concerns, once significant armed protests and riots broke out in the backcountry by 1768, he considered it his duty to put down the rebellion and restore order, using military force and the courts if necessary. The governor hoped that a special Court of Oyer and Terminer (created to adjudicate cases of treason) authorized by the Johnston Riot Act would be successful in indicting "some of the principal rioters" and "will bring the distractions of this country to a crisis, as the parties must either take their tryals or be in a state of outlawry." He also obtained returns from militia commanders in the eastern part of the colony "of such men as were willing to turn out in defence of their King and country," and convinced himself that many counties were "very favorable on the side of government."[18] In the absence of any inclination on the part of the regulators to give up their cause and with the court system in Orange County paralyzed by insurgent intimidation of the justices, Tryon determined in late March to proceed "with a Body of Forces taken from several Militia Regiments, into the settlements of the Insurgents to reduce them to Obedience." These soldiers were to be volunteers from county militia regiments, not drafted men, although it was soon apparent that enthusiasm for this service was low. Recognizing the difficulties he faced getting militiamen to serve in a campaign against the western inhabitants, Tryon provided a recruiting inducement of forty shillings for an "encouragement to serve in this expedition and to be entitled to receive two shillings a day while in Service." Each soldier was to also receive "a pair of Leggings, a Cockade and a Haversack given him," although it appears the men were to bring their own weapons on the march. Tryon advised county militia officers to accept "No Volunteer . . . but those who are hearty, spirited and can submit to a ready obedience to orders nor any soldier allowed to take his Horse as the whole will march on Foot."[19] Apparently concerned about the purported strength of the regulators, Tryon also wrote to General Thomas Gage in New York, commander of all British forces in America, to request "he would send me two field pieces to cover the passage of the forces across the broad rivers on which it is expected the insurgents will make their stand."[20]

Governor Tryon then appointed French and Indian War veteran Hugh Waddell as his second in command. Waddell planned to collect seven hundred men from the lower Cape Fear counties and the backcountry "to serve under his immediate command." Tryon's plan of operations was a broad pincer movement, in which Waddell would move his command into the "settlements of the insurgents by the way of Salisbury" while the governor marched the eastern troops to "break into their settlements on the east side of Orange county." The governor advised various militia colonels in the colony:

> Having appointed by Commission Hugh Waddell Esquire General of the Forces raised or to be raised to suppress the Insurgents in the back Settlements of this Province I have by special Instructions impowered him to embody the several Detachments ordered from the Western Counties and to march them into the Settlements of the Insurgents to join the Forces that are under orders to march from the Southern and Eastern parts of the Province in order to compel the Insurgents to a perfect obedience to Government.

Tryon expected to begin his advance from New Bern on April 23, "to join other divisions as they move up the country." He also advised the executives of Virginia and South Carolina of his military preparations "that they may prevent the insurgents from taking shelter" in those provinces.[21]

After the militia volunteers rendezvoused at Johnston Courthouse, Tryon marched at the head of his force toward Hillsborough and had with his command several swivel guns mounted on carriages and two field pieces. In addition to his artillery company and rangers, his forces included militiamen from Carteret, Craven, Duplin, Orange, Beaufort, Pitt, New Hanover, Onslow, Dobbs, Wake, and Johnston Counties who were variously armed with muskets, rifles, and "Small Fuzees." As the army advanced with its colors flying, scouts from the regulator forces began to shadow and observe the militia. By May 8, from the army's camp on the Eno River east of Hillsborough, Tryon ordered "the whole Army to march with the Greatest Caution" and that a "Sufficient Quantity of Ammunition be Immediately Delivered to the Army."[22] On May 10, Tryon wrote to General Waddell, "The Army with me is formidable from the unanimity that subsists through all Ranks independent of its Numbers which

Alamance Battleground. (*Author*)

with its Officers included will be little short of two thousand men." The governor reported that he had "a good Train of Artillery well provided with Ammunition—General Gage sent me some Brass Cannon from New York which fortunately arrived at Newbern the day before we marched."[23]

Tryon's force marched into Hillsborough on May 11 and left two companies of the Orange militia there (as well as those too ill to continue) to secure the town. He also formed a pioneer company from Surry County's recently arrived contingent, "to repair the Roads and make good the Bridges for the Army to pass over." Additionally, Tryon received the services of enough "Gentlemen Volunteers" to form them "into a Troop of Light Horse under the command of Captain Bullock, To be employed in escorting his Excellency and covering the Flanks of the Army in scouting partys." Having a troop of light horse and a sizable section of artillery certainly gave Tryon's force an advantage in flexibility and firepower over the insurgent regulators. Nevertheless, as his men marched deeper into the backcountry, Tryon maintained vigilance within the army. At their camp along the Haw River west of Hillsborough, he ordered on May 13 that "no officer or soldier [should] put off his clothes or stay out of camp without orders," and that the officers must be "particularly attentive to their Duty and not suffer the soldiers to make the least noise in case of alarm, but to remain perfectly silent after they are formed." The beating of drums was forbidden, and the troops were ordered to "remain under arms all night" and warned "to keep within their Encampment and to be ready to run to their arms on the first alarm."[24]

On May 15, Tryon's army encamped on the south side of Alamance Creek about twenty-five miles west of Hillsborough.[25] The light horse company

View of Alamance Battleground from regulators' position. (*Author*)

served as pickets one-half mile from camp to alert Tryon of any sign of the insurgents, whom he had learned were close by. The governor made plans to move farther west the next day at dawn to confront the regulators "without beat of drum, leaving the tents standing, and the baggage and Commissarys waggons in camp" under guard. As a further precaution, Tryon directed that the wagon horses were to "remain in their geer until the Army returns to the camp and the whole to be drawn into an hollow square" for protection.[26]

Originally the governor had planned to unite his regiments with those under Waddell, but in this he was disappointed. While Tryon's command moved toward the regulators from Hillsborough, Waddell began to march his troops and artillery east from Salisbury. A force of two thousand regulators surrounded Waddell's 284 men two miles east of the Yadkin River on May 9, forcing him to retreat to Salisbury the next day. The regulators threatened "to cut them to pieces, if they offered to advance to join the army under my command," wrote Tryon. Waddell and his officers were also doubtful of their soldiers' reliability against the insurgents, with whom many sympathized. Moreover, a small group of regulators known as "the Black Boys of Cabarrus" captured and burned a wagon train of gunpowder and other munitions from South Carolina destined for Waddell's command. Since Waddell's Anson, Tryon, Rowan, and Mecklenburg militia forces did not link up with the governor until three weeks after the battle, Tryon had to face the rebels near Alamance Creek with just his own troops.[27]

Tryon received intelligence on May 15 that the insurgents had embodied about five miles from his camp on the road to Salisbury. He called a council of war, at which the officers unanimously resolved to march the next morning to confront the regulators. The next morning after dawn, the army of about one thousand men left its camp and "advanced to an old field within half a mile of the rebels." Here Tryon formed his army for battle. The county regiments formed two lines, with the artillery in the center of the front line and on each flank. The ranger companies were to cover both flanks, and a small detachment of militia acted as a rear guard. While the army slowly advanced against the rebels' camp several miles west of Alamance Creek, Tryon sent an emissary to convince them to "lay down their arms, surrender their outlawed ringleaders, and submit to the laws of their country" within one hour, per the Johnston Riot Act. This effort at negotiation failed as the regulators rejected the appeal, and soon afterward "a considerable body of them appeared in sight, and waved their hats, daring us to advance," Tryon reported.[28] The size of the regulator force can only be estimated, but it appears that two thousand to three thousand men were in camp the day of the battle. These men were poorly armed and supplied, lacked an overall military organization, and had no leader to command them on the day of the engagement.[29] Some of the men who had gathered did not expect a battle but rather some kind of negotiation conference with the governor to avoid bloodshed and discuss their grievances. Tryon had no intention of negotiating anything but insisted that the rebels lay down their arms, return to their homes, and surrender their leaders to him.[30]

To force the regulators' hand, Tryon moved his men within thirty yards of the rebel position and had an aide inform the regulators that the hour was up. "Fire and be damned," came a shout from the rebels, which started the action at about noon. The opponents traded volleys of musketry, while the militia added their artillery to the salvoes in "a hot fire" that was "kept up on both sides for about an hour and a quarter." The regulators soon "took to tree fighting," and many of them concentrated their fire on the artillery crews, whose fire was particularly telling. One witness observed that Tryon's six pieces of "artillery was well served, and did great execution," and most of the rebels' casualties were felled by grapeshot. To flush the rebels from their firing positions, Tryon had his men set fire to the woods, which later burned some of the wounded to death. When he sensed that the regulators' fire "abated a little," Tryon ordered the cannons to "cease firing, and the whole army to advance." The militia fought the rebels about forty-five minutes longer, "drove the enemy out of the field, and gained a compleat victory." A newspaper printed a report that the regulators "ran in great confusion to all quarters from whence they apprehended the least danger." One witness noted that "his Excellency the Governor . . . was in the center of the line during the whole engagement, and in the most imminent danger, having had his bayonet shot away with a musket ball." Tryon afterward wrote that the "two field pieces from Genl Gage was of infinite service to us," particularly since the rebels had none of their own.[31]

Once the rebels fled the field, Tryon's militia captured their camp, "with many horses, arms, ammunitions, cloaths, and provisions." One account reported that most of the rebels' "hunting shirts, wallets of dumplings, jackets, breeches, powder-horns, shot bags, &c. were taken, with a number of horses." Government forces pursued the defeated regulators approximately one mile before returning to their camp,[32] where the governor ordered one of the fifteen captives hanged on the spot for refusing to take an oath of loyalty to the British Crown. Estimating the casualties on each side is problematic, as accounts vary widely. Tryon's losses appear to have been nine soldiers killed and sixty-one wounded, and "one officer killed and one dangerously wounded."[33] Regulator losses are unknown with certainty but may have exceeded Tryon's because of the militia's deployment of artillery. Once the smoke cleared on the field, the governor had "all the wounded of the Army . . . brought to his own Tent and the greatest care taken of them, the wounded of the Rebels brought to Camp to be taken care of" as well.[34] The day after the battle, he congratulated his troops on their victory and praised their "Valour & Steady Conduct." The army collected the dead from the battlefield and buried them near the artillery park, where they were interred with "Military Honours to the Deceased," including a "ceremony of Prayers and Thanksgiving for the Signal Victory it has pleased Divine Providence yesterday to grant the army over the Insurgents."[35]

Moravian village of Salem.

Although Tryon's militia routed the rebels in battle, most regulators managed to flee and still remained at large. To capitalize on his victory, Tryon issued a pardon to all rebels who "come into camp, lay down their Arms, take the Oath of Allegiance and promise to pay all Taxes that are due or may hereafter become due by them respectively, and submit from this day to the Laws of this Country."[36] Hundreds took advantage of this offer of immunity, but Tryon still needed to make a show of force in regulator strongholds to the west. His troops ravaged the farms of known insurgents as they marched across the Piedmont. Tryon moved to Sandy Creek, where they encamped for a week on the Orange County plantation (near modern Liberty) of Herman Husband, who had left the regulator force just prior to the battle. The army then moved across Deep River and Reedy Creek to the Moravian town of Salem, and on June 4 it joined Waddell's forces there. Before Tryon's command left the Salem area on June 9, he ordered Waddell to return to "the Southern and Western Counties to force the Inhabitants to a submission to Government." Once the rebels were cowed into submission, Waddell was to "disband your Army and order the

Commanding Officer of the Detachments to march their Men into their respective Counties and then dismiss them."[37]

After Waddell and his militia companies departed, Tryon moved his command to Hillsborough by June 14. Here fourteen insurgent prisoners taken captive during the campaign were tried, and twelve were condemned to death. Six were hanged on June 19 in front of the army, which was drawn up in an "Oblong Square," with the "Light Horse to cover the outside of the Flanks to Prevent the mobs crowding on the men." The remaining six prisoners received pardons. With this unpleasant business complete, Tryon left the army and returned to New Bern, in order to travel to New York for his new assignment as royal governor of that colony.[38] Militia Colonel John Ashe assumed command of the army at Hillsborough and marched the troops to Colonel William Bryan's plantation in Johnston County, where they were all discharged.[39]

For the regulators and their cause, the battle of Alamance was a heavy blow. Their complaints were still unresolved, and redress seemed all but impossible once they had been soundly defeated in the field. One Carolinian reported that "it is said 1,500 families departed since the battle of Alamance and to my knowledge a great many more are only waiting to dispose of their plantations in order to follow them. This is to me an argument that their grievances were real and their oppression great, notwithstanding all that has been said to the contrary."[40]

Many of these families moved to lands farther west in what is now Kentucky and Tennessee. Still, thousands of backcountry farmers took an oath of allegiance to the king, as the regulator leaders remained in hiding or had fled until the Johnston Riot Act expired in 1772. North Carolina authorities did not pursue further legal actions against the former rebels, although even as late as 1775, the British Crown refused to offer amnesty to Herman Husband, who by then was living in Pennsylvania.[41] By that time, those with regulator sympathies looked at the nascent revolutionary movement in the colony against Great Britain with distrust, since the new "rebel" leaders were not primarily backcountry farmers but men such as Francis Nash, Robert Howe, Alexander Lillington, Alexander Martin, John Ashe, Richard Caswell, James Moore, William Thomson, William Bryan, Thomas Polk, Cornelius Harnett, and Willie Jones. These notables had not been friends to the insurgents—instead they had been part of Tryon's army during the Alamance campaign, or had supported the governor. Once these North Carolina Revolutionary authorities began to mobilize support for their own insurgency, they faced a formidable obstacle in getting those whom they had battled four years earlier to join them.[42]

5. Revolution and War, 1775–1776

THE CRISIS WITH GREAT BRITAIN

Following the French and Indian War, imperial authorities in London tried to prevent conflicts with native peoples beyond the North American colonial frontier and to reduce the enormous British debt incurred since 1754 to win the recent struggle with France. To curb rapacious white settlers from encroaching on Indian lands and fomenting costly hostilities, the British Crown issued the Proclamation of 1763. This announcement barred settlement beyond the crest of the Appalachian Mountains and limited future white incursions by American and British land speculators, as well as those men who were promised western lands as a reward for their recent military service. French defeat had promised new opportunities for American colonists, but King George III's decree threatened to negate the gains won in the war. Angered by the proclamation, many colonists ignored it.[1]

A year later, after newly appointed governor William Tryon had arrived in North Carolina, the British Parliament began to enact a series of taxation measures designed to raise revenue in the colonies, including the Sugar Act (1764), the Townsend Acts (1767), and the Tea Act (1773), all of which provoked opposition in America. None of these revenue schemes engendered more opposition in North Carolina than the Stamp Act, passed March 22, 1765, and scheduled to begin November 1 that year. This act required the purchase of a stamp to be affixed to licenses, diplomas, court documents, wills, playing cards, shipping manifests, newspapers, and many similar items. Americans objected to being taxed directly by Parliament rather than their own representative governments, which they felt violated their rights as British subjects. Numerous demonstrations took place against the Stamp Act in eastern North Carolina, including an armed mob that surrounded the residence of Governor Tryon in February 1766. Opposition became so heated that Tryon grew concerned about the possession of Fort Johnston on the Cape Fear River. He asked Captain C. J. Phipps of the

"The Stamp Act denounced," from Benjamin Lossing's *History of the United States of America.*

Royal Navy to secure the fort, and when confronted by three hundred armed protesters under Colonel Hugh Waddell, Phipps's sailors spiked the fort's heavy guns to make them inoperable. Although the Stamp Act was repealed in March 1766, other matters remained in dispute with Crown officials, particularly related to the colony's court system, legal attachments to foreign debts within the province, and colonial paper currency.[2]

In August 1771, thirty-four-year-old Josiah Martin arrived in North Carolina to replace Tryon as royal governor in the wake of the regulator crisis. Born in Dublin, Ireland, and with family connections to the West Indies, Martin had been an officer in the British Army during the Seven Years' War in Canada and New York prior to taking up his new post. He was a staunch supporter of the king's prerogative and unafraid to make active efforts to quell what he determined to be a rising tide of rebellion and independence. He soon faced rising opposition to what the inhabitants regarded as parliamentary abuses and was the last royal governor of the colony.[3]

Martin had the misfortune to inherit the leadership of a colony in turmoil. In 1773, North Carolinians established a committee of correspondence to share news and coordinate responses with other American provinces regarding the growing imperial tensions with Great Britain. The following year, at New Bern on August 25, the colony's First Provincial Congress began its meeting, an extralegal convention of Carolinians gathered to consider what it called "the present alarming state of British America." The elected delegates opposed parliamentary taxation and supported an economic boycott on trade with British merchants. That summer a network of committees of public safety began to organize across the colony, which soon became local government bodies as British authority gradually eroded.[4] A second Provincial Congress met in early April 1775, appointed representatives to the Second Continental Congress in Philadelphia, and created a Council of Safety for the entire colony, which Martin called "democratical Usurpations." These conventions were loudly denounced by Martin, who tried aggressively to undermine their authority and influence, though with little effect.[5]

By late spring 1775, the governor regarded the situation within the colony as volatile and began to consider plans for the royal government's defense. He identified two groups within North Carolina that might support the king's authority: recently immigrated Highland Scots in the Cape Fear River Valley and former regulators in the backcountry. Using these two groups—"steadfast in duty and loyalty," Martin assumed—augmented with British regulars from abroad, he hoped to maintain his position, defend the Crown's authority, and stifle "the ill spirit" in the province. Soon North Carolina became a scene of open conflict in the struggle between home country and colony.[6]

A month after the Battles of Lexington and Concord, a "motley mob" led by prominent lawyer Abner Nash confronted Martin on May 23, 1775, concerned that Martin had dismounted several cannons from their carriages at the governor's official residence at New Bern to prevent them from falling into Patriot hands. Nash's group did secure several other artillery pieces nearby, demonstrating that the Patriots, too, were preparing for possible hostilities.[7] Matters quickly deteriorated between Patriots (also called Whigs) and the royal governor, and fighting erupted. On May 31, Martin felt so threatened by what he called "rebels" he fled his official residence for the safety of Fort Johnston, held by a small contingent of British troops under Captain John Collett. Martin arrived there on June 2 but soon fled to the British navy ship *Cruizer* in the Cape Fear River nearby, as the fort was so dilapidated it offered him little protection.[8] Weeks later, on July 18, several hundred local Patriot militiamen led by Cornelius Harnett, John Ashe, and Robert Howe marched to Fort Johnston and occupied it unopposed. The Patriots burned the fort, and over the next few days, the navy ships sporadically fired at militia troops onshore. Only in November did British sailors and marines go onshore for several days to reclaim their abandoned cannons, all the while under musket fire from Whig militia.[9]

On August 20, 1775, the third Provincial Congress convened at Hillsborough. Much of this body's work concerned preparing for war. The convention divided North Carolina into six military districts, issued provincial currency, and declared the colony bound to obey the Continental and Provincial Congresses. Moreover, the delegates authorized raising two infantry regiments of five hundred men each under Colonels James Moore of New Hanover County and Robert Howe of Brunswick County. These two regiments were later accepted into Continental service in November. Moore's 1st Regiment was based in New Bern and Wilmington, and Howe's 2nd Regiment served in Edenton and Salisbury. Six regiments of minutemen were also authorized for six-month tours of service. The congress also created a thirteen-member committee to oversee military preparations and ordered the printing of £125,000 in bills of credit. For the protection of commerce and its waterways, the delegates voted to allow the construction of fortifications on the Neuse and Cape Fear Rivers and the building of three state navy ships.[10]

Before Carolina Patriots could meet again in April 1776, the colony's troops were involved in several military campaigns in North Carolina, South Carolina, and Virginia. The first of these operations involved the mobilization of North Carolina militia and regulars in November 1775 to assist South Car-

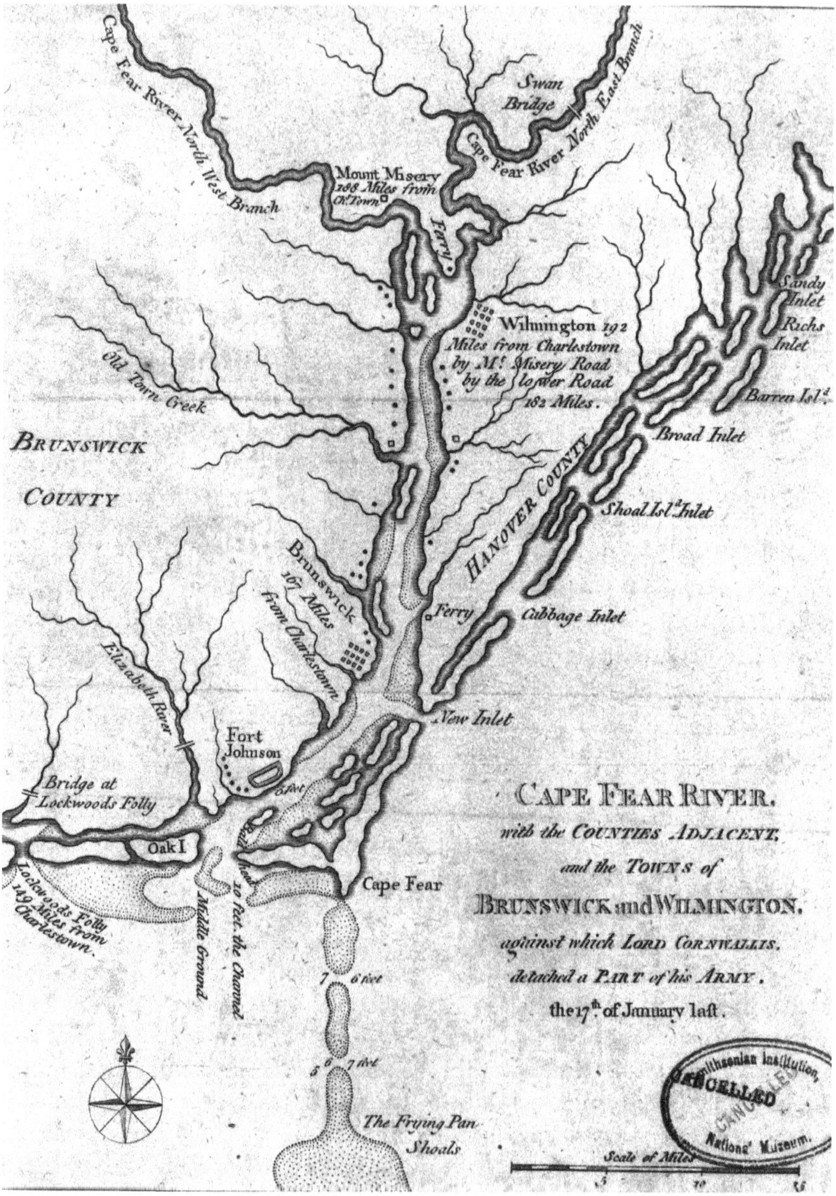

Cape Fear River, 1781.

olina troops under Colonel Richard Richardson in preventing backcountry Loyalists from embodying in western South Carolina. The long march to the South Carolina frontier culminated in a Patriot victory December 22 at the

Great Cane Brake on the Reedy River (about twenty miles south of modern Greenville). This expedition became known as the Snow Campaign because of the unusual snowfall of almost two feet encountered in late December as the Whigs marched back east. Lieutenant Colonel Alexander Martin of the 2nd North Carolina Regiment led four companies from Salisbury in this successful campaign; five hundred militia soldiers from Mecklenburg, Rowan, and Tryon Counties served as well.[11]

THE BATTLE OF GREAT BRIDGE

While some of North Carolina's soldiers marched into South Carolina in November 1775, others supported the neighboring colony to the north, Virginia. Lord Dunmore, Virginia's royal governor, used Norfolk as his base of authority, having fled the colonial capital of Williamsburg after enduring mounting Whig pressure. From Norfolk, a Loyalist enclave and the second largest city in the South, Dunmore encouraged Loyalists, sought British assistance in reasserting royal authority over the colony, and issued a series of controversial pronouncements to Virginia's inhabitants. The most inflammatory of these proclamations was his promise of freedom to slaves who entered into British military service, a shocking measure to slave owners of both Whig and Loyalist (Tory) sentiments. Virginia's revolutionary government quickly moved to isolate the governor at Norfolk with military force.

British and Virginia troops faced each other on opposite sides of the Great Bridge, a wooden structure forty yards long that crossed the southern branch of the Elizabeth River south of Norfolk on the main road to North Carolina, skirting the Great Dismal Swamp. On the east bank of the river, British forces under Dunmore built a small fort and placed in it two companies of the British 14th Regiment, Loyalist militia, and a regiment of runaway slaves called the Royal Ethiopians. Opposing him on the west side of the bridge was Colonel William Woodford and his 2nd Virginia Regiment, as well as several hundred riflemen of the Culpeper County minutemen. Almost two hundred volunteer North Carolina minutemen from Halifax under Colonel Nicholas Long were also in Woodford's camp by December 9, having heard rumors that Dunmore was recruiting Albemarle Sound Loyalists with plans to eventually march into their home state. These poorly armed Carolinians brought two cannons with them but had no powder, and the guns were not mounted and could therefore not be fired.[12]

Aware of additional troops coming from North Carolina, Dunmore ordered his troops to make a sudden attack against the Patriot camp at dawn on the ninth. The British redcoats bravely charged across the bridge and down a short causeway to dislodge the Patriot fort's defenders with fixed bayonets but instead were met with withering musket fire from the 2nd Virginia behind a low earthwork across the road and from Culpeper riflemen on high ground to the north. The oncoming column suffered heavy losses and fell back to its own defenses to regroup. "Their fire was so heavy, that, had we not retreated as we did, we

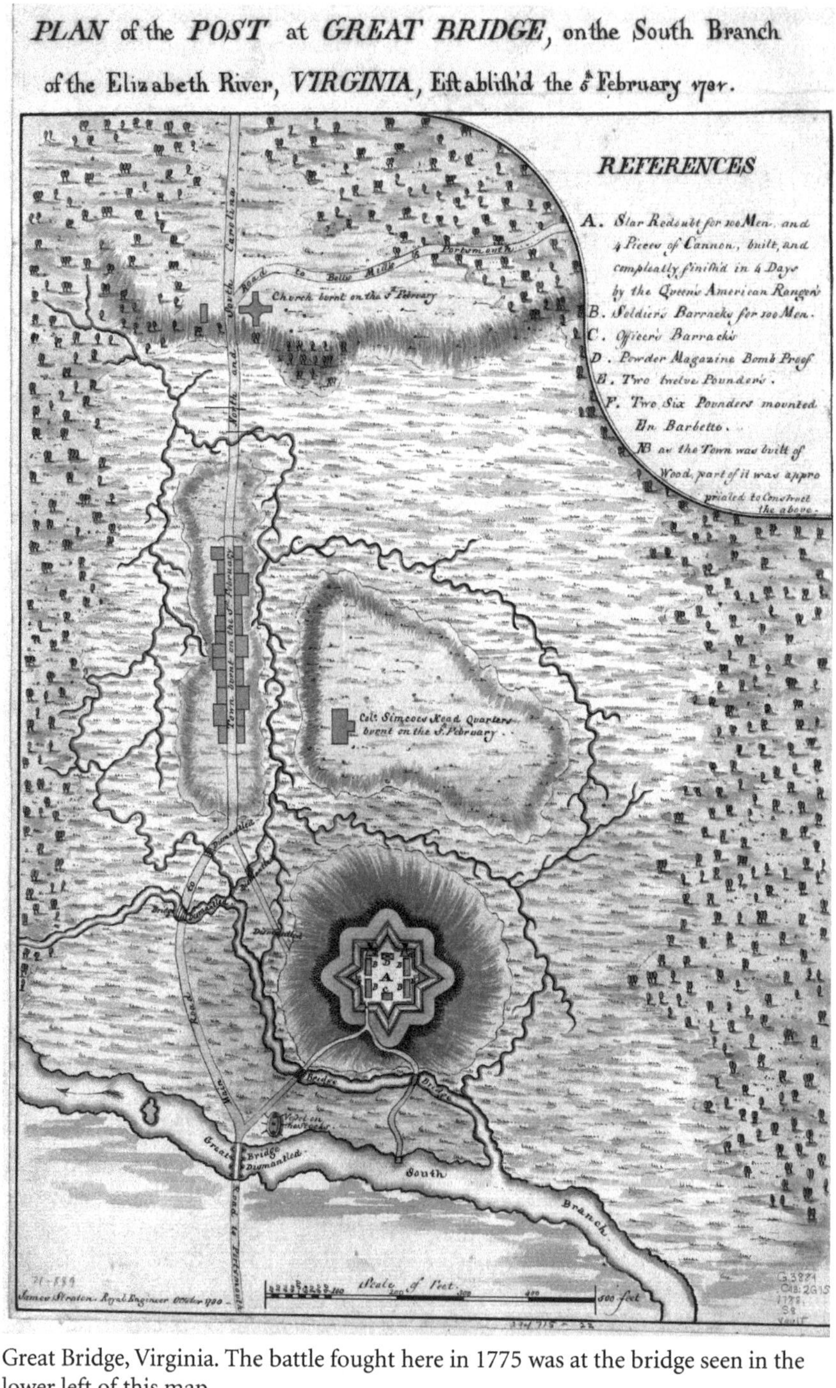

Great Bridge, Virginia. The battle fought here in 1775 was at the bridge seen in the lower left of this map.

should every one have been cut off," wrote a naval officer at the scene. Woodford called up the Carolinians from their camp four hundred yards to the rear in case Dunmore attacked again, but the British did not make another assault. Abandoning their fort, the redcoats withdrew to Norfolk that night, leaving the field and their dead and wounded to the Patriots.[13] "This was a second Bunker's Hill affair," Woodford proudly wrote the day after the fighting, "in miniature, with this difference, that we kept our post and had only one man wounded in the hand."[14]

Soon after the fighting was over, Colonel Robert Howe arrived at Great Bridge from Edenton with over four hundred men of his 2nd North Carolina Regiment on December 12, and by seniority took over all American forces there, numbering about two thousand men. Howe moved his force to Norfolk after British troops left the city on December 14. However, on January 1, 1776, the British navy ships from the Elizabeth River bombarded the port city, and landing parties set fire to the buildings and wharves. Several of Howe's soldiers were wounded during this affair, but none were reported killed as they aided in driving back the enemy shore parties. Howe and his North Carolina troops returned to Edenton in March 1776 and earned the appreciation of Virginia's new government. In late December 1775, a Virginia convention in Williamsburg published a resolution thanking "the brave officers, gentlemen volunteers, and soldiers of North Carolina as well as our brethren of that Province in general, for their prompt and generous aid in defence of our common rights against the enemies of America and of the British Constitution."[15]

THE BATTLE OF MOORE'S CREEK BRIDGE

Although Governor Martin had fled to a British navy ship in the Cape Fear River (after he sent his family to safety in New York), he was one among many royal officials in America and England who waged an active letter-writing campaign to encourage the king and his ministers to reassert the Crown's authority and control over North Carolina. In January, Martin received approval from Lord George Germain, British secretary of state for the American Department, to prepare for and conduct operations to put down the rebellion in North Carolina. Martin had already developed a plan in which he would raise loyal troops within the colony who would embody and march to the Lower Cape Fear region. "I am persuaded to believe that loyal subjects yet abound in the Western Counties of this Province," Martin wrote in late 1775. Germain advised Martin that he could also count on two thousand British regulars from Boston under Major General Henry Clinton and seven British regiments from Ireland, led by Charles, Lord Cornwallis. According to Martin's plan, all forces would unite in February at Brunswick, reestablish British rule in the province, then perhaps move on to South Carolina for the same purpose. In addition to the troops he expected from Boston and Ireland, Martin believed he could recruit thousands of men within North Carolina and requested ten thousand muskets from London to arm them.[16]

On January 10, 1776, the governor issued a proclamation calling for "all His Majesty's liege subjects within this Province" to gather in arms for the purpose of "resisting and subduing, with the assistance of the Almighty, the . . . impious and unnatural Rebellion, and to restore the just rights of His Majesty's Crown and Government."[17] He initially sought to raise troops among former regulators in the backcountry, who he assumed nursed bitter resentments against the Tidewater elites then in the forefront of the rebellion. But few of these former insurgents rallied to the British standard, and Martin had better success among the Highland Scots along the Cape Fear River, many of whom had recently immigrated to settlements at Cross Creek (modern Fayetteville) and Cross Hill (today's Carthage). Many of the Scots were beholden to the Crown for their lands, and Martin guessed that they could be enlisted to demonstrate their loyalty and secure their property. In this he was largely correct: by mid-February, about fourteen hundred Highlanders—induced to join by promises of money, land, and tax exemptions—had been raised in a regiment led by Donald McDonald, a British regular officer who was made a brigadier general of the loyal militia force for this campaign. He was assisted by another regular Highland officer, Captain Donald McLeod, and after collecting his troops, of whom about half were unarmed, General McDonald set out from Cross Creek toward the Carolina coast in order to help "restore peace and tranquillity to this distracted land."[18]

The North Carolina Whigs, well aware of the Loyalists trying to embody their forces along the Cape Fear River, began to mobilize their own soldiers to meet the growing danger posed by McDonald's Scots. Colonel James Moore led the effort to intercept McDonald's column, although his ability to control these various Carolina forces in the field was limited by distance.[19] Moore moved his 1st Regiment soldiers—augmented by hundreds of local militiamen—to Rockfish Creek, south of Cross Creek on the main road to Wilmington, to block McDonald's route. McDonald decided not to confront Moore's eleven hundred men here and instead moved east to the Black River on February 20. Realizing that the Loyalists had left his front, Moore sent word to Whig militia Colonel Richard Caswell, advancing from New Bern with eight hundred men, to intercept McDonald's force on the Black River at Corbett's Ferry, where he assumed the Loyalist host would have to march. Here McDonald prepared to attack Caswell in order to continue his progress, but a local slave informed the Loyalist leader of a little-known crossing of the Black River upstream. While part of McDonald's troops distracted the Whig militia at the ferry, the rest of the Loyalists successfully evaded Caswell's men and continued their march on the east side of the river.[20]

After McDonald had given his command the slip at Rockfish Creek, Moore sent an advance militia detachment of 150 men of the Wilmington District under Colonel Alexander Lillington and Colonel John Ashe Sr.'s one hundred New Hanover volunteer rangers southeast through Elizabethtown, then on to the Black River, in order to get below Caswell in case the enemy was able to bypass him. Moore ordered Lillington to secure Moore's Creek Bridge, seventeen miles from Wilmington, over which he surmised McDonald would have to pass with his troops to reach Brunswick. Moore followed Lillington with his own regiment and his wagons at a slower pace, part of the way in boats down the northwest branch of Cape Fear River to Dollison's Landing, a few miles northwest of Wilmington. Meanwhile, moving quickly, Lillington arrived at the bridge, deployed his men on the east side of it, and erected a small earthwork nearby.[21]

On the afternoon of March 26, Colonel Caswell also marched his troops to Moore's Creek Bridge, took up a position on the west side, and made a fortified camp. This arrangement, however, put Caswell's command with its back to the creek, a dangerous position if he were attacked in force by the approaching Loyalist troops. It also divided the Whig militia force in the face of the enemy. Later that day, one of McDonald's officers perceived Caswell's curious deployment as the Highlanders and regulators stealthily advanced toward the creek crossing. After consulting his fellow officers, McDonald decided to attack the Whigs at the bridge, knowing that Moore's regiment was on the march from the west and would soon reinforce Caswell's command. Moreover, the Loyalist army was reduced to only seven hundred to eight hundred men by this point because of numerous desertions along the line of march. From their camp six miles away, the Loyalists advanced quietly toward the bridge at about 1 AM on February 27, led by Donald McLeod, as General McDonald had become too ill to command his troops.[22]

Just before dawn, the Loyalist attackers came up to Caswell's camp and were surprised to discover that the Whig leader had moved his men to the east side of the creek to join Lillington's militia. Additionally, Caswell had his troops remove most of the planks on the bridge as they retired to the east side of the creek. McLeod decided to proceed with the attack, and with drums and bagpipes playing, he ordered his men to fire a volley and charge. Led by a company of men armed only with broadswords, the Loyalists found that the Whigs had greased the bridge's beams with tallow and soap, making the crossing even more hazardous. The Whigs fired from their breastworks about one hundred yards from the bridge and also discharged their two small field cannons at the oncoming Highlanders "with a very heavy fire." Surging forward, McLeod fell dead from multiple wounds close to Caswell's line, as did at least thirty others in the brief battle, besides those shot down at the bridge. Once the enemy was repulsed, the Whigs gave chase and routed McDonalds's panicked army, having suffered only one man killed and one wounded. Over the next few days in the nearby swamps and woods, the Patriots captured several hundred of the fleeing Tories—including McDonald and most of his officers—and £15,000 in gold.[23] About two hours after the firing had ended, Colonel Moore's troops ar-

Sir Henry Clinton.

rived at Moore's Creek Bridge to find the enemy defeated. As Moore wrote to the North Carolina Provincial Council, his troops had "terminated a very dangerous insurrection and will, I trust, put an effectual check to Toryism in this country."[24]

Soon after the battle, the second part of Governor Martin's strategic plan came to fruition, albeit several weeks too late. General Clinton finally arrived at Cape Fear with his forces from Boston in March 1776. There he learned that the ships from Ireland had not yet arrived and, more disappointingly, that Patriot forces had soundly defeated the Loyalists two weeks earlier. Cornwallis's regiments were supposed to have sailed from Cork, Ireland, by December 1, but they did not leave until February 13. Clinton, too, was delayed by following the orders of General William Howe, the British army commander in North America, to have his flotilla put in at New York and Virginia on the voyage to Cape Fear, which he reached March 12. There Governor Martin informed Clinton that "the King's friends in the backcountry . . . had been attacked by the rebels on the 27th of February, and after meeting with some loss were now totally dispersed and many of them in confinement."[25] Clinton landed some British troops to allow Martin to leave his cramped ship and enjoy dry land, and by April 18, the transport ships and Royal Navy escorts from Cork commanded by Sir Peter Parker began to appear at the cape; the last arrived May 31.[26]

While Clinton and Cornwallis remained at Cape Fear, they directed their British troops on several inland foraging expeditions and raids. Colonel Moore brought his 1st North Carolina Regiment and part of the 2nd Regiment to the Wilmington area to defend the country and support the local militia defending the lower river. In early May, British land and naval forces attacked Fort Johnston, which was used by Patriot snipers to fire on enemy ships in the river, soon eliminating the threat by patrolling inland for miles around. Clinton positioned British forces on Bald Head Island and Fort Johnston and later led a raid up the Cape Fear with three regiments to Robert Howe's plantation, Kendal, which they plundered, along with nearby Orton Mill. On June 1, Clinton's entire expedition along with Governor Martin set sail for Charles Town, South Carolina, which Clinton had been told was weakly held by Whig forces. His departure left North Carolina's Loyalists unsupported and left the Whig government free to continue its preparations for war.[27]

MOBILIZING FOR WAR

While James Moore, recently appointed by the Continental Congress to the rank of brigadier general in command of the forces in North Carolina, tried to counter British raids on the Cape Fear River in the spring, North Carolina's fourth Provincial Congress met at Halifax in April. This meeting's most significant result was the Halifax Resolves, which called on the Continental Congress to proclaim American independence and to secure foreign aid for America's war efforts. Military matters took up much of the convention's time, including financial issues. The delegates appointed a nine-member Council of Safety to supervise war preparations, led by Cornelius Harnett of Wilmington. The Provincial Congress also allowed for raising four additional Continental battalions (the 3rd, 4th, 5th, and 6th North Carolina Regiments), and £500,000 in additional North Carolina paper currency. The "Minute men and Militia battalions and troops under the command of Colonel Caswell" were disbanded and allowed to return to their homes, although other militia troops were kept on active service, including those near Beaufort, "to prevent our enemies from landing there, supplying themselves with provisions, and committing hostilities and depredations in that part of the Province." Additionally, five independent companies were raised for service on the seacoast.[28]

Halifax, North Carolina.

North Carolina leaders also endorsed measures to suppress threats from Tories within the colony and to strengthen its militia. For "the better and more effectual defence and protection of the Colony," the militia was divided into six brigades, one in each military district, and general officers appointed to lead them. All healthy men "from 16 to 60 years of age" were liable for militia duty and were to be "furnished with a good gun, bayonet, cartouch box, shot bag and powder horn, a cutlass or tomahawk." With regard to the Loyalists, the Provincial Congress decided to banish some of these "misguided people [who] . . . have raised their hands against us, and endeavoured to imbrue them in the best blood of our fellow citizens." North Carolina authorities seized Tory weapons, sent off numerous prisoners captured after the Battle of Moore's Creek Bridge to northern jails, and otherwise made life difficult for those who sought to "drench this Province in blood and slaughter."[29]

ATTACK ON CHARLES TOWN, JUNE 1776

Guessing that South Carolina would be the next target of the British force, newly promoted Brigadier General

Robert Howe traveled to Charles Town with the recently appointed Continental army commander in the South, Major General Charles Lee. Additionally, approximately twelve hundred troops of the 1st, 2nd, and 3rd North Carolina Regiments and a troop of dragoons marched south to the city later that month.[30] As was soon evident, Lee and Howe were correct in their military assessment: after General Clinton and Commodore Parker departed Cape Fear on June 1—with Governor Martin on one of the ships—they sailed south to attack Charles Town, where the Patriots had not yet finished the city's defenses.[31]

The British fleet arrived at Charles Town on June 4, while Patriot forces busily constructed earth and log fortifications around the prosperous port city. After several weeks, the British attacked the unfinished log fort on Sullivan's Island, called Fort Sullivan, on June 28, by land and sea. Parker's fleet closed in on the fort to reduce it with broadsides in what General Lee called "one of the most furious cannonades I ever heard or saw," however, the South Carolina gunners in the fort delivered a slow but destructive fire against the enemy's ships. Patriot troops, including a detachment of the 1st North Carolina Regiment, repulsed two attempts by British foot regiments to attack the fort by land. Other North Carolina troops witnessed the battle but were not directly involved in the action: Colonel Jethro Sumner's 3rd North Carolina was posted to Charles Town, while the remainder of Colonel Francis Nash's 1st North Carolina and Colonel Alexander Martin's 2nd North Carolina stayed on the mainland to the rear of the fort at Haddrells Point, acting as a reserve under Lee's direct command. After dark, the British ceased their attacks and withdrew from the harbor with heavy losses to men and ships. "The behavior of the Garrison, both men and officers, with Colonel [William] Moultrie at their head, I confess, astonished me," wrote Lee. "[I]t was brave to the last degree, I had no idea that so much coolness and intrepidity could be displayed by a collection of raw recruits, as I was witness of in this garrison." He went on to report, "I know not which corps I have the greatest reason to be pleased with [the] Virginians, or the North Carolina troops—they are both equally alert, zealous, and spirited."[32] The British ships and troops left the waters around Charles Town on July 21 for New York Harbor, where Major General William Howe was concentrating his forces for an attack on the American-held city defended by General George Washington.[33]

THE CHEROKEE CAMPAIGN OF 1776

As hundreds of North Carolinians served at Charles Town during summer 1776, on the province's western frontier, a new threat emerged from an old foe: the Cherokee Indians, who numbered perhaps twelve thousand people by the mid-1770s. Conflict stemmed from many of the same issues that caused the Cherokee War of 1759–61, namely the continued encroachment on traditional Cherokee lands and hunting grounds by white settlers. The 1775 Treaty of Sycamore Shoals, in which North Carolina land speculator Richard Henderson obtained a huge land session (primarily in Kentucky) from the Cherokees in violation of the Proclamation of 1763 and Indian law, aroused bitter feelings among the native leaders, who protested that Henderson had swindled them in the terms of the agreement. Pressured by younger warriors to stem the tide of land-hungry Carolinians moving west, Cherokee leaders demanded of colonial officials the removal of settlers on Indian territory guaranteed by prior treaties or face a border war. Elder chiefs such as Attakullakulla and Oconostota had previously entered into an alliance with the British, but they were unable to prevent militant, younger warriors from attacking white settlements in the southern colonies without waiting for a coordinated offensive with their European and Indian allies. That summer, Cherokee war parties struck colonial farms and outposts all along the southern frontier, killing settlers and burning homes. Although Carolinians had been warned of an impending Indian onslaught, devastation in the backcountry was widespread. From the backcountry Brigadier General Griffith Rutherford, commander of the Salisbury Military District, reported in July to North Carolina officials with alarm that "the Indins is making Grate prograce, in Distroying & Murdering, in the frunteers of this County," and urged them to "send us Plenty of Powder."[34]

The southern American colonies reacted to the Cherokee attacks with a coordinated campaign to strike native villages and strongholds from several avenues of approach. South Carolina raised a force of two thousand men under Colonel Andrew Williamson and advanced into the rugged mountains of North Carolina along the Little Tennessee River, the same route Montgomery and Grant had taken in 1760 and 1761. Virginia sent its troops—supported by three hundred North Carolinians under Colonel Joseph Williams—down the Holston River under Colonel William Christian to operate against the Cherokee Overhill Towns in modern Tennessee. Georgia also sent a small militia force of two hundred men into enemy territory along the Chattahoochee and Tugaloo Rivers.[35]

Maj. Gen. Charles Lee.

North Carolina's efforts to defeat the Cherokee with volunteers and drafted militia forces were led by General Rutherford, an Irish-born veteran of the French and Indian War and former Rowan County sheriff. In July, Rutherford received word from the North Carolina Committee of Safety authorizing him to raise a large force of western militia and lead a campaign against the Cherokee Middle Towns from the backcountry. He and his officers were urged by the colony's congressional delegation in Philadelphia to show no mercy to the Indian enemies, to "extinguish the very race of them," and "to carry fire and Sword into the very bowels of their country and sink them so low that they may never be able again to rise and disturb the peace of their Neighbours."[36]

Gathering men on the eastern slope of the Blue Ridge Mountains in late summer, Rutherford marched his twenty-five hundred troops west from his camp at Pleasant Garden near Davidson's Fort (now Old Fort) on the first day of September. His army crossed the mountains at Swannanoa Gap by Black Mountain, crossed the French Broad River two days later, and reached the Cherokee village of Watauga (near today's Franklin) in the Little Tennessee River Valley on the eighth. On September 10, at Sugartown on the Cullasaja River five miles from Watauga, Indians fought a three-hour battle with militia troops in which at least eighteen Carolinians were killed before the Cherokees withdrew from the village. On the same day, Rutherford's soldiers burned the large town of Nikwasi, a ceremonial and religious center (at Franklin). Most Cherokees abandoned their homes and fled before Rutherford's advancing column, so that on September 11, the general and his troops occupied Cowee, an important trade center northwest of Watauga, which they also ruined.[37]

While the North Carolina troops trekked west over steep mountains, Williamson proceeded north in search of Rutherford's column, with which he was expected to unite. Near Wayah Gap, about fourteen miles west of Franklin, the South Carolinians fought a bloody battle with Cherokee forces led by Oconostota in the dense woods and rugged hills called the Black Hole. Only when some Carolinians reached the high ground at the gap and flanked the Indians after heavy fighting did the native warriors withdraw from the battleground. One hundred fifty North Carolinians under frontier Colonel Benjamin Cleveland of Wilkes County managed to reach Williamson's position as the battle drew to a close, but by that time over sixty of Williamson's men had been killed and two hundred wounded in heavy fighting.[38]

General Rutherford continued his own expedition farther west, destroying crops and villages as he proceeded, and eventually joined with Williamson's South Carolina force at the Hiwassee River (near modern Murphy) on September 26. The next day, both commands began their return marches and continued to destroy Indian towns and supplies along the way, having turned dozens of Cherokee villages to ashes. "After burning the Indian Towns, destroying their corn and committing such other depredations upon them as they could the Army returned to North Carolina," one militiaman wrote years later. Many of the Indians captured during the campaign were sold into slavery. By early October, the militia under Rutherford had returned to Burke County, where most were discharged by November. Peace treaties with the Cherokees were concluded in May and July 1777, in which the defeated Indians lost over five million acres of land.[39]

WAR IN GEORGIA AND MILITARY PREPARATIONS

After the unsuccessful attempt in June 1776 to attack and capture Charles Town, British forces left the South Carolina coast. General Charles Lee was unsure where they would next strike and considered Chesapeake Bay and Virginia their likely objectives. The Continental commander, however, came under pressure from South Carolina and Georgia officials to strike at St. Augustine, used as a base by Tories to conduct raids from East Florida into the southern colonies. Eventually, Lee decided to send some of his troops to Savannah, in preparation for operations farther south, including the North Carolina Continental regiments. At Charles Town that summer, the troops from North Carolina were in "wretched condition," many of them lacking shoes and clothing, and with their pay in arrears, but they marched south under General Howe's command, reaching Savannah by August 18. Soon thereafter, Congress ordered General Lee to New York and replaced him with Brigadier General James Moore. Lee's departure left Howe in command in Georgia. Lee took most of the 2nd and 3rd North Carolina forces back with him to South Carolina on his way north, and later these units marched to Wilmington. At Savannah, Howe began a march along the Georgia coast toward St. Augustine in September with his ragged troops, including the 1st North Carolina.[40] These troops were, according to one of North Carolina's Continental congressmen, "Without Cloaths, Tents, Waggons," and were "Badly armed," and "ill payed." Nevertheless, they "marched in this extreme unhealthy season without repining thousands of Miles to the inhospitable Clime of Georgia." Transportation and logistical problems, as well as Georgia's inability to support the campaign, forced Howe to suspend the operation before reaching the East Florida border and return to Savannah.[41]

While Howe's expedition in Georgia proceeded with numerous challenges, at Halifax, North Carolina, the fifth Provincial Congress met in November 1776. This body drafted a state constitution and a bill of rights and elected Richard Caswell the state's first governor, an office he held for three years.[42] The Congress enacted measures to procure arms, powder, lead, "pieces of cannon," salt, canvas, ship rigging, and all manner of military stores. The delegates also voted to raise three additional regiments of Continental troops and placed General Howe in command of all of the state's regulars. A new Washington District Regiment of Militia was created for the far western settlements of the province. The Congress also allowed for two battalions of militia volunteers under Brigadier General Allen Jones "to be raised for the aid of the State of South Carolina," which expected another attack that winter. During the Halifax sessions, the assembly authorized "a Party of Light Horse, ordered in Pursuit of certain disaffected Persons in Chatham County," one of the many Loyalist threats the state faced that year, and in the future, despite their earlier defeat at Moore's Creek Bridge.[43]

At the end of 1776, North Carolinians could look back on the first eighteen months of the Revolutionary War with some satisfaction. Their troops had soundly defeated the insurgent Loyalists on the banks of Moore's Creek, assisted with the successful defense of Charles Town and Great Bridge, and wreaked havoc in Cherokee country that fall. The next two years saw the new state send its own troops to the northern seat of war and strive to provide more men, money, and materiel for its own defense and to keep the threat from Loyalists in check. By late 1778, however, Carolinians saw the clouds of war come ominously closer to their homes, and by 1781, they suffered a British invasion, Tory violence, and a major battle in the backcountry at Guilford Courthouse.

6. Fighting Redcoats and Tories: A New State at War

A LONG STRUGGLE

Despite North Carolina's defeating the Loyalists at Moore's Creek Bridge and the Cherokees in the western mountains in 1776, the Revolutionary War continued to place great military demands on the new state. Its Continental troops saw action on northern battlefields as part of George Washington's army and also sent regulars and militia forces to support its southern neighbors, trying to keep enemy incursions from crossing its own border. Tories in North Carolina remained a serious threat, and acts of violence and property destruction were common. Although the state struggled to raise troops, collect supplies, and ensure its security, the British army's late 1778 invasion of the South reached the western counties of North Carolina by early 1781 and created a scene of chaos, destruction, and military actions as redcoats marched across the Piedmont and Tidewater, making it "a Country on the verge of ruin," according to prominent Wilmington Patriot William Hooper. Even after most British forces left the state following a major battle with Continental troops and militia at Guilford Courthouse in March 1781, Tory brutality continued in North Carolina for over a year. Peace eventually came in 1783, a welcome end to the successful but bloody struggle for American Independence.[1]

TWO BATTLES FOR PHILADELPHIA, 1777

In early 1777, the state's Continental line fielded nine regiments under Robert Howe's overall command, although none were at full strength and all were poorly armed and equipped. In February that year, these troops were reorganized so that Howe commanded a brigade of the 1st, 2nd, and 3rd Regiments, James Moore led the 4th, 5th, and 6th Regiments, and newly commissioned Brigadier General Francis Nash of Hillsborough commanded the 7th, 8th, and 9th Regiments, recently allowed by law and recruited at Halifax. A tenth regiment was authorized by April and taken into Continental service in June, but recruiting for the new battalion organized at Kinston was slow. Three

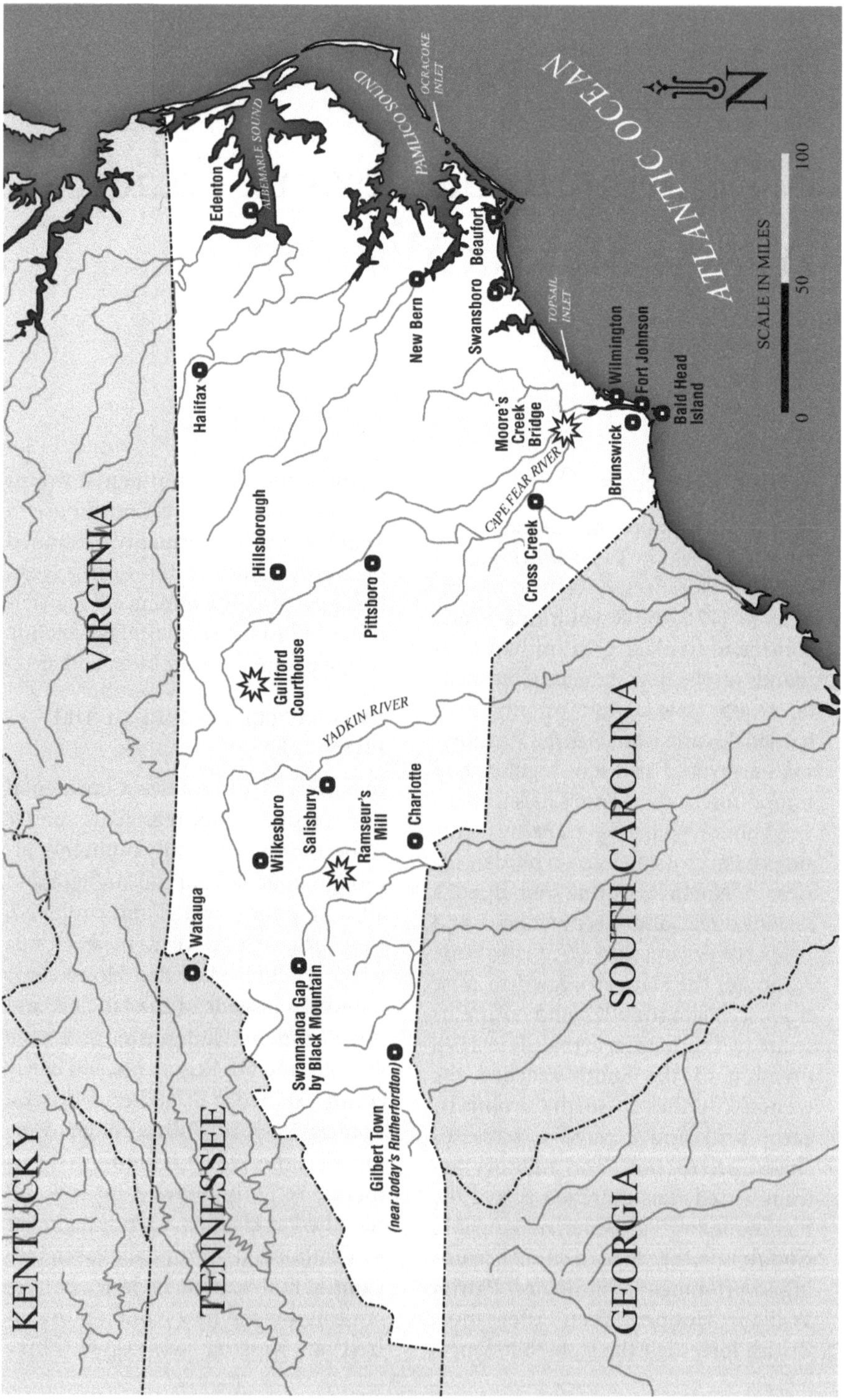
VIRGINIA
KENTUCKY
TENNESSEE
SOUTH CAROLINA
GEORGIA
ATLANTIC OCEAN
N
SCALE IN MILES
0
50
100
ALBEMARLE SOUND
PAMLICO SOUND
OCRACOKE INLET
TOPSAIL INLET
CAPE FEAR RIVER
YADKIN RIVER
Edenton
Halifax
Hillsborough
New Bern
Beaufort
Swansboro
Wilmington
Fort Johnson
Bald Head Island
Brunswick
Moore's Creek Bridge
Cross Creek
Pittsboro
Guilford Courthouse
Salisbury
Charlotte
Ramseur's Mill
Wilkesboro
Watauga
Swannanoa Gap by Black Mountain
Gilbert Town
(near today's Rutherfordton)

companies of light dragoons also became part of the Continental army that spring. After General Moore's death in April 1777 "from a fit of Gout in his stomach" and Howe's assumption of command in the Southern Department, all of the state's regiments fell under General Nash's authority in May.[2]

By late winter 1777, it became clear to Continental officers and Congress that the main British army operations during the upcoming campaign season would be around New York or Philadelphia. So Congress and General Washington called for troops to be sent from the South to bolster Washington's army at New York, including the North Carolina regiments.[3] In May, Nash sent off his fifteen hundred poorly equipped men, depleted by illness and desertion, from Halifax under the command of Colonel Alexander Martin, a Princeton graduate from Salisbury, while he remained behind several days to invigorate recruiting efforts. The troops reached Alexandria, Virginia, by May 25, where they were inoculated for smallpox. After recuperating several weeks from this procedure, they set out for Philadelphia, which they reached June 28. Nash's men served that summer in New Jersey and Pennsylvania as Washington tried to discern where the British would move their powerful army to open the campaign.[4]

The American high command finally learned in late August 1777 that General William Howe intended to capture Philadelphia. The British shipped their army of twelve thousand men led by Howe from New York up the Chesapeake Bay, and they landed at Head of Elk, Maryland. From there they began their advance north toward the seat of American government at the end of the month. Washington moved his forces south of the city and took up a blocking position on the east side of Brandywine Creek. On September 11, 1777, Howe held most of Washington's troops along the creek by feigning an attack, while seventy-five hundred of his men under General Cornwallis made a sweeping surprise attack around the Americans' right flank by way of an unguarded ford. Nash's North Carolina brigade of about one thousand men, unattached to a division, was initially posted in reserve behind Major General Nathanael Greene's division at Chad's Ford, defending the major road crossing of Brandywine Creek on the American left flank. When Cornwallis's redcoats hit the rebel right flank and threatened to rout most of Washington's army, Nash's brigade followed Greene's troops to help stall the British assault late in the day, but by the time they arrived, the overpowered American troops were in retreat. These Carolinians were not involved in the actual fighting but "were of the utmost service in covering the retreat of the other divisions," according to Major General Henry Knox, Washington's chief artillerist. A detachment of North Carolinians served as a corps of light infantry under the command of New Jersey Brigadier General William Maxwell and did see action that day. Pressured from two sides in "a very severe engagement," Washington prudently withdrew his defeated army to Philadelphia, and Howe did not pursue him until September 16.[5]

The British eventually occupied Philadelphia on September 26, having outmaneuvered Washington and forcing the Continental Congress to flee the city. Howe placed most of his troops at nearby Germantown, and with the rest he garrisoned Philadelphia. This disposition divided the British forces and provided the American commanding general an opportunity to seize the initiative against part of Howe's army. Washington elected to attack the redcoats at Germantown, with his eleven thousand men divided into four columns to strike from several directions. Nash's brigade of Carolinians was placed in reserve, to follow two of Washington's divisions south on the Germantown Road as they moved to attack on the foggy morning of October 4. The Carolinians managed to capture several pieces of British artillery during their morning advance. Unfortunately for the Americans, Washington's battle plan was too ambitious and their attacks uncoordinated, so that after some initial success, the British drove the American forces from the field.[6]

During the battle, British artillery fired on Continental troops retreating on the Germantown Road north of the Chew House. One of their shots from a 6-pounder cannon ricocheted down the road and tore into the thigh of General Nash riding at the head of his troops, nearly severing his leg and killing his horse and a nearby New Jersey officer. After urging his men forward, Nash was taken to the rear for medical attention, but he died of his ghastly wound on October 7. He was one of the "best, the most respected & regretted [missed] officers in the Continental Army," lamented Thomas Burke, a North Carolina Continental congressman. General Washington called him "a brave man who died in defence of his country." Congress later voted five hundred dollars to erect a monument in Nash's memory within a month of his death. "Poor General Nash is since dead of his wound," Cornelius Harnett reported a few days later to Gov. Richard Caswell, "his thigh being shattered by a Cannon Ball, we lost several other brave officers and many wounded" in the recent battle. Harnett referred to Colonel Thomas Polk of the 4th North Carolina, who was shot through the jaw shortly thereafter on the same road, and the 5th Regiment's Lieutenant Colonel Henry Irwin, who was killed that day.[7]

VALLEY FORGE AND THE BATTLE OF MONMOUTH, 1777–1778

After Germantown, no major battles were fought around Philadelphia until the following year. The North Carolina troops spent winter 1777–1778 at Valley Forge, Pennsylvania, in the frigid encampment of Washington's army. Here the Carolina soldiers, numbering just over one thousand men, were temporarily under the command of Brigadier General Lachlan McIntosh, a Georgia Continental army officer appointed December 20, 1777, as no replacement had yet been named for Nash.[8] The conditions at Valley Forge were difficult for all the troops. "I am sorry I have to inform you the men of my Brigade here have suffered severely this winter for want of clothing and other necessaries," General McIntosh reported to Governor Caswell in

March 1778. "[F]ifty of them died in and about Camp since the beginning of January last, and near two hundred sick here now besides as many more reported sick absent in different Hospitals of this State and Jersey, a most distressing situation!" Only one doctor had been present to treat the sick men of the North Carolina brigade from December through March.[9] Over the winter, the nine regiments in the brigade were so understrength because of illness and desertion they were consolidated into four regiments, and Wilmington native Thomas Clark, colonel of the 1st North Carolina Regiment, was given "immediate command" of the brigade when Washington assigned McIntosh to another position.[10]

In late spring 1778, Sir Henry Clinton became the British army commander in chief after General Howe sailed back to England in June. Clinton had orders to move his army from Philadelphia to New York,[11] and he marched his forces overland across the New Jersey countryside, with Washington's Continentals and militia reinforcements in pursuit. The two forces eventually collided in a sprawling battle in extreme heat near Monmouth Courthouse, about forty-five miles southwest of New York City on June 28, 1778. Most of the North Carolina brigade, which numbered fewer than four hundred men led by Colonel Clark, was part of the army's right wing under Major General Nathanael Greene, while the 2nd North Carolina served with Brigadier General Charles Scott in the advance guard. Two light infantry companies of the North Carolina Brigade were attached to a separate corps under Colonel Daniel Morgan of Virginia. After significant fighting during the day, Clinton withdrew his forces at midnight to resume his march to New York.[12]

Most of the North Carolina troops were posted in New York around the Hudson River Highlands and at West Point, and in New Jersey for the remainder of the year and into 1779, as part of the division led by Major General Alexander McDougal of the New York Continental line. One of the most significant actions in which North Carolina troops were involved in 1779 was Major General "Mad" Anthony Wayne's surprise night attack on the British defenses at Stony Point, on the west bank of the Hudson River thirty miles north of New York City. In this daring assault on July 16, the light companies of the 1st and 2nd North Carolina Regiments, commanded by young Major Hardy Murfree of Hertford County, made a successful feint on the center of the enemy's lines to divert their attention from Wayne's main thrust launched from below the fort along the river. In thirty minutes of fighting, the fort was taken by Wayne's troops, along with about five hundred prisoners. "Every officer & soldier belonging to the Light Corps discovered a zeal & Intrepidity that did & ever will secure success," Wayne reported to Congress.[13]

THE BRITISH INVADE THE SOUTH, 1778–1779

By the last few months of 1778, Washington and other Continental leaders suspected that the British would soon make a major effort to subdue the southern states. Indeed the British were planning operations in the South and anticipated great success in putting down the rebellion in those provinces. London authorities were convinced by numerous reports from American Loyalists that support for the Crown was strong in the South and that a military showing by red-coated soldiers and Royal Navy ships was all that was needed to quell the rebellion there.

The South was also considered vulnerable by the British because of the potential use of their Indian allies on the frontier, although this was a secondary factor. Under directions from Lord George Germain, the British government's secretary of state for the colonies, General Clinton sent an expedition under Lieutenant Colonel Archibald Campbell to Georgia with three thousand men in November. After arriving on the Georgia coast in late December, Campbell attacked and captured Savannah on the twenty-ninth, defeating a smaller Patriot force led by North Carolina's Robert Howe. The British operations to retake the South were off to an auspicious start.[14]

In anticipating British operations in the South, North Carolina officials tried during summer and fall 1779 to mobilize, arm, and equip the militia for service in the field. Governor Caswell and his officers met with little success, as money was lacking, arms scarce, and most Carolinians refused to muster. Still, a small militia force of about twelve hundred men eventually embodied under the command of Brigadier General John Ashe, a Harvard-educated French and Indian War veteran from Brunswick County, who marched his poorly armed men to Charles Town to serve under the Southern Department's new Continental commander, Major General Benjamin Lincoln of Massachusetts.[15] After Ashe's men joined Lincoln in South Carolina, he marched them toward Savannah and along the way met with Howe and his recently defeated troops at Purrysburg, on the Savannah River. Ashe's militia was sent to Brier Creek, south of Augusta, Georgia, to secure this backcountry region. On March 3, 1779, Ashe's troops, including his militia units and seventy Georgia Continentals, were surprised and quickly routed by veteran enemy troops, including some North Carolina Loyalists, under British Lieutenant Colonel Mark Prevost, north of the creek. Despite this victory, Prevost soon withdrew his detached and exposed force to the Georgia coast. A court-martial after the battle held that Ashe had failed to secure his camp, but he was acquitted of cowardice.[16]

After the defeat at Brier Creek, Lincoln and South Carolina Governor John Rutledge worked to collect troops from other states "with the utmost dispatch" to defend South Carolina from additional enemy incursions made from Georgia. North Carolina Brigadier General Jethro Sumner, a respected French and Indian War veteran with a home in Warren County, collected over seven hundred Continentals from his state with nine-month enlistments and brought them to South Carolina in March, organizing them into what he called the 4th and 5th North Carolina Regiments. After British forces under Prevost failed to capture Charles Town in May and began a withdrawal, Lincoln gathered his forces at the city and doggedly pursued the retreating British force to Stono Ferry. There the enemy had constructed breastworks studded with artillery to defend their rear eighteen miles south of Charles Town on the north side of the Stono River. Prevost began to evacuate his troops from John's Island and left command of the fortified Stono Ferry position to Lieutenant Colonel John Maitland of the 71st Foot. Lincoln attacked Maitland's works on the morning of June 20, 1779, with his force of three thousand soldiers, including about one thousand North Carolina militiamen under Colonel John Butler and four hundred North Carolina Continentals in a brigade led by Colonel James Armstrong, an experienced regular officer from Pitt County. The Americans' attack was initially successful, but after the enemy's resistance stiffened and Patriot ammunition ran low, Lincoln decided to withdraw from the field after an hour of fighting. Encouragingly, Colonel Butler wrote that his militia units "behaved better than could be expected of raw Troops."[17]

Three days after the battle, the British withdrew from the Charles Town area. Continental army officers and state officials in the southern states continued to try to raise and equip regulars and militia regiments to defend the South but met with limited success. Moreover, most of the North Carolina troops who fought at Stono Ferry were discharged on the expiration of their enlistments in August and returned home.[18] In October 1779, a combined French and American army laid siege to Savannah, but after British forces under Major General Augustine Prevost repulsed a rash assault on the city's defensive works made by the allies at the insistence of French commander General Le Comte d'Estaing on the ninth, the siege was lifted. That fall, at Congress' recommendation, General Washington began to send the seven hundred men of the North Carolina regiments in his army along the Hudson River to South Carolina to support the efforts of General Lincoln and the southern governors to counter the British invaders. The Carolina troops left New York in November and reached South Carolina in March 1780.[19]

THE FALL OF CHARLES TOWN AND THE BATTLE OF CAMDEN, AUGUST 16, 1780

General Clinton decided to launch a major expedition to capture Charles Town, which he thought would encourage Loyalists to come forward to support British arms and facilitate the restoration of the Crown's government in the South. With almost nine thousand soldiers, Clinton's force sailed from New York in late December 1779 and began to land its troops on February 12, 1780, south of Charles Town on Wadmalaw Island. Joined by additional troops from Savannah, Clinton's army invested the city on April 1 and compelled General Lincoln to surrender his post and all 5,660 troops and hundreds of cannons within it on May 12. Included in the garrison were 750 men in three regiments of North Carolina Continentals under Brigadier General James Hogun, a section of the North Carolina Continental Artillery, two companies of North Carolina light infantry, and the North Carolina Light

"Plan of the battle fought near Camden, August 16th, 1780."

Dragoons led by Colonel Marquis Francois DeMalmedy. Additionally, twelve hundred North Carolina militia troops under Colonel Henry William Harrington surrendered and were soon paroled. The British victory was a significant setback to Patriot hopes for a southern victory, not to mention the loss of men and materiel that could not be readily replaced.[20]

Just over a month after the capitulation of Charles Town, Congress appointed Major General Horatio Gates, a former British officer, to replace General Lincoln as commander of the Southern Department. Gates, who was the victorious commander of American forces at the decisive Battles of Saratoga in 1777, commanded the remnants of Continental forces in the

Maj. Gen. Horatio Gates.

South as well as the Maryland and Delaware lines previously sent to the Carolinas by Washington and led by German-born Major General Baron de Kalb. Congress also directed Virginia and North Carolina to call out thousands of its militia forces to augment Gates's regulars and provide all material support each could manage.[21]

In April, prior to Charles Town's fall, North Carolina's assembly elected Abner Nash to the state's governorship and appointed former Governor Caswell as major general of the state's militia forces in the field. Caswell moved his units in advance of de Kalb's men just across the border into South Carolina by early August, the men "worn down with fatigue."[22] General Gates reached de Kalb's camp on Deep River in North Carolina on July 26 and immediately decided to advance into South Carolina via the direct road south to Camden, a major British outpost in central South Carolina. Despite the protestations of his officers that this route would be barren of supplies and in an area full of Tories, Gates dismissed their suggestion that the army march toward Camden by way of Charlotte, farther west. On August 7, Gates's troops joined with Caswell's two thousand militiamen and proceeded toward Camden, joined several days later by Virginia militia troops under Brigadier General Edward Stevens. Nearby British and Loyalist troops fell back in front of Gates's army and combined with additional troops at Camden, now commanded by General Cornwallis.[23]

Coincidently, at 10 PM August 15, both commanders ordered their forces to approach the enemy's position in a night march. After blundering into each other several miles north of Camden at about 2 AM, the armies waited until dawn to begin the battle. Gates deployed his Continental forces on his right, to the west of the road, with one regiment of Maryland regulars on the road to the rear as a reserve. Caswell's three North Carolina militia brigades occupied the center of the American line, while the Virginia militia under Stevens and a light infantry unit was on Gates's left. Gates's army numbered about four thousand men. Once it was light enough to see through the open woods of tall pines, Cornwallis attacked with his veteran troops on his right flank facing Gates's inexperienced militia, and with his Loyalist troops to the left, including Lieutenant Colonel John Hamilton's Royal North Carolina Regiment and three hundred North Carolina volunteers under Lieutenant Colonel Samuel Bryan. The British counted about twenty-two hundred men in their ranks that morning.[24]

Lt. Gen. Charles, Lord Cornwallis.

The disparity of the two armies' deployments became apparent as soon as the firing started. Cornwallis's veteran redcoats on his right flank fired a volley and charged with bayonets against the untested Patriot militiamen, most of whom broke for the rear without firing a shot. The Virginia militia fled down the road the army had advanced on, followed by nearly all of the North Carolina troops. One of Gates's staff officers, Colonel Otho Holland Williams, described the scene: "they threw down their loaded arms and fled, in the utmost consternation. The unworthy example of the Virginians was almost instantly followed by the North Carolinians; only a small part of Brigadier General Isaac Gregory's brigade made a short pause." Williams was referring to Lieutenant Colonel Henry Dixon's North Carolina militia regiment in line next to the 2nd Maryland, which "fired two or three rounds of cartridge" and held fast.[25] After the militia fled, along with Caswell and Gates, the charging British regiments wheeled left to fight the Continentals. Eventually the American troops were overwhelmed in total defeat. In the struggle, in which General de Kalb was mortally wounded, his Continentals were either captured or scattered in the woods and swamps nearby. Most of the militia returned to their homes, unwilling to regroup even when they reached North Carolina or Virginia. "We owe all our misfortune to the Militia," one of Gates's aides wrote. "[H]ad they not run like dastardly cowards, our Army was sufficient to cope with theirs, drawn up as we were upon a rising and advantageous ground."[26]

VICTORIES AT KINGS MOUNTAIN AND COWPENS, 1780–1781

The defeat at Camden left North Carolina wide open to British invasion, effectively gave the British control of South Carolina, and encouraged the Loyalists to openly vie for political and military power within both states. Still, all was not lost for the cause of independence that summer. Whig forces in North Carolina routed a larger force of Tories in a surprise morning attack on June 20, 1780, at the Battle of Ramseur's Mill, in today's Lincolnton. One month later, at Colson's Mill near present-day Norwood, Patriots dispersed a force of Loyalists in a brief skirmish, although Whig militia leader (and former Continental officer) Colonel William L. Davidson was wounded in the action. General Gates struggled to regroup his forces around Hillsborough in September, but as always, arms and provisions were difficult to procure, and militiamen often refused to muster.[27]

After his victory at Camden, Cornwallis moved his army north into North Carolina and reached Charlotte by September 26. Here he met with stiff resistance from 150 mounted Whig troops under the English-born Colonel William R. Davie, who was eventually forced to withdraw from the courthouse village by the redcoats' infantry, but only with difficulty. The British found the area to be thoroughly hostile to the Crown, and intelligence on Patriot forces was impossible to obtain during their stay there of several weeks.[28]

Maj. Gen. Nathanael Greene.

Cornwallis's thrust into North Carolina was supported by a secondary offensive on his western flank, along the base of the Blue Ridge Mountains. Major Patrick Ferguson, a regular British army officer then serving as inspector of the Loyalist militia, commanded this column. In late September, Ferguson's eleven hundred troops, consisting entirely of Tories, reached Gilbert Town (near modern Rutherfordton). From there Ferguson sent an inflammatory message to Whigs in the backcountry and the mountainous frontiers of Virginia, the Carolinas, Georgia, and what is now East Tennessee. "If you do not desist your opposition to the British Arms," he threatened, "I shall march this army over the mountains, hang your leaders, and lay waste your country with fire and sword." Instead of cowing the frontier Overmountain men and backcountry Patriots, Ferguson's message instead led to the mobilization of a significant force of frontier Patriots, most of whom carried rifles and moved toward Ferguson's position on horseback. Virginians also began marching east over the mountains from around Abingdon, joined by North Carolinians along the way, and passed through Sycamore Shoals, Cathey's Plantation, and Gillespie Gap. At a large encampment at Quaker Meadows (present-day Morganton), they were joined by other Whigs from Elkin, Fort Crider (Lenoir), and Fort Defiance. Prominent North Carolina leaders who served during this campaign included Colonels Benjamin Cleveland, Isaac Shelby, and John Sevier, along with Majors Joseph Winston and Joseph McDowell. The combined forces moved south to Gilbert Town, which they reached October 4. Met by South Carolinians at the Cowpens, a picked force of about one thousand men hurried east toward Kings Mountain, a high ridge just south of the North Carolina line, where several days earlier Ferguson had taken up a defensive—but isolated—position.[29]

On October 7, 1780, Whig forces led by Virginia's Colonel William Campbell surrounded and attacked the Tories on the mountain. After a one-hour battle in which Major Ferguson was killed, the Tories capitulated, having lost 119 men killed, 123 wounded, and 698 surrendered. A large number of the captured Loyalists were from North Carolina. Some of the Whigs continued to fire at their enemies even after they had raised white flags, such was the animosity between Loyalists and Patriots. Concerned that Cornwallis would move against them after the battle, the Whig forces separated to return home, while the North Carolina and Virginia troops marched with the Tory prisoners north to Biggerstaff's Old Fields, east of Gilbert Town. There several Tory leaders were tried and hanged before Whig officers belatedly put an end to these irregular executions.[30]

The rebel victory at Kings Mountain was more than a loss of a thousand Loyalist troops. It gave southern Patriots a much-needed moral boost, temporarily quelled Tory depredations, and stopped the British invasion of North Carolina that fall. As British General Clinton concluded several years later, it was "the first link in a chain of evils that followed each other in regular succession until they had at last ended in the total loss of America." Thomas Jefferson reached a similar verdict decades later, calling the battle (with some exaggeration) the "turn of the tide of success which terminated the Revolutionary War."[31]

With Ferguson's column wiped out, Cornwallis withdrew his force from Charlotte to Winnsboro, South Carolina, by late October. Here he remained refitting his forces until January 1781.

Meanwhile, North Carolina officials and General Gates made efforts to raise more troops at Hillsborough. In October, the Continental Congress made two significant military appointments for the Southern Department. On October 25, Colonel Daniel Morgan, a Virginia Continental officer, received a brigadier general's commission to command light troops in the Carolinas. Several days earlier, Congress formally appointed Major General Nathanael Greene as Gates's replacement in command of the department. "You will . . . proceed without delay to the Southern army, now in North Carolina, and take the command accordingly," Washington informed the former Rhode Island Quaker. Greene arrived in Charlotte on December 2 and relieved Gates.[32] Greene was astounded at the wretched condition of the army. "The Difficulty of carrying on the war in this Department is much greater than my imagination had extended to," he found just a few days after reaching his command, which he described as "the Shadow of an Army in the midst of Distress."[33] Despite his frequent letters to state leaders, the Continental Congress, and military officers throughout the coming years, Greene was forced to fight the war in the South with too few men, scanty supplies, and little support until the war's termination in 1783.

Upon marshaling what forces he could in North Carolina, including about one thousand Continentals, Greene adopted a risky strategy of dividing his small force and sending Morgan's light troops southwest of Charlotte while he moved his own troops into South Carolina. Morgan was to gather militia companies, protect Whigs in the backcountry, and "annoy" the enemy in upcountry South Carolina. Should Cornwallis advance against him, the two Patriot forces could swiftly unite in North Carolina.[34] To counter Morgan's threat to his west, Cornwallis directed twelve hundred men in a mixed force of cavalry and infantry led by Lieutenant Colonel Banastre Tarleton to bring the rebels to battle while the rest of the British troops, wagons, and guns marched north. Morgan began moving away from Tarleton's fast-moving column, but at the Broad River, the American general decided to make a stand with the troops he had on hand on January 16, 1781.[35] Early in the morning the following day, Tarleton's force caught up to Morgan aligned in battle formation, militia in the first two lines, regulars in the third. The British charged impetuously and drove back the Whig militia, but Morgan's Continentals held firm, and with a timely attack by Continental cavalry they routed the British forces in a complete victory. One hundred fifty North Carolina militiamen under Major Joseph McDowell fought in the battle, posted on Morgan's right flank.[36]

Morgan retreated from Cowpens on January 18 headed for the Catawba River, followed by Cornwallis with the main British army of twenty-four hundred soldiers, intent on following the Patriots into North Carolina. At Ramseur's Mill, Cornwallis destroyed most of his excess baggage to facilitate a rapid pursuit of the American forces, who were ahead crossing the Catawba River at Sherrald's Ford. Several bodies of militia also began to gather at other fords on the river, ahead of the British advance. Cornwallis forced a crossing of the Catawba at Cowan's Ford (several miles west of modern Huntersville) on February 1, which was defended by a North Carolina militia force of several hundred men under Brigadier General William Lee Davidson. British light troops flanked the militia and forced them to fall back, and Davidson was mortally wounded during the fight.

THE BATTLE OF GUILFORD COURTHOUSE, MARCH 15, 1781

Joining his army at Guilford Courthouse a few days later, General Greene knew he was too weak to face Cornwallis's pursuing army in battle, so he elected to retreat northeast toward Virginia, where he hoped to be resupplied and reinforced with more militia troops. The British gave chase, following Greene closely in what came to be called "the Race for the Dan," a river near the Virginia border that the Patriots sought to put between their army and the enemy. Greene's men marched northeast away from Guilford Courthouse, near modern Greensboro, and Lower Saura Town, near present-day Eden, while Cornwallis's route took him from Salisbury to Shallow Ford (on the Yadkin River), to the Moravian settlement of Bethania, and finally just into Virginia to the banks of the Dan River at Irwin's and Boyd's Ferries (near present-day South Boston, Virginia). Cornwallis reached the rain-swollen river early on February 15 but was too late to catch Greene's army, whose troops finished crossing the previous day. The weary British withdrew to Hillsborough soon thereafter.[37]

Refreshed, refitted, and reinforced after crossing the Dan, although with-

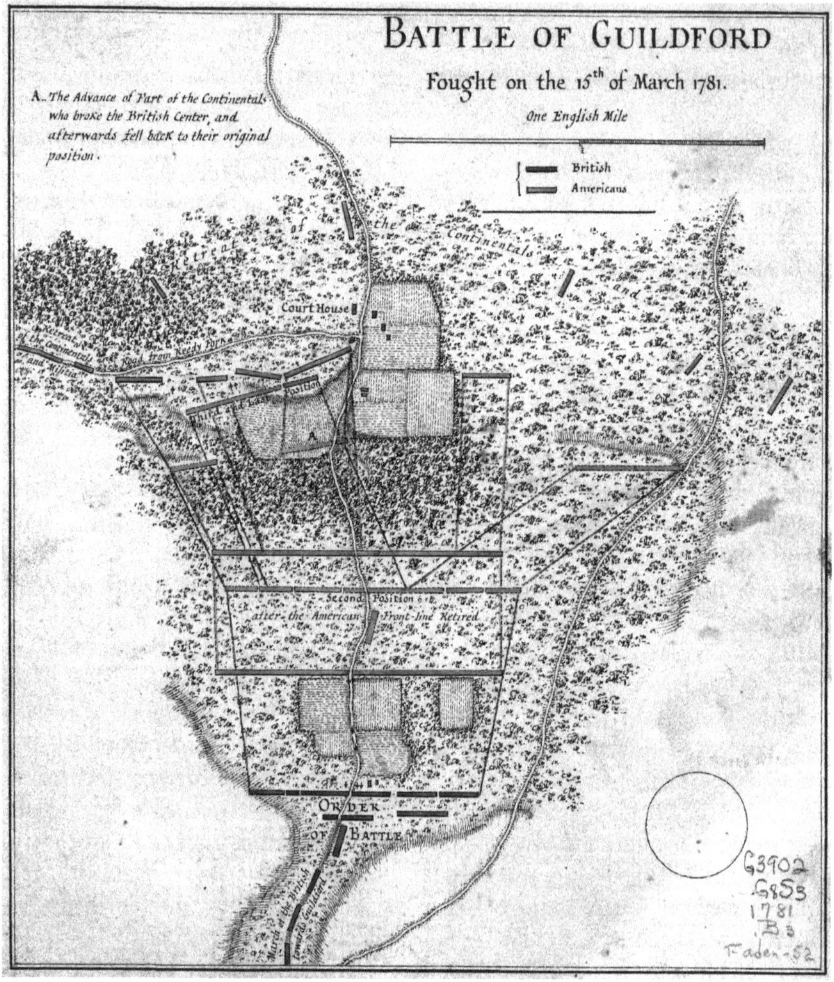

Plan of the Battle of Guilford Courthouse, 1781.

out the services of General Morgan, who left the field due to illness, Greene's forces marched back into North Carolina to face a British army weakened by their exertions and far from their base of supplies. Cornwallis was able to recruit few Loyalists on his arrival in the Piedmont and was reduced to just less than two thousand men in his ranks. After several weeks of skirmishes (particularly with Tory militiamen) and maneuvering, Greene arrived at Guilford Courthouse on March 14, with a four-thousand-man army consisting of Continental infantry and cavalry, and North Carolina and Virginia militia. On the advice of Morgan, Greene placed his army in three lines upon learning of the enemy's approach. In advance he deployed his North Carolina militiamen, over a third of whom were draftees, supported on both flanks by Continentals and dragoons. His second line consisted of Virginia militia troops, which counted many veterans in their ranks. Finally, close to the courthouse, Greene posted his Continentals—Maryland and Virginia regulars, with Continental cavalry in reserve.[38]

On March 15, 1781, Cornwallis approached Greene's position from the New Garden Quaker meetinghouse eight miles to the southwest. Tarleton's cavalry was in the British van, followed by the foot regiments and artillery, tired, cold, and hungry as they advanced in a column along the road. American cavalry under Lieutenant Colonel Henry "Lighthorse Harry" Lee sparred with Tarleton's horsemen along the Great Salisbury Road leading to Greene's position that morning, then fell back to the rebel lines.[39]

The first line of the American army, primarily untested militia companies, was deployed blocking the road in a line behind a rail fence, with riflemen and dragoons on each flank. They looked out on about four hundred yards of open ground, muddy from recent rains, across which Cornwallis's infantry would have to advance. Greene told the militia officers to have their men fire two volleys, then fall back through the woods to the second line once the British regulars closed in. Brigadier General Edward Stevens, commanding a brigade of Virginia troops in the second line, was determined that his men would not repeat their shameful performance at Camden: he ordered picked men among his soldiers to shoot down those who tried to break ranks and flee the field.[40]

After thirty minutes of artillery fire, Cornwallis sent his troops forward to attack the rebel militia shortly after noon. When the redcoats advanced to about forty yards from the militia line, the Carolinians let loose "a most galling and effective fire," wrote one British officer. The British regiments and one Hessian battalion paused to regroup after suffering casualties, returned the Americans' fire, and charged with their steel bayonets fixed. It is unclear how many of the Carolinians fired a second or even a third volley, but soon all retreated through the woods, some in a state of panic, "scattered in every direction," one of them later recalled. The Crown forces, though bloodied, pressed forward toward the Virginians in the forest and brush four hundred yards away.[41]

The wooded terrain disrupted British unit alignments so that their assault on the Virginians was disjointed and "of almost infinite diversity," according to a British army witness. The fighting in the forest was confusing, made more so by the smoke of the musketry. Eventually Cornwallis's men pressed the Virginians back with bayonet charges and superior discipline. Although some of the militiamen fled in panic, almost five hundred men from the first and second lines did regroup around the courthouse to the rear of Greene's third line.[42] Meanwhile, on the far right of Cornwallis's line, a separate battle began to develop away from the main scene of action, as British and Hessian troops, including Tarleton's feared dragoons, pushed Virginia riflemen and Colonel Lee's mixed legion of cavalry and infantry south through the woods. Many of Greene's soldiers in this part of the field were killed or wounded by saber wounds from pursuing British cavalrymen.[43]

Finally, about ninety minutes after the battle opened, tired British troops approached Greene's third line, which to that point had been unengaged in the fight. Initially the 1st Maryland and 2nd Virginia Regiments repulsed a British attack, but to their left the 2nd Maryland broke when attacked by Brigadier General Charles O'Hara's 2nd Battalion of Guards, which also captured two American 6-pounder cannons. O'Hara's successful attack put his men in the rear of the 1st Maryland, which faced about and gave "some well directed fires" in close combat. Joining the attack on the British was Lieutenant Colonel William Washington's Continental Light Dragoons, which charged into the enemy's ranks with about eighty mounted men who then made a second pass through the enemy troop formation. In the confused action, the 1st Maryland was able to recapture the lost artillery pieces and some prisoners, and the bitter fighting was hand to hand. Several blasts of cannon fire from the British lines soon checked the danger from Washington's cavalry.[44]

With all of the British regiments now up to the third line, and having engaged in heavy fighting including the rout of the 2nd Maryland, Greene concluded that a withdrawal from the field was now prudent. At about 3:30 PM, his forces withdrew in good order north on the Reedy Fork Road to Speedwell Ironworks on Troublesome Creek (in modern Rockingham County), the army's predesignated rallying point. British forces initially pursued but were checked by Virginia Continentals as rain began to fall on the dead and wounded on the field. It was "one of the most hazardous, as well as severe battles that occurred during the war," wrote Tarleton. Greene, taking some solace in the disappointing result of the contest, wrote to Congress that the British "have met with a defeat in a victory." American losses were 79 killed, 184 wounded, and 1,046 missing, most of the latter being militiamen who fled the field and did not return to the ranks. Greene's army lost four guns to the redcoats as well. Cornwallis lost 93 killed, 413 wounded, and 26 missing, a staggering casualty rate of about 25 percent. His army held the bloody field, but at great cost. "Another such victory would ruin the British Army," quipped Charles James Fox, a prominent member of the British Parliament who opposed the war.[45]

Although much of Greene's militia had left the army during the retreat to Speedwell Ironworks, he still had a force of which the British had to be wary. Given his losses, the British commander knew he had won a Pyrrhic victory. Cornwallis left about seventy of his wounded at New Garden meetinghouse and began to march his men south "by easy marches" to Cross Creek, given his lack of supplies and weakened army. He brought his worn-down troops to Wilmington on April 7, and at the end of that month started his campaign to subdue Virginia, which eventually led to his surrender at Yorktown in October 1781.[46]

As Cornwallis marched south along the Cape Fear River toward the coast, Greene followed him part of the way, then decided to move his army into South Carolina with twelve hundred Continentals and several hundred militia. Although he was unsuccessful in defeating the enemy outright in 1781 at Hobkirk's Hill near Camden (April 25), at Ninety-Six in the South Carolina backcountry (May and June), and at Eutaw Springs (September 8), these actions caused the British to withdraw their posts and eventually maintain posts only at Charles Town and Georgetown.[47]

FIGHTING THE TORIES

Greene and Cornwallis had left North Carolina with their armies by early May 1781, but the war was not over for the struggling state. The state assembly attempted to raise more troops and gather more supplies, using drafts to bring in men and impressments (which amounted to confiscation) to obtain provisions—onerous practices used since early in the war and resented by the people.[48] Additionally, a substantial threat from hostile Tories remained the most widespread, persistent, and frustrating problem for North Carolina Patriots well into 1783. The Cape Fear Valley and the backcountry (especially Randolph, Chatham, Orange, Cumberland, and Anson Counties) suffered far more than did other parts of the state in terms of violence and destruction associated with battling the Tories. Some counties, particularly those along the Cape Fear River watershed, remained heavily Tory in sentiment for much or all of the war. Gov. Abner Nash described the state in 1780 as "a Country exposed to the misfortune of having a War within its Bowels." Likewise Gov. Thomas Burke wrote two years later that "it is our misfortune to have among us a large Settlement of people who were never thoroughly United with us, and who have always become very dangerous Instruments in the hands of the Enemy."[49] No one was more concerned about the Loyalist problem than General Greene, who wrote in late 1780 that "the Whigs and Tories pursue one another with the most relent[less] Fury killing and destroying each other wherever they meet. Indeed a great deal of this Country is already laid waste & in the utmost danger of becoming a Desert."[50]

Perhaps the most notorious Tory in the eyes of the Whigs was Colonel David Fanning, who, although a commissioned provincial officer, was despised as an outlaw by his enemies. To give only two examples of his exploits, Tories under Fanning raided Pittsboro in Chatham County on a court day in July 1781 and captured "the lawyers, justices and other officers of the court"; three months later, Governor Burke himself was captured by Fanning's Loyalists while at Hillsborough and subsequently held as a prisoner in South Carolina for months.[51] Tory-Whig violence became so troublesome by 1782 that Fanning suggested a three-month truce and establishing a Tory enclave along the Cape Fear in exchange for their pacific behavior. The state's assembly eventually balked at such an agreement, and in May 1782, Fanning left the state for British-held East Florida.[52]

Limited resources, numerous Tories, British invasions, and the constant demands on the citizenry combined to create a disorganized, often chaotic wartime experience for most North Carolinians. By the end of 1782, however, the Loyalists had been suppressed and active military campaigning in the South had ended. By the end of the following year, the peace treaty ending the Revolutionary War was signed. Although this struggle with the British was over, twenty-nine years later, Carolinians would be called on to wage war against the same foe over different issues, in a conflict called the War of 1812.

7. War and the New Nation

With the winning of its independence, the United States reduced its military forces in 1784, a cost-saving measure also based on traditional republican fears of a standing army. The end of the Revolutionary War, however, did not mean the newly established country was secure or free from powerful enemies. Many Native Americans west of the Appalachian Mountains were still hostile toward settlers, surveyors, and land agents coming into their lands. Great Britain, although locked in a titanic struggle with France and its allies from 1793 to 1815, was still a dangerous threat to American security and independence. By the 1840s, a dispute with Mexico over the future of Texas and American expansion grew into a war on foreign soil. All of these conflicts enmeshed North Carolina with demands for troops and led the state to send its soldiers to distant battlefields in the Ohio Valley, Canada, and Mexico.

CAROLINA TROOPS ON THE OHIO FRONTIER

Although the new United States agreed on peace with Great Britain in 1783 with the signing of the Treaty of Paris, political and military conflict with the Indians west of the Appalachian Mountains continued after the Revolutionary War. As had been the case for decades, native peoples resented the Americans' hunger for western land and their abusive trading practices, which were ongoing throughout the 1780s. Once the war ended, a torrent of Americans crossed the mountains to claim frontier lands the Indians held as their own. Conflict was inevitable, and not long in coming.[1]

Although the administration of President George Washington attempted to avoid war with the Indians by negotiations and treaties, by the late 1780s it became clear that the military forces of the United States needed to be strengthened. In 1784, the Continental army was disbanded and quickly replaced with a new force of militia drafts for one year's service called the 1st American Regiment, under Lieutenant Colonel Josiah Harmar. After the adoption of the US Constitution in 1787, Congress ex-

Arthur St. Clair.

panded the army to an authorized strength of 1,273 officers and men, although recruiting the force to this number was difficult. Most of these troops were assigned to small isolated posts in the Ohio Valley, to keep the peace between Indians and settlers.[2]

By 1786, open warfare had erupted in the Ohio Country, with the Indians on the Wabash, Miami, and Maumee Rivers particularly hostile. Arthur St. Clair, the first governor of the Northwest Territory (which included the modern states of Ohio, Indiana, Illinois, Michigan, Wisconsin, and part of Minnesota), recommended to the American government that in light of increased Indian attacks the army should be deployed against them in a punitive expedition. With President Washington's approval, in June 1790, Secretary of War Henry Knox ordered a military strike against Indian villages on the upper Wabash River to "extirpate" the enemy warriors. Harmar, now a brigadier general, conducted the foray north of the Ohio River from Fort Washington (at today's Cincinnati) in October. Although he was able to burn a number of Indian villages and cornfields in what is now northwestern Ohio, his army of regulars and militiamen suffered heavy casualties before returning to Fort Washington by early November. It soon became clear that Harmar had not significantly weakened Indian strength during his campaign, and another expedition would be needed.

In 1791, Congress authorized the establishment of the 2nd American Regiment to serve on the frontier, along with two thousand six-month levies to be raised for another Ohio campaign. In addition, the 1st Regiment had to be brought up to full strength for these active wilderness operations, which were to be commanded by St. Clair, now a major general.[3]

Back in June 1790, Secretary Knox appointed Captain Joseph Montfort of Halifax, North Carolina, to raise and command a company of the 1st American Regiment in North Carolina. Montfort was a former Continental army officer in the 3rd North Carolina Regiment, had served seven years during the Revolutionary War, and earned for himself hundreds of acres of land grants in compensation in the immediate postwar years.[4] Montfort, who based his recruiting efforts at Halifax, had received orders to complete his company by September 1790, then march the men to the French Broad River. Here he was to attend treaty negotiations with the Cherokees and "to defend the frontiers and carry the treaty into effect." Knox expected peace on the southern frontier, but noted "it may be otherwise, in which case the citizens will expect protection from the United States."[5]

In January 1791, Montfort's company consisted of fifty men, and he was still recruiting in North Carolina, although records do not show where the captain was located.[6] War Department papers indicate that Montfort and sixty men moved to Staunton, Virginia, in early May 1791, having orders to march to Fort Pitt (Pittsburgh) by the end of the month on their way downriver to Fort Washington.[7] Other sources indicate that Montfort's men may have traveled through the Cumberland Gap or down the Kanawha River to the Ohio Country. Either way, the troops were expected to eventually reach Fort Washington to augment St. Clair's force that summer. Additionally, North Carolina was expected to raise four companies of "new levies" for the campaign, although it is unclear if these troops were fully embodied.[8]

Montfort's company of the 1st Regiment reached Fort Washington on July 14, 1791, along with about one hundred Carolinians of the new levies under Major Mathew Rhea, a former Virginia Continental officer.[9] With these men and other reinforcements, St. Clair began an expedition on September 17 to destroy the hostile Indian stronghold called Kekionga, on the headwaters of the Maumee River at modern Fort Wayne, Indiana. His army was ill fed, disgruntled, and poorly equipped as they cut a road north through the forests to reach the Indian towns. At the Miami River, the army built Fort Hamilton as a supply depot, then St. Clair had troops erect a second bastion, called Fort Jefferson, forty-five miles farther north. On October 31, about sixty disgruntled Kentucky militiamen abandoned St. Clair's column and announced they would plunder the army's supply train advancing from Fort Hamilton as they set off south for the Ohio River. Fearful for the safety of his supplies, St. Clair ordered three hundred regulars of the 1st Regiment, including Montfort's North Carolinians, to overtake the mutinous militiamen and secure the army's vital supply wagons.[10] Some of the 1st Regiment stayed at Fort Jefferson while Montfort and his men trekked back to Fort Hamilton.[11]

St. Clair's decision to send the 1st Regiment—some of his best soldiers, led by Colonel John Hamtramck—back down the trace toward Fort Jefferson was imprudent tactically but fortunate for Montfort and his soldiers. On the morning of November 4, St. Clair's army was attacked by a powerful Indian force and soundly defeated with heavy casualties on the Wabash River. The panicked survivors fled south to Fort Jefferson, leaving over half of their comrades dead or wounded on the battlefield.[12] On November 7, St. Clair and his weary troops reached Fort Hamilton, where the general ordered Captain Montfort to take part of his company and march north toward Fort Jefferson with supplies and medicine for the relief and protection of the men still straggling along the road from the battleground. Montfort's detachment returned to Fort Hamilton three days later.[13]

After St. Clair's disastrous defeat, the War Department oversaw a major reorganization of the American army. In 1792, the Legion of the United States was established, a force of 5,190 offi-

Maj. Gen. Anthony Wayne.

cers and men (at least on paper), and organized into four "sublegions." Each sublegion consisted of dragoons, artillery, infantry, and a rifle battalion. Congress appointed Revolutionary War hero Major General "Mad" Anthony Wayne to command the new army, which was to operate in the Ohio Valley against the Indians.[14] Captain Montfort received an appointment to the first sublegion and command of Fort Jefferson, but a few months later, in April 1792, he was killed outside of the fort, having been tricked by Indians using turkey calls.[15] A condescending letter from War Secretary Knox to Colonel Winthrop Sargent of General St. Clair's staff survives from three months after Montfort's death. In it, Knox opines that "Montfort was punished instantly although with rather too much severity," referring to the result of his mistake, and he hoped that "examples will introduce a proper and necessary spirit of discipline."[16]

General Wayne eventually built his legion into a superior, disciplined fighting force and began his campaign against the Indians of the Ohio Valley late in 1793. The following year, on August 20, Wayne's legion defeated an Indian force led by Blue Jacket and Little Turtle at the battle of Fallen Timbers (near present-day Maumee, Ohio). Wayne later coerced massive land concessions from the defeated warriors and pushed many of the tribes farther west, engendering further bitterness soon to be exploited by an old foe of the Americans: the British.[17]

THE SECOND WAR WITH GREAT BRITAIN

Historians debate the causes of the War of 1812 even today, and the issues involved were controversial at the time. Like other major conflicts in which the United States has fought, the struggle with Great Britain from 1812 to 1815 highlighted deep political and geographic divisions within the country and met with significant opposition. The war was unpopular in New England and among those of the Federalist Party, but others in the fledgling nation also opposed the war for a variety of reasons. The fact that the United States endured many military defeats in the conflict did nothing to make it more popular.

The European wars from 1792 to 1815 pitting Great Britain against France (along with the allies of each belligerent) resulting from the French Revolution and Napoleon Bonaparte's rise to power gradually enveloped the United States, at the time a small neutral nation attempting to commercially capitalize on the European hostilities. As the conflict grew in size and desperation, England and France each tried to monopolize American trade and to restrict it with decrees and other trade limitations. Britain's practice of impressing American sailors and seizing its ships close to US ports and on the high seas disrupted trade and violated American sovereignty. Many Americans suspected that the British encouraged Indian opposition to further American encroachment of native lands in the west and supplied them with arms and money for scalps, from forts the redcoats should have evacuated after the Revolutionary War. All these factors led to the clamoring for war in the United States, although many merchants, ship owners, and businessmen considered the British highhandedness merely a cost of doing business. While "War Hawk" congressmen called for a military response to British affronts in the name of the nation's honor, many Americans refused to support the country's war efforts. Others observed that the United States was unprepared for a war and had no business engaging in one. Nevertheless, at President James Madison's request, Congress approved a declaration of war against Great Britain in June 1812.[18]

It appears that most North Carolinians favored the war, including Gov. William Hawkins. The state assembly supported measures to raise troops and defend its ports. In Washington, the state's congressional delegation voted in favor of the declaration of war, including both its US senators. Still, there were some Federalists in North Carolina who opposed the conflict and, in the war's later years, criticized how it was waged. Many Carolinians also objected to sending the militia out of the state for military service and decried the paucity of assistance the national government gave to North Carolina for its defense. The state legislature claimed to have spent almost $31,000 for war-related necessities but was not reimbursed by Congress for these expenditures until 1916.[19]

FIGHTING ON THE NORTHERN FRONTIER

Like the French and Indian War, much of the military action of the War of 1812 occurred far away from the southern states, although the 1814 British campaign in the Chesapeake region, the Creek War in modern Alabama, and British operations to capture New Orleans are notable exceptions. Still, the northern frontier of the United States and the waters of the Great Lakes were the principal zones of conflict from 1812 to 1814.

As part of the country's mobilization process, the United States attempted to fill its army regiments to their full strength of 10,603 soldiers and increased the size of the army by creating a supplementary force of regulars. President Madison also sought to use volunteers and militia forces to bolster America's military might. In January 1812, Congress voted to recruit twenty-five thousand additional men for the US Army in regiments of two thousand soldiers each, and called for thirty thousand additional volunteers.[20]

As part of this increase in military strength, the new 10th Regiment of Infantry under Colonel James Wellborn of Wilkes County began to recruit in and around Wilkesboro, North Carolina, in January 1812 and was allowed two battalions, which the state was never able to recruit to full strength. The first battalion of the regiment was active during the conflict until 1815, at which point it was consolidated with several other regiments. The second battalion was at Richmond, Virginia, and Baltimore, Maryland, in 1813, but little else is known about its wartime service. In early 1813, the 43rd Regiment of Infantry was commanded by Colonel Nicholas Long Jr. of North Carolina, headquartered in the Raleigh area. It served in garrisons along the southern coast for the entire war and was made up primarily of Georgia enlistees. Other North Carolinians served in US Army artillery and rifle regiments, as well as the 12th, 13th, and 15th Regiments. By fall 1812, almost two thousand North Carolinians had been recruited for service.[21]

The 10th Regiment faced the enemy in battle in the War of 1812's northern theater. The regiment marched to Burlington, Vermont, in 1813 and was placed in a division commanded by Major General Wade Hampton. During a campaign to capture Montreal in October, Hampton advanced his poorly fed and equipped troops—including the Carolinians—from northern Lake Champlain to Four Corners on the Chateauguay River just south of Canadian territory. As he advanced into Canada, Hampton was abandoned by his fifteen hundred recalcitrant New York militiamen, who refused to leave the state. On the twenty-fifth, Hampton found the enemy along the Chateauguay River behind strong defenses, manned by a force of Canadian light infantry, militia, volunteers, and Mohawk Indians. During this battle, the 10th Regiment attacked the entrenched Canadians' front while Hampton sent a flanking column around the enemy's left to get in their rear. The North Carolinians exchanged heavy fire with the enemy in dense wooded terrain and expended most of their ammunition but eventually fell back with the rest of Hampton's force when the flanking column was repulsed. Subsequently, Hampton retreated to Plattsburg, New York, on Lake Champlain. The battle of Chateauguay was the only major engagement in which the 10th Regiment was involved.[22]

In the northern theater, the most successful and famous North Carolina soldier was Benjamin Forsyth, an officer in the US 1st Regiment of Rifles. From Germantown in Stokes County, Forsyth became a captain in the Rifles in 1808 and rose to brevet lieutenant colonel by 1814. He became well known for his successful and daring hit-and-run attacks in Canada, threatening supply lines and smaller outposts with his green-uniformed light troops, many of whom hailed from North Carolina. Operating from Sackett's Harbor, New York, in early 1813, Forsyth's company served with American forces in the attack on York, Canada, in April. Although his men defeated part of the British 8th Regiment of Foot in the attack, they followed their success by pillaging the town after it fell and bore part of the blame for burning it as well. In late May, the rifle regiment troops led by Forsyth, now a major, served under Colonel Winfield Scott during the successful American amphibious attack on Fort George, on the Canadian side of the Niagara River near its mouth on Lake Ontario. Promoted to lieutenant colonel, in June 1814 Forsyth was killed in action at Odelltown, Canada, at the head of his troops.[23]

In addition to providing uniformed regulars, North Carolina organized its state forces by attempting to embody its quota of seven thousand militiamen, in response to President Madison's call for up to one hundred thousand militia soldiers to serve on federal duty. In 1812, nine companies of these troops were mustered and sent to coastal fortifications for garrison duty. The following year Carolina militia served at Norfolk, Virginia, because of the threat of British expeditionary forces in Chesapeake Bay. In early 1815, fifteen militia companies mustered at Wadesboro in anticipation of marching south to defend against a British invasion of the Florida gulf coast, but when news of Major General Andrew Jackson's January 8 victory at New Orleans reached the Carolinas, these troops were sent home.[24]

FIGHTING THE CREEK WAR, 1814

In 1814, militia troops from both Carolinas joined to form a single brigade in order to support General Jackson's campaign against the Creek Indians in 1814. The Creeks were a loosely knit group of towns and villages along the Coosa and Tallapoosa River valleys in Alabama and along the Flint and Chattahoochee Rivers of western Georgia. Angered by encroaching white settlers, abusive white traders in their territory, a federal road through their homeland, and the internal divisions within the Creek people, the "Red Stick" faction of the Creeks kicked off a war with their white enemies in 1813 in what the United States called the Mississippi Territory. Many Creeks were also stirred to action by Tecumseh, a charismatic Shawnee leader who was working to create a pan-Indian alliance against the whites. Once the violence between Indians and whites began, Jackson became the primary American military leader of the conflict.[25]

US Secretary of War John Armstrong ordered Major General Thomas Pinckney, commander of the federal military district in the South, to raise the Carolina brigade in 1814. The brigade would be composed of two regiments—one from each state—of eight companies of infantry, one of cavalry, and one of artillery. North Carolina raised its men in the western counties under Colonel Jesse A. Pearson, a Rowan County Federalist, as militia forces in the east were primarily engaged in defending the seacoast. Joseph Graham, a brigadier in the North Carolina militia, was appointed to lead the new brigade. Graham was able to raise his troops and move them from Salisbury to Fort Benjamin Hawkins, Georgia, on the Ocmulgee River (at modern Macon) by late March 1814, and the men were mustered into federal service. Once the regiment moved west into Creek Country, the South Carolinians joined them.[26]

On March 27, 1814, Jackson and his small army defeated the Creeks at Horseshoe Bend on the Tallapoosa River in the culminating battle of the war. While some North Carolina volunteers fought in the battle as part of Jackson's small army, Graham's brigade did not reach Jackson's position in time to take part in the fighting. Graham thought many of

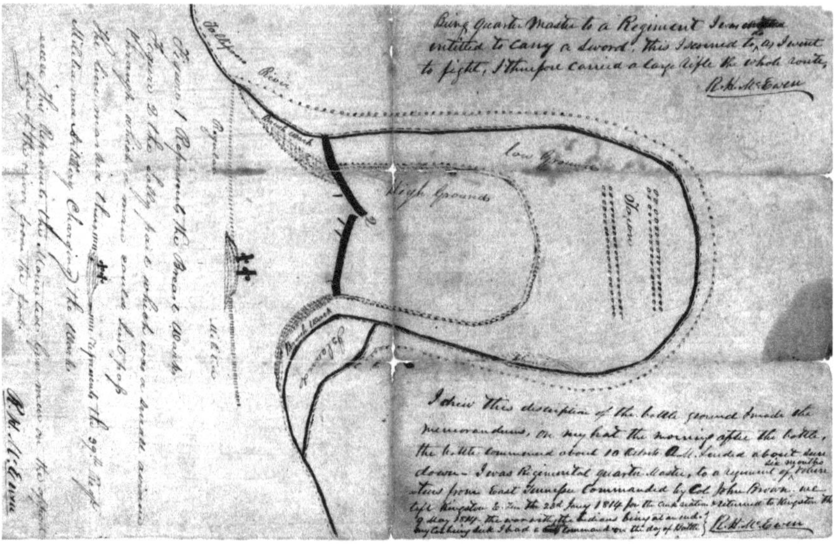

Battle of Horseshoe Bend, Alabama.

his men would be disappointed "not having any opportunity to discharge a single musket at an enemy." Upon arriving at Jackson's camp at the confluence of the Coosa and the Tallapoosa Rivers, the Tennessee general ordered the Carolina troops to construct several small forts within Creek territory. Part of Graham's force captured over five hundred Creeks during an expedition along the Alabama River in June 1814. During this period, discipline seems to have lapsed among Graham's men, even among the officers. In mid-July, the Carolinians had marched back to Fort Hawkins and returned to North Carolina once their enlistments ran out, although 350 of them volunteered to remain in service beyond their initial terms of service. General Pinckney was pleased with the service the Carolina troops had given and wrote that Graham "conducted his brigade with judgment and propriety."[27]

WAR ON THE CAROLINA COAST AND AT SEA

Because of the protective nature of the Outer Banks, North Carolina's ports were less vulnerable than other states to British naval harassment and attack. The state concentrated its efforts to protect Wilmington, Beaufort, and Ocracoke Inlet, all of which were more exposed to potential attacks. With blockading enemy ships off the coast, Carolinians were often alarmed that the British would bombard their ports or land troops on the shores to plunder and destroy public and private property. Most British incursions on the coastline occurred when they landed to obtain fresh water and supplies or chased and destroyed commercial vessels. In July 1813, British Admiral Sir George Cockburn led an expedition of several ships to Ocracoke to destroy American ships, an attack that frightened the state's coastal region.

The resulting damages were relatively light, but the alarm exposed the state's vulnerability to British raids.[28]

During the War of 1812, the Americans also fought at sea. North Carolina ports were home to a number of privateers. Also called commerce raiders, these privateers made the British navy divert royal warships from blockading American ports and protecting its own commercial vessels. Usually small, sleek, and of shallow draft, privateers could be used to import much-needed military supplies to a besieged country as well. Prizes taken by these privateers could be sold in friendly ports, often netting large profits for ship owners and crews. North Carolina's sounds and inlets provided privateers with secure havens for their daring maritime expeditions, as most British navy ships were unable to ply the shallow waters inside the Outer Banks.[29]

Otway Burns of Swansboro was perhaps the most successful North Carolina privateer during the conflict with Great Britain from 1812–1815. He and business partner Edward Pasteur purchased the eighty-five-foot ship *Snap Dragon*, a Maryland-built, 147-ton vessel with six to eight guns. After receiving authority to engage in privateering in 1812, Burns began to collect a crew in New Bern and Norfolk. With Burns as captain, the *Snap Dragon* made three privateering forays during the war, one to Newfoundland and Nova Scotia and two to the Caribbean Sea, during which he captured over forty British ships and $4 million worth of cargo. In May 1814, severe rheumatism prevented him from making a fourth voyage, and after the *Snap Dragon* sailed out of port under Captain W. R. Graham, the ship was captured by a British navy sloop off Nova Scotia on June 30.[30]

Another North Carolinian gained fame on the high seas during the War of 1812, acting in an official capacity. Irish-born Johnston Blakely of Wilmington commanded a US Navy sloop called *Wasp*, with a crew of 173 men and 22 guns, built in Massachusetts. Blakely had served in the US Navy as a midshipman, seeing action against the Tripoli pirates in 1803. When war broke out in 1812, he was stationed in Norfolk but sought out a more active command. In July 1813, he was promoted to master commandant and took over the *Wasp*. He began a cruise in May 1814, sailing for the British Isles to raid the enemy's commerce. The *Wasp* wreaked havoc in the English Channel by capturing and burning several ships. After defeating HMS *Reindeer* off Plymouth, England, in late June, he captured several merchant ships in August, then sank HMS *Avon* the next month before being driven off by three approaching enemy ships. Thereafter, the *Wasp* took three more ships, but apparently Blakely's ship and all its crew were lost at sea, as they were never sited again after October 8, 1814. Congress posthumously awarded him a gold medal and promoted him to captain.[31]

CAROLINIANS AND THE MEXICAN-AMERICAN WAR

Ultimately, the Mexican-American War (1846–48) was a conflict over territorial expansion. In 1835, American inhabitants of the Mexican province of Texas revolted against the Mexican government and sought independence. After losing the Battle of the Alamo in San Antonio (in which nine native North Carolinians were killed) in March 1836, Texans led by Sam Houston defeated Mexican forces at the Battle of San Jacinto the following month and established their independence. Soon thereafter, a strong political movement arose within Texas to have their new independent republic annexed to the United States. This sentiment attracted support within the US government. Many Texans and Americans had shared the view that the United States was destined by God to expand its territory from the Atlantic Ocean to the Pacific and anticipated the end of Mexican rule. In December 1845, Texas was admitted to the Union by congressional resolution. Mexico was not only angered by this development but also disputed the border that the new state and the US government claimed. Both countries moved troops into the disputed region, skirmishes broke out, and when diplomatic efforts failed, on May 13, 1846, the United States declared war on Mexico.[32]

Supporting the war was the new president, James K. Polk, born in Mecklenburg County, North Carolina, in 1795, and graduated from the University of North Carolina in 1818. He later trained as a lawyer, moved to Tennessee, and became a protégé of Andrew Jackson's. Polk reacted to the crisis with Mexico by sending US Army troops under General Zachary Taylor to what he claimed was the Texas border at the Rio Grande, an act he must have known would provoke the Mexicans into a military response. The country was divided in its sentiments about the morality of the war; many northerners saw it as an attempt by the South to add territory suited to slave-based agriculture to the United States. Others thought war was unjustifiable against a weaker country over debatable issues. Nevertheless, war fever had gripped many Americans, especially those in Polk's Democratic Party, and plans proceeded in Washington to invade Mexican territory.[33]

Given the small size of the US Army at the time—less than eight thousand men—volunteer regiments from the states were needed to provide enough troops to ensure success in Mexico. North Carolina's governor, William A. Graham, received word from Washington in May 1845 that his state was expected to raise one volunteer regiment of infantry. Response to his call for volunteers was enthusiastic, as thirty-two companies were raised across the state, far more than requested by the War Department. Mecklenburg County raised a separate dragoon company for service with US troops. The state's assembly voted to spend $10,000 to equip the soldiers. Since these men enlisted for only twelve months, they were rejected by the army, which required tours for the entire war. By the time North Carolina authorities issued another call for volunteers, war fever had abated and recruiting went slowly for the unit's ten companies. Graham appointed Edenton lawyer Robert Treat Paine to lead the regiment as colonel and John A. Fagg of Buncombe County as lieutenant colonel, but this led to objections among the various regimental company leaders, who expected to elect their own officers. Although Paine remained the commander of the regiment until the war's end in August 1847, the men revolted against his unpopular leadership, and only intervention by US Army regulars could control the soldiers' unrest.[34]

Paine's regiment was mostly engaged in guarding supply trains and other mundane tasks as part of the army of General Taylor while in Mexico, seeing little combat. One hundred seventy-two Carolina soldiers died of disease during the war, while others deserted, and the unit was known for being hard to handle. The regiment left Mexico in 1848 and was disbanded in July and August on its return to North Carolina.[35]

Although Paine's volunteer regiment saw no action in Mexico, other North Carolinians did see combat in the war. Two companies raised in the state became part of the 12th US Infantry Regiment in 1847, one of ten new regular army regiments created at the onset of the war. Louis D. Wilson of Edgecombe County became the colonel of the 12th, appointed by President Polk. In March 1847, the Carolina companies arrived in Mexico and joined the forces of Major General Winfield Scott, commander of the American forces at Vera Cruz, which were moving west from the coast to capture Mexico City, the country's capital city. While the regiment was engaged in active operations, however, Colonel Wilson died of yellow fever on August 12, while at Vera Cruz.[36]

As part of Scott's operations, the 12th Infantry fought at the minor battle of National Bridge, sixty miles west of Vera Cruz, on August 12, 1847, in which part of the regiment captured the arched stone bridge and drove off the enemy defenders blocking the main road to Mexico City. This engagement was two days before the more significant battle of Cerro Gordo, in which Scott's forces were triumphant over Mexican troops under General Antonio Lopez de Santa Ana.[37]

Braxton Bragg.

General Scott pushed his army on to Mexico City and, after a series of hard-fought battles, captured it on September 14, 1847. During the campaign, the 12th Infantry was commanded by Colonel Milledge Bonham of South Carolina. After a brief occupation period, the regular troops returned to the United States, and the war ended with the signing of the Treaty of Guadalupe Hidalgo in 1848.

In addition to the service of the North Carolina troops during the war, the state was also represented within the American army's officer corps by some of its sons. Captain John Henry King Burgwin of New Hanover County was mortally wounded while serving in the US 1st Dragoons. His unit was engaged in suppressing the Taos Revolt in what is now New Mexico, and Burgwin was shot while attacking a Pueblo Indian position in a chapel with his unit in February 1847.

He was also the grandson of North Carolina Governor Abner Nash, who served during the American Revolution.

Warrenton native Captain Braxton Bragg of the 3rd US Artillery won acclaim for his conspicuous bravery and martial skill at the battle of Buena Vista in February 1847. A graduate of the US Military Academy at West Point in 1837, having entered the Corps of Cadets at age sixteen, Bragg had served in the Second Seminole War (1835–1842) as an adjutant prior to the Mexican-American War but saw no action. After his notable service in the Mexican conflict, he was one of many American officers who went on to attain high rank in the American Civil War, just twelve years into the future, a struggle that engulfed North Carolina in four years of death and destruction.[38]

8. The Civil War: Opening Battles

IN THE MIDST OF REVOLUTION

The dispute over the expansion of slavery into the territories won in the Mexican-American War culminated in the Compromise of 1850, a series of legislative measures that merely postponed the sectional crisis. Soon afterward, a new conflict arose over the Kansas-Nebraska Territories and the formation of the Republican Party, which opposed the territorial expansion of slavery. In 1856, University of North Carolina Professor Benjamin S. Hedrick was driven from the state for openly supporting the antislavery party. Three years later, the radical abolitionist John Brown led a raid on the federal arsenal at Harpers Ferry, Virginia, in a futile attempt to spark a slave revolt. A small force of US marines commanded by Colonel Robert E. Lee swiftly put down the insurrection, and Brown was tried and executed soon afterward. In the wake of Brown's raid, rumors of insurrectionary plots swept through North Carolina like wildfire, prompting state officials to ban antislavery literature such as Hinton Rowan Helper's *The Impending Crisis of the South*. At the direction of Gov. John W. Ellis, North Carolina abolitionist Daniel Worth was arrested and driven from the state for distributing copies of Helper's book. "On the issue of slavery," asserts historian William C. Harris, "North Carolina had become a closed society."[1]

In the presidential election of 1860, North Carolina chose the Southern Democratic candidate, John C. Breckinridge, who ran on a platform demanding protection of slavery in the territories. Although Breckinridge carried most of the southern states, he finished a distant second in the electoral vote to Republican candidate Abraham Lincoln, whose name did not even appear on ballots in the South. Lincoln's election provoked South Carolina and six other Lower South states into seceding from the Union. Most North Carolinians, however, did not regard Lincoln's election as sufficient grounds for secession. They remained staunch Unionists who favored a watch-and-wait stance to give Lincoln a chance to unfold his

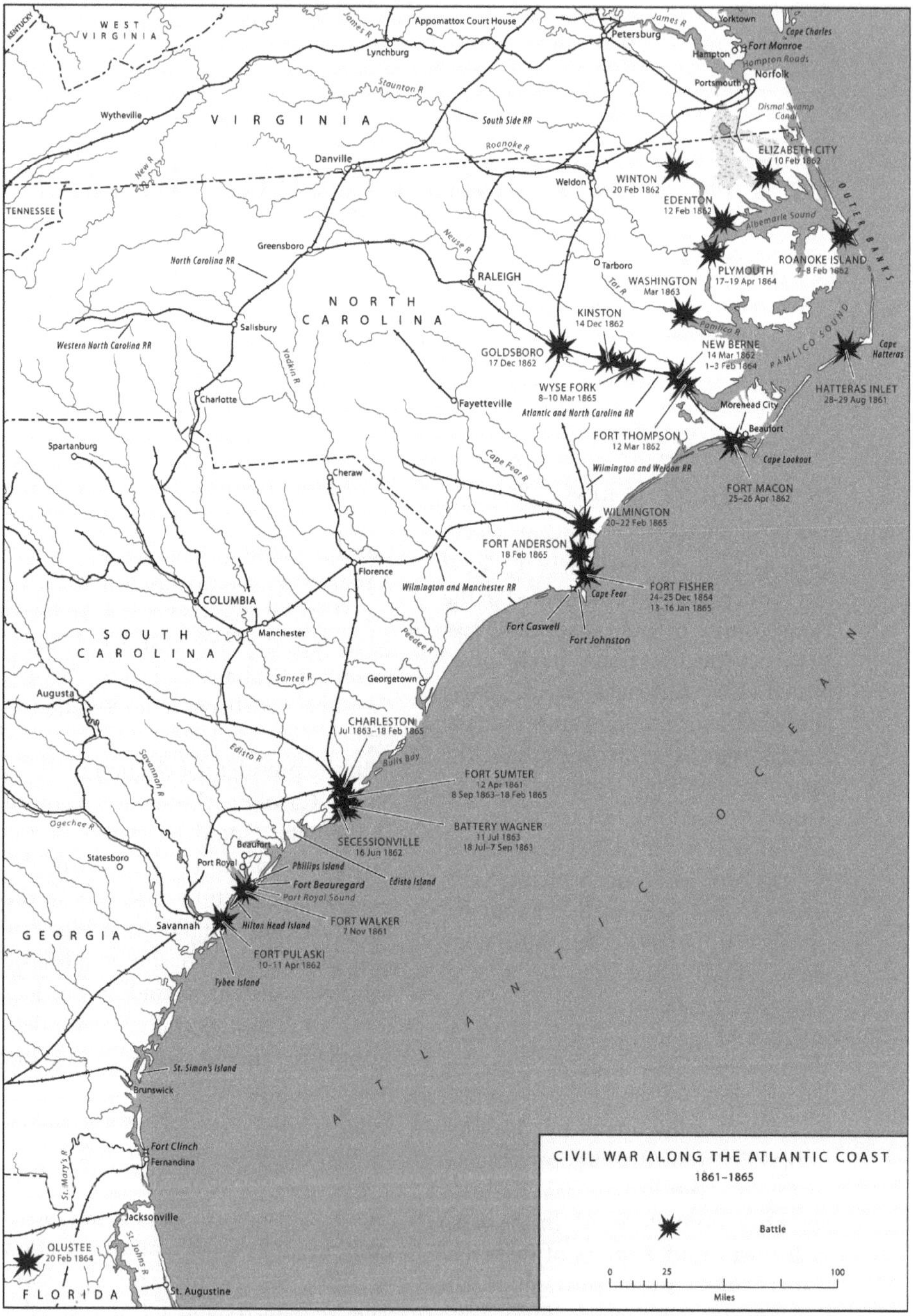

Battles Along the Atlantic Coast, 1861-1865. (*Sherry Dowdy, CMH*)

policy. Governor Ellis privately sympathized with the secessionists, but he also shared the concern of many conservatives that secession might jeopardize the state's political stability and economic well-being.[2]

On January 28, 1861, the North Carolina General Assembly adopted a bill for the people to vote on a convention to determine the state's course. In the weeks leading up to the vote, secession was the dominant topic of discussion. "We are in the midst of revolution!" wrote David Schenck of Lincolnton. "Every hour and day brings some startling news . . . and fireside conversation is confined to the great issue of the day—'Will there be Civil War?'" On February 28, North Carolinians rejected a convention by the razor-thin margin of 661 votes, indicating that pro-secession forces had gained considerable ground since Lincoln's election.[3]

Outside events ultimately determined the course that North Carolina would take. In February 1861, delegates from the seven seceded states formed the Confederate States of America and ratified a provisional constitution. They elected Jefferson Davis president and designated Montgomery, Alabama, as the nascent republic's capital. On April 12, 1861, Confederate forces fired on Fort Sumter in Charleston Harbor, South Carolina, igniting the Civil War. The federal garrison defending the fort surrendered on April 13. In North Carolina, reaction to the Battle of Fort Sumter was mixed. Secessionists rejoiced at the news of the victory at Charleston, while Unionists lamented the outbreak of civil war. On April 15, President Lincoln issued a call for seventy-five thousand troops to put down the "insurrection," and Governor Ellis fired off an immediate reply to the US secretary of war: "You can get no troops from North Carolina." Ellis then ordered the seizure of federal property within the state, including three coastal forts, the arsenal at Fayetteville, and the mint at Charlotte. The governor also issued a proclamation calling on the General Assembly to meet in special session on May 1.[4]

Former Unionists now joined radicals in supporting secession and opposing Lincoln's effort to coerce the seceded states back into the Union. Thirty-year-old Congressman Zebulon B. Vance was "addressing a large and excited crowd . . . and literally had my hand extended upward in pleading for peace and the Union . . . when the telegraphic news was announced of the firing on Sumter and [the] President's call" for troops. "When my hand came down from that impassioned gesticulation," Vance recalled, "it fell slowly and sadly by the side of a Secessionist."[5]

The General Assembly met in Raleigh, the state capital, on May 1 and acted swiftly. The House unanimously passed a bill calling for the election of 120 delegates on May 13 for a convention that would meet one week later. The Senate followed suit, though with three dissenting votes. On May 20, the convention met, unanimously adopting the ordinance of secession and then ratifying the provisional Confederate constitution. When the announcement came that North Caro-lina had left the Union, the crowd surrounding the state capitol cheered, church bells pealed, and the guns of the Ellis Light Artillery

Daniel Harvey Hill. (*University of Arkansas*)

fired a salute—the force of the blast shattering windows along Fayetteville Street. In the meantime, three other Upper South states—Arkansas, Tennessee, and Virginia—rejected Lincoln's call for troops, seceded from the Union, and joined the Confederacy. The Confederate capital was moved to Richmond, Virginia.[6]

As the news of North Carolina's secession spread, thousands of volunteers across the state flocked to the colors. Some men had volunteered in late April 1861, following the General Assembly's passing of the Convention Act in special session. The new law gave Governor Ellis the power to raise troops and begin making arms, uniforms, and equipment. Many companies bore such colorful names as the "Black River Tigers," the "Rough and Ready Guards," and the "Stanly Yankee Hunters." Confusion arose over the numbering of the new regiments. The old recruitment law stipulated the formation of twenty regiments, numbered one through twenty, composed of twelve-month volunteers. The new law, passed during the May convention, called for ten regiments of state troops serving for three years or the duration of the war. To avoid duplication, the volunteer regiments were required to add ten to their original numerical designation. For example, after the 1st North Carolina Volunteers disbanded in 1861 upon expiration of the soldiers' six-month enlistments, most of the men joined the 11th Regiment, North Carolina Infantry in 1862.[7]

Governor Ellis offered the Confederate secretary of war four regiments even before North Carolina had left the Union. This proved to be one of Ellis's last acts as governor, for he died of tuberculosis just a few months later and was succeeded by Henry T. Clark, the speaker of the state senate. The 1st North Carolina Volunteers, commanded by Colonel Daniel Harvey Hill, was the first regiment to go. The 1st Volunteers left for Virginia on May 18 and fought in the Battle of Big Bethel on June 10. By the end of August, North Carolina had mustered sixteen regiments of cavalry and infantry into service.[8]

THE HATTERAS INLET EXPEDITION

Only the 17th North Carolina Infantry and elements of the 1st North Carolina Artillery were sent to defend the North Carolina coast. The troops arrived in midsummer, as the fortifications along the coastal inlets were nearing completion. The largest of these works was Fort Hatteras, which guarded Hatteras Inlet. A second structure, Fort Clark—

Union Bombardment of Forts Hatteras and Clark. (*Harper's Weekly*)

named for Governor Clark—stood three-fourths of a mile east of Fort Hatteras and nearer to the Atlantic Ocean. On August 26, a joint Union army-navy expedition sailed from Hampton Roads, Virginia, on an operation to close Hatteras Inlet to Confederate commerce raiders and supply ships. The commander of the army contingent, Major General Benjamin F. Butler, had 860 troops of the 9th and 20th New York Infantry Regiments; the naval commander, Flag Officer Silas H. Stringham, led a flotilla of six warships and two troop transports. The Confederates had just 580 men stationed at Oregon, Hatteras, and Ocracoke Inlets, including 350 soldiers at Fort Hatteras. They also had several lightly armed, undersized vessels aptly nicknamed the "Mosquito Fleet" under Commodore William F. Lynch.

At four o'clock on the afternoon of August 27, the Union flotilla anchored near Fort Hatteras, and the next morning, an assault force of 318 federal infantrymen landed on the beach near Fort Clark. While one part of the flotilla transported the troops, the remaining vessels opened fire on the fort. Strong winds resulted in choppy surf that swamped or shattered many of the landing craft. The rough seas prevented many of the troops from landing; Butler therefore postponed the attack. By some miracle, none of the Union soldiers drowned, but their ammunition was wet, and rations and fresh water proved scarce.[9]

As difficult as the conditions were for the federals on the beach, the situation facing the Confederate garrison at Fort Clark was even worse. Having expended all of their ammunition by midday, the defenders received orders from their commander, Colonel J. C. Lamb, to spike their guns and evacuate the fort. The rebels made their way to

Fort Hatteras under a heavy fire from Stringham's naval guns, which claimed several casualties. Soon afterward, the 20th New York captured Fort Clark but briefly had to abandon it because Union naval shells continued to rain down on it until nightfall halted the bombardment.[10]

On the evening of August 28, threatening weather led Stringham to order most of his flotilla out to sea, leaving the bluecoats at Fort Clark unsupported. Across the way, the Confederates at Fort Hatteras received some reinforcements. Among the new arrivals was Commodore Samuel Barron, commander of Confederate coastal defenses in Virginia and North Carolina. He assumed command of Fort Hatteras at the request of Colonel William F. Martin, the garrison commander. Barron planned to recapture Fort Clark, but when the expected reinforcements from New Bern failed to arrive that night, the commodore abandoned the idea of retaking it and instead concentrated on improving Hatteras's defenses. The storm dissipated overnight, and the Union flotilla returned around daybreak, dropping anchor well beyond range of the Fort Hatteras artillery. Starting at seven o'clock on the morning of August 29, the federal naval guns subjected the fort to a devastating bombardment that lasted more than three hours. At 11:00 AM, Commodore Barron ordered the white flag to be run up, and General Butler demanded the fort's unconditional surrender. After an anxious forty-five-minute wait, Butler received word that Barron agreed to his demand. Later that day, Butler entered Fort Hatteras, and the Stars and Stripes were soon flying above the parapets as Stringham's flotilla fired a thirteen-gun salute.[11]

In addition to the forts, the federals captured 715 prisoners at a cost of one man wounded compared with the Confederates' loss of twelve killed and thirty-five wounded. Coming just over one month after the Union army's defeat at Manassas, the capture of Forts Clark and Hatteras boosted Northern morale while depriving Confederate privateers of a secure base and providing Union blockaders with an additional coaling station on the Eastern Seaboard.[12]

THE BURNSIDE EXPEDITION: ROANOKE ISLAND

On November 1, 1861, Major General George B. McClellan succeeded Major General Winfield Scott as general-in-chief of the Union army. McClellan decided to mount an expedition to capture Roanoke Island, and he placed his friend and trusted subordinate, Brigadier General Ambrose E. Burnside, in command of the operation. Burnside needed two months to assemble his troops and transports at Annapolis, Maryland. His Coast Division consisted of three infantry brigades led by Brigadier Generals John G. Foster, John G. Parke, and Jesse L. Reno. The commander of the naval contingent was Rear Admiral Louis M. Goldsborough. The Burnside expedition set sail from Annapolis on the morning of January 9, 1862. As the ships approached Cape Hatteras four days later, a series of winter storms swept in and battered the cape and the Union fleet for nearly two weeks. The soldiers had to remain on board until

January 26, when the weather at last improved. But the fleet had to contend with another natural obstacle in the form of the shallow channel into Pamlico Sound. Nevertheless, by February 4, the eighty federal vessels had passed into the sound and sailed for Roanoke Island.[13]

Since the fall of Cape Hatteras, Governor Clark and several high-ranking officers in North Carolina had urged the War Department in Richmond to bolster the defenses on Roanoke Island, but to no avail, for President Davis believed that no soldiers in Virginia could be spared. As a result, the Confederate commander at Roanoke, Brigadier General Henry A. Wise, had to fend off Burnside and Goldsborough's armada with a collection of undersized forts manned by just 1,400 North Carolina and Virginia troops, supported by Commodore Lynch's Mosquito Fleet. Worse yet, Wise fell ill with pneumonia and was bedridden when the Union flotilla came into view. Command thus devolved on Colonel Henry M. Shaw of the 8th North Carolina Infantry.[14]

Ambrose E. Burnside.

Early on the morning of February 7, the federal gunboats entered Croatan Sound from the south, followed by the troop transports and supply ships. Of the three Southern forts on the western edge of Roanoke Island, only one—Fort Bartow—stood within range, and just three of its guns were able to fire on the Union vessels. As a result, only one Northern ship had to withdraw from the battle for repairs. In the meantime, the Mosquito Fleet remained shielded behind a row of sunken obstructions along the northern end of the sound. Twice the Confederate gunboats ventured beyond the barrier to tempt the Union warships into pursuing them past the forts, but Commodore Goldsborough refused to take the bait. By evening, the Union gunboats had crippled two of the Southern vessels while ten thousand of Burnside's infantry and several batteries of artillery disembarked at Ashby's Harbor. Nearby a two-hundred-man Confederate detachment, armed with a few cannons, withdrew without firing on the federals, squandering a golden opportunity to delay the bluecoats' progress.[15]

On the morning of February 8, Burnside's command marched north on the only road on the island. The federals soon collided with Shaw's Confederates, who were dug in across the thoroughfare. Led by the 9th New York Zouaves, Foster's brigade assaulted the center of the Southern line and were repulsed. In the meantime, Reno's brigade on the left and Parke's brigade on the right had worked their way through knee-deep swamps and

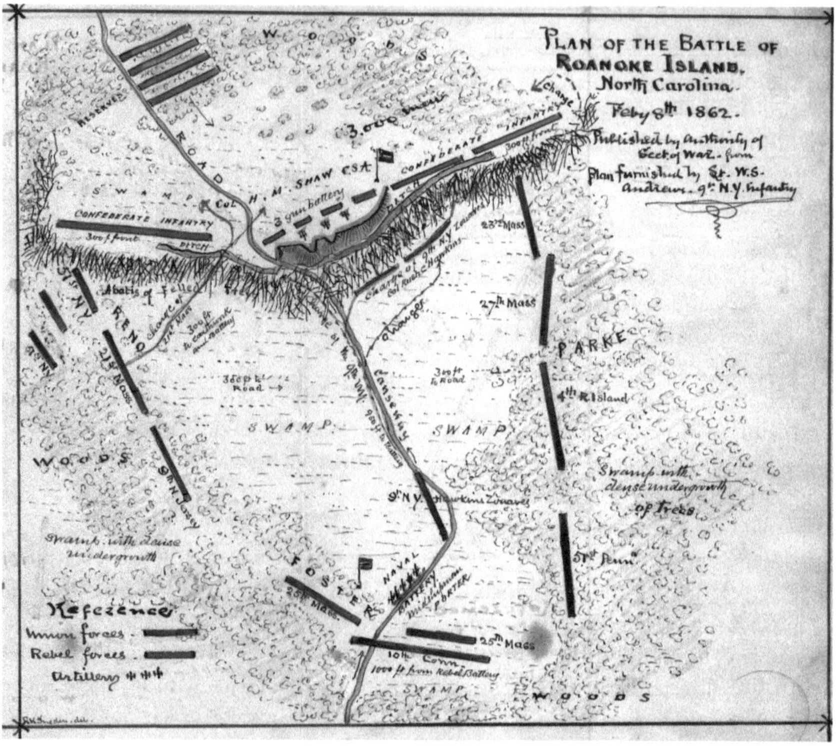

Plan of the Battle of Roanoke Island.

turned the Confederates' flanks. Outnumbered and outflanked, the Southerners were soon in full retreat. Trapped on the northern end of the island, Colonel Shaw surrendered his force to General Foster. The Confederates lost 22 killed, 58 wounded, and 2,500 captured; only a handful managed to escape by boat to the mainland. The federal casualties came to 37 killed, 214 wounded, and 13 missing.[16]

As Burnside's troops took possession of Roanoke Island, the Mosquito Fleet fled up the Pasquotank River to Elizabeth City. The town's defenses consisted of some untried militia and a four-gun emplacement that Commodore Lynch dismissed as a "wretchedly constructed affair." On the morning of February 10, thirteen Union gunboats steamed into the harbor and bore down on the Confederate vessels. In less than an hour, the federal warships drove off the militia, silenced the shore battery, and nearly destroyed the Mosquito Fleet; only one ship managed to escape via the Dismal Swamp Canal to Norfolk, Virginia. Union sailors soon landed at the wharf and occupied the town. They found some of the buildings in flames, set ablaze by Confederate soldiers at the behest of their owners. Evidently, some of the townsfolk had adopted this course "to spite the Yankees," even though it meant destroying their own property.[17]

After the federals had secured Elizabeth City, they began clearing the surrounding area of Confederate forces. A detachment of five Union vessels steamed west on Albemarle Sound to Edenton, arriving there about 8:00 AM on February 12. The federals searched the town; the only trace of the Confederates they could find was eight cannons, which they spiked. The Northerners departed around noon. On February 18, Commander Stephen C. Rowan led eight gunboats in a joint army-navy expedition to Winton on the Chowan River near the Virginia border. The infantry contingent consisted of roughly one thousand soldiers of the 9th New York Zouaves and the 4th Rhode Island Infantry under Colonel Rush C. Hawkins. The purpose of the expedition was to determine the extent of Unionist sentiment at Winton and to destroy two railroad bridges north of town. On the nineteenth, two Union ships attempted to dock at Winton but were fired on by Southern infantry and artillery. The federals managed to withdraw beyond range of the fusillade without sustaining any casualties. Early the next morning, the Union gunboats returned and began shelling the town. After the cannonade, the colonel and the 9th New York disembarked and found the streets deserted. In retaliation for the previous day's ambush, Hawkins ordered his men to torch the town; the enterprising soldiers then ransacked the burning buildings. Hawkins later justified his decision by maintaining that most of the structures had served as storehouses and quarters for the enemy. The burning and pillaging of Winton indicated the war was taking a more destructive turn and civilian property was no longer sacrosanct.[18]

THE BURNSIDE EXPEDITION: NEW BERN AND FORT MACON

Before he could embark on another campaign, Burnside had to divest himself of more than two thousand Confederate captives that burdened his command. Instead of sending them north to prisoner of war camps, he paroled them at Elizabeth City. He regarded this expedient as preferable to the loss of three regiments of troops for guard duty. But the downside was that most of the parolees soon opposed him once more, either as soldiers or guerrillas. Regardless of their status, Burnside believed he had bigger fish to fry—namely, the capture of New Bern.[19]

On March 11, a force of eleven thousand federal infantry boarded transports and headed for Cape Hatteras, where they joined the rest of the Union fleet. The next day, Burnside issued an order announcing they were embarking on an expedition "which would greatly demoralize the enemy." No sooner had the vessels gotten underway than Admiral Goldsborough was summoned to Hampton Roads, where the Confederate ironclad CSS *Virginia* had wreaked havoc on the Union blockade squadron. A disappointed Goldsborough turned over command of the naval force to Commander Rowan. In the meantime, the fleet anchored off the mouth of Slocum Creek a dozen miles south of New Bern. On

Zebulon B. Vance. (*Clark,* Histories)

the morning of March 13, the gunboats began to shell the shoreline—an unnecessary precaution given the absence of enemy troops in the area. Burnside's infantry therefore landed unopposed and began slogging north toward New Bern amid a heavy rain. The federals marched to within a short distance of the Confederate defensive position and camped for the night.[20]

About six miles south of the city, four thousand Confederates under Brigadier General Lawrence O'Bryan Branch occupied a mile-long line of entrenchments, the fortifications running from Fort Thompson on the Neuse River to the Atlantic and North Carolina Railroad. About 150 yards to the rear, a second line stretched west from the railroad to a swamp; a brickyard just west of the railroad left a gap between the two lines. Branch inexplicably weakened an already vulnerable position by using local militia to plug the gap. Although his entire force was untried in battle, the regular troops were at least well armed and equipped and had received a modicum of training, whereas the militia wielded their own arms, wore civilian clothing, and had received no training whatsoever. From left to right, starting at Fort Thompson and extending to the brickyard, the Confederate defenders consisted of four North Carolina infantry regiments—the 27th, 37th, 7th, and 35th—plus the militia battalion. Colonel Clark M. Avery's 33rd North Carolina and Colonel Zebulon B. Vance's 26th North Carolina held the line from the brickyard to the swamp. Of Branch's dozen cannons, ten were unlimbered to the left of the railroad while just two were posted on the right.[21]

Burnside's force was on the move at 7:00 AM on March 14, with Reno's brigade advancing on the left, Foster's brigade on the right, and Parke's brigade in reserve along the railroad. Foster launched an attack on the Confederate works before Reno could support him, and the result was predictable. The Southerners poured a devastating combination of small-arms and artillery fire into the attacking federals, while shells from Commander Rowan's Union naval vessels exploded among the blue-clad soldiers. Rowan later justified his rash action by declaring that it was better to kill a Union soldier or two than to lose the demoralizing effect of the big naval guns on the enemy.[22]

Up to this point, the Confederate line had held firm, but then several companies of Reno's command broke through at the brickyard and routed the militia. The panic proved contagious, for the 35th North Carolina also began fleeing to the rear. Branch im-

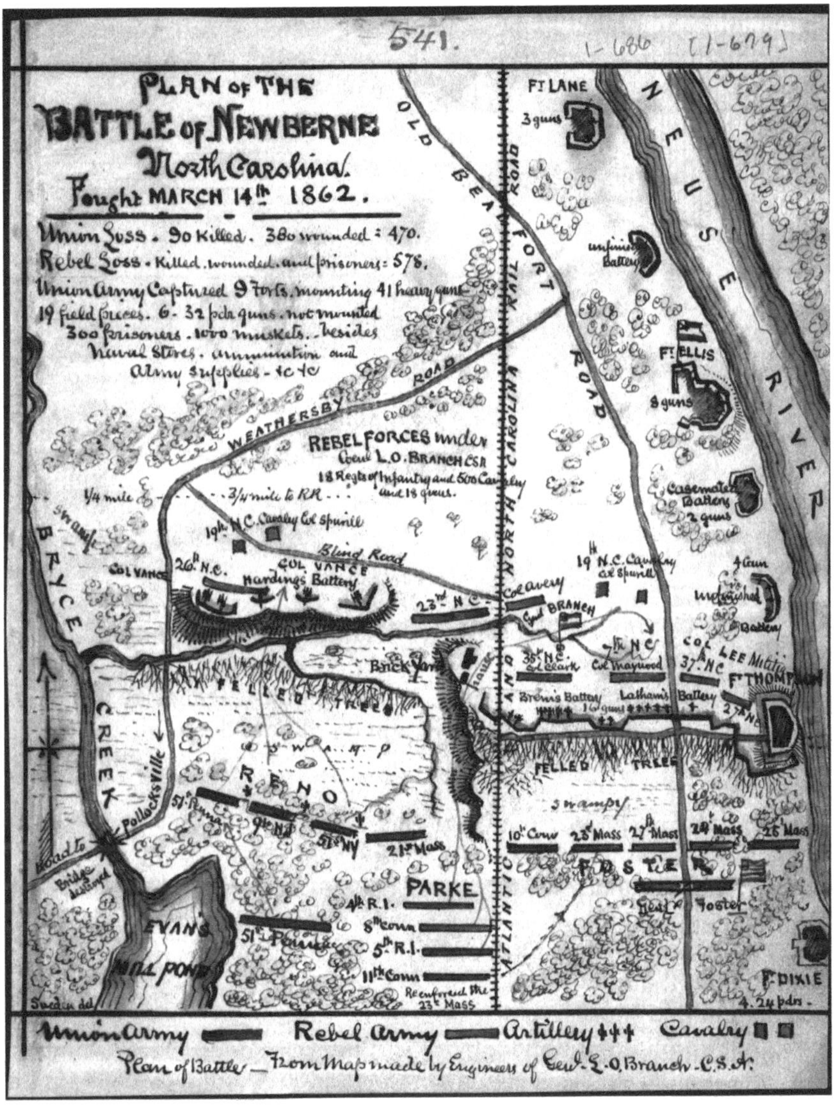

Plan of the Battle of New Bern.

mediately sent the 33rd North Carolina forward to plug the gap. Raising the Rebel yell, the men of the 33rd launched a bayonet charge, and after a savage hand-to-hand fight, they drove back the federals. But the victorious Carolinians were tired and disorganized, and a counterattack by Parke's reserve force succeeded in sweeping the left half of the 33rd North Carolina out of the brickyard. This time, Branch had no reserves to call on, and Foster

Battle of New Bern. (*Harper's Weekly*)

ordered another assault on Fort Thompson to exploit Parke's breakthrough.[23]

The Union onslaught caused the entire Confederate left flank to collapse. As the defenders fled, Parke's troops poured over the parapet in hot pursuit. On the right, Vance's 26th North Carolina fought a stubborn rearguard action as it fell back, enabling most of the regiment to cross Brice's Creek by boat. The former congressman had kept his cool while under fire for the first time. The rest of Branch's command began to panic as a bottleneck formed at the Trent River bridge. In the confusion, some of the fleeing Confederates set fire to the bridge too soon, stranding many of their comrades on the south bank. As a result, the federals captured several hundred North Carolinians, including Avery, but a portion of the 33rd North Carolina, ably led by Lieutenant Colonel Robert F. Hoke, managed to slip across Brice's Creek. The Confederates fell back to New Bern, where Branch directed them to march to Kinston about thirty miles to the west. Rowan's gunboats, meanwhile, had reached New Bern and opened fire on the retreating Southerners before falling silent when Union infantry entered the town. The Battle of New Bern cost the Confederates 578 casualties, most of them captured during the rout, while the federals lost 470 killed or wounded. Though some buildings were damaged or destroyed by fleeing Confederates and advancing federals, New Bern emerged from the campaign more or less intact. The town remained in Union hands for the rest of the war, serving as a base for federal operations in the eastern part of the state.[24]

Burnside decided that before he could advance farther inland, he must first capture Fort Macon about forty miles to the southeast. Located on the eastern tip of Bogue Banks, the pentagonal masonry fortification stood in the rear of the Union position at New Bern, and it protected Beaufort Inlet, the last passageway on the Outer Banks available to Confederate ships. Burnside launched the operation by ordering General Parke to seize Beaufort and Morehead City a few miles above the fort. Parke met with no resistance in occupying Morehead City on March 22 and Beaufort on the twenty-fourth; five days later, his force established a beachhead on Bogue Banks.[25]

While Parke prepared to assault Fort Macon, Burnside received disturbing news that the Confederates at Norfolk, Virginia, were building ironclads to send against the Union fleet in Albemarle Sound via the Great Dismal Swamp Canal. He accordingly sent General Reno with over three thousand troops to destroy the locks on the canal at South Mills. The Union transports reached Elizabeth City at 1:00 AM, and the lead element, consisting of three regiments under Colonel Hawkins, was on the march two hours later. But a local black serving as guide led the federals down the wrong road; the ensuing delay cost the bluecoats the element of surprise and the guide his life.

A Confederate force under Colonel Ambrose R. Wright numbering four hundred infantry and four pieces of artillery opposed Reno's force near South Mills. Wright's outnumbered command fought the federals to a standstill for over four hours, withdrawing only when it appeared they were in danger of being outflanked. Reno decided his troops were too exhausted to pursue, and fearful of a night attack, he withdrew that evening to Elizabeth City, returning to New Bern on April 22. The Battle of South Mills was a Confederate victory, albeit a minor one, having prevented Reno from destroying the locks. On May 10, a Union force led by seventy-eight-year-old Major General John E. Wool captured Norfolk, ending the threat of Southern ironclads from that sector. Norfolk remained in federal hands until the end of the war.[26]

In the meantime, Parke massed his forces against Fort Macon. He twice issued a formal surrender demand to the fort's commander, Lieutenant Colonel Moses J. White, who refused him both times. A Union officer claimed to have heard that White had vowed "he would not surrender until he had eaten his last biscuit and killed his last horse." The federals struck before White could find himself in that extremity. By the morning of April 25, the Union joint army-navy force was ready. At 5:50 AM, federal land-based mortars and heavy artillery opened fire, followed a few hours later by the even-larger guns of the Union fleet. Rough seas and a succession of accurate shots from Confederate cannons soon forced the warships beyond range of the fort . In any event, the federal artillery's eleven-hour bombardment had taken a severe toll on the fort's brick casemates, cracking open one section near the powder magazine. At that point, Colonel White raised the white flag and asked for terms. When told that the surrender would be unconditional, he refused. The two sides nevertheless agreed to meet again the following morning, at which time the federals proved more generous: the fort's garrison would be released on parole and could keep their personal possessions. White agreed to the terms and signed the surrender document on April 26. As the federals took possession, roughly four hundred Confederate prisoners filed out of Fort Macon, bound for Beaufort and other destinations. The Union navy now had a first-rate port on the North Carolina coast—welcome news for the North Atlantic Blockading Squadron.[27]

RUNNING THE BLOCKADE

Within a week of the fall of Fort Sumter, President Lincoln had proclaimed a naval blockade of Southern ports. The original proclamation had omitted North Carolina, but the state was quickly added to the list when it joined the Confederacy. The blockade was the most ambitious ever undertaken, encompassing 3,549 miles of Southern coastline from Virginia to Texas, including a dozen major seaports plus nearly two hundred smaller harbors and inlets. At first, the US Navy lacked the vessels and supply bases to enforce the blockade: in May 1861, just two federal warships patrolled the entire coastline of North Carolina. In June, the USS *Daylight* took its station off the Cape Fear River south of Wilmington, the state's largest port, indicating that the Union blockade was in earnest. During the war, more than 1,600 vessels had served as blockade runners, of which around 1,300 were sailing ships. By mid-1863, the Union blockade had become formidable enough that attempting to break it by wind power alone was a risky undertaking. Over 1,450 blockade runners were captured or destroyed during the war, including thirty that wrecked off the Cape Fear coast.[28]

Despite the ever-tightening noose of the blockade, roughly seventy steam-powered blockade runners bearing such evocative names as *Banshee*, *Night Hawk*, *Phantom*, and *Ranger* enjoyed an impressive 80 percent success rate at Wilmington from 1863 to 1864. They relied on speed and stealth, often waiting for a moonless night to make a dash into the Cape Fear. When hugging the coastline after dark, blockade runners were difficult to spot, thanks to a low profile and a coat of dull gray paint. The vessels were further aided by the mouth of the Cape Fear River, which nature had divided into Old Inlet and New Inlet. This geographic feature compelled the federals to station ships near both entrances, while the heavy guns of the fortifications defending the two inlets compelled the blockaders to maintain a respectful distance. By early 1865, Fort Fisher, the guardian of New Inlet, ranked as the largest bastion in the Confederacy, but in mid-1862, it was very much a work in progress.[29]

Because of the risk involved, blockade running was a lucrative business, supplying eager customers with luxury goods and military stores at inflated prices. The cargo of the *Cornubia* was typical. In August 1863, the blockade runner docked at Wilmington with 228 cases of rifles from Austria, 459 cases of Austrian and British rifle ammunition, 52 bales of cartridge paper, and 200 boxes of musket cartridges.[30]

Chronic supply shortages persuaded the state of North Carolina to enter the blockade running trade. The idea was the brainchild of the state adjutant general, James G. Martin, who recommended to Governor Clark that the state purchase a ship to import desperately needed supplies from Great Britain. Clark was lukewarm to the

The blockade runner *Advance.* (*Naval Historical Center*)

idea, but his successor, Gov. Zebulon B. Vance, proved far more receptive. Running on the Conservative Party ticket, the popular colonel of the 26th North Carolina had defeated his Confederate Party opponent, William J. Johnston, by a landslide. In September 1862, Vance assumed office with a mandate to improve the lot of North Carolina's soldiers, who were among the most poorly provisioned in the Confederate army. Unable to feed and clothe the troops, the Richmond government had resorted to paying the states a commutation fee for every soldier they supported. As Vance knew from firsthand experience, the state of North Carolina had failed to meet its obligation, leaving the troops destitute. He therefore seized on the idea of a state-sponsored blockade-running enterprise based at Wilmington.[31]

To finance the venture, Vance persuaded the state legislature to appropriate $2 million to purchase and store cotton. The state then issued warrants, or bonds, based on the cotton, and Vance sent two agents to England to find investors. After months of fruitless negotiations, they entered into an agreement with Alexander Collie, an English trading company. Using the cotton as collateral, the agents purchased the 902-ton, side-wheel steamer *Lord Clyde*. On June 28, 1863, the vessel ran the blockade into Wilmington with a cargo of dry goods, blankets, and shoes. Soon after reaching port, the ship was renamed the *Advance*—probably in honor of the governor, who had made the blockade-running venture possible. The *Advance* proved to be one of the most successful blockade runners of the war, enabling Collie to turn a profit while North Carolina received the supplies its soldiers urgently needed. Collie found blockade running so profitable that the company bought several more steamers. Vance saw the advantages of expansion and secured the state legislature's approval to purchase one-fourth interest in four of the Collie-owned vessels: the *Don*, the *Hansa*, and two others under construction. The *Advance*, meanwhile, made eight successful runs between

Bermuda and Wilmington before the Union blockader USS *Santiago de Cuba* captured it on September 10, 1864.[32]

LINCOLN APPOINTS A MILITARY GOVERNOR

Having taken Roanoke Island, New Bern, Fort Macon, and Beaufort, Burnside had accomplished all the objectives General McClellan had assigned him on the eve of the expedition. He now contemplated advancing inland to seize Goldsboro and Raleigh in support of McClellan's Peninsula Campaign to capture Richmond, which had begun in March. While awaiting the go-ahead from his superior, Burnside launched several minor expeditions from New Bern. On March 21, a joint federal force consisting of three gunboats and the 23rd Massachusetts Infantry occupied the town of Washington on the Pamlico River. Many residents warmly greeted the Union soldiers as they marched past, and a few even displayed the Stars and Stripes. In May, Union gunboats made several trips to Plymouth on the Roanoke River. In answer to the request of the town's Unionist element, a small force consisting of one gunboat and Company F of the 9th New York Infantry remained behind to provide security.[33]

Reports of widespread Unionist sentiment in eastern North Carolina reached President Lincoln, inducing him to establish a loyal government there. He appointed New Bern native Edward Stanly as military governor of the state with the rank of brigadier general. A five-term congressman from North Carolina between 1837 and 1853, Stanly had since moved to California and had run unsuccessfully in 1857 as the Republican candidate for governor. He arrived at New Bern on May 26 determined to nurture Unionism wherever he found it. "My chief hope & aim in coming here," he later wrote, "was to protect loyal men, and to encourage the people to return to their allegiance to the Union." He made several overtures to Governor Vance, a former Union Whig like himself, but the latter rebuffed him. Stanly soon learned that most North Carolinians had branded him a traitor. He nevertheless attempted to form a Unionist government in the Tar Heel State. With Lincoln's approval, he held a congressional election, but the House of Representatives refused to seat the victor, Jennings Pigott. When Lincoln's Emancipation Proclamation became law on January 1, 1863, Stanly concluded that the document snuffed out any hope for a conciliatory peace. He therefore resigned his post a few weeks later. Realizing that he had overestimated Unionist sentiment in North Carolina, Lincoln made no further attempts to establish wartime Reconstruction in the state.[34]

FOSTER'S RAID

Burnside, now a major general, had been only too happy to turn over all civil and political matters to Stanly, for he expected to receive McClellan's order to commence his Goldsboro expedition at any moment. The order arrived on June 25. As Burnside prepared to march, an urgent message from President Lincoln reached his headquarters, summoning him to Virginia with all the soldiers he could spare. On June 26, the Army of Northern Virginia under General Robert E. Lee had launched the first in a series of assaults—known collectively as the Seven Days Battles—that would drive McClellan's Army of the Potomac from the outskirts of Richmond thirty miles south to Harrison's Landing on the James River. On July 6, Burnside sailed with two divisions numbering seven thousand men to reinforce McClellan, leaving General Foster in command in North Carolina with just nine thousand troops—too small a force to attempt the Goldsboro expedition. The Confederate force in North Carolina likewise shrank, as Lee summoned most of the Department of North Carolina troops to Virginia in response to McClellan's advance on Richmond.[35]

John G. Foster.

For the next several months, Foster contented himself with strengthening the fortifications around New Bern and with sending small raiding parties into the surrounding area that accomplished little aside from destroying some civilian property. Despite their diminished numbers, the Confederates attempted to recapture Washington on September 6 and Plymouth three months later; in each case, the Southerners had to withdraw after briefly occupying their objective.[36]

Perhaps the most notable event to occur in eastern North Carolina that fall was a daring raid up the New River by the USS *Ellis*, a Union gunboat commanded by Lieutenant William B. Cushing. On November 23, the twenty-year-old Cushing set out to capture the town of Jacksonville, destroy any enemy salt works he found there, and intercept the mail bound for Wilmington. Cushing succeeded in reaching Jacksonville and burning an enemy schooner along the way. He also captured the Wilmington mail, confiscated several of the postmaster's slaves, and commandeered two schooners loaded with cotton and turpentine. During the retreat from Jacksonville on the twenty-fourth, the crew of the *Ellis* exchanged fire with several Confederate batteries posted along the river. When the federal gunboat ran aground, Cushing had most of his crew make their escape in one of the captured vessels, along with most of the valuable cargo. In the meantime, Cushing and six volunteers set fire to the *Ellis* and then rowed to safety in a small boat. Expecting to face a court of inquiry for the loss of his ship, Cushing instead received a commendation for bravery from the US Navy. This was but the first of several exploits that made him a war hero in the North.[37]

As winter approached, Foster planned to launch his long-anticipated raid on Goldsboro. His force had almost doubled since Burnside's departure, and Burnside (who had replaced McClellan as commander of the Army of the Potomac) had opened a new campaign to capture Richmond. Foster thus hoped to prevent reinforcements from being transferred from the Tar Heel State to Lee's army, and by destroying the Wilmington and Weldon Railroad bridge spanning the Neuse River at Goldsboro, he sought to cut one of Lee's vital supply lines as well. On the morning of December 11, Foster left New Bern with over ten thousand infantry and cavalry and forty pieces of artillery. Three days later, the federals encountered their first serious resistance at Southwest Creek near Kinston. The Confederates had burned the bridge there and were posted along the opposite bank. Early on the morning of the fourteenth, Foster directed the 9th New Jersey and 85th Pennsylvania Infantry Regiments to ford the stream and turn the Southern flank, which proved easier said than done. The federals managed to cross the treacherous creek by wading, floating on debris, and swimming.[38]

At this point, the Confederate commander, Brigadier General Nathan G. "Shanks" Evans, arrived at the front. Seeing that the federals were turning his position at the creek, he ordered his command to withdraw on the Wilmington Road toward the Neuse River. Evans halted his command two miles south of the bridge below Kinston and posted his North Carolina units on the right and his South Carolina troops on the left. Though numbering only 2,014 soldiers, the Carolinians occupied a strong position in the woods. The ground in the Confederates' immediate front formed a natural breastwork, while their right flank rested on a large swamp and their left on the Neuse.[39]

Foster's skirmishers advanced through thick woods until they came to within seventy yards of the well-concealed Southerners. The two sides blazed away at each other, and as the woods filled with gunpowder smoke, some confused bluecoats began firing on their comrades. The confusion was not confined to the Union ranks. During the fight, the federals succeeded in turning the Confederate left. After the South Carolinians had retreated across the bridge, Evans ordered the structure put to the torch, unaware that the North Carolinians holding the center and right of his line had not received orders to withdraw. Assuming they were enemy soldiers, he ordered his artillery to open fire on them. The Confederate fusillade, combined with the attacking Union soldiers, induced the Tar Heels to fall back toward the bridge. Panic ensued when the North Carolinians reached the burning span. The men struggled to get across, and in the chaos, the federals captured over four hundred Confederates who were unable to escape.[40]

Once the rest were across the bridge, Evans rallied his demoralized troops on the 47th North Carolina, which had just arrived, and he formed a new line about two miles above Kinston. As the federals crossed the half-burned bridge, Foster sent a courier to Evans with a demand for his surrender. "Tell your General to go to h—l," was the defiant Evans's reply. Thus refused, Foster prepared to launch an assault, but the Confederates withdrew before he could attack. Rather than resume the pursuit, Foster had his men make camp. The federals had won an impressive victory. In addition to the prisoners, they had seized eleven pieces of artillery with one thousand rounds of ammunition, five hundred small arms, and a large quantity of quartermaster and commissary stores. That night, word arrived from Virginia that Lee had defeated Burnside in the Battle of Fredericksburg, and that Confederate reinforcements were en route to North Carolina. Despite the distressing news, Foster decided to press on to Goldsboro and do as much damage to the railroad as possible before returning to New Bern. On the morning of December 15, the Union expeditionary force recrossed the Neuse River and headed west on the Dover Road toward Goldsboro. The federals left a thoroughly ransacked town of Kinston in their wake.[41]

That evening, Foster halted his marching column a few miles from White Hall, a village on the south side of the Neuse about eighteen miles from Goldsboro. The north bank of the river just east of the bridge served as the dry dock for the CSS *Neuse*, a 150-foot ironclad gunboat under construction. The Union commander sent forward a small force of cavalry and artillery to reconnoiter, and the detachment reached the bridge just as the retreating Confederates set it on fire using barrels of rosin and turpentine. The wooden structure was soon wrapped in flames, and burning sections of it began to crash into the river. The Union horsemen decided to create their own bonfire by stacking two thousand barrels of turpentine and other naval stores. In the immediate area, the mammoth conflagration transformed night into day, and the towering flames could be seen for miles around.[42]

Eager to destroy the *Neuse*, Major Jeptha Garrard of the 3rd New York Cavalry called for volunteers to carry out the mission. Only one man stepped forward—Private Henry Butler. As the federals unleashed a furious fire on the Confederates, the daring Butler jumped into the cold, deep waters of the Neuse and swam to the opposite shore. Grabbing a flaming piece of wood from the bridge, he raced toward the gunboat, only to find his path blocked by Rebel soldiers eager to capture the bold Yankee. Amid a hail of bullets, Butler abruptly turned and plunged back into the river, returning safely to his comrades. The *Neuse* was thus spared a fiery end, but it sustained some minor damage from Union projectiles.[43]

Foster's main column reached White Hall on the morning of December 16. Finding the bridge over the Neuse burned and the Confederates occupying a strong position, Foster decided to feign an attack to pin down the enemy and then resume the march to Goldsboro. He sent the 9th New Jersey and Colonel Thomas J. C. Amory's brigade forward to engage the Confederates, who were commanded by Brigadier General Beverly H. Robertson. Although the Union artillery devastated the thickly wooded landscape occupied by the Confederates, the federal infantry deployed along the river suffered heavier casualties because they were caught in the open. In any event, soldiers on both sides commented on

Thomas L. Clingman. (*Duke University*)

receiving an intense volume of fire.[44]

Breaking off the attack, Foster resumed the march to Goldsboro; on the morning of December 17, the federal advance reached the Wilmington and Weldon Railroad a few miles below town. The Union commander ordered a detachment of his cavalry south to wreck railroad track and equipment at Mount Olive, and he sent five infantry regiments north to burn the covered railroad bridge over the Neuse. Defending the bridge was Brigadier General Thomas L. Clingman's brigade and several artillery units. The brunt of the Union attack fell on the 51st and 52nd North Carolina Infantry Regiments on the south side of the river. As the two Tar Heel regiments withdrew across the bridge, a federal detachment dashed forward to burn it. According to one Union soldier, the Confederates "directed their fire upon them with terrible fury," but the detail managed to set fire to the wooden span, and the flames soon engulfed the entire structure. Foster ordered his artillery to fire on the bridge to speed its destruction and to prevent Clingman's troops from dousing the blaze. He also directed some of his men to stack arms and tear up several miles of railroad track south of the bridge. Satisfied that he had accomplished his mission, Foster directed his force to begin the return march to New Bern.[45]

In the meantime, General Evans reached the battlefield with his South Carolina brigade. He assumed command and ordered an attack on the Union rear guard, which consisted of Colonel Horace C. Lee's brigade. The onrushing Confederates had to charge uphill toward eighteen Union guns supported by Lee's infantry. Colonel Lee reported that the Carolinians "bore up steadily in the face of a well-directed and most destructive fire." But, he continued, "the crushing fire of the batteries" proved to be too much, and the attackers "broke and fled in disorder to the wood[s]." Soon afterward, darkness brought the Battle of Goldsboro Bridge to an end. Union losses in Foster's Goldsboro Expedition totaled 591 killed, wounded, and missing. The Confederate casualties are less certain, but given the four hundred men captured at Kinston, their losses probably equaled, if not exceeded, the federals'.[46]

Following his return to New Bern, Foster informed the War Department that his raid had been "a perfect success," boasting that he had burned the railroad bridge at Goldsboro and had then "whipped the enemy" at Southwest Creek, Kinston, White Hall, and Goldsboro. But his triumph proved short lived. Foster noted that the Con-

Sinking of the USS *Monitor.* (*Harper's Weekly*)

federates in North Carolina had since been heavily reinforced by Lee's army in Virginia, rendering future operations in the state doubtful until his own numbers were increased. As for the damage to the railroad, the Confederates repaired it within a few days and even replaced the Goldsboro railroad bridge. After a brief interruption, the crucial supply line linking Wilmington to Lee's army was once more intact.[47]

The year 1862 ended on a somber note for the Union navy. On December 31, the USS *Monitor* foundered off Cape Hatteras during a squall, as it was being towed from Hampton Roads, Virginia, to Beaufort, North Carolina. Sixteen of the sixty-three men on board perished. On March 9, 1862, the *Monitor* had fought the CSS *Virginia* to a draw in the famed Battle of the Ironclads, the first naval engagement of its kind. Now the legendary vessel rested among countless other shipwrecks in the Graveyard of the Atlantic.[48]

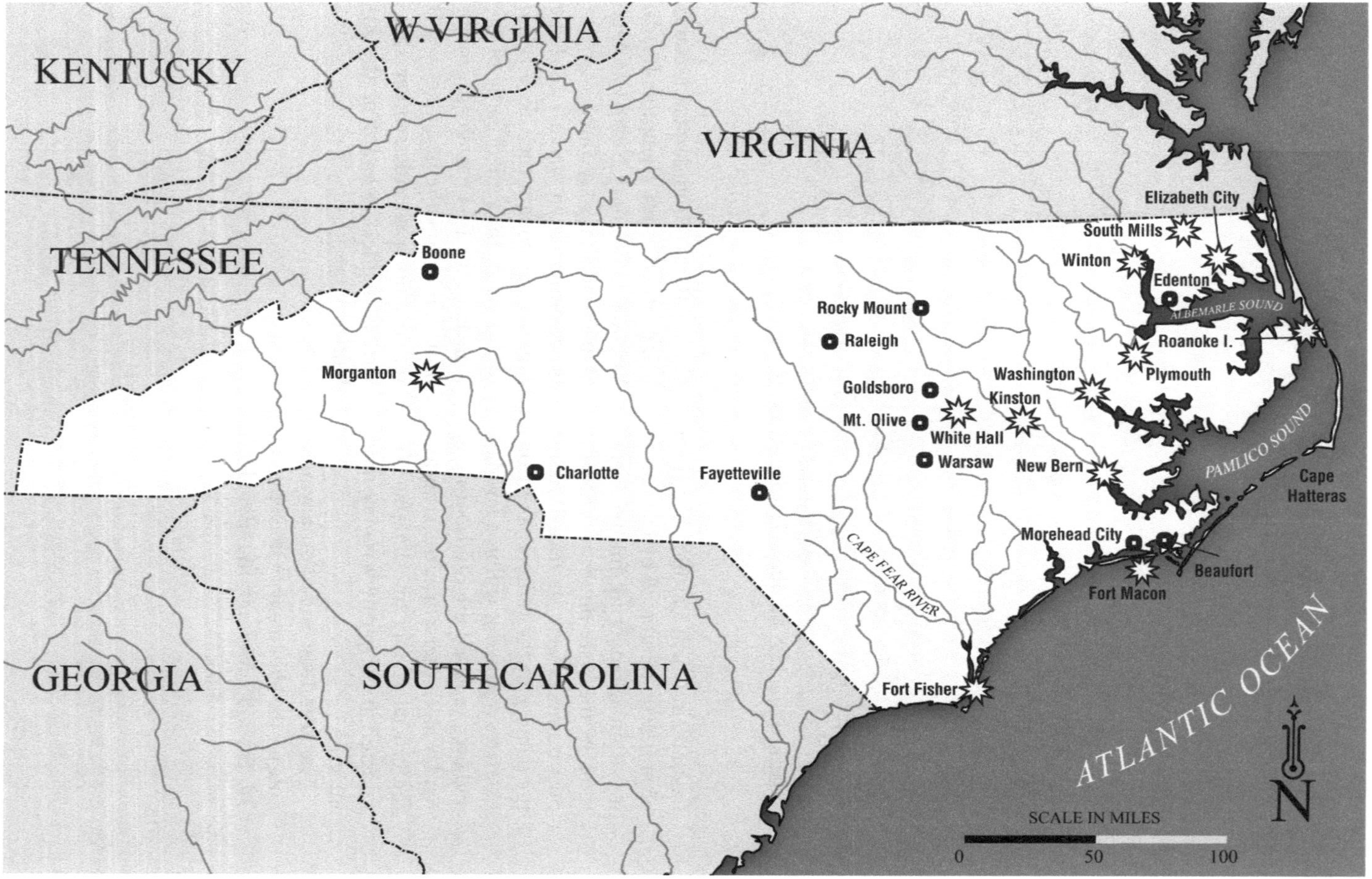

KENTUCKY
W. VIRGINIA
VIRGINIA
TENNESSEE
SOUTH CAROLINA
GEORGIA
ATLANTIC OCEAN
Boone
Morganton
Charlotte
Fayetteville
Rocky Mount
Raleigh
Goldsboro
Mt. Olive
White Hall
Warsaw
Kinston
Washington
New Bern
Plymouth
Roanoke I.
Edenton
Winton
South Mills
Elizabeth City
ALBEMARLE SOUND
PAMLICO SOUND
Cape Hatteras
Morehead City
Beaufort
Fort Macon
CAPE FEAR RIVER
Fort Fisher
SCALE IN MILES
0
50
100
N

9. The Civil War Grinds On

D. H. HILL'S NEW BERN-WASHINGTON EXPEDITION

In February 1863, General Lee sent one of his corps commanders, Lieutenant General James Longstreet, south with two divisions to protect the vital supply lines extending from eastern North Carolina to Petersburg, Virginia. On February 25, Lee appointed Longstreet commander of the Department of North Carolina and Virginia. Well aware that Lee's army was short of rations, Longstreet planned to gather provisions in the rich farming region of his department. To give his foragers a free hand, Longstreet intended to fix the Union forces inside their bases. To accomplish this, he would besiege the federals at Suffolk, Virginia, while his subordinate in North Carolina, Major General D. H. Hill, moved on New Bern and Washington. Hill returned to the Tar Heel State after a two-year absence. In spring 1861, Hill had been sent to the Virginia theater, where he served with distinction and ultimately rose to division-level command. He owed his transfer to North Carolina to his reputation as an able and aggressive combat commander, as well as to his open criticism of Lee's generalship, which made his future in the Army of Northern Virginia uncertain at best.[1]

On March 13, 1863, Hill launched a three-pronged attack on New Bern from Kinston. The three Confederate columns consisted of Brigadier Generals Junius Daniel's and James J. Pettigrew's infantry brigades and Brigadier General Beverly H. Robertson's cavalry brigade. Daniel's column struck first, driving the federals from a line of earthworks at Deep Gully. Heavily reinforced later that day, the Union force assaulted Daniel's troops on the morning of March 14. The Confederates repulsed the federals, and the bluecoats withdrew eight miles to the fortifications around New Bern. In the meantime, Pettigrew's brigade prepared to attack Fort Anderson on the north bank of the Neuse River opposite the town. But Union gunboats arrived offshore, and Pettigrew decided to call off the attack rather than risk sacrificing his men in a futile charge. Robertson likewise failed to cut the Atlantic and North Carolina Railroad as directed.

Despite Daniel's success, the failure of Pettigrew and Robertson to achieve their objectives induced Hill to withdraw from New Bern and focus his attention on Washington.[2]

Lee and Longstreet advised against storming the town's defenses because of the heavy losses that the Confederates might incur. Instead, Longstreet urged Hill to collect all the provisions he could and keep the federals at New Bern and Washington occupied to prevent them from being used elsewhere. By the end of March, Hill was besieging Washington. On receiving word of Hill's intentions, General Foster hurried to Washington and arrived there just ahead of the Confederates. The Union garrison numbered 1,200 troops, supported by three gunboats. A West Point-trained engineer, Foster had his men strengthen the existing fortifications and build new ones at critical locations in town, on the river, and along the roads. The federal and Confederate guns exchanged a steady fire but took few casualties. The siege nevertheless enabled Hill's troops to gather large amounts of corn and bacon from the countryside, and it prevented supplies and reinforcements from reaching Foster at Washington. The Union commander knew that the federal defenders' only hope was that a relief column from New Bern would soon arrive and break the siege.[3]

Unfortunately for the beleaguered garrison of Washington, the three generals at New Bern ranked among the most incompetent in the Union army. Foster's second in command, Brigadier General Innis N. Palmer, left the relief effort to Brigadier General Henry Prince, who led a river-borne expedition up the Pamlico. Prince took one look at the Confederate defenses surrounding Washington and beat a hasty retreat to New Bern. His replacement, Brigadier General Francis B. Spinola, was a political general with no experience commanding troops in the field. Although Palmer and Prince were professional soldiers, they chose to remain behind at New Bern while Spinola made a feeble attempt to relieve the federals at Washington. On April 9, the Confederates repulsed Spinola's force at Blount's Creek by firing a few rounds of artillery.[4]

Foster soon realized he would have to run the blockade and lead the relief column himself. On the night of April 13, the steamer *Escort* ran the Confederate batteries on the Pamlico River and safely reached Washington with the 5th Rhode Island Infantry on board. Two days later, Foster boarded the *Escort* and made his way back to New Bern, even though the vessel was hit forty times and the ship's pilot was mortally wounded. Seeing that the federals were able to move supplies and reinforcements up the Pamlico, Hill abandoned the siege of Washington. The withdrawal came as a bitter disappointment to most of Hill's troops, who had eagerly anticipated capturing the town. In any event, General Lee had begun to transfer most of Hill's soldiers north to participate in a Northern offensive following his brilliant victory at Chancellorsville, Virginia, in early May.[5]

The Confederate troop withdrawal suddenly put Hill on the defensive, encouraging Foster to launch a minor expedition along the Atlantic and North Carolina Railroad toward Kinston in mid-May with a brigade-size force of infantry, cavalry, and artillery. During a skirmish at Gum Swamp about eight miles east of Kinston, the federals captured 165 Confederates, but Colonel John Richter Jones, the able fifty-nine-year-old commander of the 58th Pennsylvania Infantry, was killed during the fight. After this operation, Foster chose to bide his time before making another move.[6]

Edward E. Potter. (*National Archives*)

POTTER'S RAID

In early July, following a two-month respite, Foster sent Lieutenant Colonel George W. Lewis at the head of the 3rd New York Cavalry and a few other mounted units west toward the Wilmington and Weldon Railroad. On the Fourth of July, the 640-man force struck at Kenansville, burning the Louis Froelich and Company arms, knapsack, and saddle factories there to the ground. The federals then continued west, reaching the railroad at Warsaw early the next morning. They destroyed two miles of track and telegraph wire, two rail cars, a supply depot, four thousand barrels of resin and turpentine, and some gunpowder. On July 7, Lewis's horse soldiers returned to New Bern with 30 prisoners, 150 livestock, and about 400 black refugees. Lewis estimated that his raid eliminated "nearly a million dollars worth of property."[7]

Foster was so pleased with the result of the Kenansville-Warsaw raid that he ordered a second raid, which he placed under the command of his chief of staff, Brigadier General Edward E. Potter. The raiders' two main targets were Tarboro and Rocky Mount. Tarboro was an important port town on the Tar River where the Confederates had several warehouses and an ironclad warship under construction. Rocky Mount boasted the largest cotton mill in North Carolina, producing huge quantities of Confederate uniform cloth, and it was the site of the Wilmington and Weldon Railroad's bridge over the Tar River. Destroying that bridge would prevent Lee's army from receiving much-needed supplies following its defeat in the Battle of Gettysburg.[8]

On July 18, Potter left New Bern at the head of a large cavalry force and four pieces of artillery; he reached Greenville the following afternoon, pausing long enough to destroy about $300,000 worth of property as well as the bridge across the Tar River. The Union cavalry resumed the march at 6:00 PM and charged into Tarboro around 8:00 AM on the twentieth, driving a small force of the enemy before them. During their brief occupation of the town, the federals burned the half-finished ironclad, two steam-

William H. C. Whiting. (*North Carolina State Archives*)

ships, some railroad cars, one hundred bales of cotton, and a large store of supplies. Late that afternoon, they burned the bridge across the Tar River and then began the return march to New Bern. While the main column raided Tarboro, a detachment commanded by Major Ferris Jacobs Jr. rode on to Rocky Mount about fifteen miles west. Jacobs's force captured some Confederates there and destroyed the railroad depot, a locomotive and some rail cars, several cotton mills and a flour mill, a machine shop, over three-dozen wagons filled with supplies, and both the wagon bridge and railroad bridge across the Tar River. Jacobs's detachment rejoined the main Union column shortly after its departure from Tarboro. The Confederates maintained a relentless pursuit of the federal raiders until the latter reached New Bern on July 23.[9]

Potter's raid had been a great success. The general returned to New Bern with over one hundred Confederate prisoners and three hundred newly freed slaves, and his losses were low, totaling seventy-five killed, wounded, and missing. His command had destroyed the only Confederate ironclad in the Tar-Pamlico region as well as a vast quantity of supplies and had closed the Wilmington and Weldon Railroad at Rocky Mount for about a week.[10]

In late July, Foster led a raid on the Wilmington and Weldon Railroad bridge at Weldon. Setting out from the ruins of Winton at the head of five infantry regiments and one artillery battery, Foster's force linked up with a cavalry detachment under Colonel Samuel P. Spear on the twenty-seventh. In the meantime, the newly appointed commander of the Confederate Department of North Carolina, Major General William H. C. Whiting, received word of Foster's advance on Weldon. He informed his superiors at Petersburg and urged that a force be rushed south to intercept the Union raiders. Brigadier General Matt W. Ransom's brigade of five North Carolina regiments immediately boarded trains bound for Weldon.[11]

Ransom directed his men to deploy at Boone's Mill east of Weldon, behind the pond and stream. As the troops went into position, Ransom and his staff rode out to reconnoiter and nearly collided with Spear's federal cavalry. Ransom raced back to the mill and was chagrined to find the men bathing in the pond. The general ordered his troops to form in line of battle and remove the planks from the bridge across the millstream. The Confederates—many of them naked and dripping wet—instantly obeyed and either set to work dismantling the bridge or opened fire on the charging federal cavalry. Finding himself opposed by what appeared to be a superior force, Spear halted and had his men dismount. The federals made several attempts to advance down the main road or to outflank the Southerners but were repulsed each time. Ransom's Confederates thus prevented Foster's raiders from burning the railroad bridge at Weldon. Aside from some skirmishing, the action at Boone's Mill marked the last combat in eastern North Carolina for the year 1863.[12]

THE TAR HEEL STATE IN TURMOIL

For most of the war, bands of Confederate deserters, draft dodgers, and Unionists roamed the eastern and the western counties of the state. Soon the central region—namely Guilford, Randolph, Forsyth, Davidson, Yadkin, Davie, and Wilkes Counties—also became a haven for dissidents. In the east, they were called "buffaloes," in the central counties "outliers," and in the west "bushwhackers" or "Tories." This state of affairs stemmed from the Conscription Act passed April 16, 1862, authorizing the Confederate government to draft all able-bodied white males eighteen to thirty-five. By January 1863, the situation had become so critical that Governor Vance requested the General Assembly to make aiding and abetting deserters a crime while offering clemency to those who voluntarily returned to their regiments. State militia and regular Confederate units attempted to round up deserters and draft dodgers, bur their efforts were largely ineffectual. The resulting frustration often led to harsh reprisals when Confederates captured Unionists.[13]

Perhaps the most brutal such incident occurred in the Shelton Laurel district of Madison County in the western part of the state. In January 1863, a band of men from Shelton Laurel raided Marshall, the Madison County seat, to obtain salt they claimed was denied them because of their reputation as Unionists. In addition to plundering the depot where the salt was stored, the raiders also pillaged several homes, including that of Colonel Lawrence M. Allen of the 64th North Carolina Infantry. Some of the raiders were deserters from the 64th. At Governor Vance's request, the commander of that district, Brigadier General Henry Heth, sent a detachment to restore order in Madison County. In January 1863, the commander, Lieutenant Colonel James A. Keith of the 64th North Carolina, rounded up thirteen suspects—including several boys—and had them shot. Vance was outraged by the "Shelton Laurel Massacre" and demanded an investigation, but Keith's superiors allowed him to resign on the grounds of incompetence. After the war, he was tried for thirteen counts of murder and acquitted of the first count. He appealed the remaining charges on the grounds that an 1866 state amnesty law shielded him from further prosecution. On February 21, 1869, he broke out of jail and fled to Arkansas. He escaped just days before the North Carolina Supreme Court ruled in his favor. Keith was never heard from again.[14]

One month after the Shelton Laurel incident, a few dozen Yadkin County militia briefly exchanged fire with a comparable number of dissidents hiding out in a schoolhouse near Yad-

Robert F. Hoke. (*North Carolina State Archives*)

kinville. The skirmish resulted in two men killed on each side and the capture of three Tories. The prisoners requested a writ of habeas corpus from the North Carolina Supreme Court. The chief justice, Richmond M. Pearson, ordered their release on the grounds that state militia had no authority to enforce Confederate law, as the prisoners were charged with violating the Conscription Act. Pearson's ruling remained unchallenged because there was no Confederate supreme court to hear an appeal. As a result, Vance reassigned the militia to other duties, but when desertions increased, he once more ordered the militia to round up deserters. The problem became so serious that in July 1863, he established the Guard for Home Defense to assist the militia in arresting deserters and protecting Confederate supporters. The Home Guard consisted of all able-bodied white males eighteen to fifty, including those exempt from Confederate service. These part-time soldiers faced a daunting task, for many of the deserters were combat veterans who were usually better armed and organized than the Home Guard units.[15]

Realizing that neither the militia nor the Home Guard could cope with the situation, Vance appealed to General Lee for assistance, and Lee sent him two regiments of North Carolina infantry and a squadron of cavalry commanded by a Tar Heel native, Brigadier General Robert F. Hoke. The Confederate force swept into Wilkes and several other counties and succeeded in rounding up over five hundred deserters by late October 1863. Law and order returned to central North Carolina, but quiet prevailed only as long as Hoke's detachment remained there.[16]

If there was a law as unpopular as the Conscription Act, it was an act that the Confederate Congress passed in April 1863 to levy a series of taxes on a populace already suffering keenly from privation. One tax law required merchants and professional men to pay a fee for a business license, while another—known as a "tax-in-kind"—assessed farmers one-tenth of their output, which local agents collected for the army. A third law authorized agents to impress provisions, livestock, wagons, and even slaves for the Confederate army, and to set prices for them. The much-despised tax act not only marked the first time many North Carolinians had to pay a tax but also left numerous families on the verge of starvation.

Even before the tax act had passed, food shortages led some Tar Heel civilians to resort to desperate measures.

On March 18, 1863, a group of fifty to seventy-five local women calling themselves "Soldiers' Wives" descended on Salisbury and demanded that the local merchants sell them provisions at government prices, which stood at one-half the market value. When the store owners refused to comply, the women—many of them armed with axes and hatchets—broke into one shop and made off with thirteen barrels of flour, one barrel of molasses, two sacks of salt, and twenty dollars in cash. Flushed with success, the women moved on a small Confederate quartermaster store at the North Carolina Railroad depot and, ignoring the threats of the railroad agent, took ten more barrels of flour. The "Female Raid" concluded the next morning when the women divided their plunder. The perpetrators were never arrested or charged with a crime, indicating that their neighbors sympathized with them. A similar raid in nearby Greensboro one month later ended less happily for the women involved. Local law enforcement officials arrested several of the protestors and briefly jailed them. The possibility of severe punishment did not discourage women in other towns across the state from staging bread riots to the end of the war.[17]

In July 1863, the fall of Vicksburg and Lee's defeat at Gettysburg spurred the rise of the peace faction in the Tar Heel State. The members borrowed their rallying cry from the Peace Democrat—or "Copperhead"—faction in the North: "The Constitution as it is, and the Union as it was." The chief spokesman of the peace movement was Raleigh newspaper editor William W. Holden. In the pages of his *North Carolina Standard*, Holden called for an end to the war, branding it "this awful evil." But he did not advocate peace at any price, rather insisting that any cessation of hostilities must "preserve the rights of the sovereign States and the institutions of the South"—above all, slavery. From July to September, Holden's appeal inspired about a hundred peace rallies in North Carolina, with most of them occurring in the central counties.

That summer, the peace movement split the Conservative Party of North Carolina into the peace faction headed by Holden and the war faction headed by Vance. The two sides often clashed in print and sometimes in face-to-face confrontations such as a peace meeting in Cabarrus County that ended with a brawl. The ensuing notoriety made Holden a target for reprisal. On September 9, a brigade of Georgia soldiers traveling by train took advantage of a brief stopover at Raleigh by vandalizing the office of Holden's *Standard*. Receiving word of the incident, Vance rushed to the scene and persuaded the troops to disperse by reminding them of the price in blood "their patriotic fathers" had paid to secure freedom of the press. On returning to the Governor's Palace, Vance found that Holden had fled there seeking sanctuary. The following day, Vance had to break up a mob that was destroying the presses of the pro-Confederate *State Journal*, followed by a third riot involving a trainload of Alabama troops who threatened to kidnap Holden. At this point, Vance urged President Davis to prohibit Confederate soldiers from stopping at Raleigh, and the latter is-

Edward A. Wild.

sued the necessary orders. Quiet soon returned to the streets of the state capital, but the party schism set the stage for a bitter gubernatorial contest in 1864 pitting incumbent Vance against Holden.[18]

A MORE RIGOROUS STYLE OF WARFARE

On November 11, 1863, Major General Benjamin F. Butler replaced Foster as commander of the Department of Virginia and North Carolina. Three weeks later, Butler authorized Brigadier General Edward A. Wild to launch a raid into northeastern North Carolina. A native of Massachusetts, Wild had been a physician before the war, but he enlisted as an infantry captain rather than as a surgeon. Though battlefield wounds that maimed his right hand and cost him his left arm made Wild unable to resume his medical practice, he remained a capable combat officer, rising to brigadier general. In April 1863, Wild was placed in charge of recruiting in eastern North Carolina, enabling him to raise a brigade of black troops led by hand-picked white officers. By December, "Wild's African Brigade," as it was called, made up all or part of seven regiments: the 1st, 2nd, and 3rd North Carolina Colored Volunteers; the 1st, 5th, and 10th US Colored Troops (USCT); and the 55th Massachusetts Volunteer Infantry. Wild would lead roughly 1,800 soldiers on the raid.[19]

Wild's objectives were to open the Great Dismal Swamp Canal to friendly traffic, clear the area of guerrillas, liberate slaves, and obtain recruits for his brigade. The route of march led from Union-held Norfolk, Virginia, to Elizabeth City. On December 5, Wild's command departed Norfolk in two columns; it reached South Mills, North Carolina, three days later. Two supply steamers were to accompany the federals, but they took a wrong turn and failed to arrive at South Mills as planned. Though disappointed, Wild refused to let this setback discourage him. Instead, he directed his force "to live on the country for a few days . . . judiciously discriminating in favor of the worst rebels." After camping at South Mills on the night of December 8, the federals resumed the march the next morning and arrived at Elizabeth City on the eleventh.[20]

In addition to foraging, Wild's troops had liberated slaves along their route and had demolished a notorious Rebel's house and barn to rebuild the Pasquotank River bridge after guerrillas had burned it. When the supply ships reached Elizabeth City, Wild ordered them to ferry the former slaves to the freedpeople's colony on Roanoke Island, unaware that the community was overcrowded and undersupplied. The refugees' arrival soon left the residents on the verge of starvation.[21]

During the federals' weeklong occupation of Elizabeth City, Wild sent out detachments to destroy guerrilla camps and to forage. He also sent out a four-hundred-man detachment into Currituck and Gates Counties under Colonel Alonzo Draper to liberate slaves and collect recruits, and he held military trials for twenty or so local citizens accused of various crimes. One of the accused, Daniel Bright, was tried as a guerrilla, convicted, and sentenced to hang. Bright was executed on December 18. On the same day, Wild began the return march to Norfolk. While en route to Indiantown to link up with the main body, Colonel Draper's detachment skirmished with a stubborn guerrilla force that finally gave way before a bayonet charge launched by men of the 5th USCT. Draper's command then resumed the march, reaching Indiantown on the evening of the eighteenth. The main column arrived a few days later, and Wild sent out a detachment to corner the guerrillas. Although the federals failed to pin down the enemy, the soldiers in blue succeeded in finding the guerrillas' camp, which they plundered and then burned.[22]

Wild resumed the march and arrived at Currituck Courthouse on December 20. Once again, he sent out a detachment under Draper to destroy another guerrilla camp and "burn pretty freely" any Rebel farms he might encounter. In addition to destroying the enemy camp, Draper's men confiscated a stockpile of weapons and took a sixteen-year-old white girl hostage. The last action had serious repercussions. Shortly after Draper's detachment reached the presumed safety of the federal outpost at Pungo Bridge, the commander of the outpost, Colonel Frederick F. Wead, ordered his white troops into formation against Draper's black soldiers. Wead had just learned that Draper had a teenage white girl in his custody and demanded that he hand her over. Draper refused and was slightly wounded when he drew his sword to prevent Wead from seizing his female prisoner. Some tense moments followed as Draper led his black troops past Wead's all-white command to rejoin Wild near Norfolk. Wead later preferred charges against Draper, and though they were eventually dismissed, the possibility of a court-martial delayed for several months the girl's return to her home in North Carolina.[23]

Wild "adopted a more rigorous style of warfare" because, as Major General William T. Sherman had also concluded, "ordinary measures [are] of little avail." In the course of his raid, Wild burned a dozen Rebel homes, four guerrilla camps, and two distilleries. He also liberated 2,500 slaves (including one hundred recruits), confiscated horses, devoured provisions, took several prisoners, and executed one guerrilla. Wild's raid gave hope to North Carolina Unionists while spreading disaffection among the Confederates, many of whom fled the region to avoid further devastation. Frustration and embarrassment over his inability to stop Wild probably induced the Confederate department commander,

William H. Thomas. (*Clark,* Histories)

Major General George E. Pickett, to hang one of Wild's black soldiers in retaliation for the execution of Confederate guerrilla Daniel Bright. Although conceding that Wild had resorted to "the most stringent measures," General Butler nevertheless maintained that the success of his subordinate's raid muffled any criticism as to its harshness.[24]

THE WAR IN THE MOUNTAINS INTENSIFIES

On September 2, 1863, a Union force commanded by Major General Ambrose E. Burnside captured Knoxville, Tennessee. The loss of eastern Tennessee induced Colonel William H. Thomas, the commander of the main Confederate force in that region, Thomas's Legion (69th North Carolina), to withdraw into western North Carolina. Thomas decided to take just two companies with him and leave the remainder in Tennessee. Up to then, Thomas' Legion had been a combined arms unit with contingents of infantry, cavalry, and artillery. At one time, as many as four hundred Cherokee Indians had served under Thomas. As he made his way through the Great Smoky Mountains, Thomas left detachments to block the major passes. In late October, a portion of Thomas' Legion joined a small force of Confederate cavalry and the Cherokee County Home Guard in pursuit of Unionist raiders led by Goldman Bryson. After routing Bryson's force in a skirmish near Murphy, North Carolina, the Confederates followed the Tory leader to his home and killed him.[25]

In Madison County, meanwhile, a 150-man Confederate force suffered a defeat that spread panic among local secessionist sympathizers, but it proved to be a minor setback. In November, Brigadier General Robert B. Vance, the governor's brother and commander of the Western Military District, led several raids into eastern Tennessee from Madison County, seizing numerous horses, cattle, and hogs. General Vance informed his brother that he was "threatening the enemy . . . and keeping him uneasy, and drawing some of his force away to watch me."[26]

At the behest of General Longstreet, Vance led an expedition into eastern Tennessee in January 1864 to protect the Confederate supply line at Newport. Following his unsuccessful campaign to capture Knoxville from Burnside, Longstreet had gone into winter quarters. Vance's force consisted of five hundred infantry and cavalry plus a section of artillery that had to be manhandled over the Great Smoky Mountains. After sending part of his force to Gatlinburg, Vance continued with the remainder toward Newport to capture a Union supply train. He seized the supplies, but on January 14, a Union cavalry force captured Vance and fifty-two of his men at Schultz's Mill. Command of the Western District thus devolved on Colonel John B. Palmer of the 58th North Carolina.[27]

PICKETT'S NEW BERN EXPEDITION

Concern over the reverses in North Carolina and their demoralizing effect spurred General Lee to propose a bold counterstroke to President Davis: capture New Bern and the federal garrison there. Writing on January 2, 1864, Lee indicated that he could now spare the troops for the campaign but warned that would probably not be the case when spring arrived. Davis approved Lee's proposal, and he even suggested that the general himself lead the expedition. Lee demurred, however, and recommended that General Hoke be given the assignment. But that was not to be, for Davis believed that such an important operation required a more senior commander. The task thus fell to Major General George E. Pickett of Gettysburg fame. Davis chose his personal aide and nephew, Commander John Taylor Wood, to lead the supporting naval contingent.[28]

The Confederates collected a force of roughly thirteen thousand soldiers and fourteen gunboats at Kinston. On the morning of January 30, Pickett moved out toward New Bern, his infantry divided into three columns. The column commanded by Brigadier General Seth M. Barton was to assault New Bern from the southeast via the railroad bridge, thus preventing the arrival of Union reinforcements from Beaufort and Morehead City. Colonel James Dearing's column was to approach from the north along the Neuse River and capture Fort Anderson, while General Hoke's column, accompanied by Pickett, was to advance between the Neuse and the Trent Rivers and, after overrunning the federal position at Bachelor Creek, strike from the west. The three columns were slated to attack New Bern on February 1.[29]

Hoke defeated the Union force at Bachelor Creek, but neither Barton nor Dearing even attempted to accomplish their objectives. Both men were convinced that the Union defenses they faced were impregnable given the resources at their disposal. Pickett still hoped to continue the operation by having Barton join Hoke's column. But when the Confederate commander learned that Barton could not reach him until February 4, if then, he decided to abandon the campaign and withdraw from New Bern.[30]

In the meantime, Commander Wood and his contingent of sailors and marines enjoyed some success on the Neuse River. On the night of February 1, the Confederates boarded the Union steamer *Underwriter* near New Bern, fought the crew hand to hand, and captured the ship. But Wood had to burn his prize after discovering he could not move beyond range of the federal guns. A Confederate expedition from Wilmington led by Brigadier General James G. Martin likewise succeeded in capturing the Union depot at Newport Barracks near Morehead City and in focusing federal attention on that region during Pickett's New Bern campaign. In addition to routing the garrison, Martin's force captured

The ironclad ram CSS *Albemarle.* (*Photographic History of the Civil War*)

eighty prisoners and destroyed a vast quantity of supplies before returning to Wilmington.[31]

After his failure to capture New Bern, Pickett returned to Lee's army in Virginia, little suspecting that one of his actions would later cause him considerable distress. In February 1864, twenty-two Union prisoners were hanged at Kinston by order of General Pickett after they were tried and found guilty of desertion from the Confederate army. After the war, Pickett learned that he was under investigation for his role in the hangings and fled to Canada. Pickett owed his freedom—and perhaps his life—to his old West Point chum and Mexican War comrade, Ulysses S. Grant, who intervened on Pickett's behalf and thus ensured he would never be charged with war crimes.[32]

HOKE'S PLYMOUTH EXPEDITION

With Pickett's departure, General Hoke assumed command of the Confederate expeditionary force and set his sights on the town of Plymouth, an important outpost for the Union army. Like Pickett's New Bern expedition, this was a joint army-navy operation. Hoke sought to ensure the success of his assault by securing the services of the newly commissioned ironclad ram CSS *Albemarle*, the sister ship of the CSS *Neuse*. Built in a cornfield on the Roanoke River, the *Albemarle* measured 158 feet long and was armed with two 6.4-inch Brooke rifled cannons. Crewed by 150 officers and men, it was propelled by two three-blade screw propellers powered by a pair of two-hundred-horsepower steam engines. The vessel's four inches of iron plating and sloping sides deflected enemy projectiles, and its ax-head-shaped iron ram proved effective in sinking wooden-hulled vessels. The commander of the *Albemarle* was Captain James W. Cooke, a former officer in the US Navy.[33]

Cooke's mission was to sail down the Roanoke to Plymouth and support Hoke by sinking or driving off any Union naval vessels in the area. Hoke reached the outskirts of Plymouth on April 17, 1864, and he began to invest the town. His force consisted of three infantry brigades, a cavalry regiment, and three artillery battalions totaling roughly seven thousand men. The Confederates faced a difficult task. A ring of fortifications protected the landside, and the Union garrison numbered 2,834 troops commanded by a veteran officer, Colonel Henry W. Wessells. Though outnumbered by more than two-to-one, the federals were well trained, capably led, and amply supplied. On April 18, following a six-hour artillery barrage, Hoke's brigade under Colonel John T. Mercer succeeded in capturing Fort Wessells west of town, but only after several failed attempts. During one attack, Mercer fell mortally wounded. That night, a "rain of shells" screamed across the moonlit sky above Plymouth. One Union soldier who endured the artillery barrage described the ordeal as "a night of terror."[34]

Early on the morning of April 19, the *Albemarle* slowly steamed into view before Plymouth and passed several Union forts defending the town. The federals trained a heavy fire on the ironclad that included a direct hit from a hundred-pound shell that bounced harmlessly off its sturdy armor. The *Albemarle* then shifted its attention to the Union gunboats, sinking the USS *Southfield* and driving off the USS *Miami*, shortly after the death of the federal naval commander, Lieutenant Commander Charles W. Flusser. His primary mission accomplished, Cooke asked Hoke for orders, and the general directed him to open fire on Plymouth.[35]

Just after daybreak on April 20, Brigadier General Matt W. Ransom's brigade overran the Union fortifications to the east and entered the town. The federals withdrew into Fort Williams, their last sanctuary, and then had to endure a fierce Confederate artillery barrage. A few hours later, Wessells surrendered his entire command, including 2,500 men, twenty-eight guns, five thousand rifle-muskets, five hundred horses, and seven hundred barrels of flour. Plymouth was once more in Confederate hands. A grateful President Davis rewarded Hoke by promoting him to the rank of major general.[36]

Many federals feared retribution at the hands of the victorious Confederates. Bearing in mind Pickett's execution of twenty-two deserters at Kinston, soldiers of the 2nd North Carolina Union Volunteers either attempted to flee or adopted the identities of fallen comrades from other federal regiments. Some of the men bearing assumed names later met their end in the notorious prison camp at Andersonville, Georgia. Among the Union captives were a handful of black army recruits. The victorious Confederates refused to treat the African American troops as prisoners of war and either shot them on sight or hunted them

William B. Cushing.

down in the swamps. The authors of the definitive work on the subject, Weymouth T. Jordan Jr. and Gerald W. Thomas, estimate that Confederate soldiers massacred at least fifty black soldiers at Plymouth. The killings at Plymouth thus joined the more notorious butchery of black captive soldiers at Fort Pillow and the Crater, the latter battle occurring later that summer.[37]

The seizure of Plymouth provided the *Albemarle* with a port to use in keeping Union gunboats out of the Albemarle and Pamlico Sounds. Hoke followed up his success by laying siege to the town of Washington, which fell without a fight on April 30. Before their departure for New Bern, federal troops plundered the town and set fire to several buildings. The conflagration spread quickly, and before it could be brought under control, over one-half of the town was consumed by flames.[38]

Flushed with success, Hoke advanced to the outskirts of New Bern in early May, determined to capture the town even though the *Albemarle* had not yet arrived. Before he could launch an attack, however, Hoke received orders from General Lee to rejoin the Army of Northern Virginia, for the Union army's senior officer, Lieutenant General Ulysses S. Grant, had begun his spring campaign to capture Richmond and Petersburg. Before withdrawing, Hoke attempted to bluff the federals into surrendering, but they rejected his demand. His gambit having failed, Hoke and his troops reluctantly turned their backs on New Bern and headed north. The Confederates made no further attempts to recapture the town.[39]

The *Albemarle* did not rendezvous with Hoke's force at New Bern, because a flotilla of seven Union warships commanded by Captain Melancton Smith blocked its path. Late on the afternoon of May 5, the *Albemarle* attacked the federal vessels, whose fire seemed to have little effect on the Confederate ironclad. But then the USS *Sassacus* rammed the *Albemarle*, causing it to take on water. The ironclad retaliated by firing a hundred-pound shot into one of the boilers on the *Sassacus*, disabling it. Although the *Albemarle* managed to break free of the *Sassacus*, its colors were shot away, its steering mechanism was damaged, and its smokestack was so riddled with holes that reaching New Bern was out of the question. The crippled ironclad barely made its way back to Plymouth.[40]

SINKING OF THE *ALBEMARLE*

Though damaged, the *Albemarle* remained a viable threat to federal warships in the region, and the Union naval high command decided the ironclad had to be eliminated. They chose the audacious Lieutenant William B. Cushing for the mission. On the night of October 27, 1864, Cushing and his men steamed up the Roanoke River aboard a launch with a manned cutter in tow. As they approached the *Albemarle*, which was berthed at Plymouth, a dog began to bark, alerting the sentries. At this point, Cushing abandoned his plan of capturing the ironclad and resolved to destroy it instead. Amid a hail of rifle fire, Cushing guided the launch over the log obstructions barring his path and then extended a spar with a torpedo attached to the end, detonating it against the hull of the *Albemarle*. The explosion tore a six-foot hole beneath the water line, and the vessel soon sank. But the geyser of water thrown up by the blast damaged the launch. Cushing ordered his men to save themselves and plunged into the frigid waters of the Roanoke. Only he and one other man escaped; of the remainder, two drowned and twenty-one were captured.[41]

As a result of Cushing's daring exploit, the federals recaptured Plymouth on October 31, and Washington fell just a few days later. Union forces once more controlled the sound region of North Carolina.

George W. Kirk. (*North Carolina Division of Archives and History*)

KIRK'S RAID

With most of eastern Tennessee in federal hands, Confederate officials dreaded the prospect of Union raids into western North Carolina, which was defended by a scratch force of five hundred regular troops and a somewhat larger contingent of highly unreliable part-time soldiers attached to the state Home Guard. As feared, the federals launched cavalry raids into Jackson and Cherokee Counties in early 1864. In June, Colonel George W. Kirk, a Tennessee native commanding two small Unionist regiments designated the 2nd and 3rd North Carolina Mounted Volunteers, led a bold raid on Morganton in which his small force captured Camp Vance, a training facility then occupied by a few hundred seventeen-year-old Junior Reserves conscripts who were untrained and unarmed. On June 28, Kirk attacked the camp after the Confederates refused his surrender demand. The new recruits surrendered following a brief struggle in which twelve soldiers were killed and an unknown number wounded. Kirk's men then proceeded to burn every building on the grounds except the hospital.[42]

Kirk's next objective was to seize a train on the Western North Carolina Railroad so he could travel to Salisbury, liberate the Union prisoners incarcerated there, and burn the Yadkin River railroad bridge north of town.

But on reaching the railroad near Morganton, he failed to cut the telegraph line before the Confederates could send word of the federals' presence. Kirk therefore decided to abandon his raid on Salisbury. Instead, he ordered his men to burn the depot as well as an engine and four rail cars, and began the return march to Tennessee. While en route, Kirk fought several skirmishes, including one in which he used his Confederate prisoners as human shields. On reaching Mitchell County, Kirk managed to find time to burn the home of Colonel John B. Palmer and to destroy the Cranberry Iron Mills. By early July, Kirk's force had reached federal lines in eastern Tennessee. His raid gained about forty recruits for his command and liberated thirty-two slaves, some of whom later joined the Union army. Kirk's raid also demonstrated the Confederacy's and the state government's lack of authority in western North Carolina. This lawlessness encouraged bushwhackers and deserters from both sides to hide out there, making the region a dangerous place to live.[43]

THE GUBERNATORIAL ELECTION OF 1864

In November 1863, mounting dissatisfaction with the war and the hardships arising from it enabled the peace faction of the Conservative Party to win six of the state's ten seats in the Confederate Congress. Eager to exploit these gains, the state's foremost peace advocate, William W. Holden, called for a state convention to open peace negotiations with the US government. He also promised to support Vance in the election of 1864 if the governor endorsed the convention. But Vance refused to support the peace movement, and despite his many disputes with the Davis administration, he argued that the Tar Heel State should remain in the Confederacy. Separation from the Southern states, he believed, would open North Carolina to invasion by both Union and Confederate forces and lead to revolution and anarchy. Vance also maintained that the preservation of slavery depended on the survival of the Confederacy. In short, the governor would only support a peace that secured Confederate independence and guaranteed the institution of slavery.[44]

Vance's opposition to a peace convention led Holden to run against him in the 1864 gubernatorial election. During the campaign, the governor denounced Holden and his peace convention proposal in numerous speeches across the state and to North Carolina troop units stationed in Virginia. All the while, Holden remained on the sidelines. Lacking the charismatic Vance's talent for oratory, he refused to take to the hustings. Holden also waited until May 18 to resume regular publication of the *Standard*, which he had shut down in protest over President Davis's suspension of the writ of habeas corpus. He thus missed his best opportunity to exploit North Carolinians' outrage over Confederate transgressions, which he could have used to advantage against Vance. The incumbent received a further boost that summer by an apparent improvement in the Confederate military situation and by rumors of waning support in the North for the war effort. The defeat of Lincoln in the upcoming presidential election seemed a real possibility, and North Carolinians became more willing to heed Vance's exhortations to stay the course.[45]

As a result, Vance won the August election for governor by a landslide, receiving over 77 percent of the civilian vote. The soldier vote was even more lopsided, with Vance garnering 13,209 votes to Holden's 1,824. The evidence, however, suggests that fraud accounted for some of the disparity, though not enough to have altered the outcome. Vance's reelection thus signified North Carolina's renewed commitment to Confederate independence.[46]

TARGET: WILMINGTON

For the first three years of the war, the Union high command had focused its main effort on capturing Richmond, the Confederate capital, and other key inland cities of the South. Of the seaports, only Charleston, South Carolina—where the Civil War had begun—and New Orleans, Louisiana—the Confederacy's largest city and busiest port—had generated sufficient interest in the North to merit military operations. Federal combined forces captured the Crescent City in April 1862 and laid siege to the "Cradle of Secession" the following year. From their stations off the river approaches to Wilmington, meanwhile, Union naval officers on blockading vessels watched in frustration as Confederate blockade runners came and went almost at will. Without the aid of an army expeditionary force, the US Navy was powerless to halt the smuggling of vital goods into the Tar Heel port. Worse yet, two Confederate commerce raiders, the CSS *Tallahassee* and the CSS *Chickamauga*, began to use Wilmington as their base as they preyed on Union shipping along the Atlantic coast from North Carolina to Nova Scotia.

The navy had made several proposals for capturing Wilmington earlier in the war, but it was not until summer 1864 that Secretary of the Navy Gideon Welles could persuade President Lincoln to support such an operation. The impetus came from the navy's closing of Mobile Bay, Alabama, on August 5, 1864; Mobile had been the last open seaport on the Gulf of Mexico. That left Wilmington as the only major Confederate port still able to trade with the outside world, making it the "Lifeline of the Confederacy." Although Lincoln favored Welles's proposal, he deferred final approval to the general in chief of the US Army, Ulysses S. Grant.[47]

At first, Grant was lukewarm to the idea of sending a large expeditionary force to assist the navy in seizing Wilmington. Since June 1864, Grant's immediate command—the Army of the James and the Army of the Potomac—had been battling Lee's Army of Northern Virginia around Richmond and Petersburg. Despite incessant fighting and heavy casualties, the two sides remained deadlocked, and Grant believed he could ill afford to detach up to ten thousand soldiers for an amphibious operation in distant southeastern North Carolina. Not one to be easily dissuaded, Welles countered that the stalemate in Virginia could be broken by depriving Lee's army of the supplies entering the Confederacy via Wilmington. "Could we seize the forts at the entrance of Cape

David D. Porter. (*National Archives*)

Fear and close the illicit traffic," the navy secretary argued, "it would be almost as important as the capture of Richmond on the fate of the Rebels, and an important step in that direction." Yielding to mounting political pressure, Grant at last agreed to send an expeditionary force but did not specify when he would do so.[48]

The new commander of the North Atlantic Blockading Squadron, Rear Admiral David D. Porter, responded to Grant's verbal commitment by assembling the largest naval task force of the war. Porter believed it would take all the firepower he could muster to destroy his main target—Fort Fisher, the strongest coastal fortification in the South. Located on Confederate Point near the mouth of the Cape Fear River, Fort Fisher was the key to the Confederate river defenses. Capturing it would prevent blockade runners from reaching Wilmington via either New Inlet or Old Inlet, the two passageways into the Cape Fear. By fall 1864, Fort Fisher was a mammoth, two-sided, sand-and-marsh-grass fortification that looked like a giant number "7" from above. Stretching for over a mile, the fort mounted forty-seven cannons—eight fewer than the fifty-five-gun USS *Colorado*, the largest frigate in the Union fleet.[49]

The fort was largely the brainchild of its commander, Colonel William Lamb, a self-taught military engineer who transformed Fort Fisher from a handful of detached batteries into the most imposing fortress in America. Lamb received plenty of moral support and technical guidance from his superior, Major General William H. C. Whiting, commander of the District of the Cape Fear. Since assuming command of the district in November 1862, Whiting had repeatedly warned the authorities in Richmond of an impending federal attack on Wilmington. With each warning came an appeal for reinforcements. The Confederate War Department soon grew weary of Whiting's continual badgering. Although a talented engineer, Whiting had a reputation for drunkenness, which did nothing to enhance his credibility. As a result, his warnings went unheeded—that is, until after the closing of Mobile Bay, when Confederate military intelligence and Northern newspaper reports began to indicate that Wilmington would soon be attacked.

In October 1864, President Davis replaced Whiting with General Braxton Bragg as commander of the District of the Cape Fear. In doing so, Davis was placing the fate of the South's last open seaport in the hands of the most reviled man in the Confederate army. As commander of the Army of Tennessee, the acerbic Bragg had been dogged by intrigue and accusations of incompetence and ultimately resigned his post in disgrace. Davis's faith in Bragg remained unshaken, however, and it was his opinion that ultimately mattered. But the *Richmond Enquirer* expressed a sentiment shared by many Southerners when it announced, "General Bragg is going to Wilmington. Goodbye Wilmington."[50]

Within a few weeks of Bragg's arrival, Major General William T. Sherman's army group in Georgia began the March to the Sea. Striking out from Atlanta on November 16, the federals cut a swath of devastation as they headed east toward the port city of Savannah. To bolster the Confederate forces opposing Sherman, on November 22, Davis ordered Bragg to Georgia with over two thousand soldiers taken from the Cape Fear defenses. The detachment was sent even as Whiting renewed his pleas for reinforcements, seconded by Governor Vance.[51]

Learning of Bragg's troop transfer from Southern newspapers, Grant decided the time to attack Fort Fisher had arrived. He chose Major General Godfrey Weitzel to lead a 6,500-man expeditionary force drawn from two divisions of the Army of the James. Just before departure, Major General Benjamin F. Butler, Weitzel's superior and the commander of the Union Department of Southeastern Virginia and North Carolina, assumed command of the expedition. Grant inexplicably allowed Butler to supersede Weitzel, which infuriated Admiral Porter. Butler and Porter had despised each other since their first encounter three years earlier, and yet their close cooperation in the coming assault on Fort Fisher was essential to its success. Their acrimony augured ill for the expedition.[52]

William Lamb. (*Museum of the Confederacy*)

"THERE'S A FIZZLE!"

On December 13, Porter's fleet and Butler's troop transports sailed from Hampton Roads, Virginia, planning to meet off the Cape Fear coast a few days later. Butler had hatched a scheme to fashion a massive floating bomb by packing a ship with three hundred tons of gunpowder, running it aground at Fort Fisher, and then detonating it. He believed that the explosion of so much gunpowder would generate powerful winds that would blow down the fort's sand walls, incapacitate the defenders, and enable the Union forces to capture the fort without a struggle. Although ridiculed by some in the War Department, others deemed it worth a try if the lives of federal soldiers might be saved. The navy chose the USS *Louisiana*, a steamship in Porter's blockading squadron, for the mission.[53]

Due to bad weather and the need for more supplies, Porter's and Butler's ships had to stop for several days at Beaufort, North Carolina. When Porter's fleet arrived off Fort Fisher on December 23, the army transports were nowhere in sight. After a short wait, the admiral decided to detonate Butler's powder boat despite the general's absence. Porter thus hoped to reap all the credit if the experiment succeeded or deflect all the blame onto Butler if it failed. Shortly after midnight on Christmas Eve, the *Louisiana*, loaded with just 215 tons of gunpowder, exploded. The shock waves briefly shook the sails and rigging of the Union vessels, and the noise awoke Fort Fisher's sleeping garrison, but that was all. "There's a fizzle!" commented Commander Alexander C. Rhind, the Union naval officer who had steered the *Louisiana* toward Fort Fisher. Unknown to Rhind, the powder vessel had drifted too far from the fort to do any damage. "Butler's Folly"—as the ill-fated powder boat experiment was dubbed—not only failed to demolish Fort Fisher but also convinced Butler that Porter had deliberately botched the effort to embarrass him. The consequences would be devastating to Butler and the expedition.[54]

FIRST BATTLE OF FORT FISHER

On Christmas Eve morning 1864, a fleet of sixty-four federal warships bore down on Fort Fisher. "A grander sight than the approach of [the Union] armada towards the fort was never witnessed on our coast," recalled Colonel Lamb. He was well aware that Fort Fisher had to be held at all costs. A deeply concerned General Lee had just sent word that if Wilmington fell, he would be unable to maintain his army. For the past seven months, Lee and Grant had been locked in a desperate war of attrition in the trenches surrounding Richmond and Petersburg that favored the numerically superior and better supplied Union forces. Without the supplies brought in through the blockade to Wilmington, Lee's army could not hold out and the Confederacy would soon collapse.[55]

Starting shortly after noon on December 24, Union warships began firing shot and shell at the fort, and they maintained the thunderous barrage until late on Christmas Day. The federal naval guns fired 20,271 rounds in all, ranging from 3-inch bolts to 15-inch cannonballs weighing more than 300 pounds each. One Union soldier compared the noise that filled the air to "the rattling of a thousand railway trains." Those who witnessed the spectacle had seen nothing like it before—for the simple reason that it was the largest naval bombardment in American history up to that time.

For all the smoke and noise, the barrage inflicted relatively few casualties and caused little damage to the fort. The failure of the powder boat experiment had left Butler ill-disposed to work with Porter, which is why he landed just one-third of his troops above Fort Fisher on Christmas Day. General Weitzel led a small force on a reconnaissance of the fort, and he reported that the mammoth structure and its guns remained more or less intact, rendering an assault suicidal. Butler briefly considered the matter and

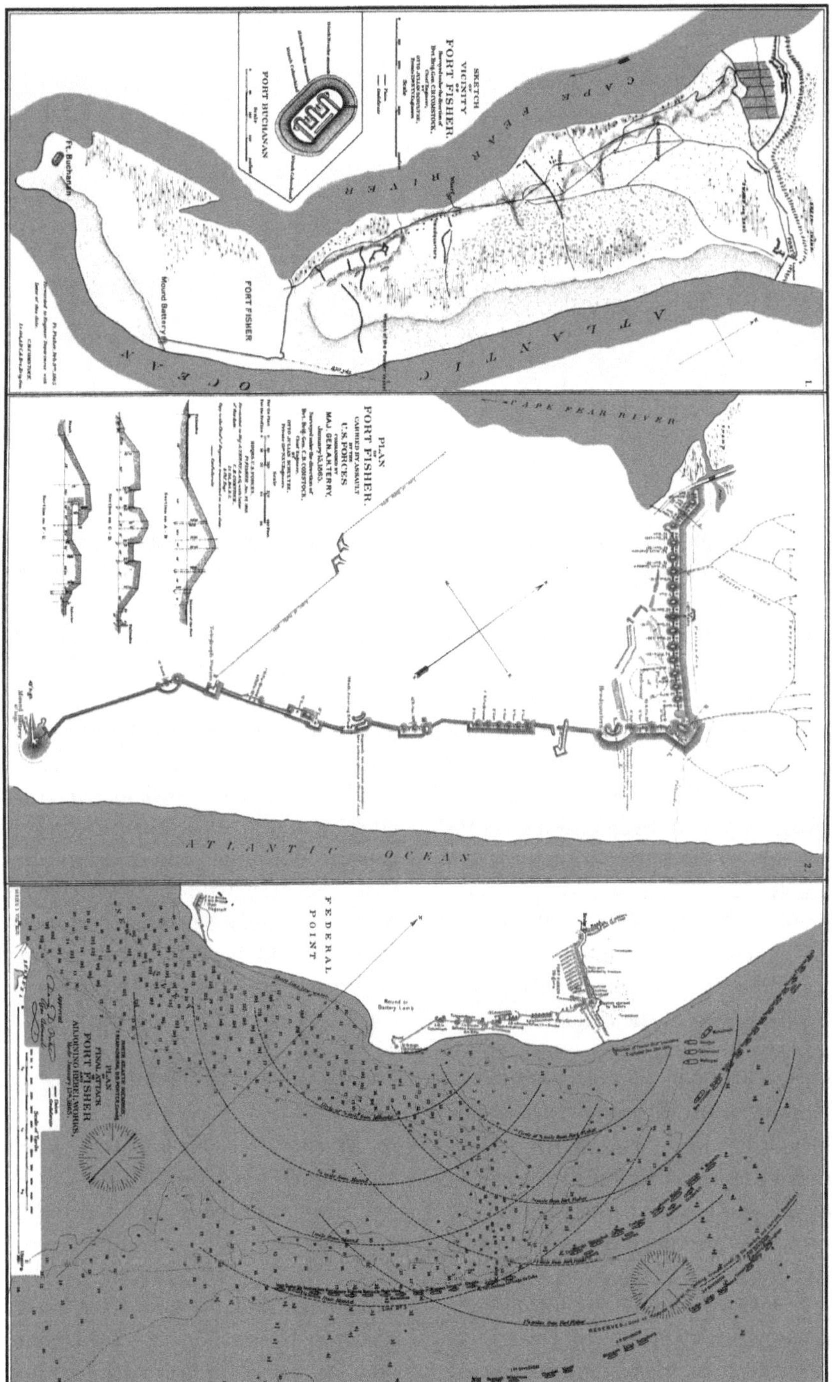

Battle of Fort Fisher map. A distant view of the fort complex on the left, a closeup of the fort in the center, and the Union fleet on the right.

Union Fleet Bombarding Fort Fisher.

decided to cancel the attack. He withdrew his infantry from the beach and returned to Virginia.[56]

From their station at Fort Fisher, Lamb and Whiting were shocked yet delighted to watch the Union fleet withdraw on December 27. But they were certain that the federals would soon return and remained as vigilant as ever. In Wilmington, meanwhile, Bragg seemed as overconfident as his two subordinates were concerned. On January 12, 1865, he staged a grand review of Major General Robert F. Hoke's veteran division, which General Lee had sent to bolster the Cape Fear defenses. Two of the brigades, Clingman's and Kirkland's, consisted of North Carolina regiments.[57]

In the North, outrage over the failed Fort Fisher expedition led to a congressional investigation of the causes as well as Butler's dismissal from the army. After sacking Butler, Grant made preparations for a second attack on Fort Fisher. Though unenthusiastic about the first expedition, Grant now took a personal interest in ensuring the success of the second. This was because his most trusted subordinate, General Sherman, had just completed the March to the Sea by capturing Savannah and planned to advance north through the Carolinas with his army group. His ultimate destination was Virginia, where he would join Grant. Together they would defeat Lee's army and bring the war to a victorious conclusion. But first Grant intended to capture Wilmington in order to provide Sherman with a coastal haven midway between Savannah and Richmond should he need one. Capturing Fort Fisher now assumed top priority for the Union general in chief.[58]

SECOND BATTLE OF FORT FISHER

As Sherman readied his army group for a winter march through the Carolinas, Grant sent the second Fort Fisher expeditionary force on its way. His replacement for Butler was the capable Brigadier General Alfred H. Terry, whose Provisional Corps—as his command was officially designated—numbered almost ten thousand troops. The Union fleet—reduced to a still-formidable fifty-eight ships—arrived off Fort Fisher on the night of January 12, 1865. Because Bragg had reviewed Hoke's division at Wilmington that day, they were in no position to contest the federals' landing the next morning. By the time the Confederates arrived on January 13, the Union infantry was already ashore and deploying for the assault. While a part of the federal armada provided covering fire for the soldiers on the beach, the remainder subjected Fort Fisher to a bombardment lasting two-and-a-half days. From January 13–15, the six-hundred-odd Union guns fired 19,682 rounds in what proved to be the second-largest naval barrage of the Civil War. Porter ordered his gunners to concentrate their fire on the fort's landface artillery on the northern end of the fort to knock out the guns trained on the ground across which Terry's infantry would soon attack. The intensive shelling disabled all but one gun along the landface and inflicted over three hundred killed and wounded among the defenders. Overcome by the relentless storm of iron and lead, the survivors huddled inside the fort's bombproof shelters.[59]

Alfred H. Terry.

Whiting sent several messages to Bragg warning him of the dire situation inside the fort and pleading for support. That morning, Bragg had led Hoke's division to Sugar Loaf, a hill about five miles north of Fort Fisher, and had the men dig in there. He attempted to land reinforcements at Battery Buchanan at the tip of Confederate Point, but only five hundred troops managed to disembark before Union gunboats drove off the transport. After that, Bragg made no further effort to relieve the fort but awaited the outcome behind Hoke's entrenchments. Whiting, Lamb, and the rest of the Fort Fisher garrison were on their own.

At 3:25 PM on January 15, Porter's warships blew their steam whistles to signal the attack. While the 3,500 blueclad soldiers of Brigadier General Adelbert Ames's division rushed the shell-torn landface, a naval force of more than two thousand sailors and marines raced down the beach toward the Northeast Bastion, where the fort's seaface and landface ramparts converged. (The seaface was the eastern part of the fort that faced the Atlantic Ocean.) The Union tars ran headlong into the deadly musketry of five hundred Confederates under the personal command of Whiting and Lamb. Within thirty minutes, the defenders killed or wounded roughly three hundred federals and forced the remainder to withdraw.[60]

"Siege of Fort Fisher" by J. O. Davidson. (*National Museum of the U.S. Navy*)

Although the assault of Porter's naval contingent had failed, it drew the attention of most of the fort's defenders, enabling Ames's infantry to force its way into Shepherd's Battery on the western end of the landface. Though heavily outnumbered, Whiting attempted to lead a desperate counterattack against the federals inside the fort, but he was severely wounded and had to be carried off. Thirty minutes later, Lamb led a second counterattack and was also gravely wounded. After the two ranking Confederates were knocked out of action, the defense of the fort settled into a brutal hand-to-hand struggle that raged for several hours along the parapets and on the parade ground below. By 9:00 PM, the Union attackers had driven the Confederates out of the fort toward Battery Buchanan. The garrison—including the wounded Whiting and Lamb— arrived there expecting to escape by ship to the west side of the Cape Fear River, but the Confederates stationed at Buchanan had fled with all of the boats.[61]

Stranded, the garrison waited for the federals, who overtook them about 10:00 PM. Whiting surrendered to Terry while lying on a stretcher; a few months later, he died of complications from his wounds while in a military prison in New York City. Lamb survived his injuries and became a hero to the people of Wilmington after the war. Bragg, however, came under fire from Whiting and others for failing to act while Fort Fisher was under attack. The entire Confederate force of 1,900 became casualties—five hundred killed or wounded and the remainder captured. Union losses totaled more than one thousand. The fort was now in federal hands, and though Wilmington itself had not yet fallen, it was closed to blockade-running traffic. As General Lee had feared, the Confederacy could no longer obtain supplies for his army from the outside world. And with Sherman once again on the move, the situation was about to become even more desperate.[62]

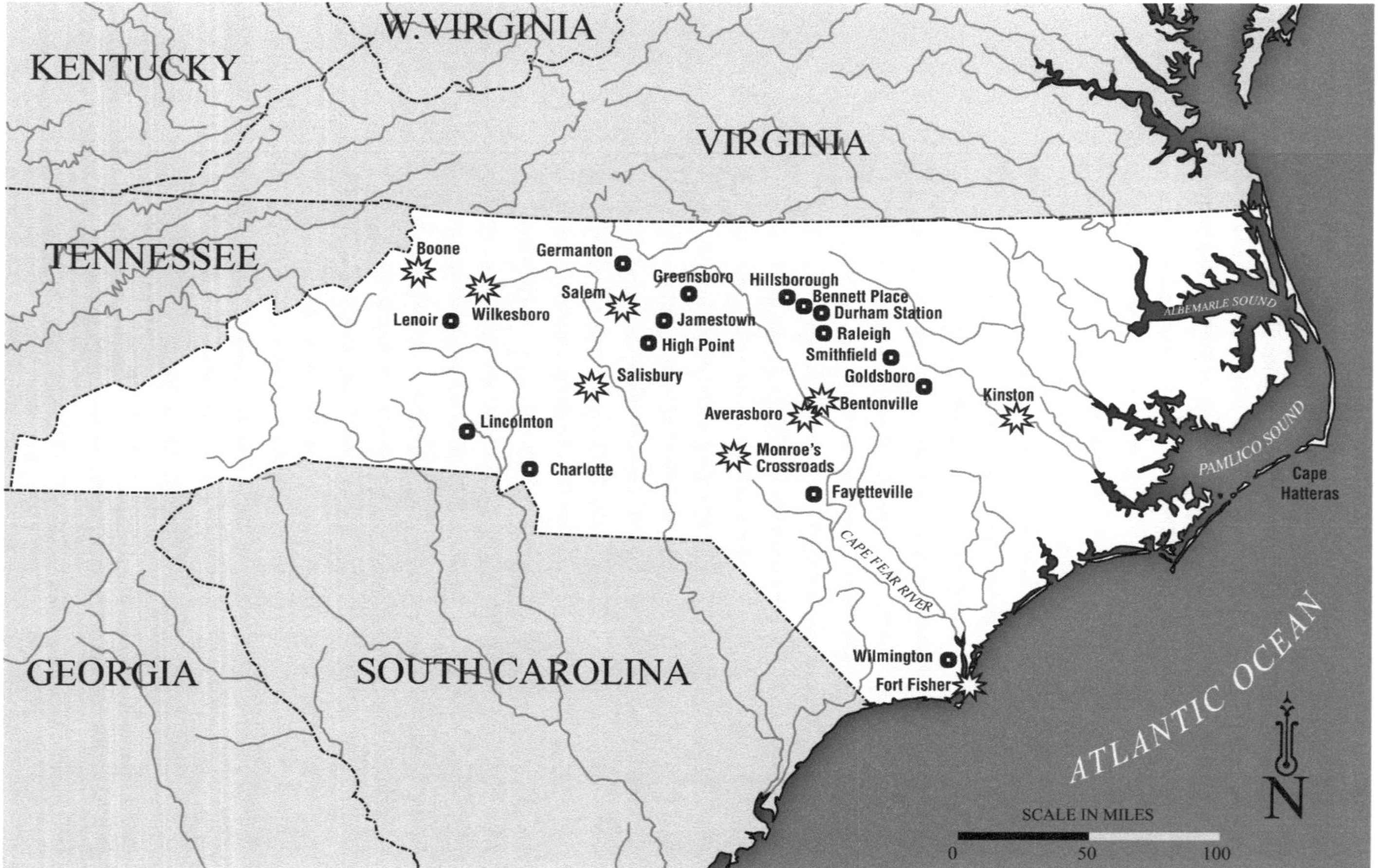
KENTUCKY
W. VIRGINIA
VIRGINIA
TENNESSEE
GEORGIA
SOUTH CAROLINA
Boone
Germanton
Greensboro
Hillsborough
Bennett Place
Durham Station
Salem
Lenoir
Wilkesboro
Jamestown
High Point
Raleigh
Smithfield
Goldsboro
Salisbury
Bentonville
Averasboro
Kinston
Lincolnton
Monroe's Crossroads
Charlotte
Fayetteville
CAPE FEAR RIVER
Wilmington
Fort Fisher
ALBEMARLE SOUND
PAMLICO SOUND
Cape Hatteras
ATLANTIC OCEAN
N
SCALE IN MILES
0
50
100

10. The Final Months of the Civil War

SHERMAN STRIKES NORTH

After concluding his March to the Sea by presenting the city of Savannah to President Lincoln as a Christmas gift, General Sherman planned his next move—a march north through the Carolinas to Richmond, Virginia, the capital of the Confederacy. Sherman would combine forces with Grant, and together they would defeat Lee's army, bringing the war to a victorious conclusion for the Union. As he had done on the March to the Sea, Sherman divided his army group into two wings comprising two infantry corps each. Major General Oliver O. Howard's Army of the Tennessee was the right wing, while Major General Henry W. Slocum's Army of Georgia was the left wing. In addition, Sherman had a cavalry division commanded by Brigadier General Judson Kilpatrick.

At the start of the Carolinas Campaign, Sherman's army group numbered 60,079 officers and enlisted men. Most of the soldiers were veteran volunteers who had enlisted during the first two years of the war and then reenlisted after their two- or three-year enlistments had expired. They were the survivors of what one soldier described as "a rigorous weeding-out process" effected by Rebel bullets, hardship, and disease. Moreover, prior to the Savannah and Carolinas Campaigns, Sherman ordered the Medical Department to examine all soldiers and ship out those unfit for campaigning. As a result, the force Sherman led in the closing months of the war had no equal.[1]

"Uncle Billy"—as Sherman's men called him—had hoped to begin his campaign in early January 1865, but torrential winter rains that flooded the Savannah River and transformed the South Carolina roads into quagmires compelled him to postpone the start for about a month. While Sherman waited for the deluge to subside, Grant directed Major General George H. Thomas, the Union commander at Nashville, to transfer Major General John M. Schofield's XXIII Corps to North Carolina, where it would combine with Terry's Provisional Corps, which had just captured Fort Fisher. On December 16, 1864, Thomas's

William T. Sherman.

Army of the Cumberland had routed General John Bell Hood's Army of Tennessee, the Confederacy's second-largest field army. With Hood's army virtually eliminated, the XXIII Corps and other units in Thomas's army became available for duty elsewhere.

Assuming command of the newly reestablished Department of North Carolina, Schofield's first task was to capture Wilmington to provide Sherman with a safe haven on the coast should he need one. But Grant identified an even more desirable objective about ninety miles north of Wilmington: Goldsboro. It was the inland junction of two coastal railroads, providing rail connections with New Bern and Wilmington. Goldsboro thus became the site where Sherman's army group would rest and resupply before resuming the march to Richmond.[2]

In preparing for the Carolinas Campaign, Sherman stripped his army down to fighting trim. He reduced the wagons to 2,500 and the ambulances to six hundred, and while the ordnance trains carried plenty of ammunition, the commissary wagons hauled just seven days' forage and twenty days' provisions. As on the March to the Sea, the federals lived off the land, relying on detachments of foragers, or "bummers," to feed the army. Sherman also held the number of cannons to sixty-eight, or roughly one gun per thousand men.

Opposing the Union invasion of South Carolina was a ragtag collection of Confederate forces led by General Pierre G. T. Beauregard, the commander of the Military Division of the West. He claimed to have 33,450 troops, but this figure was based on anticipated reinforcements as well as soldiers on hand. The actual number of officers and men present came to about one-half of Beauregard's optimistic estimate. Rather than risk losing his heavily outnumbered command by offering battle to Sherman at the start of the campaign, Beauregard sought to hold Charleston, South Carolina, and Augusta, Georgia, "for as long as it was humanly possible" in order to negotiate from a position of strength. The "pending negotiations for peace" on which he based his strategy proved to be the Hampton Roads Conference. Held on February 3, 1865, the meeting at Hampton Roads, Virginia, between President Lincoln and Confederate Vice President Alexander H. Stephens was amicable but failed to end the war. Beauregard's decision to divide his forces thus played into Sherman's hands, for it enabled the federals to march virtually uncontested through the center of the state.[3]

As Sherman's army group marched into South Carolina, the scattered

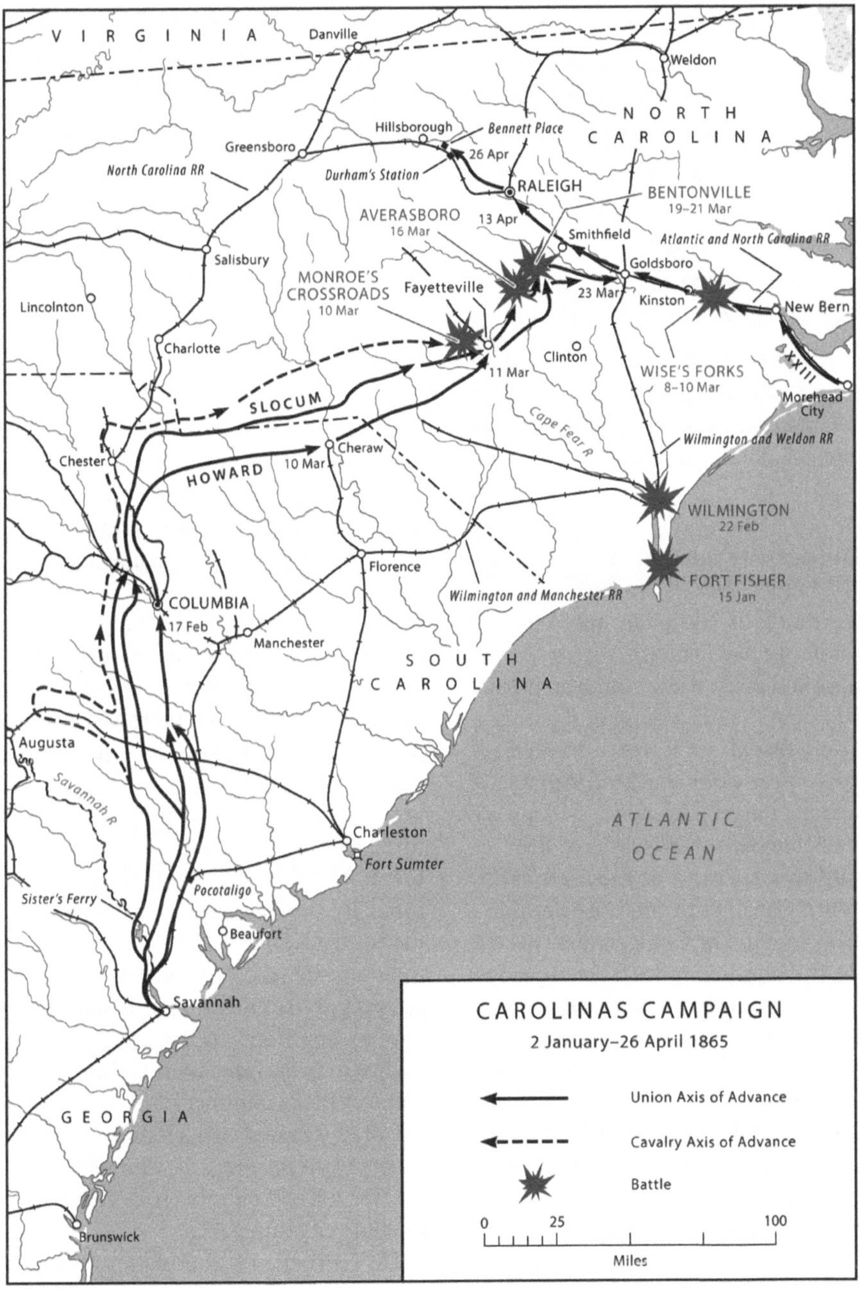

The Carolinas Campaign, 1865. (*Sherry Dowdy, CMH*)

Joseph E. Johnston. (*National Archives*)

Confederates attempted to unite and give battle. After its crushing defeat in the Battle of Nashville, the Army of Tennessee had fled into eastern Mississippi and made winter camp at Tupelo. "If not in the strict sense of the word a disorganized mob," reported inspection officer Colonel Alfred Roman, "it was no longer an army." In January 1865, President Davis ordered Beauregard to send most of the remnant to South Carolina to oppose Sherman's army group. The Confederates covered the five hundred miles from Tupelo to Augusta on foot, by boat, and by train. Discipline was uncertain at best. Beauregard's quartermaster, Captain John M. Goodman, was less charitable than Colonel Roman. He called the Army of Tennessee "a complete mob. I have never witnessed so much demoralization in my life. I have feared for my life in contending with our own troops and in the attempt to keep them in some kind of discipline."[4]

Sherman's Carolinas Campaign began on February 1 under less than auspicious circumstances. Beauregard and other Confederates hoped that the heavy winter rains would cause Sherman's long wagon trains to bog down in the swampy terrain, forcing the federals to abandon the undertaking. General Joseph E. Johnston, who lived in Columbia, South Carolina, at the time, later noted that Lieutenant General William J. Hardee, the Confederate commander at Charleston, had assured him Sherman's army group could never pass through the swamps bordering the Salkehatchie River in the southern part of the Palmetto State. But Hardee was wrong. "When I learned that Sherman's army was marching through the Salkehatchie swamps, making its own corduroy road at the rate of a dozen miles a day or more, and bringing its artillery and wagons with it," Johnston confessed, "I made up my mind that there had been no such army in existence since the days of Julius Caesar."[5]

Sherman's modern-day legions captured Columbia on February 17 after brushing aside a small Confederate force. By the next morning, much of the South Carolina capital was reduced to ashes, the result of a conflagration caused by burning cotton—initially set afire by Southern cavalry—spread by high winds and drunken Union soldiers. In the meantime, Hardee's command evacuated Charleston under orders from Beauregard, who realized that the fall of Columbia had rendered the port city untenable.

On February 19, Sherman resumed his march north, and Beauregard once again misjudged his route. Convinced that Sherman was on his way to Petersburg, Virginia, via Charlotte and

Greensboro, North Carolina, Beauregard ordered Hardee to board his troops on trains at Wilmington and rush them to Greensboro. There was only one problem: Schofield's Union force was about to capture Wilmington.

The Wilmington Campaign had begun February 11. General Terry's Provisional Corps advanced from Fort Fisher up the east side of the Cape Fear River, only to find that Hoke's division still blocked his path at Sugar Loaf. Concluding that the Confederate fortifications were too strong to carry by frontal assault, Schofield crossed a division of the XXIII Corps to the west side of the river, supported by Admiral Porter's gunboats. On February 18, the Union division attacked Confederate-held Fort Anderson about fifteen miles south of Wilmington. While Porter's gunboats silenced the fort's artillery, the federal infantry encircled the stronghold, forcing the garrison back to Town Creek, while Hoke withdrew to Forks Road on the east side. The Confederates now occupied a line just a few miles south of Wilmington. Terry attempted to overwhelm Hoke's well-fortified position, launching several assaults with roughly 1,600 US Colored Troops. Hoke's men repulsed the attacks, buying time for the Confederates to evacuate or destroy their stores, but by the afternoon of February 21, it was apparent to General Bragg, the commander of the Department of North Carolina, that the fall of the city was at hand.[6]

The deteriorating situation at Wilmington meant a change of plans for Hardee's corps. Bragg warned Hardee that the federals had cut the Wilmington and Manchester Railroad, necessitating an alternate route to Cheraw, South Carolina. As expected, Wilmington fell to Schofield's command on February 22, while Sherman's army group abruptly shifted its advance more easterly and threatened to beat Hardee to Cheraw.[7]

By now, the Confederacy's newly appointed general in chief, Robert E. Lee, had concluded that Beauregard could not stop Sherman. A subsequent message from Beauregard outlining a grandiose scheme in which the Confederate army would defeat Grant and Sherman separately and then "march on Washington to dictate a peace" convinced both Lee and President Davis that Beauregard could not come to grips with military reality.

Lee wished to replace Beauregard with General Johnston, but Davis had dismissed him from command of the Army of Tennessee the previous July and had since kept him in virtual retirement. Lee was persistent, however: he obtained Secretary of War John C. Breckinridge's permission—and by implication Davis's grudging consent—to return Johnston to duty. On February 22, Lee wired Johnston: "Assume command of the Army of Tennessee and all troops in the Department of South Carolina, Georgia, and Florida. Assign General Beauregard to duty under you, as you may select. Concentrate all available forces and drive back Sherman."[8]

Like many other refugees from Columbia, Johnston had fled to Lincolnton, North Carolina, in late February, hoping Sherman would bypass that backwater of the Confederacy. But Lee's order thrust Johnston back into the thick of it. "It is too late to expect me to concentrate troops capable of driving back Sherman," Johnston replied. "The remnant of the Army of Tennessee is much divided. So are other troops."

On February 23, Johnston traveled to Charlotte to begin concentrating his scattered forces. After meeting with Beauregard and appointing him second in command, Johnston examined the remnants of his old Army of Tennessee. As the commanding general passed each brigade on review, "three cheers were given in a joyful tone and manner expressive of great satisfaction," wrote an Alabama soldier. "The old general looks as usual hearty and soldier like. . . . He is as well loved in this army among the men, as an officer can be. They have every confidence in him, and that alone will benefit the army and the service."[9]

Though Johnston was grateful for the enthusiastic welcome from the Army of Tennessee veterans, the reviews merely confirmed what he had suspected about his army's condition. On February 25, he informed Lee that his small force was "too weak to cope with Sherman." Altogether, the Army of Tennessee contingent, Hardee's command, and the Confederate cavalry led by Lieutenant General Wade Hampton totaled fewer than twenty-five thousand troops.

On March 3, Hardee's corps evacuated Cheraw just ahead of the Union right wing and marched toward Fayetteville, North Carolina. When it became apparent that Sherman would enter the Old North State, Lee transferred Bragg's Department of North Carolina troops to Johnston's command. Bragg's force consisted mainly of Hoke's division from the Army of Northern Virginia and the North Carolina Junior Reserves Brigade, whose ranks were filled with teenage boys. Johnston, meanwhile, traveled from Charlotte to Fayetteville to be nearer Sherman's line of march. Encouraged by the federals' difficult South Carolina river crossings, Johnston planned to unite the Army of Tennessee contingent with Hardee's corps in time to contest Sherman's crossing of the Cape Fear River at Fayetteville. But Bragg, whose small force had retreated to Kinston, North Carolina, about eighty miles east, saw a better opportunity on his front and asked Johnston to send the Army of Tennessee troops to him instead.[10]

THE BATTLE OF WISE'S FORKS

In early March, Schofield sent the Union XXIII Corps under Major General Jacob D. Cox, about thirteen thousand strong, inland from New Bern to secure Goldsboro for Sherman. But Bragg had other plans. He intended to defeat Cox and prevent the junction of the XXIII Corps and Sherman's army group. Canceling his plan to attack Sherman at Fayetteville, Johnston instead granted Bragg's request but directed him to send the Army of Tennessee troops to Smithfield, North Carolina, as soon as possible for use against Sherman. The troop transfer led to an uneasy alliance between Bragg and Major General D. H. Hill, the commander of the Army of Tennessee contingent. The two men had been bitter enemies since Bragg had dismissed Hill from corps command eighteen months earlier. Johnston closed his dispatch to Hill ordering him to join Bragg with a plea "to forget the past for this emergency." Hill swallowed his pride and reported to Bragg as ordered. The addition of the Army of Tennessee contingent gave Bragg a total of about 6,100 troops.[11]

On March 8, Cox's federals collided with Bragg's Confederates at Wise's Forks, about four miles east of Kinston. Early in the battle, the Southerners routed a portion of the Union force, capturing over eight hundred men. The remainder of Cox's troops dug in that night, and the two sides skirmished the following day. On March 10, the Confederates renewed the offensive, but the well-entrenched federals inflicted heavy casualties on the Southern attackers, including Kirkland's North Carolina brigade. Learning that Cox had been reinforced, Bragg withdrew to Kinston that night. Once again, the hapless Bragg had seen an apparent victory end in retreat. In the Battle of Wise's Forks, the federals had sustained 1,337 casualties compared to the Confederates' 800.[12]

While Bragg fell back toward Goldsboro, Johnston resumed his efforts to field an army against Sherman by means of the North Carolina Railroad, which formed a 220-mile arc from Charlotte in the western part of the state to Goldsboro in the east. Unfortunately for the Confederates, a 120-car backlog of troops, artillery, and supplies had piled up at Salisbury, while sixty-five more carloads waited at Chester, South Carolina. The bottlenecks resulted from a narrowing of the track gauge at Salisbury, and most of the narrow-gauge rolling stock sent to Bragg at Kinston had not yet returned

Jacob D. Cox. (*Gilder Lehrman Institute of American History*)

from the front. Although Bragg's monopolization of the railroad had caused the backlog, Johnston's failure to intervene only worsened the problem. At stake was the Confederate chieftain's ability to strike Sherman with every available soldier. When the moment of truth arrived, many of Johnston's troops were still stranded at Salisbury.

With the federals advancing in superior force on two fronts, the concentration of his own army impeded by delays on the railroad, and that army dependent on a sparsely settled region for subsistence, prospects appeared bleak for Johnston. "I will not give battle with Sherman's united army," he informed Lee on March 11, "but will if I can find it divided." In the meantime, Johnston attempted to gather his own scattered army in the desperate hope he could defeat either Sherman or Schofield before the two Union forces combined.[13]

Judson Kilpatrick.

THE BATTLE OF MONROE'S CROSSROADS

As Sherman's army group swept into North Carolina during the first week of March, Kilpatrick's cavalry division led the way, clashing repeatedly with Hampton's Confederate cavalry, which served as the rear guard for Hardee's corps during the march to Fayetteville. On March 7, Hampton discovered that Kilpatrick had slipped around his flank and gotten between him and Hardee. "As soon as my command can be concentrated," Hampton informed Hardee, "I shall move round the left flank of the enemy to his front." This maneuver proved more difficult to execute than Hampton had anticipated, and Kilpatrick continued to obstruct his progress. The Union cavalry commander nevertheless remained unaware of his advantage until the afternoon of March 9, when some captured Confederates revealed that a large force of Yankee cavalry had driven a wedge between Hampton and Hardee. Despite a recent order from Sherman to avoid battle for the present, Kilpatrick decided to block the roads to Fayetteville in order to prevent Hampton from rejoining Hardee. In doing so, Kilpatrick recklessly divided his command, which contained about the same number of horsemen as Hampton's cavalry. Kilpatrick was inviting Hampton to defeat him in detail, and the latter eagerly accepted his invitation.[14]

On the evening of March 9, Kilpatrick and two of his four brigades—numbering about 1,500 troopers in all—made camp at Monroe's Crossroads. A torrential downpour and the presence of Confederate cavalry prevented his two remaining brigades from taking up their assigned positions, leaving the Union cavalry commander's bivouac isolated and vulnerable to attack—which was exactly what Hampton had in mind. Several thousand Confederate troopers spent the cold, rainy night deploying for an assault on Kilpatrick's camp. Hopes ran high among the Southerners that they would deal the federals a stunning blow at Monroe's Crossroads and perhaps bag "Little Kil" in the process. Hampton's force consisted of Major General Joseph Wheeler's cavalry corps and Major General Matthew C. Butler's cavalry division from the Army of Northern Virginia, totaling roughly four thousand horse soldiers.[15]

As dawn broke on the morning of March 10, Butler's cavalry burst out of the woods from the north and Wheeler's horsemen from the west. Shrieking the Rebel yell, they overran the lightly guarded federal camp. Kilpatrick witnessed the onslaught from the porch of the Monroe house, which served as his headquarters. He later recalled that his first thought was, "My God, here's a Major General's commission after four years' hard fighting gone up with an infernal surprise." Dressed only in his shirt, pants, and slippers, Kilpatrick fled into a nearby swamp along with many of his men, but a large number had the presence of mind to carry their weapons with them. This enabled the federal troopers to launch a counterattack when the initial Confederate charge lost momentum.

After a furious close-quarters struggle that lasted over an hour, the federals drove off the Confederates and regained their camp. But the Southerners had opened the road to Fayetteville and freed all their captured comrades. The Battle of Monroe's Crossroads was a moral victory for the Confederates, who had demonstrated that they still posed a serious threat to an unwary adversary. It was also something of an embarrassment for Sherman's cavalry commander—after all, waggish Union infantrymen dubbed the Rebel surprise attack "Kilpatrick's Shirttail Skedaddle."

Casualty figures for Monroe's Crossroads are sketchy at best. Although Kilpatrick reported a total of 190 killed, wounded, and missing, the actual figure is probably closer to 250. The Confederate casualty figures are likewise incomplete, amounting to fewer than ninety, and yet Kilpatrick reported that his men had buried about eighty Southern dead and captured thirty prisoners. Regardless of the Confederates' total casualties, the battle cost Hampton's cavalry dearly, resulting in the loss of one regimental commander killed and six division and brigade commanders with wounds of varying severity.[16]

Wade Hampton.

THE BATTLE OF AVERASBORO

Sherman's army group entered Fayetteville on March 11 and remained there for four days. While most of the men rested, the 1st Michigan Engineers and Mechanics demolished the Confederate arsenal there under orders from the commanding general. Sherman, meanwhile, plotted the final leg of his 450-mile march to Goldsboro. As usual, the plan included a feint—this time toward Raleigh, the North Carolina capital, with Kilpatrick's cavalry and four divisions of Slocum's wing in light marching order. The remaining two divisions would escort all nonessential wagons in the rear of Howard's wing. Slocum would advance up the Plank Road to within four miles of Averasboro and then head east on the Goldsboro Road via Bentonville. In the meantime, Kilpatrick's cavalry and one division of

William J. Hardee.

infantry would continue feinting on Raleigh before veering off toward Goldsboro. Of Slocum's march toward Bentonville, Sherman wrote, "I do think it is Johnston's only chance to meet this army before an easy junction with Schofield can be effected."

While Sherman's army group rested at Fayetteville, Hardee's Corps halted at Smithville (not to be confused with Smithfield, North Carolina), about five miles south of Averasboro. Since evacuating Charleston in mid-February, Hardee had lost one-half of his thirteen thousand troops to straggling, desertion, and South Carolina Governor Andrew Magrath's militia recalls. The general decided he had better fight before the rest of his demoralized command melted away. He also sought to buy time for the concentration of Johnston's army. Hardee deployed his corps in three lines, placing the relatively inexperienced soldiers of Brigadier General William B. Taliaferro's division on the first two lines and entrusting the third and main line to the more seasoned troops of Major General Lafayette McLaws's division.[17]

Sherman's army group resumed the advance on March 15, with Kilpatrick's cavalry preceding Slocum's wing up the Plank Road. About midafternoon, Kilpatrick's lead regiment collided with Confederates from Hardee's command, and the two sides skirmished for several hours. While working their way through no-man's-land, three Union cavalry scouts captured one of Taliaferro's brigade commanders, Colonel Alfred M. Rhett, who was riding between the lines with just one staff officer. Before being turned over to the provost marshal, Rhett spent the evening with some old acquaintances—namely Generals Sherman, Slocum, and XIV Corps commander Jefferson C. Davis, who had all been stationed at Charleston, Rhett's hometown, before the war. At nightfall, the fighting ceased, and the two sides frantically dug fieldworks in preparation for a battle the next day. "Hardee is ahead of me and shows fight," Sherman wrote early on March 16. "I will go at him in the morning with four divisions and push him as far as Averasborough before turning toward Bentonville and [Goldsboro]."[18]

The Battle of Averasboro began at dawn on March 16, amid a steady rain that fell for most of the day. Throughout the morning, Kilpatrick's cavalry and the federal XX Corps probed Hardee's first line for weaknesses. About noon, Sherman directed Slocum to send a brigade around the Confederate right flank. Slocum chose Colonel Henry Case's XX Corps brigade, whose surprise flank attack routed the Confederates of Rhett's brigade manning the first line. "[T]he Johnnies showed their heels as fast as God would let them," wrote an Illinois soldier who participated in the assault. Soon afterward, the federals drove back the second line held by Brigadier General Stephen Elliott's brigade. As Brigadier General James D. Morgan's division of the Union XIV Corps attacked on the left in order to outflank Hardee's third line, two small divisions of Wheeler's Confederate cavalry arrived just in time to plug the gap. With Hardee's line now extending from the Cape Fear River on his right to the swamps bordering the Black River on the left, Sherman decided to postpone making a general assault until the next morning. At nightfall, however, Hardee began to evacuate his position. When federal skirmishers advanced at dawn on March 17, they discovered that the Confederates had withdrawn.[19]

Hardee's delaying action at Averasboro had succeeded in checking Sherman's advance for one day, buying Johnston invaluable time to concentrate his forces. In addition, Hardee had given his green troops their first taste of field combat and had boosted their sagging morale. For his part, Sherman had driven Hardee toward Smithfield, thus opening the road to Goldsboro. The Confederates suffered about 500 casualties—most of them coming from Rhett's Brigade—while the federal losses amounted to 682. Of that number, 533 were wounded who had to be transported with the column. Hence Sherman's decision to press Hardee on March 16 rather than risk a full-scale assault, because he knew that each additional wounded man would further slow his progress.[20]

Henry W. Slocum.

JOHNSTON SETS A TRAP FOR SHERMAN

The day before the Battle of Averasboro, Johnston had traveled to Smithfield, where his army was converging. He chose that point to concentrate his forces because it stood midway between Raleigh to the west and Goldsboro to the east, Sherman's two most likely objectives. Arriving at Smithfield were Hoke's division under Bragg and the remnant of the Army of Tennessee, which the Confederate commander placed under Lieutenant General Alexander P. Stewart. Johnston formed the Army of the South from the four distinct forces under his command: Hardee's corps, Hoke's division (which now included the teenage Junior Reserves Brigade), the Army of Tennessee contingent, and Hampton's cavalry. By mid-March, Johnston could field about twenty thousand troops against Sherman's sixty-thousand-man army group.[21]

After the Battle of Averasboro, Hardee marched toward Smithfield to join Johnston's army. He told the Confederate chieftain that he believed Sherman was heading to Goldsboro. On the evening of March 17, Johnston notified Hardee that it was time to act. "Something must be done to-morrow morning," Johnston wrote, "and yet I have no satisfactory information as to the enemy's movements. Can you give me any certain information of the force you engaged yesterday?" Hardee's reply is lost, but it probably indicated that Hampton was better informed as to the federals' current status. Johnston ordered Bragg and Stewart to be prepared to march at dawn. He then sent a message to Hampton instructing him to send all the information he had regarding the position and strength of the federal columns, their distance from Goldsboro, and whether Hampton thought it possible to intercept one of the columns before it reached its destination.

Hampton replied that the two federal wings were indeed heading toward Goldsboro and were widely separated. He noted that the nearest Union column—Slocum's wing—advancing up the road from Averasboro was more than a day's march from his headquarters at the Willis Cole plantation south of Bentonville. The cavalry commander suggested that the plantation would make an excellent site for a surprise attack and assured Johnston that he could delay the federal advance long enough to enable the Confederate army to arrive from Smithfield.

Johnston received Hampton's reply at dawn on March 18. A glance at the state map told him that the two federal wings were a dozen miles apart and separated by a day's march. He therefore decided to attack Slocum's wing as it moved up the Goldsboro Road. "We will go to the place at which your dispatch was written," Johnston informed Hampton. "The scheme mentioned in my note, which you pronounce practicable, will be attempted." But the Confederates were unaware that the maps of the area were wildly inaccurate, leading Johnston to underestimate Hardee's distance from Bentonville while exaggerating the distance separating the Union columns. Although Bragg and Stewart reached Bentonville at nightfall, Hardee's corps was still six miles north of the village when it halted at 9:00 PM.[22]

In the meantime, the federals marched to within five miles of the Cole plantation on the afternoon of March 18. Sherman remained cautious as his army group approached Bentonville, the two Union wings marching only a few miles apart. "I think it probable that Joe Johnston will try to prevent our getting Goldsboro," he wrote Howard about 2:00 PM. A few hours later, Sherman received two messages that caused him to drop his guard. First, Kilpatrick informed him that Hardee was retreating toward Smithfield and Johnston was concentrating his army a few miles south of Raleigh. Second, XIV Corps skirmishers reported that the Rebels had burned the bridge across Mill Creek on the Smithfield-Clinton Road. According to Sherman's faulty map, the Confederates had just cut their only approach route to Bentonville, indicating a retreat toward Raleigh. Unknown to the federals, Sherman's map omitted the Smithfield-Bentonville Road—or the "Devil's Race Path"—that Bragg and Stewart were using. Sherman now believed that Johnston had conceded Goldsboro to him. Although several Union foraging details returned to camp that night reporting stiff resistance from Confederate cavalry, Union generals ignored their warnings. On the evening of March 18, the federals' point of vulnerability was not the distance separating their columns but their growing overconfidence.[23]

While Sherman camped several miles to the southwest, Johnston conferred with Hampton at his headquarters near Bentonville. Having arrived too late to reconnoiter the proposed battlefield, Johnston relied on Hampton to devise a plan of attack based on his study of the ground. The plan exploited the densely wooded terrain surrounding the Cole house, where Hampton recommended launching the assault. The Confederate cavalry commander suggested that Johnston deploy Hoke's division across the Goldsboro Road to block the federals' advance and conceal Hardee's corps and Stewart's Army of Tennessee in the thick woods north of the road. At a designated time, Hardee and Stewart would burst out of the woods and rout the Union column before it could deploy into line of battle. Although he regretted that Hardee's corps stood farther than the federal advance from the battlefield, Johnston approved Hampton's plan and directed the deployment to begin at dawn, bearing in mind that this might be his final opportunity to strike Sherman with any hope of success.[24]

THE BATTLE OF BENTONVILLE

Sunrise on Sunday, March 19, revealed a beautiful spring day. The awakening Union soldiers enjoyed the mild early morning air and the sight of budding apple and peach trees. Their thoughts were far removed from battle and focused instead on reaching Goldsboro, where new shoes, clean clothes, and mail from home awaited them. "We feel in excellent spirits," Lieutenant John M. Branum of Morgan's XIV Corps division jotted in his diary. "Everything promises for a smooth entry into Goldsboro." This entry was Branum's last, for within a few hours, he would be killed in action.[25]

Believing that the danger of a Confederate attack had passed, Sherman prepared to rejoin Howard's wing at dawn on March 19 to communicate with General Schofield. Before his departure, Sherman conferred with Slocum and other Union generals at the crossroads leading to Howard's column. During the conversation, the XIV Corps commander, Brigadier General Jefferson C. Davis, said he thought his command would have to face more than the usual cavalry opposition. "No, Jeff," Sherman replied. "There is nothing there but [Colonel George G.] Dibrell's cavalry. Brush them out of the way. . . . I'll meet you tomorrow morning at Cox's Bridge." With that, Sherman led his staff and escort down the road toward Howard's column, unaware that Slocum's wing would not reach Cox's Bridge for another four days.[26]

Although Union foraging detachments reported that "the Rebels don't drive worth a damn," the federal advance, consisting of Brigadier General William P. Carlin's XIV Corps division, easily drove back Dibrell's small cavalry division. But the Southerners' re-

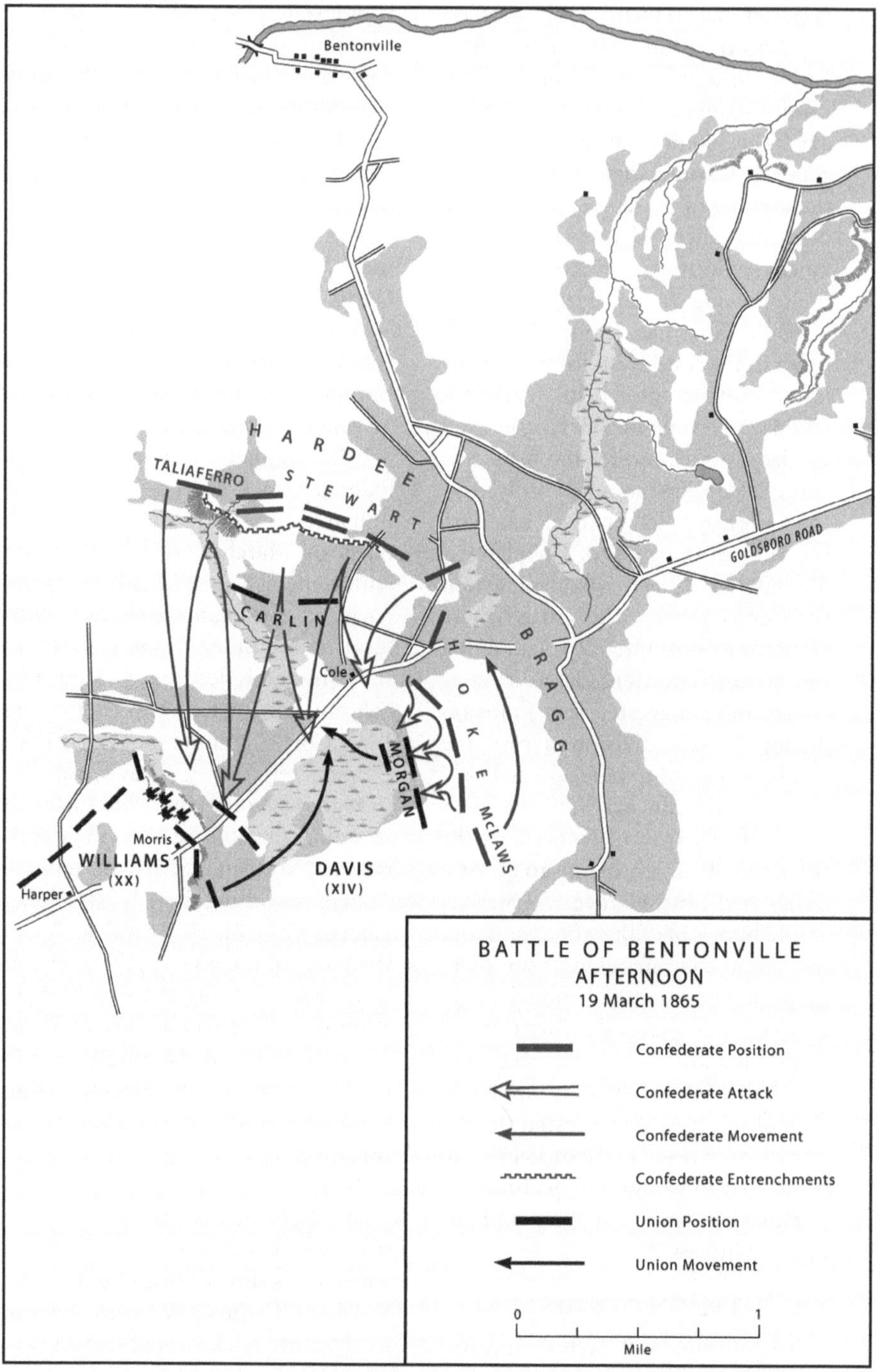

The Battle of Bentonville, March 19, 1865. Action during the afternoon. (*Sherry Dowdy, CMH*)

sistance stiffened at the Cole plantation, where Carlin's foot soldiers collided with a force far larger than Dibrell's cavalry. Carlin deployed all three of his brigades and still met with fierce opposition. Ignoring Carlin's plight, Slocum sent word to Sherman that he was merely skirmishing with stubborn Rebel cavalry and needed no assistance from Howard. Growing impatient, Slocum then ordered Carlin to launch an attack to develop the enemy's position and strength. About noon, Carlin assaulted the Confederate line at several points, only to meet with a bloody repulse.[27]

Undaunted, Slocum brought up Morgan's XIV Corps division on Carlin's right and was preparing to deploy the XX Corps on the same line in a more determined effort to outflank Johnston's position. But a Union prisoner of war who had made his escape during Carlin's repulse brought Slocum some startling intelligence: Johnston's entire army was on the field, and Joe Johnston himself had ridden among his troops, telling them they would crush one wing of Sherman's army at Bentonville and then attack the other wing and destroy it as well. If Slocum needed additional evidence of his predicament, he received it from a XIV Corps staff officer who reported, "Well, General, I have found something more than Dibrell's cavalry—I find [Confederate] infantry intrenched along our whole front, and enough of them to give us all the amusement we shall want for the rest of the day."

Slocum received the staff officer's report about 1:30 PM and immediately shifted to the defensive. The left wing commander kept his two XIV Corps divisions at the front to absorb the shock of the expected Confederate onslaught while deploying his two XX Corps divisions on more defensible ground at the Reddick Morris farm a mile to the rear. Slocum also sent Sherman a far more accurate assessment of the situation. As the afternoon wore on, Slocum's messages to the commanding general became increasingly urgent and were invariably accompanied by appeals for reinforcements from Howard's wing.[28]

For Johnston, the afternoon of March 19 was filled with annoying delays. With only one approach route from Bentonville to the battlefield, the Confederate deployment "consumed a weary time." When Carlin launched his noontime strike, only Hoke's division and Stewart's Army of Tennessee contingent were in position, while Hardee's corps was just arriving on the field. Worse yet for the Confederates, Carlin's probing attack delayed Johnston's own assault and led Bragg, the commander of Hoke's division, to plead for reinforcements. In response, Johnston sent him McLaws's division of Hardee's corps. This proved to be the Confederate chieftain's worst blunder of the day. By the time McLaws reached Bragg's position, Hoke's division had already repulsed the federal attack. Bragg then held the four-thousand-man division for much of the afternoon, depriving Johnston of one-fourth of his infantry when he needed it most.[29]

Johnston finally launched his assault at 2:45 PM. Hardee led the right wing of Johnston's army, consisting of the Army of Tennessee contingent and Taliaferro's division of Hardee's corps. An onlooker thought the Confederate advance "looked like a picture and . . . was truly beautiful." He also found it "painful to see how close their battle flags were together, regiments being scarcely larger than companies." Despite its depleted ranks, Hardee's wing overran Carlin's position north of the Goldsboro Road. "[We] stood as long as man can stand," wrote a Michigan soldier in Carlin's division, "& when that was no longer a possibility, [we] run like the duce." During the rout, Hardee's men captured two Union cannons and drove off Carlin's troops south of the road. Thus far, the Confederate assault was an unqualified success.[30]

The Confederates' accomplishment might have been greater still had Bragg's wing, consisting of Hoke's and McLaws's divisions, attacked when ordered. Instead, Bragg waited until 4:00 PM, more than an hour after the time Johnston had designated. Bragg may have delayed his assault pending the outcome of Hardee's charge, but such a course was indefensible because it would have been in defiance of Johnston's orders. In any event, Bragg gave the federals of Morgan's division a precious extra hour to strengthen their field fortifications, and they made the most of their opportunity.[31]

Morgan's stand south of the Goldsboro Road proved to be the turning point of the March 19 battle at Bentonville. Attacked in quick succession by Hoke's division along their front and left flank and by several brigades of the Army of Tennessee from their rear, Morgan's federals stubbornly clung to their swampy salient. During the desperate struggle, the soldiers in blue fought on both sides of their log works. One of Hoke's units, Lieutenant Colonel John D. Taylor's contingent of North Carolina "Red Infantry"—so called in recognition of the red trim on the artillerymen's uniforms—launched a desperate assault on Morgan's strong position. The charge cost the Tar Heels 152 losses out of 267 officers and men, a casualty rate of 57 percent. Colonel Taylor was severely wounded, losing his left arm to a Yankee bullet. Aided by the timely arrival of Brigadier General William Cogswell's XX Corps brigade, Morgan's troops repulsed the Confederates and turned the tide in the federals' favor.[32]

The Southerners' final assaults of the day were launched against the XX Corps' position on the Morris farm. Spearheaded by troops from Taliaferro's division and Major General Benjamin F. Cheatham's corps of the Army of Tennessee, the attacks constituted the Confederate army's high-water mark at Bentonville. Advancing several times to within point-blank range of the Union line, the Southerners braved a blistering small-arms and artillery fire before Johnston called off the offensive and ordered his army to return to its jump-off point. After some anxious moments, the federals had held on at Bentonville, and the March 19 fight ended in a draw.[33]

Sherman, meanwhile, received Slocum's appeals for reinforcements and rushed Howard's command to the left wing's support. Early on the morning of March 20, the Union right wing marched west on the Goldsboro Road toward the Confederate rear. While

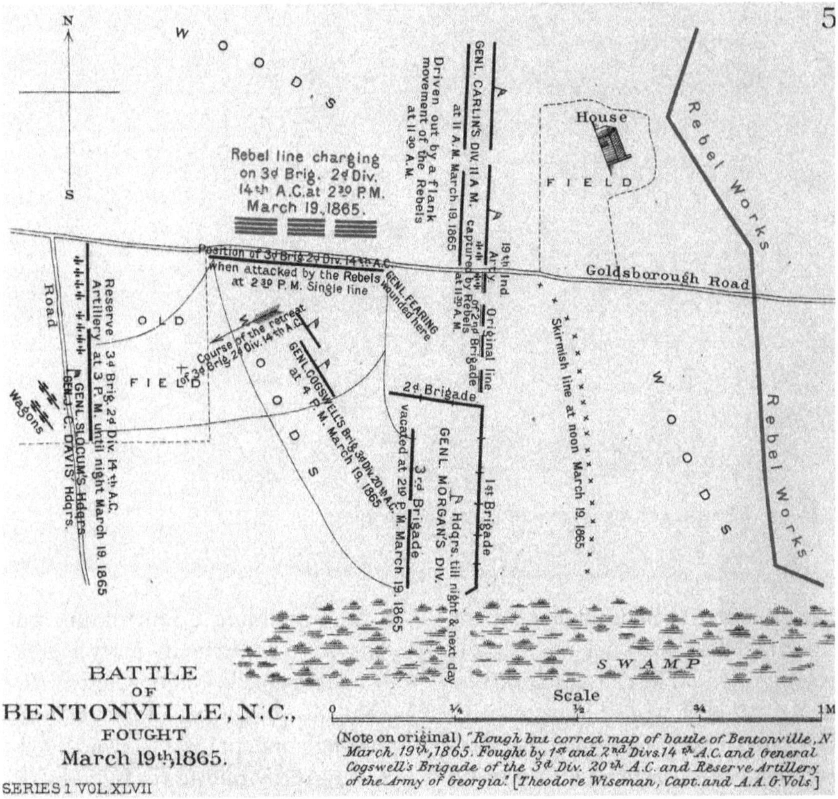

The Battle of Bentonville showing the position of Morgan's Union Division south of the Goldsboro Road. (*Official Records Atlas*)

using his cavalry to delay the federals' advance, Johnston swung back Hoke's and McLaws's divisions on a new left flank that slanted northeast toward Bentonville. Howard's advance reached the vicinity of Bentonville around noon. Johnston now faced a federal force numbering almost three times the size of his own army. The Confederates occupied a tenuous, four-mile-long bastion that guarded their sole line of retreat across a flooded Mill Creek at Bentonville. For the next two days, skirmishing erupted along the entire line. A teenage officer in the North Carolina Junior Reserves, Major Walter Clark, described the combat in his sector as "a regular Indian fight of it behind trees."[34]

Sherman was surprised that Johnston—contrary to his usual cautious nature—held his ground. "I cannot see why he remains," Sherman wrote Slocum, "and still think he will avail himself of night to get back to Smithfield. I would rather avoid a general battle if possible, but if he insists on it, we must accommodate him." Why *did*

Mower's Charge. (*Frank Leslie's Illustrated Newspaper*)

Johnston stay at Bentonville? Having failed to defeat one wing of Sherman's army group, did he expect to fare better against both wings? Johnston provided two reasons for remaining. First, he intended to evacuate his wounded before retreating, and second, he hoped that Sherman might attempt a costly frontal assault against his well-entrenched line. Perhaps Johnston had a third reason—his army's morale. By standing toe to toe with Sherman's much larger army while evacuating his wounded, Johnston would achieve a moral victory, whereas if he abandoned the field on the night of March 19–20, he would admit defeat. Johnston doubtless believed that his army's morale was worth the risk of staying at Bentonville.[35]

The Confederate commander's decision to remain nearly proved to be his undoing. On the morning of March 21, the 1st Division of the XVII Corps deployed on the extreme right of the Union line. Commanding that division was Sherman's most aggressive subordinate, Major General Joseph A. "Fighting Joe" Mower. Although under orders to avoid a general engagement, Mower intended to assail the Confederates, perhaps hoping to draw Sherman into the pitched battle he did not want. Facing Mower's division was Hampton's cavalry, spread out in a futile attempt to cover the Confederates' vulnerable left flank.

Mower began his assault about noon in a driving rain. His two attacking brigades struggled through the briar-infested swamp that separated them from Hampton's position and then drove back the heavily outnumbered Confederates. Hampton, meanwhile, reported the breakthrough to Johnston, who assigned Hardee the task of repulsing the assault. At stake was Johnston's only avenue of escape across Mill Creek, which could not be forded in its flooded state. Fortunately for the Confederates, Mower halted his main line even as his skirmishers overran Johnston's headquarters at Bentonville, enabling Hardee to counterattack with a hastily assembled force. One of the regiments was the 8th Texas Cavalry—or "Terry's Texas Rangers"—whose newest recruit was General Hardee's only son, sixteen-year-old Private Willie Hardee. The youth was mortally wounded while charging in the Rangers' front rank. The Confederates managed to repulse Mower's charge, but "Fighting Joe" was preparing to attack again when Sherman sent him orders to halt. The Army of the South had survived to fight another day, but Bentonville would be Sherman and Johnston's last battle.[36]

On the night of March 21–22, the Confederates retreated across the Mill Creek bridge and marched toward Smithfield. Aside from a rear-guard action the following day, the Battle of Bentonville was over. The Confederates sustained about 2,600 casualties, while the federals lost roughly 1,500 killed, wounded, or captured. Most of the losses occurred on March 19, by far the bloodiest day of the battle. Among the Southern casualties were two high-ranking Tar Heels: Colonel William S. Devane, the commander of Clingman's brigade in Hoke's division, and Lieutenant Colonel Edward B. Mallett, the commander of the 61st North Carolina in Clingman's brigade. Devane was severely wounded and Mallett killed in the fighting on March 21. The culminating event of Sherman's Carolinas Campaign, the Battle of Bentonville nevertheless proved indecisive. Although the federals had opened the road to Goldsboro, they had failed to crush Johnston's army, and while the Confederates had won a moral victory, the Southerners had been unable to defeat even Slocum's wing.[37]

STONEMAN'S LAST RAID

In March and April 1865, while Sherman conducted his Carolinas Campaign, Union Major General George Stoneman led his four-thousand-man cavalry division on a raid from Knoxville, Tennessee, through western North Carolina and southern Virginia. The long-deferred operation occurred at General Grant's urging. The objective was to support Sherman's and Grant's campaigns by destroying facilities, equipment, and supplies in North Carolina and Virginia that could aid the Confederates. Grant directed that, "As this expedition goes to destroy and not to fight battles, but to avoid them when practicable . . . it should go as light as possible."[38]

Stoneman was fortunate to be leading the cavalry operation. He enjoyed the dubious distinction of having been the highest-ranking Union prisoner of war, following his capture near Macon, Georgia, during the disastrous raid in July 1864 led by him and Brigadier General Edward M. McCook. Secretary of War Edwin M. Stanton was no admirer, calling Stoneman "one of the most worthless officers in the service." But he had a staunch supporter in General Schofield. In September 1864, after Stoneman's release from captivity, Schofield, then commanding the Department of the Ohio, had appointed the cavalryman as his second in command. Stoneman had repaid Schofield's unwavering faith in him by leading a successful strike into south-

George Stoneman.

western Virginia in December 1864. Two months later, Stoneman became commander of the District of East Tennessee. He had been eager to launch a raid into South Carolina in support of Sherman's march, but several delays had forced him to abandon that undertaking and shift his focus to North Carolina and Virginia.[39]

Stoneman's raiders first struck in western North Carolina. As he would do throughout the operation, Stoneman divided his force to maximize its destructive potential. On March 28, one Union mounted column rode into Boone, where the bluecoats routed a local Home Guard unit and burned the town's jail. That evening, a second federal column headed south and torched Patterson's Factory, a large cotton mill in Caldwell County. The raiders next headed east to Wilkesboro and then swung north in early April, making a brief detour into southern Virginia. On April 9, the day of Lee's surrender to Grant, Stoneman's cavalry reentered North Carolina. The timing was fortuitous, for Lee's surrender had made Johnston's army the main target of Stoneman's raid.[40]

In late March, as Stoneman headed east, Johnston had entrusted General Beauregard, his second in command, with the task of stopping the federal raiders. He also had directed General Bragg—left without a command since the Battle of Bentonville—to assist Beauregard. Together, Beauregard and Bragg assembled a patchwork defensive force consisting of various infantry, cavalry, and artillery units, which they deployed at several key points on the railroad from Chester north to Danville.[41]

Unaware of these dispositions, Stoneman once again divided his force. At Germanton, North Carolina, he directed Colonel William J. Palmer's brigade to strike Salem, twelve miles to the south, and then proceed twenty-five miles east to Greensboro, destroying railroad bridges and supply depots on his route. Stoneman, meanwhile, led his other two brigades toward Salisbury, his main geographic objective. Colonel Palmer reached Salem on the afternoon of April 10 and burned seven thousand bales of cotton. That night, he sent out several detachments to the south and east. At noon the following day, the first detachment destroyed the Piedmont Railroad bridge spanning Reedy Creek, ten miles north of Greensboro. Unknown to the federal raiders, the train carrying President Davis and his cabinet had crossed that bridge just an hour before. When informed of his close call at Reedy Creek, Davis remarked, "A miss is as good as a mile." But the destruction wrought by other detachments of

Stoneman's cavalry prevented the Davis party from traveling beyond Greensboro by rail.

Palmer's second detachment made a bold feint on Greensboro. After routing the 3rd South Carolina Cavalry in a surprise assault, the federals rode to within a few miles of Greensboro, where they cut a telegraph line and burned the North Carolina Railroad bridge across Buffalo Creek. The third detachment attacked Florence and Jamestown, about fifteen miles southwest of Greensboro, burning a gun factory, some Confederate cotton and commissary stores, and the North Carolina Railroad bridge over Deep River. A few miles south of Jamestown, Palmer's fourth detachment hit High Point, burning 1,700 bales of cotton and two trains loaded with medical and commissary supplies. Having completed its work of destruction, Palmer's brigade rejoined Stoneman's main column on the evening of April 12. Palmer's multipronged strike wreaked untold havoc on the enemy, but Stoneman could not judge his raid a success until he had captured Salisbury.[42]

Salisbury had strategic and symbolic importance. The town was the junction of two railroads—the North Carolina and the Western North Carolina. It also boasted a foundry, an arsenal, and numerous warehouses filled with supplies, and it was the site of a notorious military prison. Stoneman hoped to redeem his reputation by liberating the Union prisoners there.

When Stoneman reached Salisbury early on the morning of April 12, the town was defended by a scratch force of three veteran artillery batteries, a few hundred prison guards, several companies of Home Guards and reserves, four hundred state employees, a handful of civilian volunteers, and some "galvanized Yankees"—foreign-born Union captives who had agreed to serve in the Confederate army rather than rot in Southern prisons. Oddly enough, most of the regular Salisbury garrison and its commander, Brigadier General Bradley T. Johnson, were at Greensboro because General Beauregard believed the latter town was Stoneman's main target.[43]

Brigadier General William M. Gardner, a journeyman officer, commanded the motley crew protecting Salisbury. Gardner established his defensive position along Grant's Creek north and west of town, deploying his one-thousand-man force on a tenuous two-mile line to cover the incoming roads. At dawn, Stoneman divided his two available brigades into five columns and launched a general assault. Deploying into line of battle, the Union horsemen easily turned Gardner's right flank, capturing most of the defenders in that sector, including a contingent of galvanized Yankees who threw down their weapons when the blue-clad riders approached. The Confederates on the left proved more stubborn. The Southern batteries repulsed the initial Union charge by firing double-shotted canister, but the federal cavalrymen rallied, forded the creek beyond range of the cannons, and then attacked from the rear. The Northerners' sudden appearance panicked the Confederates, who abandoned their guns and fled. Stoneman then ordered a general charge, and the federals routed the entire Southern line. According to Stoneman's second in command, Brigadier General Alvan C. Gillem, "The pursuit was kept up as long as the enemy retained a semblance of organization and until those who escaped capture had scattered and concealed themselves in the woods." By noon on April 12, Salisbury was firmly in Union hands. The Battle of Salisbury cost the federals about 40 casualties, while the Confederates lost 1 killed, 6 wounded, and roughly 1,300 captured.[44]

Stoneman was chagrined to discover that the thousands of prisoners he hoped to liberate had been transferred elsewhere in March and that the handful of inmates who remained were either too lame or too sick to travel. He was further disappointed to learn that a detachment sent to destroy the 660-foot Yadkin River bridge north of town had been repulsed by a Confederate force under Brigadier General Zebulon York. But Stoneman was unaware that Colonel Palmer's detachments had already shut down rail traffic in central North Carolina by destroying three railroad bridges and several miles of track to the north.[45]

In addition to intercepting some railroad trains attempting to escape, Stoneman's troopers seized an enormous quantity of supplies at Salisbury, including one million rounds of small arms ammunition, two hundred fifty thousand army blankets, thirty-five thousand pounds of cornmeal, and seven thousand bales of cotton. The raiders piled the goods in the street and took what they wanted. The civilians then helped themselves to the remainder. About 8:00 PM on April 12, the federals set fire to the last of the supplies and to the prison, the arsenal, the foundry, several hospitals, and four cotton mills. That night, the red skies above Salisbury could be seen for miles, and the resulting explosions reached the volume of a pitched battle.[46]

On the morning of April 13, Stoneman's horsemen headed west in a driving rainstorm. Four days later, Stoneman left the main column at Lenoir, North Carolina, and returned to Knoxville, having fulfilled his mission. Although his raid had done considerable damage to Confederate resources, the destruction did not hasten the end of the war. Rather, the outcome would be determined by the armies of Grant and Lee in Virginia and of Sherman and Johnston in North Carolina.[47]

CLOSING OPERATIONS

After the Battle of Bentonville, Sherman's army group resumed the march to Goldsboro and began arriving there on March 23; Schofield's XXIII Corps had arrived a few days earlier. With his army group united and camped around Goldsboro, Sherman traveled north to Grant's headquarters at City Point, Virginia, hoping to persuade the Union general in chief to postpone his upcoming campaign long enough to enable Sherman's army group to participate in the defeat of Lee's army. Much to Sherman's dismay, Grant refused to delay the operation for even one day. While at City Point, Sherman had an opportunity to confer with President Lincoln aboard the steamship *River Queen*. Although they briefly discussed the end of the war, Lincoln gave no inkling of the precise terms he would offer the defeated

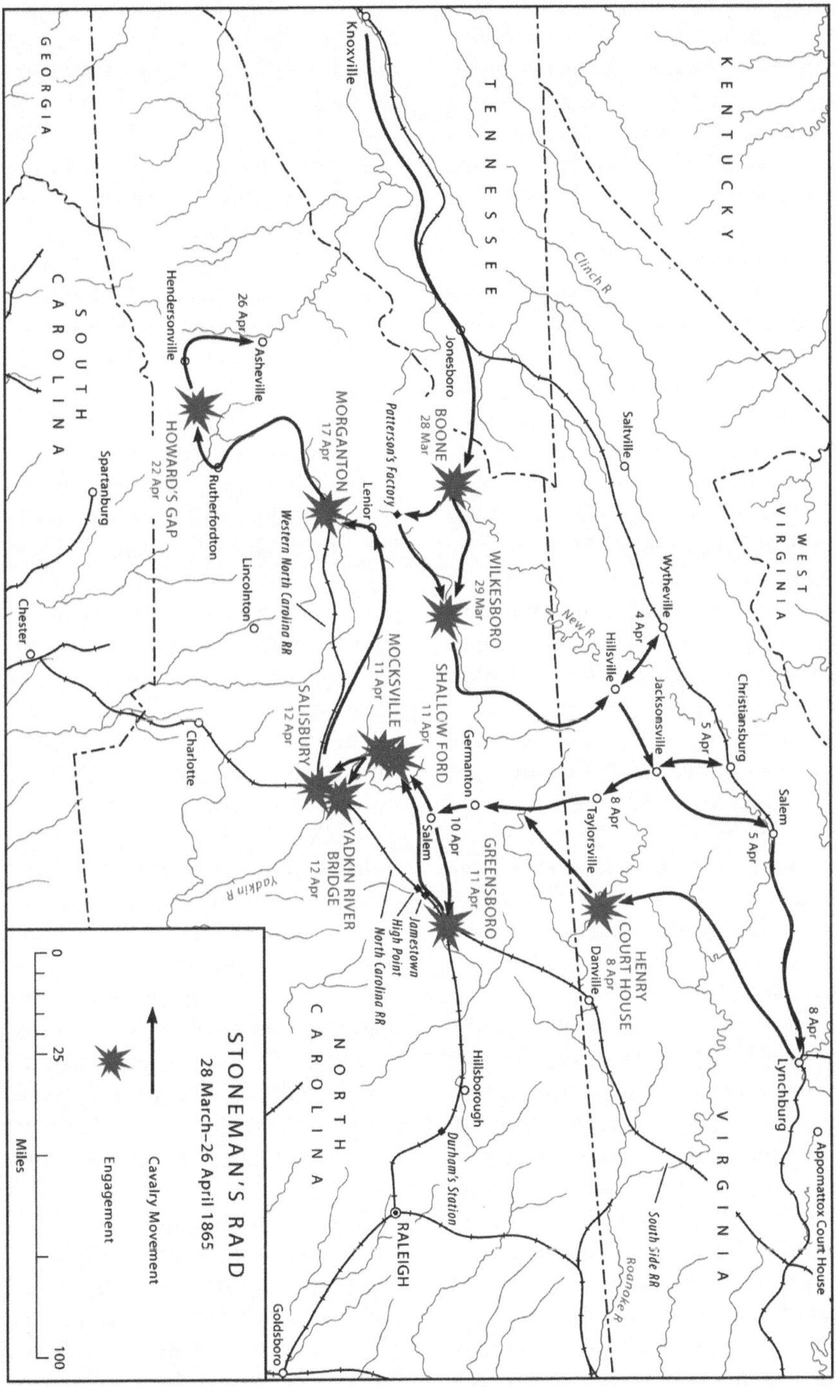

Stoneman's Raid. (*Sherry Dowdy, CMH*)

South. Sherman nonetheless left City Point convinced that Lincoln "contemplated no revenge—no harsh measures, but quite the contrary. . . . I know, when I left him, that I was more than ever impressed with his kindly nature, his deep and earnest sympathy with the afflictions of the whole people, resulting from the war."[48]

When Sherman returned to Goldsboro, he was pleased to find "all things working well." As supplies rolled in from the coast, his command began to look like an army once more. On April 6, momentous news arrived from Virginia: Richmond had fallen, and Grant's forces were pursuing Lee's army as it fled toward Danville, Virginia, and the North Carolina border in a desperate bid to link up with Johnston's army. "Great rejoicing among us tonight—Victory! Victory!" Union staff officer Lieutenant C. C. Platter scribbled in his diary. In response, Sherman shifted his destination from Richmond to Raleigh, and he ordered the campaign to begin on April 10. With the addition of Schofield's command—which Sherman designated the Army of the Ohio—Sherman's army group numbered roughly ninety thousand soldiers.[49]

While the federals celebrated the news of the Confederate capital's fall, morale plummeted in Johnston's army, which was camped around Smithfield. "The shades of sorrow are gathering upon us—horrible rumors!" wrote Confederate staff officer Captain Bromfield Ridley. "We, today, have heard of the distressing news that the fall of Richmond took place the [second] day of the month. . . . Heavens, the gloom and how terrible our feelings!" Johnston, meanwhile, renamed his force the Army of Tennessee and reorganized it into three corps commanded by Hardee, Stewart, and Lieutenant General Stephen D. Lee, with Hampton retaining command of the cavalry. On April 7, Johnston's army numbered around thirty-one thousand soldiers, making it larger by half than the command he had led at Bentonville, and yet it remained just one-third the size of Sherman's army group.[50]

The federals broke camp early on April 10 and began the sixty-mile trek from Goldsboro to Raleigh. In the meantime, the Confederate infantry at Smithfield fell back toward the state capital about a day's march ahead of the Union advance, which skirmished with Hampton's cavalry for much of the way. Sherman reached Smithfield on the afternoon of April 11 and made his headquarters in the courthouse square. About 5:00 AM on April 12, two riders arrived at the commanding general's tent with a dispatch from General Grant announcing Lee's surrender at Appomattox Court House on April 9. The news spread like wildfire through Sherman's army group. As an excited courier galloped down the marching column of the XXIII Corps, shouting, "Lee has surrendered! Lee has surrendered!" one wag yelled back at him, "Great God! You're the man I've been looking for these last four years."[51]

That evening, Sherman met with a deputation from Governor Vance requesting a cease-fire to open peace negotiations with the US government. The peace commissioners were North Carolina Senator William A. Graham and University of North Carolina President David L. Swain. Although Sherman told Graham and Swain that an immediate suspension of hostilities was unlikely, the general informed them that he planned to let Vance remain in office. In a message, he assured the governor, "I will aid you all in my power to contribute to the end you aim to reach, the termination of the existing war." The elder statesmen returned to Raleigh the next morning. When the two men reached the state capital, they learned that Vance had fled with Johnston's army after receiving inaccurate news that his peace commissioners had been captured.[52]

While Sherman's army group converged on the state capital, Johnston was trying to convince President Davis that the war was lost. After the fall of Richmond, Davis and his cabinet had fled by train to Danville. While there, the Confederate president received an unofficial report of Lee's surrender and passed it on to Johnston. Continuing south to Greensboro, Davis met there with Johnston and Beauregard on April 12. Instead of inviting the generals to brief him on the military situation, Davis launched into a scheme to raise a large army in a few weeks by recalling the men who had deserted or evaded conscription. Johnston said it would be a mistake to expect such men to rejoin or enter the army "upon mere invitation" when the cause appeared lost. At that point, Davis abruptly adjourned the meeting with the announcement that Secretary of War Breckinridge was expected to arrive that evening with news of Lee's army.

Breckinridge arrived as anticipated, confirming that Lee had indeed surrendered. Johnston told Breckinridge that the president "had but one power of government left in his hands—that of terminating hostilities." He offered to so advise Davis if the secretary of war provided him with the opportunity, and Breckinridge said he would arrange a conference for the next day.

Johnston and Beauregard met with Davis for a second time on the morning of April 13. Despite Lee's surrender, the president remained confident that the Confederacy would prevail "if our people will turn out." When Johnston at last had the opportunity to speak, he described a Confederacy on the verge of collapse and argued that "it would be the greatest of human crimes to continue the war." The general then urged Davis to "exercise at once the only function of government still in his possession, and open negotiations for peace." The president asked Beauregard and his cabinet for their opinions; with one exception, they agreed with Johnston. Davis yielded to the majority and dictated a letter to Sherman requesting a suspension of hostilities "to permit the civil authorities to enter into the needful arrangements to terminate the existing war." Johnston then signed the letter and ordered it sent at once to General Hampton for delivery to the federals.[53]

The Union army, meanwhile, entered Raleigh on the morning of April 13. A lone Confederate cavalryman fired on Kilpatrick's advance as it rode into town, violating Mayor William H. Harrison's formal surrender of the state capital. The federals captured the Southern horseman and hanged him for his futile gesture. Soon afterward, Sherman established his headquarters at the Governor's Palace and discovered that Vance had fled with Johnston's army after receiving an erroneous report that his peace commissioners had been captured.[54]

At midnight on April 15, Johnston's letter proposing an armistice reached Sherman's headquarters. The Union chieftain dashed off a reply accepting his Confederate counterpart's proposal. "That a basis of action may be had," Sherman wrote, "I undertake to abide by the same terms and conditions as were made by Generals Grant and Lee at Appomattox Court-House." Sherman sent his message to Kilpatrick at Durham's Station with instructions to forward it at once to Hampton's headquarters near Hillsborough. After receiving Hampton's dispatch proposing a conference midway between the opposing picket lines on the Hillsborough Road, the Union commander wired his acceptance to Kilpatrick with an order to forward it at once.[55]

THE BENNETT PLACE NEGOTIATIONS

On the morning of April 17, as Sherman prepared to board a train for his meeting with Johnston, a cipher dispatch from Secretary of War Stanton arrived at the depot. The message informed Sherman that an assassin had shot President Lincoln on the evening of April 14, and that he had died the next morning. After ordering the telegraph operator to say nothing to anyone about the contents of the message, Sherman rode the train to Durham's Station, where he was met by Kilpatrick. The generals and their escort of federal cavalry headed west on the Hillsborough Road until the Union flag-of-truce bearer met his Confederate counterpart about four miles west of Durham's Station. Sherman and Johnston saluted, shook hands, and introduced their respective subordinates. The two commanders then entered the James and Nancy Bennett farmhouse and began their conference.[56]

Sherman opened the meeting by showing Johnston the telegram announcing Lincoln's assassination. The Union commander then stated that he had not yet announced the news to his army and dreaded the reaction of the troops. Johnston agreed that Sherman's situation was "extremely delicate" indeed. Observing that Johnston's army was hopelessly outnumbered, Sherman offered his Confederate counterpart the same terms that Grant had given Lee at Appomattox Court House. While acknowledging that those terms were generous, Johnston also noted that Lee's army had been surrounded, whereas he and Sherman were a four days' march apart, with the federals camped around Raleigh and the Confederates around Greensboro. The Confederate commander then played his trump card, proposing that they "make one job of it" by negotiating the surrender of all remaining Confederate forces. When Sherman asked how he intended to arrange such a capitulation, Johnston replied that he would obtain President Davis's authorization.

The two generals discussed the terms of the proposed surrender. The Confederate chieftain recalled that he and Sherman agreed to terms with one important exception—the Union commander's refusal to include Davis and his cabinet in a general amnesty.

Sherman, however, remembered that his sole concern was whether Johnston could secure Davis's approval of the terms. The two men ended their conference at 2:30 PM to give Johnston time to communicate with Davis and to enable Sherman to reach Raleigh before word of Lincoln's assassination could spread. They agreed to meet at the Bennett house at noon the next day.[57]

When Sherman arrived at Raleigh, he discovered that the news had already spread throughout the capital. A crowd of angry soldiers met him at the depot, shouting, "Don't let Johnston surrender! Don't let the Rebels surrender!" After writing the order announcing Lincoln's assassination, Sherman strengthened the guard patrolling the state capital, posted pickets on the roads into town, and ordered all unauthorized soldiers in Raleigh arrested and jailed. He also spent the night riding through his camps, attempting to calm his men.

Despite these precautions, a mob of several thousand soldiers of the XV Corps advanced on the capital amid shouts that Raleigh was "a Rebel hole and ought to be cleaned out." Major General John A. Logan, the XV Corps commander, confronted the mob on the outskirts of town and tried to reason with the men. When that failed, he brought forward an artillery battery and warned them that if they did not disperse, he would order the cannons to open fire. The men returned to their camps. After an anxious night, dawn revealed that Raleigh had been spared the fate of Columbia.[58]

While Sherman attempted to save Raleigh, Johnston spent the early

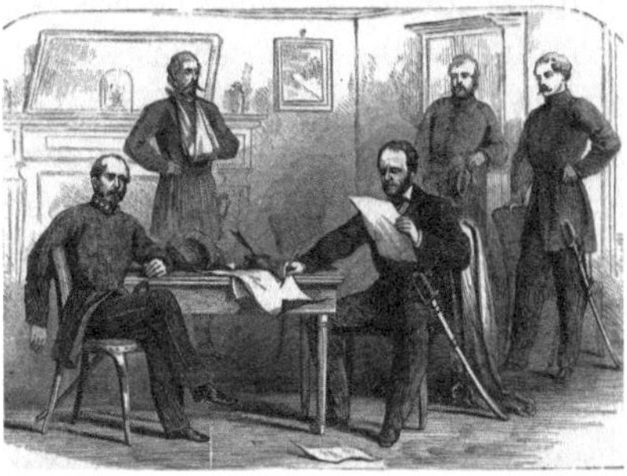

General Johnston surrenders to General Sherman. (*Frank Leslie's Illustrated Newspaper*)

morning hours of April 18 at Hampton's headquarters discussing the proposed terms with two Confederate cabinet officials: Secretary of War Breckinridge and Postmaster General John H. Reagan. Johnston related the details of his meeting with Sherman, noting that the Union commander refused to grant amnesty to Davis and his cabinet—a matter of obvious concern to Breckinridge and Reagan. When Johnston had finished his briefing, Reagan offered to write down the surrender terms. Later that morning, as Reagan made a clean copy of the terms, Johnston announced that he was going to his second meeting with Sherman. Leaving Reagan to complete his memorandum, Johnston and Breckinridge rode off for the Bennett farm at 10:00 AM.[59]

The flags of truce met before the Bennett house at noon on April 18. Sherman and Johnston entered the dwelling, and the Confederate chieftain said he now had the authority to surrender all remaining Confederate forces. Johnston also requested that Breckinridge be allowed to participate in the negotiations, since he was responsible for the comprehensive surrender. Sherman initially refused because the former US vice president was a member of Davis's cabinet but relented when Johnston stated the Kentuckian was also a major general in the Confederate army. The commanders repeated the main points of their discussion for Breckinridge. The two Southerners conceded that slavery was dead, but they stated that the Confederate soldiers desired some guarantees concerning their political status.

During the conversation, Reagan's memorandum arrived from Hampton's headquarters. Johnston read the document aloud, noting that it differed from the terms discussed only insofar as it guaranteed universal amnesty. Sherman was unimpressed, finding Reagan's document "so general and verbose" that he deemed it "inadmissible." Johnston nevertheless handed him the paper to study. Breckinridge then gave a short speech in favor of the Reagan document. At the conclusion, Sherman took out pen and paper and wrote his "Memorandum or Basis of Agreement," while bearing in mind his conversations with Lincoln at City Point.[60]

Having dismissed Reagan's terms as too verbose, Sherman's own memorandum ran twice the length of the Texan's, and it offered the Confederates a good deal more. There were four key items. First, the units composing the remaining Confederate armies were to proceed to their respective state arsenals and deposit their arms there for use in maintaining law and order. Second, the president of the United States would recognize the Southern state governments, provided their officials and legislatures took the oaths prescribed by the US Constitution. Third, the president would guarantee the Southern people their personal, political, and property rights as defined by the US and state constitutions. As a courtesy to Johnston and Breckinridge, who conceded that slavery was dead, Sherman omitted any mention of its demise in this clause. Fourth, the president would grant a general amnesty to the Southern people for their part in the war if they lived in peace and obeyed the laws in force in their respective states. Although he had not consciously intended to, Sherman was thus granting a full pardon to all Southerners, including Davis and his cabinet officers. Realizing that he had delved into matters beyond his authority as a military commander, Sherman inserted a clause at the end of his memorandum stating that he and Johnston pledged to obtain the prompt approval of their respective civilian leaders before carrying the terms into effect.[61]

After the two commanders signed the agreement, Sherman returned to Raleigh. Late that night, he sent a staff officer to Washington, DC, with the surrender document and a letter to Grant. Supremely confident that his agreement would meet with no opposition, Sherman asked Grant "to get the President to simply indorse the copy and commission me to carry out the terms."

Grant received Sherman's papers late on Friday afternoon, April 21. Reading the terms with growing concern, the Union general in chief realized he had to notify Secretary of War Stanton at once. Stanton read Sherman's agreement and then called a special cabinet meeting for 8:00 PM at President Andrew Johnson's temporary residence. An outraged Stanton voiced his objections to the document, calling it "a practical acknowledgement of the Rebel government" that would enable "the Rebels to renew their efforts to overthrow the US government at a later time." He also contended that the agreement relieved the rebels of all "pains and penalties" for their crimes and would enable them to maintain slavery. The president and his cabinet unanimously rejected Sherman's terms. Stanton then ordered Grant to "proceed immediately" to Sherman's headquarters "and direct operations against the enemy."[62]

Ulysses S. Grant.

Grant's appearance at the Governor's Palace in Raleigh on April 24 both "surprised and pleased" Sherman, but he was neither surprised nor pleased to learn that the president had rejected his terms and ordered him to resume hostilities. Since penning his agreement, Sherman had learned that the mood in the nation's capital was hardly conciliatory. As instructed, Sherman notified Johnston that the truce would end in the agreed-upon forty-eight hours, that there could be no civil negotiations, and that the troops affected would be limited to Johnston's immediate command. "I therefore demand the surrender of your army on the same terms as were given General Lee at Appomattox . . . purely and simply," Sherman wrote. Pleased with Sherman's handling of the situation, Grant disregarded Stanton's order to "direct operations."

At 5:00 PM on April 24, Johnston received President Davis's approval of Sherman's terms. (Davis and his entourage had since moved to Charlotte.) One hour later, Sherman's dispatches arrived ending the truce, rejecting the agreement, and demanding the Confederates' surrender in accordance with the Appomattox terms. Johnston immediately wired Breckinridge for instructions, but he was at no loss for a course of action: "We had better disband this small force to prevent devastation to the country." This was the last piece of advice Davis wanted from his ranking field commander. The Confederate president expected Johnston to maintain his army if the federals refused to offer acceptable terms. Breckinridge adroitly couched Davis's order as a suggestion to disband the infantry and artillery while sending a mounted force to the Trans-Mississippi Department, which consisted of Missouri, Indian Territory (present-day Oklahoma), Arkansas, Louisiana west of the Mississippi River, and Texas. (While the first two places provided Confederate troops, only the last three were Confederate states.) In response, Johnston summoned Beauregard and his corps and division commanders to a conference at 10:00 AM on April 25. This meeting proved to be the Army of Tennessee's final council of war. Johnston asked his subordinates to assess Breckinridge's proposal and the condition of their forces. The consensus was that the troops would no longer fight and the secretary of war's plan was impractical. Johnston notified Breckinridge and suggested, "We ought to make terms for our troops and give an escort of cavalry to the President." In the meantime, Johnston replied to Sherman's dispatches, proposing another armistice to resume negotiations.

Due to a railroad accident, Johnston arrived at the Bennett farm at 2:00 PM on April 26, two hours behind schedule. Although Grant had remained in Raleigh, Sherman brought several high-ranking subordinates with him, including General Schofield. The two commanders shook hands and entered the Bennett house. Their third conference began inauspiciously. Sherman offered the Appomattox terms, but Johnston called them inadequate and insisted on additional guarantees for his men. While he conceded the need for supplementary terms, Sherman doubted they would be approved in Washington. After further discussion proved fruitless, Sherman summoned Schofield to resolve their impasse.

Schofield suggested drafting a surrender document almost identical to the Appomattox agreement and a second document listing the terms that Johnston sought for his men. "I think General Schofield can fix it," Johnston said. Sherman directed his lieutenant to put the "new" terms in writing. Schofield's "Terms of a Military Convention" strongly resembled the terms Grant had offered Lee at Appomattox Court House. The crucial fifth provision ensured that all officers and men in Johnston's army could return to their homes, not to be disturbed by the US government if they observed their paroles and the laws in force where they resided. On April 27, Johnston drafted a list of eight "Supplementary Terms" based on his discussion with Sherman and Schofield at the Bennett house. Schofield then wrote a revised version consisting of six "Supplemental Terms" that permitted each brigade or independent unit to retain one-seventh of its small arms, that enabled the soldiers to keep their horses and other personal property, and that provided water-borne transportation for troops from the Trans-Mississippi. A few days later, he offered rail transportation to Johnston's troops as well. The Bennett Place surrender was the largest of the war, embracing almost ninety thousand Confederates stationed in North Carolina, South Carolina, Georgia, and Florida. Sherman and Johnston announced the momentous news to their troops on April 27.[63]

On the evening of April 26, Sherman returned to Raleigh and submitted the surrender agreement to Grant, who approved the terms and complied with Sherman's request to sign the document. The general in chief then carried the agreement back to Washington. Johnston, meanwhile, traveled to Greensboro. In compliance with the surrender agreement, he ordered his corps commanders to make out their muster rolls in duplicate and to collect all cannons, equipment, and draft animals, as well as four-fifths of the soldiers' small arms, ammunition, and accoutrements. (He did not receive Schofield's stipulation to collect six-sevenths of the arms until April 30.) For the final time, the Army of Tennessee lurched into action, as long lines of troops stacked arms and headquarters staffs filled out rolls. To maintain a semblance of cohesion during the journey home, the men remained with their units for as long as possible and received their paroles only when they neared their homes.[64]

Sherman directed Schofield's Army of the Ohio and Kilpatrick's cavalry to remain in the state while Howard's Army of the Tennessee and Slocum's Army of Georgia marched to Washington, DC, to be mustered out of the service. In the meantime, Sherman conducted an inspection tour of his command that took him to Wilmington, Savannah, and Hilton Head, South Carolina. He rejoined his army group in time to lead it in the Grand Review down Pennsylvania Avenue on May 24.[65]

On May 6, ten days after the Bennett Place surrender, a skirmish near Waynesville in western North Carolina marked the last shots fired between Union and Confederate soldiers in the Tar Heel State. One man, a federal soldier named James Arwood, was killed. Surprised by the Confederates' sudden appearance, the soldiers in blue withdrew into Waynesville. On May 7, the Union commander, Colonel William C. Bartlett, sent out a flag of truce requesting a meeting with his Confederate counterpart, Colonel Thomas, the commander of Thomas's Legion. Unknown to Bartlett, the senior Confederate officer present was Brigadier General James G. Martin, who introduced himself to the Union colonel. After a brief discussion, the two men agreed to terms. On May 9 (the exact date is in dispute), the remaining Confederate forces in western North Carolina surrendered, and Bartlett led his command back to its base in eastern Tennessee.[66]

The war in North Carolina was over.

11. North Carolina Troops Who Fought Outside Their Home State

FIRST BLOOD

On June 10, 1861, the 1st North Carolina Volunteer Regiment fought in the Battle of Big Bethel, Virginia, marking the first time that Tar Heel soldiers came under fire. A Union force numbering 3,500 troops led by Major General Benjamin F. Butler attacked 1,400 Confederates under Colonel John B. Magruder. The commander of the 1st North Carolina was Colonel D. H. Hill. Though heavily outnumbered, the Confederates emerged victorious in an engagement that amounted to little more than a skirmish. The lone Southern fatality was a North Carolinian, Private Henry L. Wyatt. He was the first Tar Heel to fall in the war.[1]

Just six weeks later, three North Carolina regiments fought in the much larger Battle of Manassas about thirty miles southwest of Washington, DC. The battle pitted the Confederate forces commanded by Generals Joseph E. Johnston and P. G. T. Beauregard against the federal army under Major General Irvin McDowell. The Union war cry that summer was "On to Richmond," a reference to the newly relocated capital of the fledgling Confederacy. On the morning of July 21, the men of the 6th North Carolina Infantry Regiment stepped off the train at Manassas Junction and soon afterward attacked a Union battery posted on Henry House hill. The regiment suffered heavy casualties during the assault, including its commander, Colonel Charles F. Fisher, who was killed. Though unable to seize the battery, the 6th North Carolina participated in the rout of the Union army later that day. The victory cost the regiment twenty-three killed and fifty wounded. The Confederates lost a total of 1,982 killed, wounded, and missing, while the federals sustained 2,709 casualties.[2]

The next campaign in the eastern theater began in March 1862. Union Major General George B. McClellan transported his one-hundred-fifteen-thousand-man Army of the Potomac by sea from Alexandria, Virginia, to Fort Monroe. On their arrival, the federals advanced cautiously up the peninsula toward Richmond, opposed by General Johnston's army of roughly eighty thousand. Forced out of their entrenchments at Yorktown, the Confederates withdrew to Williamsburg, where the rear guard fought a delaying action against the Union advance. The 5th North Carolina Infantry Regiment launched a desperate assault that resulted in 302 casualties, but its sacrifice bought invaluable time for the Southerners to make their escape.[3]

By late May, Johnston had fallen back to the eastern outskirts of Richmond. Aware that his army could not withstand a protracted siege, the Confederate commander decided to strike McClellan's army while it straddled the Chickahominy River, intending to attack thirty thousand federals south of the stream with roughly fifty thousand Confederates. The Battle of Seven Pines began shortly after noon on May 31. Johnston's complicated plan of attack soon unraveled, and the Southerners failed to crush the Union force south of the Chickahominy. The 4th North Carolina Infantry Regiment was in the thick of the fight, sustaining a loss of 369 officers and men, while the 16th North Carolina's commander, Colonel Champion T. N. Davis, was killed. Johnston was severely wounded at dusk and had to be carried from the field. On the following day, the two sides once again fought to a draw. The battle cost the Confederates 7,997 casualties, and the federal losses totaled 5,739. On the evening of June 1, President Davis appointed General Robert E. Lee to command the Army of Northern Virginia. One of Lee's first moves was to obtain reinforcements for his army, which came to include thirty-four North Carolina infantry regiments.[4]

Henry L. Wyatt. (*North Carolina Museum of History*)

LEE ASSUMES COMMAND

In late June, Lee launched a series of attacks against the Union Army of the Potomac that became known as the Seven Days Battles. Starting on June 26, the Confederates struck the federals at Mechanicsville, Gaines' Mill, Savage's Station, Glendale, and Malvern Hill. Although unable to achieve a decisive victory, Lee nevertheless succeeded in driving McClellan from the gates of Richmond to Harrison's Landing on the James River—a distance of thirty-five miles. The 20th North Carolina sustained 272 casualties in the attack on Union entrenchments at Gaines' Mill, and Colonel Charles C. Lee of the 37th North Carolina was mortally wounded by an artillery shell while leading his regiment in a charge at Glendale. The week-long campaign proved costly to both sides, with Confederate casualties exceeding twenty thousand while Union losses amounted to 18,849.[5]

Lawrence O'Bryan Branch. (*North Carolina Collection, UNC-Chapel Hill*)

Believing that McClellan was too shaken to make another push on Richmond, Lee began moving his army north to threaten Washington, DC. On August 28-30, the Confederates defeated the federal Army of Virginia under Major General John Pope in the Battle of Second Manassas. Flushed with victory, Lee's army advanced into Maryland in hopes of demoralizing the Northern populace and gaining foreign recognition for the Confederacy. McClellan led the federal pursuit of Lee's army. The Maryland Campaign culminated in the Battle of Antietam on September 17, 1862, the bloodiest day in American history. Though heavily outnumbered, the Confederates staved off a succession of Union assaults in savage fighting that resulted in a combined total of around twenty-three thousand casualties. The 27th North Carolina Infantry Regiment entered the battle with 325 soldiers and sustained 203 killed or wounded, a loss of 63 percent. Brigadier General Lawrence O'Bryan Branch, whose brigade helped repulse the last Union assault of the battle, was killed late in the day by a federal sharpshooter.[6]

The two armies rested for several months following the Battle of Antietam. President Lincoln tired of McClellan's lack of aggressiveness and replaced him with Major General Ambrose E. Burnside, whose recent operations in eastern North Carolina had been so successful. In November 1862, Burnside made a rapid march south to get between Lee's army and Richmond, but the pontoon bridges he needed to cross the Rappahannock River at Fredericksburg did not reach him until after the Confederates had occupied Marye's Heights overlooking the town.[7]

On December 13, 1862, Burnside attacked Lee's army, sending a total of seven divisions against the strong position on Marye's Heights held by Lieutenant General James Longstreet's corps. One Union brigade after another advanced into a storm of small-arms and artillery fire that mowed down the soldiers in blue before they could reach the stone wall at the base of the heights. By the time nightfall brought the assaults to a close, roughly eight thousand federals on that part of the field were killed, wounded, or missing.

On Longstreet's right, the line occupied by Jackson's corps had a flaw that the Union attackers exploited. A dense swamp left a six-hundred-yard gap between the right flank of Brigadier General James H. Lane's North Carolina brigade and Brigadier General James J. Archer's brigade. The advancing federals drove a wedge between Lane and Archer; Lane's Tar Heels nevertheless continued to fight until they ran out of ammunition, at which time they began to fall back. By then, Southern reinforcements had arrived, and the Confederates launched a counterattack that sealed the breakthrough and drove off the federals. Led by the six-foot, six-inch Colonel Archibald C. Godwin, the 57th North Carolina Infantry Regiment of Brigadier General Evander M. Law's brigade charged down the Richmond, Fredericksburg & Potomac Railroad and into the Union right flank. The 57th sustained heavy casualties in the fight, losing fifty-five killed and eighty-nine wounded. The Battle of Fredericksburg cost the federals 12,653 casualties compared to the Confederates' 5,400 losses. It was one of the most lopsided Union defeats of the war.[8]

Archibald C. Godwin.

TAR HEEL UNITS IN THE WEST

Most of North Carolina's Confederate regiments served in the eastern theater with the Army of Northern Virginia. In December 1862, only a handful—namely the 29th, 39th, and 60th North Carolina Infantry Regiments—served in the western theater. They were attached to the Army of Tennessee, whose commander was North Carolina native General Braxton Bragg. On December 31, 1862, the Confederates attacked Major General William S. Rosecrans's Army of the Cumberland at Murfreesboro in Middle Tennessee. The three-day battle ended in a tactical draw, with both sides utterly exhausted. Numbering just over seventy-eight thousand troops at the start, the two armies lost a total of 24,645 killed, wounded, and missing. The 30 percent casualty rate was the highest of the war for a major battle. The 60th North Carolina sustained seventy-five casualties at Murfreesboro, while the 29th North Carolina lost sixty, and the 39th North Carolina forty-four killed, wounded, and missing. On January 3, 1863, Bragg reluctantly withdrew to Tullahoma forty miles to the south, having learned that Rosecrans, who now occupied Murfreesboro, was being reinforced. The two armies then went into winter quarters.[9]

CHANCELLORSVILLE AND GETTYSBURG

After the Battle of Fredericksburg, Burnside attempted to restore his reputation and the morale of his men by launching a new campaign on January 20, 1863. The onset of unseasonably mild weather led Burnside to believe that his army would be able to cross the Rappahannock River before the Confederates could oppose him. That night, however, an icy rain set in that transformed the roads and fords into quagmires. The winter storm continued for three days, foiling Burnside's attempt to catch Lee off guard. The Union commander reluctantly ordered his wet and weary troops to return to their camps. Disgruntled soldiers of the Army of the Potomac dubbed the abortive campaign the "Mud March."[10]

President Lincoln replaced Burnside with Major General Joseph Hooker on January 26, 1863. The Union and Confederate armies made winter camp on opposite sides of the Rappahannock. For all his bluster, Hooker proved to be a capable administrator whose reforms helped restore the soldiers' confidence in themselves and their leaders. But it remained to be seen how the latest Union commander would fare on the battlefield against Lee.[11]

Hooker opened his campaign on April 27, 1863. His plan was to crush Lee's army between two large Union forces. Hooker would attack with the main body from the west, driving Lee's army against Major General John Sedgwick's force at Fredericksburg to the east. The odds appeared to favor the federals. Lee had sent Longstreet with two divisions to forage for provisions in southeastern Virginia, leaving him with about sixty thousand troops against Hooker's army of one hundred thirty thousand, a disparity of more than two to one. By May 1, seventy thousand federals had crossed the Rappahannock and Rapidan Rivers and had converged on a roadside inn known as Chancellorsville, while the Union I and VI Corps threatened Fredericksburg. The Confederate commander defied the odds and divided his army in the face of his numerically superior foe. On May 2, Lieutenant General Thomas J. "Stonewall" Jackson led his entire corps of thirty-three thousand troops—including twenty-five North Carolina infantry regiments—in a daring march around the Union right flank near Chancellorsville. Lee, meanwhile, held off the rest of Hooker's army with fifteen thousand infantry. Although Hooker became aware of Jackson's flank march and attempted to warn Major General Oliver O. Howard, whose XI Corps held the Union right flank, Howard evidently did not take the threat seriously and made few dispositions to guard against a flank attack.[12]

At 5:00 on the afternoon of the second, Jackson launched a sudden attack on the Union right flank, routing the soldiers of the federal XI Corps, who had been preparing supper. Darkness ended the Confederate onslaught, but Jackson, eager to mount a night assault, led his staff on a scout between the lines. The return of the general and his staff officers startled pickets of the 18th North Carolina Infantry Regiment. Major James D. Barry of the 18th had glimpsed blue-clad soldiers lurking near his lines that night, and he assumed the approaching figures on horseback must be Union cavalry. Barry therefore gave his men the order to fire on the riders. Among the casualties of that fateful smoothbore volley was General Jackson, who was shot once in the right hand and twice in the left arm. His shattered limb was amputated soon afterward; several days later, Jackson developed pneumonia and died on May 10, 1863.[13]

Lee replaced the mortally wounded Jackson with his cavalry commander,

Major General J. E. B. Stuart. On May 3, Lee and Stuart launched a series of assaults on the federals at Chancellorsville and slowly drove them back toward the Rappahannock while stalling the advance of Sedgwick's VI Corps at Salem Church. Hooker's army withdrew across the Rappahannock on the night of May 5–6. The Battle of Chancellorsville cost the federals 17,324 casualties compared to Confederate losses of 13,460. The 33rd North Carolina went into the battle with 480 soldiers and lost 199 killed and wounded for a casualty rate of 41.4 percent. Among the wounded were Brigadier General Robert F. Hoke and twenty-two-year-old Colonel Thomas F. Toon, the commander of the 20th North Carolina Infantry Regiment. Although Lee had succeeded in repulsing another Union advance on Richmond, the two armies once more occupied the same ground they had held for the past six months.[14]

Thomas F. Toon. (*North Carolina State Archives*)

Determined to turn the tide of the war in the Confederacy's favor, Lee obtained President Davis's authorization to launch a second Northern offensive. In doing so, he hoped to win a decisive victory on Union soil and thereby strengthen the peace movement in the North. Lee also planned to subsist his army on Northern provisions while buying time for Virginia farmers to raise a crop.

On June 4, the Army of Northern Virginia began filing out of its fieldworks and marching north, with Stuart's cavalry leading the way. Unknown to the Confederates, Hooker sent a combined force of Union cavalry and infantry under Major General Alfred Pleasonton in hot pursuit. Before dawn on June 9, Pleasonton launched a surprise attack on Stuart's horsemen at Brandy Station. In a day-long struggle that proved to be one of the largest mounted clashes of the war, the federals initially scattered Stuart's troopers and nearly captured the Confederate cavalry chieftain himself. Four North Carolina cavalry regiments—the 1st, 2nd, 4th, and 5th—fought in the battle. The commander of the 2nd North Carolina Cavalry, Colonel Solomon Williams, was forming his regiment for a charge when he was killed by a bullet in the head. The Confederates ultimately turned the tide and forced the federals to withdraw, but the Battle of Brandy Station served notice that the cavalry corps of the Army of the Potomac had arrived.[15]

The Army of Northern Virginia continued marching north into Maryland and Pennsylvania, with Lee keeping the bulk of his troops west of the Blue Ridge Mountains. The audacious move north thoroughly tested the new

Solomon Meredith. (*National Archives*)

organizational structure of Lee's army. After Jackson's death, Lee had increased the number of his infantry corps from two to three. He left Longstreet in command of the First Corps while placing two newly promoted lieutenant generals, Richard S. Ewell and Ambrose Powell Hill, in command of the Second and Third Corps, respectively. Most of the Tar Heel troops served in Ewell's and Hill's units. By late June, the advance of Lee's army had reached the outskirts of Harrisburg, the Pennsylvania state capital, but on receiving word that the federals were closing the gap and Major General George G. Meade was now in command, Lee decided to concentrate his scattered forces at Cashtown. Hill's corps was the first command to arrive there. Learning that Union cavalry had occupied the crossroads town of Gettysburg about five miles to the east, Hill sent two of his divisions there to drive off the federal horsemen.[16]

The Battle of Gettysburg began early on the morning of July 1, 1863. Major General Henry Heth's division of Hill's corps had the advance and slowly drove Brigadier General John Buford's Union cavalry division back to McPherson's Ridge. The Confederates assaulted Buford's line, but the blue-clad horsemen, fighting dismounted, held their ground. Soon afterward, foot soldiers of the Union I and XI Corps under Major General John F. Reynolds reached the battlefield and began to deploy on Buford's line. Reynolds was killed by a bullet in the back of the head as he was leading the famed Iron Brigade—commanded by North Carolina native Brigadier General Solomon Meredith—into Herbst's Woods for a counterattack. The fighting ceased around noon, when Midwesterners of the Iron Brigade and New Yorkers captured several hundred Confederates who had become trapped by the steep walls of a railroad cut they were using for cover.[17]

The battle resumed around 2:00 that afternoon. In the meantime, both sides had been heavily reinforced, and their lines now extended from the west to the north side of town. The fighting intensified along McPherson's Ridge, especially in Herbst's Woods, where the left flank of Brigadier General James J. Pettigrew's North Carolina brigade assaulted Meredith's Iron Brigade. The 11th North Carolina Infantry Regiment lost 40 killed and 160 wounded; among the casualties were the regimental commander, Colonel Collett Leventhorpe, who was severely wounded in the left arm and later captured, and twenty-year-old Major Egbert A. Ross, who was killed.[18]

The 26th North Carolina Infantry Regiment sustained even heavier losses than the 11th. At the start of the battle, the Tar Heel unit numbered 843 soldiers, the largest regiment in either army at Gettysburg. The 26th North Carolina struck the 24th Michigan Infantry Regiment, which was drawn up along Willoughby Run, and the two regiments became locked in a desperate struggle. As the numerically superior 26th slowly drove back the Michiganders toward Seminary Ridge, the fight became a bloodbath in which each regiment sustained higher casualties than any other regiment in its army. Within half an hour, the 26th North Carolina had lost its colonel, twenty-one-year-old Henry K. Burgwyn (killed), its lieutenant colonel (severely wounded), and fourteen color bearers. A lieutenant in the 26th exclaimed, "No man can take those colors and live," and yet each time a color bearer fell, a comrade took his place. During the three-day battle, the 26th North Carolina incurred 687 casualties, an attrition rate of 82 percent.[19]

Henry K. Burgwyn Jr. (*North Carolina Collection, UNC-Chapel Hill*)

In the meantime, Ewell's corps deployed on the north end of Gettysburg, with Major General Robert E. Rodes's division forming on the left of Hill's corps. Wrongly believing that his division faced the Union flank, Rodes decided to launch an attack with three of his five brigades. Two of them—Brigadier General Junius Daniel's and Brigadier General Alfred Iverson Jr.'s—consisted of North Carolina troops. The attack was mismanaged from the start. The three Confederate brigades stepped off at different times and soon became separated, enabling the federals to repulse one brigade at a time. Worse yet, Iverson had neglected to send a skirmish line ahead to locate the enemy, nor did he reconnoiter the ground beforehand. As a result, the North Carolinians advanced blindly toward the Union line shielded by a stone wall on top of Oak Ridge, unaware of the bluecoats' presence. When the Confederates came to within eighty yards of the wall, the federals let loose a devastating volley and then continued to load and fire into the astonished Tar Heels. Hundreds of soldiers from the 5th, 12th, 20th, and 23rd North Carolina Infantry Regiments fell, either killed or wounded. A Virginia artilleryman who arrived there after nightfall awoke to discover "[with]in a few feet of us, by actual count, seventy-nine (79) North Carolinians laying dead in a straight line . . . all evidently killed by one volley."[20]

The assault of Iverson's brigade was an unmitigated disaster. General Rodes later reported that the unit lost 130 men killed, 382 wounded, and 308 missing, for a total of 820 casualties among the 1,400 engaged. After the de-

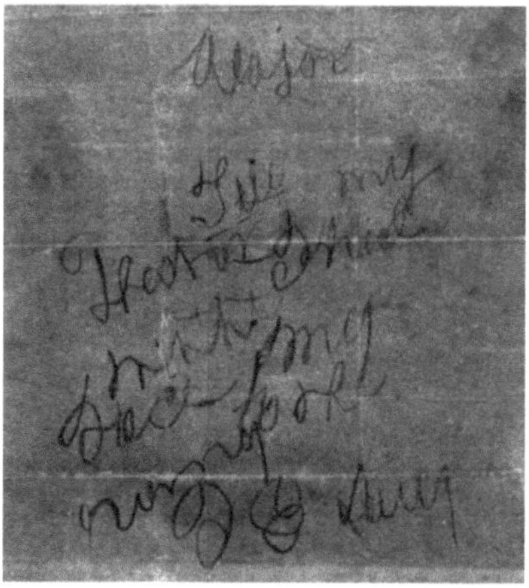

Isaac Avery's Final Note to His Father. (*North Carolina State Archives*)

bacle, Iverson's days with the Army of Northern Virginia were numbered. He briefly served as the army's provost marshal and then was transferred to a cavalry command in Georgia, his native state.[21]

Soon afterward, the Confederates outflanked the federals and drove them through the streets of Gettysburg. During the rout, a piece of shrapnel struck General Meredith in the head, fracturing his skull and giving him a severe concussion. In the meantime, several projectiles tore through his horse, causing the dying animal to collapse onto the general, breaking his ribs and heavily bruising his right leg. The six-foot, seven-inch Meredith survived his injuries, but they left him permanently disabled and unfit for field command.[22]

That evening, the Confederates occupied the town and much of Seminary Ridge to the west, while the federals deployed on Cemetery Ridge to the east, their fishhook-shaped line extending south from Culp's Hill and Cemetery Hill down to the Round Tops. On July 2, Lee's army attacked the flanks of the Union line. Longstreet's command struck first on the Confederate right and overwhelmed the Union III Corps, whose line was stretched dangerously thin. But Meade and several of his subordinates rushed reinforcements where they were most needed, and after four hours of brutal combat, the Union left flank and center had held. Aside from the artillery batteries of Captains Alexander C. Latham, Basil C. Manly, and James Reilly, few North Carolina troops participated in this fight.[23]

On the Confederate left, meanwhile, General Ewell launched an assault at dusk against the federals on Culp's Hill and Cemetery Hill. The only mounted Confederate on that part of the field, Colonel Isaac E. Avery, led his Tar Heel brigade up the eastern slope of Cemetery Hill. About halfway to the Union line, a bullet struck Avery in the neck, knocking him from his horse. Speechless and partially paralyzed, the mortally wounded colonel scrawled a note to a fellow officer: "Major: Tell my father I died with my face to the enemy." Avery's three regiments—the 6th, 21st, and 57th North Carolina Infantry—broke through the Union line, but federal reinforcements arrived and sealed the gap. Among the Confederate casualties on July 2 was North Carolina native Major General William Dorsey Pender, who was wounded in the thigh. The twenty-nine-year-old Pender died of complications from his wound sixteen days later.[24]

Believing that Meade had weakened the center of his line to bolster his

William Dorsey Pender. (*North Carolina State Archives*)

E. Fletcher Satterfield. (*North Carolina State Archives*)

flanks, Lee ordered Longstreet to attack that point on July 3. The bulk of the troops making the frontal assault consisted of Major General George E. Pickett's division, Heth's division under General Pettigrew (replacing the wounded General Heth), and two brigades of Pender's division led by Major General Isaac R. Trimble. Longstreet's assault force numbered about thirteen thousand soldiers.[25]

Lee ordered an artillery bombardment of the Union center to precede the attack. Many Confederate projectiles found their targets, disabling cannons or exploding caissons and killing or wounding numerous soldiers and draft animals. Union counterbattery fire proved no less deadly. When Longstreet received word that his artillery was running low on ammunition, he gave the signal for the attack to begin. From the moment the troops in the front rank stepped off, the Confederate assault lasted less than an hour. Although the soldiers in gray managed to break through in a few places, the federal center held, proving far stronger than Lee had anticipated. Fifteen Tar Heel regiments took part in the Picket-Pettigrew-Trimble charge, including the 26th and 47th North Carolina of Pettigrew's brigade. Both regiments lost their colors in the hand-to-hand fighting along the stone wall on Cemetery Ridge. Based on the spot where Captain E. Fletcher Satterfield of the 55th North Carolina reportedly fell, the Tar Heel State claimed the farthest Confederate advance on July 3.[26]

Lee rested his exhausted army on July 4 and then began the long retreat south early the next morning. He reached the Potomac River on July 10, well ahead of the federals, but flooding due to heavy rainfall at Williamsport and the destruction of his pontoon bridge at Falling Waters by Union cavalry prevented him from crossing for several days. By the time Meade arrived with the bulk of his army, Lee's men had dug strong fortifications, in-

James J. Pettigrew. (*North Carolina Museum of History*)

ducing the federal commander to delay an attack. After all, the federals had already sustained about thirty thousand casualties during the campaign. Such losses would have given any general pause. By the time Meade was ready, Lee had escaped with most of his army. The Confederate rear guard, consisting of Heth's division, fought a delaying action with Buford's cavalry at Falling Waters. General Pettigrew was mortally wounded there and died three days later. The two units that had opened the Battle of Gettysburg thus clashed in the final engagement of the Gettysburg Campaign.

The campaign cost Lee's army 27,125 killed, wounded, and missing—losses that the Confederacy could ill afford. The defeat also tarnished the Army of Northern Virginia's aura of invincibility. Lee's defeat at Gettysburg, combined with the surrender of Vicksburg, Mississippi, on the Fourth of July 1863, marked a devastating reversal in the Confederacy's fortunes.[27]

In fall 1863, three North Carolina infantry regiments—the 6th, 54th, and 57th of Hoke's brigade—met with disaster in the Second Battle of Rappahannock Station during the Bristoe Campaign. On November 7, a Union attack led by Colonel Emory Upton overran the three Tar Heel regiments and the bridgehead across the Rappahannock River they were defending along with the rest of Major General Jubal A. Early's division. More than nine hundred North Carolina soldiers were killed, wounded, or captured, including their commander, Colonel Archibald C. Godwin, who remained a prisoner of war until the following year. Rappahannock Station was a humiliating defeat for the Army of Northern Virginia, and it dashed General Lee's hopes for an autumn offensive.[28]

CHICKAMAUGA AND CHATTANOOGA

In summer 1863, General Rosecrans advanced southeast from Murfreesboro, maneuvering General Bragg out of middle Tennessee and forcing him back to Chattanooga in the southeastern part of the state. The Tullahoma Campaign (named after the location of Bragg's headquarters at the start of the operation) cost the federals just 569 casualties. Rosecrans completed his lightning campaign on July 3, during the Battle of Gettysburg and the day before the fall of Vicksburg, which explains why his achievement went largely unnoticed.

In early August, Rosecrans began preparing for his campaign to capture Chattanooga, a vital railroad hub and manufacturing center. He would act in conjunction with General Burnside, who was planning to launch an offensive from Lexington, Kentucky, into eastern Tennessee, a Unionist stronghold that President Lincoln had long been anxious to "liberate." Burnside moved first, capturing Knoxville on September 2 and seizing the Cumberland Gap one week later. Among the Confederate units that surrendered to the federals at the Cumberland Gap were the 62nd and the 64th North Carolina Infantry Regiments. Most of the Tar Heels were sent to Camp Butler, a prisoner of war facility near Springfield, Illinois, and many of them died there.

Rosecrans opened his campaign in mid-August. By September 4, the Union Army of the Cumberland had crossed the Tennessee River and was advancing into Georgia. Seeing that the federals threatened his line of communications, Bragg evacuated Chattanooga on September 8 and retreated to LaFayette, Georgia, twenty miles to the south. To bolster Bragg's forces, the Confederate War Department sent two small divisions from Mississippi and two divisions of Longstreet's corps from the Army of Northern Virginia. Bragg had also summoned Major General Simon B. Buckner's corps from eastern Tennessee to join him. North Carolina infantry regiments were scattered here and there in Bragg's army, including the 29th North Carolina in Ector's brigade, the 39th North Carolina in McNair's brigade, the 58th North Carolina in Kelly's brigade, and the 60th North Carolina in Stovall's brigade. There was also one Tar Heel cavalry regiment, the 6th North Carolina, which was attached to Davidson's brigade of Brigadier General Nathan B. Forrest's cavalry corps. They all participated in the Battle of Chickamauga, in which Bragg sought to crush Rosecrans's army and drive the federals from eastern Tennessee.

North Carolina regiments took part in some of the heaviest fighting on September 20, the third and final day of the battle. The 60th North Carolina participated in the assault of Major General John C. Breckinridge's division, which struck the left flank of the Union line and threatened to cut Rosecrans's line of retreat. But the attack lost momentum, enabling federal reinforcements to repulse the Confederates. The 60th North Carolina brought 150 men into the futile charge and lost eight killed, thirty-eight wounded, and sixteen missing—a casualty rate of 43 percent.[29]

Later that day, the 39th North Carolina participated in Longstreet's assault. The ten-thousand-man attack began just as a Union division was pulling out of the line in Longstreet's front. Positioned on the right of the Confederate line of battle, the 39th drove the federals steadily back, capturing the guns of the 8th Indiana Battery. During the breakthrough, McNair was wounded, and command of his brigade devolved on Colonel David Coleman, the 39th's commander. The bulk of Rosecrans's army retreated to Chattanooga, while a small Union force remained behind on Snodgrass Hill. The 58th North Carolina participated in the late-afternoon assault, which resulted in the federals' surrender after several hours of sustained combat. The Battle of Chickamauga cost the Tar Heel regiment 161 casualties—roughly one-half of all the soldiers the 58th had brought into the fight.[30]

After the battle, the Confederates occupied Lookout Mountain and Missionary Ridge overlooking Chattanooga. Bragg besieged the city in order to starve the Army of the Cumberland into surrendering. He also reorganized the Army of Tennessee. Among the changes affecting Tar Heel units, the 6th North Carolina Cavalry was transferred to Harrison's brigade of Major General Joseph Wheeler's cavalry corps, while the understrength 58th North Carolina Infantry Regiment was consolidated with the 60th North Carolina, and the regiment was assigned to Reynolds's brigade. The 29th and 39th North Carolina Infantry Regiments were transferred to the Department of Mississippi and East Louisiana.[31]

Within hours of receiving word of the Confederate victory at Chickamauga, the Union high command began rushing reinforcements to the area. In late September, Major General Ulysses S. Grant received orders to assume command of the effort to relieve Chattanooga. One of his first actions was to replace Rosecrans with Major General George H. Thomas. He also authorized a plan to establish a reliable supply line to the beleaguered city. The operation, known as Opening the Cracker Line, proved successful and effectively lifted the Confederate siege of Chattanooga.[32]

By late November, Grant's forces were ready to attack the Confederate positions south and east of Chattanooga. On November 24, the federals captured Lookout Mountain, and on the following day, they assaulted the Confederate positions on Missionary Ridge, where the 60th North Carolina was located. The rapidity of the Union advance caused many Tar Heels to panic and flee, leaving only a handful of their comrades to battle the oncoming federals. The heavily outnumbered Confederates soon gave way and retreated toward Chickamauga Station. The victorious Union forces thus secured Tennessee, enabling them to use Chattanooga as a logistical base in the coming campaign to capture Atlanta. Federal losses came to 5,824 killed, wounded, and missing, while Confederate casualties exceeded six thousand.[33]

OLUSTEE

In February 1864, while the principal Union and Confederate armies were in winter camp, a federal expedition from Hilton Head, South Carolina, was on the move in northern Florida. Brigadier General Truman Seymour landed a seven-thousand-man force at Jacksonville with orders to secure the town and promote Unionism in the area, which meant liberating slaves and recruiting black volunteers. Seymour's command included a half-dozen black regiments, most notably the 54th Massachusetts Infantry, which had gained fame for its assault on Fort Wagner at Charleston, South Carolina, the previous July. The 1st North Carolina and the 54th Massachusetts formed a two-regiment brigade commanded by Colonel James Montgomery. During the Florida expedition, the War Department designated the 1st as the 35th US Colored Troops (USCT).[34]

On January 1, 1863, President Lincoln's Emancipation Proclamation had made raising regiments of black troops official Union army policy. One of the many regiments of African American soldiers formed that spring was the 35th USCT. Most of the enlisted men were former slaves from the coastal region of Virginia and the Carolinas, and the officers were veterans of white regiments. Unlike the 54th Massachusetts, the 35th USCT had yet to fight its first battle, having mostly served behind the lines on guard duty and work details.[35]

"Sergeant Furney Bryant of the 1st North Carolina Colored Troops [later 35th USCT]," by Vincent Colyer. (*North Carolina State Archives*)

Despite considerable uncertainty as to his course of action, Seymour at last decided to launch a raid west into the interior of the state with the possible objective of capturing the port of St. Mark's on the Gulf Coast. On the afternoon of February 20, 1864, Seymour encountered a comparable Confederate force commanded by Brigadier General Joseph Finegan near Olustee Station on the Florida Atlantic and Gulf Central Railroad. The federals were fatigued by hard marching with little rest and no food, and a bungled order by one of the brigade commanders spread confusion in the ranks. As a result, many of the federals panicked and fled. Some Union troops managed to form ranks and return the Confederates' fire, but the men in blue sustained heavy casualties and began to run low on ammunition. Marching at the rear of the column, the 35th USCT and the 54th Massachusetts received orders to hurry to the front.[36]

After advancing at the double-quick for six or seven miles, the 35th USCT formed on the left of the 7th Connecticut Infantry, and the 54th Massachusetts on the right. Their arrival stabilized the Union line and enabled the rest of Seymour's force to make an orderly retreat. Forming the federal rear guard, the 54th and the 35th held the Confederates until Finegan sent in his reserves, forcing the two black regiments to fall back. The exhausted Northerners reached Jacksonville on the evening of February 22. In their first battle, the 35th USCT behaved like seasoned veterans, displaying a coolness under fire that impressed their officers. The regiment suffered 230 casualties, including their commander, Lieutenant Colonel William N. Reed, who was mortally wounded. The federals lost a total of 1,861 killed, wounded, and missing, roughly one-third of the soldiers Seymour took into battle, while the Southern losses totaled 946. The largest engagement of the Civil War in Florida, the Battle of Olustee was an overwhelming Confederate victory.[37]

THE OVERLAND CAMPAIGN

With the arrival of spring, the main Union armies launched new offensives. In the eastern theater, Lieutenant General Ulysses S. Grant, the Union army's new general in chief, led the Army of the Potomac against Lee's Army of Northern Virginia, while Grant's handpicked successor in the West, Major General William T. Sherman, commanded a federal army group against General Joseph E. Johnston's Confederate Army of Tennessee. Though Richmond and Atlanta were the geographical objectives, Grant's intent was to achieve a decisive victory by destroying Lee's and Johnston's armies. To facilitate this, Grant and Sherman maintained constant pressure on Lee and Johnston to prevent one from reinforcing the other, as Lee had done the previous fall when he sent the bulk of Longstreet's corps to Tennessee.

On May 4, 1864, Grant crossed the Rapidan River and attempted to position his command between Lee's army and Richmond, the Confederate capital, to force him into a battle in the open. Instead, Lee intercepted the federals in the Wilderness, a densely wooded area that prevented Grant from exploiting his two-to-one numerical superiority. On May 5, the Battle of the Wilderness began along the Orange Turnpike with a Union attack across Saunders Field that succeeded in driving back Ewell's corps. But the Confederates rallied and then counterattacked. After a fierce hand-to-hand struggle, the Southerners drove off the federals, and the 1st and 3rd North Carolina Infantry of Brigadier General George H. "Maryland" Steuart's brigade captured several Union guns.[38]

Off to the south in Lieutenant General A. P. Hill's sector, Brigadier General William W. Kirkland's North Carolina brigade repulsed several federal assaults along the Orange Plank Road before launching a futile counterattack late in the day. Early on the morning of May 6, the Union II Corps assaulted Hill's corps in overwhelming force. As Hill's troops streamed to the rear, reinforcements from Longstreet's corps arrived after a grueling night march. According to Captain V. E. Turner of the 23rd North Carolina Infantry, Brigadier General Robert D. Johnston's North Carolina brigade—comprising the 5th, 12th, 20th, and 23rd Regiments—"covered sixty-six miles in twenty-three hours." Using an unfinished railroad cut, the Confederates surprised the attacking federals and were forcing back the soldiers in blue when Longstreet was severely wounded by his own men less than five miles from the spot where Stonewall Jackson was mortally wounded the previous year. With Longstreet out of action, the Confederate attack soon sputtered out. The Battle of the Wilderness thus ended in a draw. Union losses numbered about seventeen thousand compared with roughly eleven thousand Confederate casualties.[39]

After battling Lee's army, previous commanders of the Army of the Potomac had opted to disengage and fall back behind the nearest river. But Grant established a precedent. Instead of retreating, he ordered his marching columns to advance southeast toward the hamlet of Spotsylvania Court House in another attempt to slip between the Army of Northern Virginia and Richmond. The Confederates arrived at the junction before the federals and were waiting behind strong entrenchments when twelve Union regiments in massed lines of battle led by Colonel Emory Upton attacked on the evening of May 10. The attackers managed to break through a portion of the line called Doles' Salient; one of the regiments under assault was the 32nd North Carolina Infantry of Brigadier General Junius Daniel's brigade. During the fight, the commander of the 32nd, Colonel Edmund C. Brabble, was killed.[40]

Junius Daniel. (*Archive.org*)

General Lee rushed one unit after another into the gap, including Brigadier General Stephen D. Ramseur's Tar Heel brigade. When Lee attempted to ride with Ramseur's men into the fight, several North Carolina soldiers took hold of the general's horse and led it to the rear. The Confederate counterattack succeeded in driving the federals back, and the Southerners were able to reclaim their fortifications. Believing that Grant was moving his army toward Fredericksburg, on the night of May 11–12, Lee drew off his artillery from a salient in the line called the Mule Shoe. In the meantime, the federals were preparing to launch a massed columnar assault with the entire II Corps along the Mule Shoe sector.[41]

The attack began at 4:35 on the morning of May 12. The Union columns broke through and pushed into the Confederate rear. The defenders on either flank swung back their lines and poured a devastating fire into the blue ranks, which were twenty deep in places. Grant and Lee fed reinforcements into the tip of the Mule Shoe, which became known as the "Bloody Angle." Daniel's Tar Heel brigade stood on the left of the breakthrough, and Brigadier General James H. Lane's North Carolina brigade was on the right. "It was more than human flesh could stand," recalled Sergeant Cyrus B. Watson of the 45th North Carolina, a regiment in Daniel's brigade. During the assault, Watson was severely wounded in the shoulder. Though he later recovered and returned to duty, the injury troubled him the rest of his life. General Daniel was mortally wounded and died the following day.[42]

Other Confederate brigades counterattacked, including Johnston's brigade, whose commander fell with a severe wound. Colonel Thomas M. Garrett of the 5th North Carolina Infantry assumed command but was killed soon afterward. Command of the brigade then devolved on twenty-

Bryan Grimes. (*North Carolina Museum of History*)

three-year-old Colonel Thomas F. Toon of the 20th North Carolina Infantry. In the meantime, Ramseur's brigade struck the federals at the Bloody Angle, and when General Ramseur received a severe wound, Colonel Bryan Grimes of the 4th North Carolina led the brigade. The Confederates drove the federals back to the front side of their entrenchments, but for twenty hours, the two sides continued to grapple along the Bloody Angle in some of the most savage combat of the war. The volume of musketry was so great it obliterated the surrounding vegetation, cutting in half an oak tree that reportedly measured twenty inches in diameter. For much of the time, a steady rainfall drenched the combatants, who fought to a bloody stalemate.[43]

While the infantry clashed at Spotsylvania Court House, Major General Philip H. Sheridan led twelve thousand Union cavalry in a raid on Richmond, with Jeb Stuart's Confederate cavalry in hot pursuit. On May 11, Stuart attempted to ambush Sheridan at Yellow Tavern six miles north of the Confederate capital. But the numerically superior federals broke through two successive blocking positions, and Stuart was mortally wounded while trying to rally his men in a driving thunderstorm. On May 12, the Confederates also lost Brigadier General James B. Gordon, a native Tar Heel who commanded a brigade that consisted of the 1st, 2nd, and 5th North Carolina Cavalry. Gordon was mortally wounded while fighting a delaying action at Meadow Bridge to prevent Sheridan from capturing Richmond. The Union cavalry commander decided to bypass the Confederate capital and instead rode south to the James River and the Union position at Haxall's Landing. Sheridan's unsuccessful raid on Richmond left Grant blind until the cavalry's return on May 24.[44]

On the night of May 18–19, Grant left his Spotsylvania line and began another flanking maneuver to sidle around Lee's right and drive all the way to Richmond. But Lee withdrew only as far as the south bank of the North Anna River to defend the crossing points there. After an indecisive clash with the Confederates at Ox Ford, Grant decided to maneuver once more to the southeast, but Lee responded quickly and concentrated a strong force at Cold Harbor to block the federal advance. On June 3, Grant launched a frontal assault against the well-entrenched Southern line; among the defenders were over three dozen North Carolina regiments and battalions. The attack was an abject failure. Over five thousand Union soldiers were killed, wounded, or missing—most within the first hour of the assault—compared with fewer than 1,500 Confederates. The disaster at Cold Harbor led to the first real pause of the Overland Campaign. During the past two months, the Army of the Potomac had sustained over fifty-five thousand casualties while the Army of Northern Virginia had lost more than thirty-three thousand. If Grant was shaken by the setback at Cold Harbor, it was only momentary, for within a few days, he was already planning his next move. Having run out of room to maneuver Lee into the open for a decisive blow, he decided to cross the James River and capture Petersburg to cut Lee's supply lines to the rest of the South.[45]

THE ATLANTA CAMPAIGN

While the armies of Grant and Lee fought in Virginia, the main armies of the western theater were battling in Georgia. The Atlanta Campaign began on May 7, 1864, as three Union armies under General Sherman advanced against the Confederate Army of Tennessee under General Johnston. Four North Carolina infantry regiments served in Johnston's army: the 58th and 60th of Brigadier General Alexander W. Reynolds's brigade, and the 29th and 39th of Brigadier General Matthew D. Ector's brigade.[46]

One of Sherman's subordinates, Major General James B. McPherson, found Snake Creek Gap on the enemy's western flank unguarded. Had McPherson exploited this opportunity, the Atlanta Campaign might well have ended then and there with a decisive Union victory. His mission had been to cut the Western and Atlantic Railroad—Johnston's supply line—and then strike the Confederates from the rear. Instead, McPherson lost his nerve and failed to advance beyond the gap. This enabled Johnston to withdraw to Resaca, where the Southerners dug in on high ground.[47]

On May 14, Sherman launched a diversionary assault on the main Confederate line while a Union XVI Corps division crossed the Oostanaula River to cut the Western and Atlantic Railroad in Johnston's rear. The Southern defenders repulsed the attack and at 4:00 that afternoon, Confederate corps commander Lieutenant General John Bell Hood counterattacked the open Union left flank and nearly overwhelmed it. The 58th and 60th North Carolina were among the regiments that took part in the attack. At dusk on the fifteenth, Hood assaulted the Union left flank a second time and was repulsed with heavy losses. The federals, meanwhile, had crossed the Oostanaula and now threatened Johnston's Western and Atlantic supply line. The Army of Tennessee evacuated its fortifications that night and began retreating south, ending the Battle of Resaca. Union losses totaled about four thousand, while Confederate casualties came to roughly three thousand. The 58th and 60th North Carolina sustained seven killed, thirty-six wounded, and eighteen captured.[48]

For the next three days, the Confederates fell back until they reached Cassville on May 19, where Johnston planned to ambush an isolated federal column. But when Hood warned the commanding general that an enemy force of unknown strength was advancing on his rear, Johnston canceled the attack and retreated instead. The Confederates halted at Allatoona Pass and then fell back to block Sherman; the Southerners established a line that ran northeast from Dallas to New Hope Church and Pickett's Mill. On May 25, Reynolds's brigade fought in the Battle of New Hope Church. The battle was a defensive victory for Hood's corps. The attacking federals suffered 1,600 casualties to the Confederates' 350. Though not heavily engaged, the 58th and 60th North Carolina took part in the fight. Their brigade commander, General Reynolds, nevertheless was severely wounded, and Colonel Robert C. Trigg assumed command of the brigade.[49]

By mid-June, the Confederates had fallen back to the Kennesaw Mountain line, a formidable position anchored on Big Kennesaw Mountain, Little Kennesaw Mountain, and Pigeon Hill. On June 19–20, the Union XX and XXIII Corps probed the Confederate left flank along the Powder Springs Road. On the evening of the twenty-first, Johnston ordered Hood to block the federal advance, and the Confederate corps commander decided to attack the XX Corps in the mistaken belief that it alone held the Union right. The Confederate assault began at 5:00 PM June 22. Hood was so confident of success that he sent no skirmishers forward to probe the enemy's defenses. No fewer than five federal batteries fired case shot and canister into the gray-and-butternut ranks as they advanced across the vast open fields of the Kolb farm. The attack soon collapsed, with the survivors hugging the ground to avoid the iron-and-lead firestorm. The Battle of Kolb's Farm cost the Confederates 1,000 casualties compared with the federals' 350 losses. The 58th and 60th North Carolina took part in the futile assault and lost heavily.[50]

Although Hood's attack was a failure, it convinced Sherman that the Confederate left flank was secure. The Union commander therefore decided to attempt a frontal assault on Johnston's Kennesaw Mountain line in the belief it was overextended. Sherman launched the attack on the morning of June 27. The federals met with a bloody repulse, costing them three thousand casualties, while the Confederates sustained one thousand killed, wounded, and missing. Afterward, General Thomas commented that "one or two more such assaults would use up this army."[51]

After the failed assault on Johnston's Kennesaw Mountain line, Sherman resumed his flanking tactics on the night of July 2. Early the next morning, Union skirmishers found the Confederate trenches empty, the soldiers in gray having withdrawn toward Atlanta. On July 5, the Army of Tennessee occupied a line of fortifications situated along the north bank of the Chattahoochee River covering the Western and Atlantic Railroad, but the federals crossed at several points farther north, forcing Johnston to abandon the Chattahoochee line. As the Southerners fell back toward the earthworks ringing Atlanta—their final line of defense—the Union forces paused to rest and resupply.[52]

Disappointed with Johnston's handling of the campaign thus far, Confederate President Davis replaced him with General Hood on July 17. Hood knew that Davis expected him to be far more aggressive than his predecessor had been, and he wasted no time in attacking Sherman's army. In a span of nine days, Hood launched three sorties. The first occurred south of Peachtree Creek on July 20. Holding the left of the Confederate line was Ector's brigade. So far in the Atlanta Campaign, the undersized brigade had been lightly engaged, but that would soon change. In addition to the 29th and 39th North Carolina Infantry, Ector's brigade comprised the 9th Texas Infantry as well as the 10th, 14th, and 32nd Texas Cavalry (dismounted). The brigade was attached to Major General Samuel G. French's division of Hardee's Corps.[53]

The Confederate assault was supposed to strike the federals while they were crossing Peachtree Creek, but most of the bluecoats had crossed the day before and were now dug in. The Southern attack began around midafternoon on the twentieth. Ector's brigade attempted to turn the Union right flank but was easily repulsed. The Battle of Peachtree Creek cost the Confederates about 2,500 casualties, while the federals lost 1,750. Ector's brigade reported thirty-nine losses, twenty-eight of whom were missing from the 29th North Carolina.[54]

Hood launched his second sortie just east of Atlanta on July 22. The Battle of Atlanta, as it became known, was the bloodiest day of the four-month campaign, resulting in 5,500 Confederate and 3,600 Union casualties; the highest-ranking fatality was General McPherson, commander of the federal Army of the Tennessee. On July 27, meanwhile, the 29th and 39th North Carolina lost their brigade commander to a Union shell fragment, which struck General Ector in the left leg above the knee, necessitating amputation. Colonel William H. Young of the 9th Texas Infantry assumed command of Ector's brigade. On July 28, Hood ordered a third sortie, which Hood's youngest corps commander, Stephen D. Lee, badly mismanaged. Of Hood's three assaults to relieve Atlanta, the Battle of Ezra Church was his most lopsided defeat, costing the attacking Confederates 3,000 casualties, compared with the defending federals' 650 losses.[55]

While fending off these attacks, Sherman continued to encircle Atlanta and cut the Confederates' remaining supply lines. In late August, he sent most of his army south of the Gate City to Jonesboro in order to cut Hood's last open rail line. Among the Confederate units rushed to defend Jonesboro were the 58th and 60th North Carolina. On the afternoon of August 31, the Southerners under Lieutenant General William J. Hardee launched a series of disjointed assaults against the strongly fortified Union line west of Jonesboro. The result was a bloody fiasco for the Confederates. On the afternoon of September 1, the federals counterattacked and broke through the Southern line. In the meantime, Union forces cut the Macon and Western Railroad north of Jonesboro, sealing Atlanta's fate. The two-day Battle of Jonesboro cost the Confederates over 2,000 casualties, compared with 1,149 losses for the federals. Realizing that he had lost his last open supply line and Atlanta with it, Hood began evacuating the city that night. At 9:00 PM on September 1, Ector's brigade led French's division out of Atlanta. They were the last Confederate troops to leave it.[56]

THE TENNESSEE CAMPAIGN

Hood then led the Army of Tennessee north to cut Sherman's supply line. On October 5, he sent French's division to attack the Union depot at Allatoona Pass, the main facility between Chattanooga and Atlanta. The federal garrison barely held out against a ferocious Confederate assault that resulted in over 1,500 casualties out of roughly four thousand total combatants. While the 39th North Carolina's casualties were light, the 29th North Carolina lost twelve killed, thirty-nine wounded, and three missing of 138 soldiers—a casualty rate of 37 percent.[57]

Hood continued pushing north before veering west into Alabama, but Sherman tired of the chase and returned to Atlanta in mid-October. He sent two Union corps to Chattanooga and placed them under General Thomas's command, while he readied the rest of his army group for the March to the Sea. In the meantime, Hood decided on a bold plan to defeat Thomas at Nashville before the latter could collect his scattered forces. As Sherman set out for Savannah in mid-November, Hood began crossing the Tennessee River into the Volunteer State. The Army of Tennessee captured Columbia on November 27; the 58th North Carolina remained there to garrison the town and guard 1,700 federal prisoners while the rest of the army continued north in pursuit of Union forces under Major General John M. Schofield.[58]

On November 29, Hood believed he had trapped the federals at Spring Hill, but they managed to slip past the sleeping Confederates that night. Furious over the missed opportunity, Hood was determined to crush Schofield's command before it could reach Nashville. Reaching Franklin on the morning of November 30, Schofield discovered that the wagon bridge across the Harpeth River was destroyed. Lacking a pontoon bridge, the Union commander decided to deploy most of his force south of town, and he placed it under the command of Brigadier General Jacob D. Cox. By the time the Confederates began to arrive, the federals occupied a strong line of entrenchments. Ignoring the advice of subordinates, Hood launched a frontal assault against the Union position at 4:00 PM. Although the Southerners broke through Cox's line at the Fountain Branch Carter house, the federals ultimately repulsed them. In the process, the Confederates sustained 6,252 casualties, almost 25 percent of their total strength. The losses included eight hundred commissioned officers, among them thirteen generals and over fifty regimental commanders. No North Carolina regiments took part in the Battle of Franklin. Ector's brigade was well to the rear guarding the army's pontoon train, the 58th North Carolina was on garrison duty at Columbia, and the 60th North Carolina was guarding a portion of the army's wagon train.[59]

Schofield began to withdraw his force from Franklin at midnight on December 1; by noon, the first of the federal troops staggered into Nashville, exhausted from marching and fighting on little or no food and sleep. Hood followed at a respectful distance and reached Nashville on December 2. He deployed his battered army, whittled down to just twenty-one thousand troops, along a four-mile front. A reconnaissance of Nashville convinced Hood that he lacked the force to storm the heavily fortified city. He instead decided to launch an attack against the eight-thousand-man Union garrison at Murfreesboro thirty miles to the southeast and force Thomas to march to its relief. Hood placed the Murfreesboro expedition under the command of the hard-charging cavalryman Major General Nathan Bedford Forrest, whose six thousand-man force included the 60th North Carolina, which now belonged to Brigadier General Joseph B. Palmer's brigade. Palmer's brigade had been formed in November 1864 by consolidating Brown's and Reynolds's brigades. Forrest intended to capture Fortress Rosecrans, a heavily fortified Union depot located about half a mile northwest of Murfreesboro. On December 7, the federal garrison routed Forrest's command. The Union force lost 225 killed, wounded, and missing in the Third Battle of Murfreesboro. Among the 197 Confederate casualties was Lieutenant Colonel James T. Weaver, the commander of the 60th North Carolina, who was killed in action. Although the attack on Fortress Rosecrans had failed, the 60th North Carolina continued to menace the federal garrison at Murfreesboro by tearing up railroad track and capturing a troop train. The Tar Heel regiment rejoined the army on December 18.[60]

James T. Weaver.

The 58th North Carolina was also on the move. On December 14, the regiment received orders to take their prisoners to Corinth, Mississippi. At the time, the 58th numbered 311 men present. Reaching their destination on December 23, the Carolinians turned over their prisoners to the provost marshal, and on the twenty-sixth, they were ordered to Okolona, Mississippi, to drive off a Union cavalry force that had cut the railroad there.[61]

While the two Tar Heel regiments performed detached duty, the bulk of Hood's army came under attack at Nashville on December 15. The federals staged a diversionary assault on the Confederate right before launching the main attack on the left and sweeping everything before them, including Ector's brigade under Colonel David Coleman of the 39th North Carolina. The Army of Tennessee fell back to a chain of hills a few miles south of their previous position, and Hood deployed his heavily outnumbered force to the right of Ector's brigade on a line that was far more compact than the previous one.[62]

The federals resumed the offensive on the afternoon of the sixteenth, and it unfolded much as the attack of the previous day had. Union commander Thomas launched a diversionary assault on the Confederate right to deceive Hood into shifting troops from the left, where the main attack would occur. The diversion worked, inducing Hood to detach two brigades from his already overextended left flank. In the meantime, Union cavalry swept around the Confederate left, where it clashed with Ector's brigade, while blue-clad infantry overwhelmed the center of Hood's line, which collapsed as panic-stricken Southerners turned and fled south down the Granny White Pike and the Franklin Pike. The two-day Battle of Nashville cost the Confederates roughly 6,800 casualties compared with the federals' 3,061 losses. In less than three weeks, the Army of Tennessee had sustained nearly fourteen thousand combat casualties, over one-third of the men Hood had led into Tennessee.[63]

On December 19, Hood placed General Forrest in command of the army's rear guard. In addition to cavalry, the rear guard included Ector's brigade and seven other infantry brigades under Major General Edward C. Walthall. The rear guard enabled the army to safely cross the Tennessee River by driving back pursuing federal cavalry with a few well-timed ambushes. The remnant of the Army of Tennessee then marched to Tupelo, Mississippi, where it went into winter camp. By January 20, 1865, the army was down to just 18,708 men due to sickness and desertion. Hood submitted his resignation to President Davis, and Davis accepted it on January 23. Soon afterward, Hood's successor, Lieutenant General Richard S. Taylor, transferred the 29th and 39th North Carolina (having just rejoined the army after a furlough) and the rest of French's division to Mobile, Alabama, where they fought in the Battle of Spanish Fort on April 8. Taylor also sent the 58th and 60th North Carolina east with the remnant of the army that fought under Johnston in the Battle of Bentonville. Following the battle, the 58th and the 60th surrendered with Johnston's army on April 26, 1865. On May 4, the 29th and the 39th surrendered with Taylor's Department of Alabama, Mississippi, and East Louisiana forces at Meridian, Mississippi.[64]

THE PETERSBURG CAMPAIGN, 1864

Following the failed frontal assaults at Cold Harbor on June 3, 1864, Grant decided to change tactics. Rather than attack Richmond directly, he chose to sever Lee's line of communications and compel the Confederates to abandon Richmond's defenses due to a lack of supplies. The Union commander accordingly began moving a part of his army south of the James River to capture the vital rail hub at Petersburg. Finding himself heavily outnumbered, the Confederate commander at Petersburg, General P. G. T. Beauregard, pleaded for reinforcements, and on June 15, Lee sent him Hoke's division—which included Brigadier General James G. Martin's and Brigadier General Thomas L. Clingman's Tar Heel brigades—as well as several other

"Battle of the Crater" by Alfred R. Waud.

units. By the morning of the sixteenth, Beauregard's force manning the fortifications east of the city totaled fourteen thousand men. Late that afternoon, the federals attacked Beauregard's line and were repulsed with heavy losses. Union forces made repeated assaults on the seventeenth and achieved a limited breakthrough, but the Confederates rushed in reinforcements, including Ransom's Tar Heel brigade led by Colonel Leroy McAfee, and counterattacked. The fighting was hand to hand, and Colonel John G. Jones of the 35th North Carolina Infantry was killed while leading his regiment in the charge.[65]

Having failed to seize Petersburg, Grant attempted to cut the railroads supplying Lee's army south and southwest of the Cockade City. The Union raiders destroyed large sections of railroad track, but the Confederates were quick to repair the damage. With his forces unable to penetrate Lee's defenses either north or south of the James River, the Union commander concluded that the siege of Petersburg had begun. In July, the federals prepared to detonate a mine under the Confederate fortifications east of the city. Grant ordered an attack on Richmond to draw Confederate forces away from Petersburg prior to the mine explosion. The federals crossed the James at Deep Bottom, and the Confederates struck the right flank of Sheridan's cavalry. A Union counterattack in turn threatened the right flank of Lane's Tar Heel brigade, which was held by the 7th North Carolina. Although the federals failed to open the road to Richmond, their actions induced Lee to concentrate over five divisions at Richmond, leaving just four divisions to defend Petersburg.[66]

At 4:45 on the morning of July 30, 1864, the mine detonated with a deafening blast, blowing a gigantic hole in the Confederate line and killing or wounding hundreds of Southern soldiers. "The Crater," as it was later called, measured about 30 feet deep, 120 feet wide, and 170 feet long. A Union eyewitness called the explosion "a magnificent spectacle" in which a "mass of earth went up into the air, carrying with it men, guns, carriages, and timbers, and spread out like an immense cloud." The blast stunned not only the Confederates but also the federals, who delayed attacking for ten minutes. The assault proved to be a debacle. The soldiers in blue, including a division of US Colored Infantry, swept into the Crater and became trapped. Dug in to the left of the Crater, Ransom's Tar Heel brigade was one of the first units to counterattack. The commander of the 49th North Carolina, Lieutenant Colonel John A. Flemming, was killed, and the commander of the 25th North Carolina, Major William S. Grady, was mortally wounded in fierce hand-to-hand fighting. Confederate reinforcements flooded into the Crater and drove back the Union attackers, killing many wounded or surrendering black soldiers. The Battle of the Crater cost the federals 3,798 casualties and the Confederates 1,491 losses. "It was the saddest affair I have witnessed in this war," Grant wrote.[67]

The fighting continued into August, with the federals attacking the Confederate fortifications shielding both Richmond and Petersburg. On August 18, the Union V Corps cut the Weldon Railroad at Globe Tavern and managed to hold the position despite a series of ferocious counterattacks launched by A. P. Hill's corps. Grant attempted to exploit this success by sending the II Corps south to Ream's Station, but after an initial repulse, Heth's and North Carolina native Major General Cadmus M. Wilcox's divisions of Hill's Corps—in which roughly half the soldiers were Tar Heels—succeeded in routing the federals, taking over two thousand prisoners and capturing nine cannons. Even so, the loss of the Weldon Railroad at Globe Tavern forced the Confederates to haul supplies by wagon along a twenty-four-mile detour from Stony Creek Station north to Petersburg.[68]

The next Union offensive began on the night of September 28–29, when Major General Benjamin F. Butler sent an assault force from the Army of the James across the James River from Bermuda Hundred to Deep Bottom. Confident that black soldiers could be relied on in battle, Butler selected Brigadier General Charles J. Paine's division of US Colored Infantry to lead the assault on New Market Heights south of Richmond. Colonel Samuel A. Duncan's two-regiment brigade launched the first charge on the Confederate works and was repulsed with heavy losses. "It was a deadly hailstorm of bullets sweeping men down as hailstones sweep the leaves from trees," wrote Sergeant Major Christian A. Fleetwood of the 4th USCT. "It was sheer madness."

As Duncan's brigade withdrew in disarray, the brigades of Colonels Alonzo G. Draper and John H. Holman advanced into the leaden hailstorm. Two of the regiments, the 36th and the 37th USCT, had been raised in

North Carolina. The assault stalled, but the men rallied and then rushed forward, driving the Confederates back to nearby Fort Harrison. For heroism in the Battle of New Market Heights, fourteen USCT soldiers received the Medal of Honor, the first black soldiers to be awarded the nation's highest decoration for valor. In the fighting at Chaffin's Farm to the south, New Bern resident Private Joseph H. Shea of the 92nd New York Infantry displayed conspicuous gallantry in bringing wounded comrades off the field while under a heavy fire, for which he received a Medal of Honor.[69]

After a brief rest, the federals resumed the advance and captured Fort Harrison. On September 30, Lee sent Major General Charles W. Field's and Hoke's divisions to recapture the fort. Hoke's two Tar Heel brigades, Clingman's and Martin's, participated in the poorly executed assault that resulted in 1,200 Confederate casualties. At Petersburg, meanwhile, the federals attempted to seize the Boydton Plank Road and the South Side Railroad and thus place a stranglehold on Lee's remaining supply lines. Two divisions of Confederate troops that included the Tar Heel brigades of Lane and Brigadier Generals John R. Cooke, William MacRae, and Alfred M. Scales counterattacked and succeeded in routing the federals, but Union infantry reinforcements and devastating artillery fire brought the advancing Southerners to an abrupt halt. During the Battle of Jones Farm, the commander of the 37th North Carolina in Lane's brigade, Colonel William M. Barbour, was mortally wounded in the hip and died on October 3. Four days later, Lee struck the Union right flank near Richmond, sending Field's and Hoke's divisions on an attack along the Darbytown Road. The soldiers in gray succeeded in routing federal cavalry and capturing eight cannons, but Union infantry repulsed a later assault along the New Market Road. The Confederates sustained a total of 1,300 casualties. The battle marked Lee's final offensive operation in 1864.[70]

EARLY'S RAID AND THE 1864 VALLEY CAMPAIGN

Since the Battle of Cold Harbor, Lee's army had been fighting in a much wider area than the Richmond-Petersburg front. In June 1864, he detached Lieutenant General Jubal A. Early's (formerly Ewell's) corps and Major General John C. Breckinridge's division to defeat a Union force operating in the Shenandoah Valley. Among the troops in Early's command were four North Carolina brigades spread over two divisions led by two Tar Heel major generals: Stephen D. Ramseur and Robert E. Rodes. After securing the railroad center at Lynchburg, Virginia, Early headed north to threaten Washington, DC, in order to draw off Northern troops from Grant's army group besieging Richmond. On July 9, he defeated a smaller Union force at Monocacy near Frederick, Maryland, and then unsuccessfully attacked Fort Stevens on the northwestern perimeter of the Washington defenses. Following that setback, Early withdrew into the valley, where, on July 24, he routed a Union force in the Second Battle of Kernstown. Less than a week later, Confederate cavalry raiders burned much of Chambersburg, Pennsylvania,

Stephen D. Ramseur. (*North Carolina Collection, UNC-Chapel Hill*)

Robert E. Rodes. (*digitalcollections.vmi.edu*)

after local officials proved unable to pay a ransom.[71]

In mid-August, General Sheridan assumed command of the Union force pursuing Early's Confederates. On September 19, the federals routed the heavily outnumbered Southerners in the Battle of Third Winchester, despite valiant fighting by the veteran troops of Ramseur's and Rodes's divisions. The Confederates lost about two thousand casualties, including General Rodes, who was killed by flying shrapnel from an artillery shell. One of Ramseur's brigade commanders, Colonel Archibald C. Godwin, was also a fatality. Three days later, Sheridan once again routed Early in the Battle of Fisher's Hill. On October 9, a cavalry fight at Tom's Brook ended with the Union horsemen pursuing their Confederate adversaries for twenty miles—an incident that became known as the "Woodstock Races." On the morning of October 19, Early attacked the federals at Cedar Creek and drove them for a considerable distance but failed to crush them. About four o'clock that afternoon, Sheridan arrived and rallied his demoralized troops, and they succeeded in sweeping the Southerners from the field. Having just learned of the birth of his first child, General Ramseur fell from the saddle with a mortal wound and died the following day. Soon after the Battle of Cedar Creek, Lee recalled most of Early's depleted command to the Richmond-Petersburg theater, leaving his subordinate to defend the Shenandoah Valley with just a skeleton force.[72]

THE PETERSBURG AND APPOMATTOX CAMPAIGNS, 1865

Fall 1864 saw the federals attempting to defeat the Confederates on either side of the James River. On a rainy October 27, General Butler sent two corps toward Richmond. General Longstreet commanded the Confederate troops north of the James, having returned to Lee's army after a lengthy recuperation following his wounding in the Battle of the Wilderness. Longstreet's men succeeded in stopping Butler's advance at Fair Oaks. On the same day, the federals attempted to seize the Boydton Plank Road south of Petersburg but failed to do so. Six weeks later, on December 7, Grant sent a force of infantry and cavalry on a raid to close the Weldon Railroad. Lee responded by sending his own combined force to stop their progress and managed to save a key railroad bridge over the Meherrin River. But the federals had destroyed fifteen miles of track before they suspended operations.

For most of the winter, the Union and Confederate soldiers hunkered down in their cold, wet trenches and waited for spring. By January 31, 1865, Lee's army totaled about seventy thousand troops, barely half the number of federal forces in the Richmond-Petersburg theater. The soldiers in blue were better clothed, fed, and equipped than their Confederate counterparts. Desertions were becoming epidemic in Lee's army, especially within the Tar Heel contingent in Hill's corps. General Lee wrote a letter to North Carolina Gov. Zebulon B. Vance, indicating that the desertions were "occasioned to a considerable extent by letters written to the soldiers by their friends at home." Lee urged Vance to do all in his power to "change public sentiment and cheer the spirits of the people." Although the Confederate government attempted to negotiate peace terms with the Lincoln administration, culminating in the Hampton Roads Conference of February 3, 1865, those efforts came to naught. On February 5, Grant once again attempted to seize the Boydton Plank Road and the South Side Railroad. When the Battle of Hatcher's Run ended on February 7, the federals had failed to capture the railroad, but they had pushed their lines to within three miles of that crucial objective.[73]

By March 1865, Lee realized that if his army were to survive, he would have to abandon his present position and join General Johnston's army in North Carolina. Lee designated Major General John B. Gordon, his junior corps commander, with the task of breaking through the Union line. About one-fourth of the soldiers in Gordon's assault force were North Carolinians. Gordon chose Fort Stedman as his objective because of its proximity to the Confederate line and its heavily damaged state. If successful, the attackers would overrun Fort Stedman and push deep into the rear of the federal position and thereby threaten City Point, the site of both Grant's headquarters and the main Union supply depot. The assault began at 4:00 AM on March 25, with the Confederates capturing Fort Stedman as well as the batteries on either flank. But the defenders soon recovered from their initial shock, and several nearby Union batteries subjected the attackers to a deadly crossfire. Gordon's assault began to lose momentum, and by 8:00 AM Lee concluded that the fortifications beyond Fort Stedman "could only be taken at great sacrifice." He therefore directed Gordon to fall back. The failed assault cost the Confederates about 2,700 killed, wounded, and missing, while the federals suffered 1,044 casualties. The repulse was a severe blow to Confederate morale.[74]

Rufus Barringer. (*Archive.org*)

Less than a week later, Grant began the offensive that culminated in the fall of Richmond and Petersburg. On April 1, 1865, Union infantry and cavalry commanded by General Sheridan routed the Confederate force defending the crossroads known as Five Forks on Lee's right flank. Sheridan's capture of Five Forks emboldened Grant to order an attack on the Confederate lines around Petersburg on the morning of April 2. The assault began at 4:30 AM. The Southerners repulsed the attack that struck in and around Fort Mahone, but they were unable to turn back the federals, who assaulted the Rebel earthworks held by Hill's corps along Hatcher's Run. The men of Lane's Tar Heel brigade were spread out at five-foot intervals, having to defend a section of the line that was once occupied by at least two brigades. The Union troops swarmed into the trenches, and for about twenty minutes, the fighting was hand to hand. During the melee, the federals captured the colors of the 37th North Carolina, and A. P. Hill was killed. Overwhelmed, the Confederates at last broke and ran, while the victorious soldiers in blue raced to capture Lee's last supply lines—the Boydton Plank Road and the South Side Railroad. The federals also seized four miles of defensive line extending from the western outskirts of Petersburg to Hatcher's Run.[75]

As his position at Richmond and Petersburg collapsed, Lee advised President Davis to evacuate the Confederate capital. The Army of Northern Virginia withdrew on the night of April 2–3, heading toward Amelia Court House on the Richmond and Danville Railroad, thirty-six miles northwest of Petersburg. Lee had arranged to have three hundred fifty thousand rations and other supplies waiting there for his retreating army, which would then march south to join Johnston's army in North Carolina. To shorten the columns, Lee's forces used several roads. The rear guard for Lieutenant General Richard H. Anderson's corps was Brigadier General William P. Roberts's cavalry brigade, which consisted of the 4th North Carolina Cavalry and the 16th North Carolina Cavalry battalion. On the morning of April 3, Roberts's brigade skirmished with elements of Brigadier General George A. Custer's mounted division until it was relieved by Brigadier General Rufus Barringer's Tar Heel cavalry brigade at Namozine Church. Barringer's command held off the federal horsemen long enough for Anderson's foot soldiers to escape, but Barringer and his staff were captured along with the colors of the 2nd North Carolina Cavalry.[76]

While Grant pursued Lee toward Amelia Court House, federal forces entered Richmond. Leading the procession was the 36th USCT, formerly known as the 2nd North Carolina Colored Troops. They were met by crowds of former slaves who gathered along the roadside to greet them. As the troops marched past, Richmond Mayor Joseph Mayo surrendered the city to Union Major General Godfrey Weitzel.[77]

On April 4, the Confederates arriving at Amelia received quite a shock, for they found only train cars loaded with ammunition and not the rations the famished soldiers so desperately needed. The army's commissary officers had no choice but to forage on the countryside. This delay cost the Confederates dearly, for it enabled the pursuing federals to overtake them. When the rebels approached Jetersville on April 5, the advance guard found a strong federal force blocking the road to North Carolina, so they headed west toward Farmville instead. In the meantime, Grant directed the commander of the Army of the James, Major General Edward O. C. Ord, to halt at Burkeville for the night. On the sixth, Ord was to block Lee's route to Farmville at High Bridge while Sheridan and the commander of the Army of the Potomac, Major General George G. Meade, attacked the Confederates from the rear.[78]

On the afternoon of April 6, the federals overtook the Confederates at Sailor's Creek and struck them hard at three points: Ewell's force near the Hillsman house, Anderson's force at Marshall's Crossroads, and Gordon's force at the Lockett farm. The Union attackers overcame stubborn resistance and routed the rebels on all fronts. "My God," Lee exclaimed in disbelief as he beheld his fleeing soldiers, "has the army dissolved?" In the Battle of Sailor's Creek, the Confederate commander lost one-fourth of his army; almost eight thousand soldiers in gray were captured, including six generals. Among the trophies taken were the flags of the 4th, 6th, and 21st North Carolina Infantry. For good reason, April 6, 1865, became known as "Black Thursday" among veterans of the Army of Northern Virginia.[79]

A few miles to the west at High Bridge, however, Southern cavalry defeated a small Union force from Ord's Army of the James, enabling Lee's army to cross the Appomattox River and reach Farmville on April 7. But the Confederates had managed to burn only a section of the railroad bridge before the federals drove them off, leaving the wagon bridge intact. Grant, meanwhile, sent a letter to Lee urging that he avoid "any further effusion of blood" by "surrendering that portion of the Confederate States army known as the Army of Northern Virginia." Lee responded by asking Grant to specify the terms of surrender.[80]

After a skirmish at Cumberland Church on April 7, the Confederates continued the westward retreat at midnight, with many soldiers dropping out of the column from hunger, fatigue, and despair. Lee's army reached the village of Appomattox Court House on the afternoon of April 8. Five miles to the west, Sheridan's cavalry had captured Appomattox Station and the trainload of rations intended for Lee's army. The two commanders exchanged additional dispatches on the topic of surrender, though Lee maintained that he "did not think the emergency has arisen to call for the surrender of this army." On the morning of April 9, Lee made a final, desperate attempt to break through the Union forces that had encircled his army. He sent a combined force of infantry and cavalry under General Gordon on a sweeping attack to the southwest that succeeded in scattering the federal horsemen and briefly opening the road, but an overwhelming force of Union infantry soon closed the gap and shoved the Confederates back toward the village. During the fight, Sergeant Ivy Ritchie of the 14th North Carolina was struck down by canister. He was thought to be the last soldier in the Army of Northern Virginia killed in action.[81]

Gordon's repulse convinced Lee that the end was at hand. He sent a messenger under a white flag to Grant with a request to discuss surrender terms, and a cease-fire soon went into effect. Lee and Grant met at the Wilmer McLean house in Appomattox Court House that afternoon, and the Confederate commander surrendered the Army of Northern Virginia. "The life of the C.S. is gone," wrote a soldier in the 37th North Carolina. On April 12, roughly twenty-eight thousand Confederates stacked arms and furled their colors for the last time. "Not a word was spoken," recalled Lieutenant Walter A. Montgomery of the 12th North Carolina Infantry, "we did not even look into each others faces." A total of 5,012 North Carolinians received their paroles and then made their way home.[82]

The Commerce Raider CSS *Shenandoah.* (*Naval History and Heritage Command*)

The last surrender of the Civil War occurred on November 6, 1865, when Commander James I. Waddell of Pittsboro, North Carolina, the skipper of the Confederate commerce raider CSS *Shenandoah*, surrendered to the captain of the British man-of-war HMS *Donegal* at Liverpool, England. After lowering the Confederate colors for the final time, Waddell walked to the Liverpool Town Hall and presented a letter to the mayor offering his vessel to the British government. The US government took possession of the *Shenandoah* in 1866.[83]

12. From Reconstruction to the Spanish-American War

COMING HOME

The thousands of veterans who returned to North Carolina in spring 1865 found their homes, farms, and businesses devastated by four long years of war. A substantial number of Tar Heels had made the ultimate sacrifice and never came home. Tradition has it that forty thousand North Carolina soldiers died during the war, but recent scholarship shows the actual figure to be closer to 31,954 Confederates, 630 white federals, and 834 US Colored Troops, for a total of 33,418 fallen men. Many returning veterans had lost an arm or a leg, and their missing limbs served as a reminder of the war's heavy toll. The state government assumed the task of ensuring that each disabled man should receive an artificial limb at no cost. At the behest of the General Assembly, in February 1866, Gov. Jonathan Worth asked each county sheriff to provide the number of artificial arms and legs needed for amputees in his jurisdiction. The state received 1,508 applications, and it equipped a former bayonet factory in Raleigh to manufacture prosthetic limbs. The state covered all costs, including the out-of-pocket expenses of veterans who had to travel to Raleigh. By the time the factory closed its doors in June 1867, the state had spent just over $80,000 on the program.[1]

When the war ended, North Carolina's civil government was replaced by martial law. The bulk of General Sherman's army group had departed the state shortly after the surrender, leaving behind an occupation force under General Schofield. Despite the presence of Union garrisons in the larger towns, lawlessness racked many rural areas of the state from the coast to the mountains. The desperadoes consisted of Union deserters, former Confederate soldiers, and local civilians, with the gangs sometimes masquerading as federal units. "At first we were threatened by armed mobs of Confederate soldiers, deserters &c," wrote Lincolnton resident David Schenck, "but, the Yankees put them down where they were, and in our town we dispersed a large mob by promptly arming our citizens and de-

John M. Schofield.

fying their power." After arresting nine of the ringleaders, the soldiers and civilians quickly restored order in Lincolnton.[2]

PRESIDENTIAL RECONSTRUCTION

On May 29, 1865, President Andrew Johnson took the first step in restoring civil government in the South. He issued two proclamations outlining his Reconstruction policy. The first granted amnesty to all former Confederates except those who fell into fourteen classes owing to factors such as military rank, wealth, or high position in state or Confederate government, but the excluded men could apply for a presidential pardon. The second proclamation designated *Raleigh Standard* editor William W. Holden as provisional governor of North Carolina. It also provided a mechanism to restore the Tar Heel State to its former relations with the federal government by means of a constitutional convention called by the new governor. At minimum, the convention had to repeal the secession ordinance, abolish slavery, and repudiate the state's war debt. Holden would also appoint loyal men to state and local offices.[3]

Of greatest interest to Schofield, no doubt, was the paragraph regarding the military's role in Presidential Reconstruction. The military commander and his officers and men were to "assist the said provisional governor in carrying into effect this proclamation." They were also "to abstain from in any way hindering, impeding, or discouraging the loyal people from the organization of a State government as herein authorized." That was all—Johnston's proclamation was silent on martial law and lacked a clear definition of the army's role. The president's vague guidance led to a clash between the provisional governor and the military commander over their respective powers.

With Holden's accession, the new occupation commander in the state, Brigadier General Thomas H. Ruger, began transferring authority to the state's civil officials. On July 5, 1865, Ruger announced that Holden had appointed mayors and boards of commissioners for eighteen North Carolina towns, with more to follow. As soon as the mayors indicated their readiness to govern, the federal garrisons would withdraw, with small detachments left to guard public property and inspect railroad trains. On July 6, Ruger announced that the state would be divided into five military districts, and four days later he reminded his district and post commanders that the transfer of authority did not relieve them of responsibility for the sanitary condition of towns within their commands, nor did it re-

William W. Holden. (*North Carolina State Archives*)

Thomas H. Ruger. (*New York Public Library*)

move the liquor traffic from their "exclusive control."

On August 30, Holden called a convention, which met in Raleigh on October 2, to amend the state constitution. The convention wasted no time in passing ordinances that prohibited slavery and repealed North Carolina's secession ordinance. But the delegates became deadlocked over repudiating the state's war debt of nearly $19 million, and only a note from President Johnson instructing the convention to refute the debt broke the impasse. The issue nevertheless cost Holden the support of political allies such as the state treasurer, Jonathan Worth, who defeated him in the election for governor and assumed office on December 28.

Although the US Army remained in the background during the convention and the election, federal soldiers committed numerous acts of violence. Black soldiers clashed with white soldiers and white policemen in Wilmington and several other towns, while in Raleigh, gangs of white troops robbed and vandalized black-owned businesses and beat the proprietors. The freedpeople on Roanoke Island complained that white soldiers brazenly stole from them and that any attempt to resist invariably resulted in their being jailed. On the other hand, the majority of Freedmen's Bureau agents were army officers who spent most of their workday as arbitrators in disputes or contract negotiations between black laborers and their white employers, often handling dozens of cases per day. Officially designated the Bureau of Refugees, Freedmen, and Abandoned Lands, the Freedmen's Bureau was an agency of the War Department. The bureau's mission was to help those displaced and impoverished by the war, to protect the former slaves from injustice, to provide them with a basic education, and to help them find work and receive fair wages.[4]

Rumors of a freedmen's Christmas insurrection plot led the state senate's

Committee on Military Affairs to meet with Ruger on December 13 and request that he provide the state militia with arms and ammunition. The general refused, explaining that he lacked the authority to do so and then indicating he could find no evidence of a conspiracy by the freedpeople. He added that the remaining black troops in the state were now stationed at remote coastal forts and that white soldiers garrisoned Wilmington and New Bern. As a further precaution, Ruger dispatched one company each of the 28th Michigan Infantry, a white regiment, to Edenton and Elizabeth City, two potential flash points on the coast. The holidays were free of disturbances, so on January 3, 1866, Ruger returned the two companies to their permanent station at New Bern. In Wilmington, meanwhile, Brigadier General George Crook permitted the town's freedpeople to hold an Emancipation Day parade on January 1, which the *Wilmington Dispatch* described as a "harmless enjoyment." Similar parades were held in Fayetteville, Halifax, and New Bern. And so ended the Christmas insurrection scare of 1865.

The surest indication of Ruger's opinion regarding the scare was his steady reduction of troop strength in his department until just three regiments—two white and one black—remained at the close of 1865. Between June and December 1865, about forty-two thousand troops departed from North Carolina, leaving Ruger with an occupation force of 2,209—a reduction of 95 percent. He knew that his volunteers were homesick, bored, and often undisciplined. Citizens at Morganton complained of outrages committed by soldiers of the 5th Ohio Cavalry. The regimental commander's flagrant misconduct resulted in his court-martial and conviction on several charges. Though Ruger was understandably eager to replace his volunteer soldiers with more-disciplined regulars, the latter were in short supply. Only after the arrival of four companies of the 5th US Cavalry and six companies of the 8th US Infantry in spring 1866 could he authorize the mustering out of his two remaining white volunteer regiments.

In January 1866, the General Assembly passed legislation to define the rights of the freedpeople. These and similar laws passed by other Southern state legislatures became known collectively as the Black Codes. While North Carolina's Black Code proved more liberal than most of the others, the laws still placed the former slaves under the same discriminatory restrictions as antebellum free blacks. Under the Tar Heel State's Black Code, freedmen could not testify in court against whites, serve on juries, or intermarry with whites. The laws also discriminated in matters such as mobility, vagrancy, apprenticeship, contracts, gun ownership, and in the punishment for assault to commit rape, a capital offense only when the assailant was a black man and the victim a white woman.

In Congress, the Republican majority responded to the Black Codes by passing two bills intended to protect blacks from white oppression. The Freedmen's Bureau Act extended the life of the agency and authorized military tribunals to intervene in cases involving freedmen who were denied rights enjoyed by whites or who faced unequal punishment for the same crime. The Civil Rights Act granted citizenship to all native-born Americans except Indians. President Johnson vetoed both bills because he deemed them unconstitutional and believed they would require "a permanent military force" to enforce them. In April 1866, Congress passed the Civil Rights Act over Johnson's veto and two months later did the same with the Freedmen's Bureau Act.

The army found itself caught squarely in the middle of the feud between the president and Congress. In eastern North Carolina, it also had to deal with an ominous threat in the form of outlaw gangs called regulators. Although blacks and white loyalists bore the brunt of the regulators' criminal activity, which ranged from vandalism and armed robbery to murder, they should not be confused with the later Ku Klux Klan. In fact, some of the criminal bands were either biracial or consisted entirely of African Americans. By early 1867, the civil authorities' failure to halt the regulators' depredations compelled the army to intervene. On February 20, the acting department commander, Brigadier General John C. Robinson, issued General Orders No. 17, directing all post commanders "to use every means at their disposal to rid the country of these banditti." If the outlaws resisted arrest, the order stated, they were to "be treated as guerrillas and summarily punished."

Wishing to solidify the gains made by the Civil Rights Act, Congress passed the Fourteenth Amendment—in effect, the North's peace terms to the defeated South. The first section restated the Civil Rights Act in terms that established the supremacy of the federal government in defining and protecting the rights of its citizens. The second section allowed the states to continue determining voter eligibility but reduced congressional representation in proportion to the number of adult males denied the franchise, thereby penalizing any Southern state that barred freedmen from voting. The third section excluded persons from federal or state office who had supported the rebellion after taking an oath to uphold the Constitution. The fourth section reaffirmed the government's commitment to pay the federal war debt, repudiated the Confederate war debt, and denied compensation for the loss of slave property. The fifth and final section granted Congress the power to enforce the amendment.

MILITARY RECONSTRUCTION

Acting on Johnson's advice, ten of the former Confederate states, including North Carolina, rejected the Fourteenth Amendment. On March 2, 1867, Congress replaced the president's plan of Reconstruction with one of their own—the penalty for the states' failure to ratify the Fourteenth Amendment and protect blacks and white loyalists from the kind of organized violence perpetrated by the regulators. Tennessee, however, was excluded because it had already ratified the amendment and rejoined the Union. Congress passed the Reconstruction Act over Johnson's veto and thus placed North Carolina and nine other Southern states under military rule. The act divided the South into five military districts and directed the

Daniel E. Sickles.

president to appoint a general to command each district. North Carolina and South Carolina formed the Second Military District.

Three weeks later, the Second Reconstruction Act passed over yet another presidential veto. It specified the procedure that the ten Southern states had to follow to reenter the Union. The first step was for the district commanders to call elections for each of their states to decide on a constitutional convention and elect delegates. Should the convention measure pass, the delegates would meet and draft a new constitution guaranteeing the vote for freedmen. Once the state had ratified the constitution and the Fourteenth Amendment, Congress would review its action. If approved, the state's US representatives and senators would be seated, signifying readmission to the Union. At that point, Congress would declare Military Reconstruction finished in that state.

On March 21, 1867, Major General Daniel E. Sickles assumed command of the Second Military District and made his headquarters in Charleston, South Carolina. He announced that civil government in the Carolinas was merely provisional "and subject to the paramount authority of the United States," which the general believed he embodied. During his tenure, Sickles issued a series of general orders that formed a new—albeit temporary—legal code for North Carolina. These orders introduced fundamental economic, social, judicial, and political changes that ranged from debtor relief and gun control to removing all property qualifications for holding public office and abolishing the death penalty for burglary and larceny. One forward-looking directive anticipated civil rights legislation of a later century by prohibiting racial and class discrimination on public transportation and rendering violators liable to civil lawsuits and trial by military tribunals.

In addition, Sickles intervened in a murder case involving a freedman in Fayetteville who was murdered while being escorted to jail after being charged with the attempted rape of a white woman. When the coroner's inquest ended inconclusively, Sickles ordered a Freedmen's Bureau officer to conduct a criminal investigation to identify suspects, and the accused were tried and convicted of murder by a military commission. Though sentenced to death, the three perpetrators were pardoned by President Johnson. But the case induced Sickles to replace most of Fayetteville's civil officials, including the mayor and the county coroner, in the belief that the local authorities had shown a determination to deny justice to the freedpeople. He intervened in the civil affairs of several other North Carolina towns. Besides appointing and removing civil officials, he suspended local elections and placed local law enforcement personnel under the supervision of post commanders. Sickles also had to contend with the regulators in the eastern part of the state as well as numerous outbreaks of violence in the Piedmont and western regions. Civilian law enforcement officials sometimes harassed large gatherings of freedpeople on the grounds of preserving law and order, but these assemblages invariably proved to be peaceful political rallies.

Determined to bring Sickles and several other generals under firm control, President Johnson directed his attorney general, Henry Stanbery, to draft an opinion defining the powers of the district commanders in the South under the First Reconstruction Act. Several of Stanbery's comments referred indirectly to Sickles. "The military commander is made a conservator of the peace, not a legislator," the attorney general argued. "He has no authority to enact or declare a new code of laws for the people within his district under any idea that he can make a better code than the people have made for themselves."

Believing that Stanbery's opinion undermined his authority, on June 19, Sickles requested that he be relieved of his command and granted a court of inquiry to answer Stanbery's accusations. For reasons known to him alone, Johnson passed up the opportunity to replace Sickles with a more acceptable general. The president instead directed the adjutant general to refuse Sickles's resignation and deny his request for a court of inquiry. On July 19, Congress upheld Sickles's actions as district commander by passing the Third Reconstruction Act over Johnson's veto. The act declared the Southern civil governments organized during Presidential Reconstruction illegal, yet it retained them on a provisional basis under the supervision of Congress and the district commanders. To preempt future legalistic assaults, the act also declared that the district commanders were not bound "by any opinion of any civil officers of the United States."

But Sickles soon offered Johnson a golden opportunity to dismiss him. On July 27, the post commander at Wilmington prohibited a deputy US marshal from enforcing a judgment issued by the US Circuit Court for the District of North Carolina. Sickles upheld the officer's action, and on August 26, the president replaced Sickles with Brigadier General Edward R. S. Canby. On August 30, Sickles wrote a lengthy report to General Grant justifying his course of action in the federal court case, and he defended his tenure as commander of the Second Military District. "The work of reconstruction has all been done quietly," he maintained, "without violence, without the actual exercise of force." One statistic challenges that rosy assessment: during Sickles's five-month tenure, military commissions in the Second Military District had to try 280 citizens for crimes ranging from larceny to murder. He nevertheless provided the Carolinas with expanded civil rights, debtor relief, alcohol and gun control, racially integrated public transportation, and penal reform. Yet nearly all of Sickles's reforms were swept away

Edward R. S. Canby.

within a few years. From the standpoint of longevity, "Sickles's code" must be accounted a failure. Even so, the general had failed in a worthy enterprise.

On September 5, 1867, Canby officially assumed command of the Second Military District. From the start, the general and Governor Worth clashed over Sickles's code, the appointment or removal of judges and other civil officials, the military's intervention in the state's judicial process, and the civil courts' alleged persecution of blacks and white loyalists. Canby also had to contend with the regulators, who were still running amok in the east.

One of Canby's most important tasks was to hold a statewide election to decide on a constitutional convention and to choose delegates. When Canby assumed command, voter registration in the Tar Heel State was already underway. He held the election on November 19 and 20. North Carolina voters overwhelmingly approved the convention measure. Of the state's 179,653 registered voters, 93,006 voted for the convention and 32,961 voted against it. The white vote split, while the black vote was unanimous—61,722 for and 0 against. Not only did the Conservatives suffer a lopsided defeat in the convention vote, but they also enabled the Republicans to gain 107 of the convention's 120 delegates.

After the election, Canby decided to reduce the number of army posts from eleven to five to simplify the logistical requirements and to minimize the erosion of discipline that often befell units on detached duty. Alarmed by the news that the occupation troops would soon be withdrawn from their communities, prominent citizens in Fayetteville, Greensboro, New Bern, and Smithville petitioned Canby to cancel the removal order. "In our opinion the presence of troops here is absolutely necessary for the preservation of order and the enforcement of the laws," pleaded the mayor of Greensboro and eleven other town officials. Although Canby refused to retain the garrison at Greensboro, he did leave the company at New Bern to deal with the regulators.

In response to several petitions from citizens living in the eastern part of the state, on New Year's Day 1868, Canby authorized four counties to organize special police forces to capture the outlaw gangs. The general stipulated that a portion of the forces consist of blacks. On receiving Canby's order, the citizens wasted no time in forming police companies and apprehending the criminals. Within a month of their formation, the county police either jailed or drove off most of the outlaws and quickly restored law and order in their communities. By April 1868, only a few of the most diehard regulators remained at large, but a detachment of federal troops finished them off, albeit at the cost of two men killed.

The state convention, meanwhile, met in Raleigh on January 14, 1868, and after two months of deliberation, the Republican majority had drafted a new constitution. The document made numerous changes to the state's laws and government. State senate seats would be apportioned according to population rather than wealth; instead of receiving lifetime appointments, state supreme court justices would be elected to eight-year terms. In addition, the voters rather than the county courts would choose sheriffs and other local officials. The new constitution mandated a free public-school system for black and white children alike, while the revised penal code was less draconian than its predecessor; plans for a state penitentiary indicated that whipping and other corporal punishment would soon be abolished.

RISE OF THE KLAN

The ensuing political campaign during spring 1868 proved to be as boisterous as it was brief. The contest for governor pitted the incumbent Worth against his bitter rival Holden. In response to outbreaks of violence, Canby and his subordinates sent troop detachments to Fayetteville and several towns in eastern North Carolina to restore peace and arrest the perpetrators. The federal officers received reports that a mysterious organization called the Ku Klux Klan was alarming the African American community. Since its formation in Pulaski, Tennessee, in early 1866, the Klan had expanded into every Southern state from Virginia to Texas. The emergence of the Ku Klux Klan and other white supremacist organizations prompted Canby to issue an order warning that conspiracies to obstruct the execution of federal law or to prevent voting would be severely punished. Tar Heel Klansmen, meanwhile, limited their actions to parading at night in fantastic costumes and posting crude signs containing skull-and-crossbones imagery and ominous messages such as, "The hour is arrived—the graves are opened, and Hell yawns." The apparent intent of these actions was to frighten superstitious blacks into not voting.[5]

Judging from the results, the night riders failed miserably. The election was a Republican triumph. Voter turnout was 84 percent, the new constitution was ratified 93,084 to 74,015, and Holden was elected governor. Republicans captured all other state offices and gained a substantial majority in both houses of the General Assembly. Nevertheless, in Camden County—a Republican stronghold due to its large black population—a freedman named Albert Rogerson was murdered about a week before the election. The local Freedmen's Bureau agent maintained that the killers sought "to terrify the Col[ore]d people, and thus prevent them from voting." One freedman stated that Rogerson's murder and threatening Klan posters had induced many blacks to keep away from the polls.[6]

On the Fourth of July, 1868, as Holden was inaugurated, Worth relinquished the governorship under protest, claiming he was compelled to surrender his office under "military

Nelson A. Miles.

duress." Nevertheless, on July 6, Congress admitted three members of the Tar Heel State's congressional delegation. North Carolina had rejoined the Union.

Holden entered the governor's office knowing that President Johnson was powerless to impede the Republicans. Congress had impeached Johnson earlier that year, and while the conviction vote fell one short of the necessary two-thirds majority, the president would serve out the remainder of his term as a political pariah. Ten days after Holden's inauguration, however, Raleigh's city hall became the scene of a violent confrontation when Republican appointees attempted to replace the Conservative mayor and town commissioners. In answer to an appeal from the state attorney general, Major George A. Williams rushed two companies of the 6th US Infantry into Raleigh to restore order. This incident marked the beginning of the Conservatives' increasingly violent resistance to Republican rule in North Carolina.[7]

After the closing of the Second Military District, Canby relinquished command of the army in the Carolinas. With his departure, overall command devolved to Major General George G. Meade, the commander of the Department of the South, with headquarters in Atlanta. The commander of the newly established District of North Carolina was Colonel Nelson A. Miles. The twenty-nine-year-old Miles's command consisted of two companies of the 5th US Cavalry, two companies of the 5th US Artillery, and the 40th US Infantry, a regiment composed of white officers and black enlisted men.[8]

As the electoral campaign season shifted into high gear, Conservatives disrupted several Republican campaign rallies, and the Ku Klux Klan embarked on a campaign of terror in several eastern and central counties. At the urging of Governor Holden and Colonel Miles, General Meade ordered troop detachments sent to nearly two dozen trouble spots across the state. Although certain areas of North Carolina could scarcely have been called peaceful before the election, the presence of federal soldiers in most of the larger towns and communities resulted in a quiet election day on November 3. Thanks to the bluecoats, the Republican Party in the Tar Heel State enjoyed another triumph at the polls. In the presidential election, General Grant carried the state with 96,939 votes to Democratic nominee Horatio Seymour's 84,560, and Republicans won six of the state's seven congressional seats.

Despite the warnings issued by Freedmen's Bureau agents across the state, Miles recalled the troop detachments to their permanent stations within a week of the election, squandering an opportunity to curtail the Ku Klux Klan's lawless activities. That opportunity soon evaporated, for on March 3, 1869, Congress passed an army manpower reduction act. The War Department accordingly transferred the 40th Infantry to Louisiana and replaced it with five companies of the 8th US Infantry from South Carolina. The number of federal troops in North Carolina fell from one thousand to about three hundred. The message from Congress was clear: in keeping the peace, the state and local authorities would have to rely on their own resources.

In December 1868, the Klan's late-night raids began in deadly earnest. In several Piedmont counties, Klansmen dragged freedmen from their homes and whipped or beat them severely. On January 24, 1869, heavily armed night riders abducted five prisoners—four of them black—from the Lenoir County jail in Kinston. The outlaws took their victims to a bridge outside town, shot them to death, and then dumped their bodies into the Neuse River. Around the same time, Klansmen burst into the home of Moore County resident Daniel Blue and opened fire, wounding Blue and killing his pregnant wife and one daughter. The night riders set fire to the house; although Blue and three of his daughters managed to escape, the remaining four children became trapped and burned to death.

These are just a few of the many atrocities the Ku Klux Klan committed in North Carolina over two years. The public regarded the Klan as a monolithic entity, but the organization consisted of many small cells that bore different names depending on the region. Initiates knew the Klan as the Constitutional Union Guard in the east, the White Brotherhood in the Piedmont, and the Invisible Empire in the west. Confident that their crimes would go unpunished, Klansmen became ever bolder, their numbers swelled, and their crimes multiplied. By March 1869, the White Brotherhood in Alamance County numbered about seven hundred members, slightly more than one-half of the county's white voters.[9]

In May 1869, the Constitutional Union Guard assassinated Orson R. Colgrove, the sheriff of Jones County, and M. L. Shepard, a Jones County commissioner. Governor Holden responded by sending detectives into Jones and Lenoir Counties to hunt down the perpetrators, and one of the operatives, Lewis H. Mowers, succeeded in persuading three suspects to turn state's evidence. With the Lenoir County sheriff's help, Mowers arrested twenty-five suspects. On October 20, 1869, Holden issued a proclamation warning that he would declare Jones and Lenoir in a state of insurrection if the crime wave continued. After peace had returned to the two counties, Holden freed the prisoners as a conciliatory gesture. No suspects were tried for their alleged crimes.

In December 1869, Alamance and Caswell Counties teetered on the brink of anarchy. Klansmen were rampaging through the countryside on a nightly basis, and their raids were becoming more lethal. Their victims included Caswell Holt, an Alamance County freedman whom the night riders shot six times. Holt somehow escaped with his life. The two counties became a vortex of Klan violence because the Republicans' success in mobilizing the black vote spurred local Klan chieftains to a comparable level of activity. Although Conservatives held most of the local offices, the state senators for the two counties—T. M. Shoffner of Alamance and John W. Stephens of Caswell—were homegrown white Republicans with strong black followings. During the holidays, Senator Shoffner became the local Klan's primary target. He recently had sponsored a bill intended to strengthen Holden's hand in combating the Klan. The Shoffner Act passed on January 29, 1870, but the bill's sponsor was fortunate to be alive for the occasion. After narrowly avoiding assassination at the hands of a band of night riders, Shoffner loaded his family's belongings into a wagon and moved with his wife and small child to Indiana.[10]

THE KIRK-HOLDEN WAR

In early 1870, the federal government's inaction as the Ku Klux Klan's reign of terror spread across much of the state had terrible consequences in Alamance and Caswell. Shortly after midnight on Saturday, February 26, a column of one hundred horsemen clad in white robes and hooded masks rode south down Graham's Main Street toward the Alamance County Courthouse. They abducted a fifty-year-old woodworker, town commissioner, and Union army veteran named Wyatt Outlaw, who was the county's foremost African American political leader. The night riders took Outlaw to a tree near the courthouse and hanged him. Outlaw's body remained there until midday, when the sheriff finally cut it down. Two days later, five Graham Republicans notified Holden of Outlaw's lynching, and Holden urged the post commander at Raleigh, Lieutenant Colonel Samuel B. Hayman of the 17th US Infantry, to send a detachment to Graham. Hayman dispatched a forty-man force to the town two days later.[11]

The Klan also struck in neighboring Caswell County. On May 21, Klansmen lured the Republican state senator, John W. Stephens, into the basement of the county courthouse at Yanceyville and stabbed him to death. Thus far, the army had failed to apprehend suspects in the Outlaw murder, and it appeared unlikely they would succeed in doing so in the Stephens case. Left with no alternative, Holden declared the two counties in a state of insurrection, and he called up the state militia.

Until now the governor had refused to mobilize the militia because of fears that white militiamen might also be Klan members. Holden chose two Civil War veterans as his militia commanders: Colonels William J. Clarke and George W. Kirk. A former Confederate colonel, Clarke commanded a regiment of white and black troops from the eastern part of the state. Kirk was a Tennessee native and an ex-Union colonel notorious for several destructive raids into western North Carolina. Kirk's regiment consisted of white soldiers from the wartime Unionist stronghold of eastern Tennessee and western North Carolina. Holden secured a pledge from President Grant that militia recruits would receive the same uniforms, equipment, rations, and pay as federal soldiers. As a result, the militia regiments soon met their enlistment quotas. The president also promised to send four companies of federal troops to North Carolina.

While the state militia was recruiting and organizing, two companies of the 4th US Artillery—the men armed and equipped as infantry—deployed to Yanceyville and several other Piedmont communities. They arrived during the second week of July. The commander at Yanceyville, Captain George B. Rodney, reported that the town was peaceful and that "there is no danger of any outbreak or resistance to authorities." Soon afterward, Holden instructed Kirk to occupy Yanceyville, and the governor gave him a list of suspects to arrest. When Kirk arrived on July 18, he learned that there was a debate in the county courthouse between two congressional candidates. The colonel surrounded the building and then arrested two dozen men, including Sheriff Jesse Griffith and John Kerr, a former US congressman. Kirk also ordered his second in command to arrest several Klan leaders in Alamance County, including Sheriff Albert Murray.

Concerned that the Klan might try to free the prisoners at Yanceyville, Kirk warned Holden, who in turn appealed to Grant for a regiment of federal soldiers. The president responded swiftly. On July 27, General Meade established the temporary District of North Carolina and placed Colonel Henry J. Hunt in command. When Hunt set up his headquarters in Raleigh on August 1, about seven hundred soldiers were stationed at Raleigh, Graham, Yanceyville, and two other Piedmont towns. The presence of the state militia and the federal garrisons in Raleigh and Yanceyville led to several confrontations between the two forces, including an incident at the state capital in which a black militiaman shot a drunken white soldier who had blundered into the militia regiment's camp. Despite these conflicts, the actions of the state militia, combined with the presence of the federal troops, succeeded in breaking up the Klan in Alamance and Caswell. Although state prosecutors arraigned forty-nine men, not one suspected Klansman had to stand trial. On September 13, General Meade discontinued the temporary District of North Carolina in the belief that the emergency was over.[12]

Henry J. Hunt.

Despite the success of the militia and the army in suppressing the Ku Klux Klan, the damage was done. The election of 1870 was nothing less than a resounding triumph for the Conservative Party. Due to a thirteen-thousand-vote drop-off in the Republican total from the presidential election of 1868, the Conservatives elected their candidate for state attorney general, and they gained six of the state's seven congressional seats as well as almost a two-to-one majority in the state legislature. Of the fifteen counties added to the Conservative column, ten had experienced considerable Klan activity.

In December 1870, Governor Holden himself became the target of a Klan attack launched from within the Conservative-dominated General Assembly. On December 9, a representative (who happened to be a former Klansman) introduced a resolution to impeach Holden, and ten days later, the house passed the resolution and eight articles of impeachment. The trial lasted three months and ended with the senate voting to expel the governor from office. Holden thus became the first state governor in the United States to be ousted by impeachment. A victim of political assassination, he was the last and the highest-ranking casualty of the so-called Kirk-Holden War.[13]

Holden's story does not end in 1871 with his removal from office. On April 12, 2011, the North Carolina state senate voted unanimously to pardon him, affording the deposed governor some long-overdue vindication, yet the gesture failed to acknowledge the other victims of the Klan's many acts of terror.[14]

In 1871, the Ku Klux Klan continued to terrorize counties in the Piedmont and the foothills regions of North Carolina. On April 20, Congress passed the so-called Ku Klux Act to enable the president to call in the military and suspend the writ of habeas corpus whenever Klan conspiracies proved too powerful for civil authorities to suppress. President Grant at last authorized the army to assist federal law enforcement agents in arresting night riders, and the Department of Justice prosecuted its first Klan cases. Once committed, the army, US marshals, Secret Service detectives, and federal prosecutors went about their work with a will. By the end of 1871, federal officers had made twelve hundred arrests in North Carolina. The federal judiciary found 763 indictments that resulted in twenty-three guilty pleas, twenty-four convictions, thirteen acquittals, and nine dropped cases. But as the case backlog mounted, the Justice Department lost interest in tackling Klan cases. At the close of 1874, Attorney General George H. Williams ordered all remaining Klan cases dismissed from the docket—in effect granting clemency to hundreds of former Klansmen.[15]

Although the Klan ceased to exist in North Carolina, the organization had served its purpose. The Conservatives—or Democrats, as they increasingly called themselves in the 1870s—had the Klan's three-year reign of terror to thank for their political resurgence. Yet state Democratic leaders had found the Klan too volatile to control. Although grateful for the Klan's support, the Democratic elite was no less thankful for its demise.

END OF RECONSTRUCTION

In the election of 1876, the Democratic gubernatorial candidate, Zebulon B. Vance, defeated his Republican opponent, and the Democrats secured a stranglehold on both houses of the General Assembly and won seven of eight congressional seats. The election marked Vance's triumphant return to the governorship. Although barred from public office for a decade after the war, Vance had long been the leading Democrat in North Carolina, due in part to his heroic status as the state's war governor from 1862 to 1865.

In contrast to the Democrats' decisive victory in the Tar Heel State, the presidential election between Republican Rutherford B. Hayes and Democrat Samuel J. Tilden was deadlocked, with rival election boards in three Southern states—South Carolina, Florida, and Louisiana—declaring for their party's candidate. To secure the election, Hayes in effect abandoned blacks and white Republicans in the South, though he persuaded himself that such was not the case. In backroom negotiations between his representatives and Southern Democrats, Hayes pledged to withdraw US troops from the Southern states. In return, the Southerners promised to respect the rights of African Americans. The agreement became known as the Compromise of 1877. A few months after the inauguration, Hayes fulfilled his end of the bargain. In April 1877, the Post of Raleigh concluded a dozen years of continuous operation that had begun with Sherman's entry into the state capital on April 13, 1865. In November, the Post of Morganton also closed, ending the use of federal troops to arrest moonshiners in the western counties. Reconstruction was over in North Carolina. In the words of the southern Democrats, the Tar Heel State was "redeemed."[16]

FRONTIER SOLDIERS

The campaigns to settle the western frontier began with the establishment of Fort Leavenworth, Kansas, in 1827. Between the late 1840s and 1891, the US Army maintained over thirty major forts and numerous smaller outposts in the western territories. North Carolina soldiers served on these frontier posts, and several of them achieved distinction. General John Gibbon became famous for his service in the US Army in the Civil War and in the western campaigns. As a boy, he lived with his family in Charlotte, North Carolina, before entering West Point Military Academy in 1843. Davidson County native Private Lorenzo D. Brown of the 7th US Cavalry received a Medal of Honor for continuing to do his duty "in a most courageous manner" despite suffering a severe shoulder wound in the Battle of the Big Hole in present-day Montana, on August 9, 1877. Gibbon commanded the army force in that battle, which occurred during the campaign to defeat the Nez Perce Indians. A second Davidson County native, William H. Jones, a farrier, or blacksmith, with the 2nd US Cavalry, received a Medal of Honor for gallantry in an attack on hostile Lakota and Cheyenne Indians in the Battle of Little Muddy Creek, Montana, on May 7, 1877. Jones's Medal of Honor citation also notes his bravery in the Battle of Camas Meadows, Idaho, on August 20, 1877, against the Nez Perce, "in which he sustained a painful knee wound."[17]

The second African American soldier from North Carolina to receive a Medal of Honor was Sergeant William

John Gibbon.

William McBryar. (*Schubert,* Black Valor: Buffalo Soldiers and the Medal of Honor)

McBryar of the 10th US Cavalry. The 10th Cavalry was one of four regiments composed of black troops in the post-Civil War US Army, the others being the 9th Cavalry, the 24th Infantry, and the 25th Infantry. They served on the western frontier and became known as "Buffalo Soldiers." The name originated with the 10th Cavalry but was soon applied to all the black regiments. The Indians apparently bestowed the name on them in recognition of their courage and because their hair and skin color resembled the buffalo's.

McBryar received his Medal of Honor by distinguishing himself for "coolness, bravery, and marksmanship while his troop was in pursuit of hostile Apache Indians" in the Arizona Territory. The two-hundred-mile chase culminated in the capture of the fugitives on March 7, 1890. The Elizabethtown native served in the army fourteen years, commanding a platoon in the 25th Infantry in Cuba during the Spanish-American War. McBryar later served in the Philippine Insurrection, rising to the temporary rank of first lieutenant before his unit was mustered out in 1901. Four years later, he reenlisted as a private in the cavalry, but rheumatism compelled the army to discharge him after barely a year. While in his mid-fifties, he tried to enlist in the army during World War I. McBryar eventually settled in Greensboro, North Carolina. He died on March 8, 1941, at age eighty, and was buried in Arlington National Cemetery.[18]

THE SPANISH-AMERICAN WAR

In 1898, the mysterious explosion of the warship USS *Maine* in Havana Harbor, Cuba, spurred the United States into declaring war against Spain on April 14. When President William McKinley issued a proclamation calling for one hundred twenty-five thousand volunteers, North Carolina immediately responded. Andrew D. Cowles, the state adjutant general, directed the captains of State Guard companies volunteering to serve in the US Army to recruit their companies to at least eighty-four men ages eighteen to forty-five, though officers could be older. The Tar Heel State eventually mobilized three infantry regiments, one of which consisted of black officers and enlisted men.[19]

Within a week of the call for volunteers, the companies of the 1st Regiment began to arrive at Camp Bryan Grimes on the western outskirts of Raleigh. The State Guard units were poorly trained and disciplined, and they lacked even basic supplies and equipment. When the regiment conducted its first parade in early May, only the officers and 60 percent of the enlisted men were in uniform, and just 70 percent of the regiment was armed. While the soldiers at Camp Grimes awaited shipments of rifles and uniforms, they engaged in a semblance of military drill under the watchful eye of their commander, Colonel Joseph F. Armfield, who had served in the State Guard since 1882.

On the morning of May 22, the men boarded trains bound for Tampa, Florida. While en route, the regiment learned that its destination was changed to Jacksonville, Florida. Soon afterward, the troop train collided with a freight train near Savannah, Georgia, killing one man and casting a dark cloud over the rest of the journey. The 1st Regiment numbered 982 officers and men when it arrived at Camp Cuba Libre on the outskirts of Jacksonville. The North Carolinians joined the Seventh Army Corps commanded by Major General Fitzhugh Lee, a former governor of Virginia and a Confederate cavalry officer during the Civil War.[20]

The soldiers of the 1st Regiment were eager to see action in Cuba, but they lacked the training and equipment to do so. An acute shortage of uniforms compelled General Lee to purchase clothing and shoes from local merchants. Firearms proved largely obsolete and defective, and when the regiment finally held its first target practice exercise on July 29, it revealed that most of the men did not even know how to load and fire their rifles. While at Cuba Libre, a large percentage of soldiers fell prey to various illnesses, and some were poisoned by a shipment of spoiled canned beef. In combination with the boredom of camp life, these maladies led to widespread desertion in the ranks, and the 1st Regiment proved unable to recruit a full quota of replacements.

It was fortuitous that the American land and naval forces won a swift victory and that hostilities ended on August 12, 1898, for the 1st Regiment was unfit for battle. With the fighting at an end, most of the enlisted men wished to be mustered out. Instead, the regiment was moved to a more favorable location on the St. Johns River near Jacksonville, army surgeons having condemned the former site as pestilential. On December 3, 1898, the soldiers traveled to Savannah, where they boarded a troop ship on the seventh and sailed for Cuba. They remained on occupation duty in the Havana area for three months. The 1st Regiment departed Cuba on March 25, 1899, and

W. H. S. Burgwyn. (*Archives.org*)

James H. Young. (*North Carolina Collection, UNC-Chapel Hill*)

arrived at Fort Pulaski, Georgia, two days later. The men were mustered out on April 23.

No sooner had the 2nd Regiment arrived at Camp Daniel Russell in Raleigh than rumors began to circulate that the unit would not be deployed to Cuba but would instead be sent to Florida for coastal defense. This disappointing news caused recruiting to plummet and desertion to spike, forcing several companies to drop out for failing to reach their quotas. During the first dress parade on May 27, the commander, Colonel W. H. S. Burgwyn, noted that many of his men lacked uniforms and rifles, leading him to make a special trip to Washington, DC, in a vain attempt to obtain those items for his troops. Worse yet, seven men died of typhoid fever, which induced the transfer of the regiment's twelve companies to posts on the South Carolina and Georgia coast. In November 1898, Burgwyn received orders to muster out the 2nd Regiment. They returned to Raleigh to receive their pay and be discharged. The guards at Camp Dan Russell were notoriously undisciplined, often clashing with local blacks and using the town's streetlights for target practice. Regardless of their race, the citizens were relieved to see the troops depart for their homes.[21]

Unlike the 2nd Regiment, the 3rd Regiment had no difficulty in recruiting enough men to meet its quota. In recognition of his debt to African American voters in the 1896 election, Republican Gov. Daniel L. Russell formed a black volunteer unit. The 3rd Regiment was originally intended to be a battalion, but the response of black volunteers was so great that the unit was expanded into a regiment. Starting with the commander, Colonel James H. Young, it consisted of black officers and enlisted men. The 3rd Regiment was the only African American unit raised by a Southern state for the Spanish-American War. The volunteers viewed their service as an opportunity to prove themselves as citizens as well as soldiers. But they had to face scathing criticism, starting with the state adjutant general, Andrew Cowles, who predicted that the 3rd Regiment would refuse to fight in Cuba. The troops also chafed under the rigid discipline that Colonel Young imposed on them to ensure their good conduct. In addition to racism, the regiment had to contend with the same shortages of weapons, uniforms, and equipment that had plagued the 1st and 2nd Regiments. At least the troops were stationed on the coast near Fort Macon, where the sea breezes helped offset the sweltering summer heat.

Worth Bagley. (*North Carolina Museum of History*)

In September 1898, the men boarded trains and traveled across the state to Camp Poland near Knoxville, Tennessee. At first, the 3rd Regiment had to endure repeated insults and assaults by white citizens and soldiers. The North Carolina volunteers often found themselves the scapegoats for the misconduct of other troops. Only after the transfer of the rival units did the men of the Tar Heel State receive the recognition for good order and discipline they deserved. By November, the men were anxious to return home, for the fighting was over, and they were deeply troubled by the Democrats' triumph in the state election as well as the Wilmington Race Riot, which ended with a coup that toppled the local Republican government. Soon afterward, the regiment traveled to Camp Haskell, near Macon, Georgia. Racial violence between the white citizens and black soldiers resulted in the killing of four members of the 3rd Regiment. Friendly juries acquitted the accused on the grounds of justifiable homicide. In January 1899, the troops received the welcome news that they were to be mustered out the following month. They traveled to Raleigh to turn in their arms and equipment and be paid. Although the returning veterans received no official recognition for their service, the 3rd North Carolina became a symbol of pride for African Americans across the Tar Heel State.[22]

Two North Carolinians were killed in action during the Spanish-American War. Ensign Worth Bagley fell on May 11, 1898, while serving on the torpedo boat USS *Winslow*, becoming the first US naval officer to die in the war. Lieutenant William E. Shipp was killed on July 1, 1898, while leading soldiers of the 10th Cavalry Regiment in the charge on San Juan Hill. Bagley's funeral was held in the rotunda of the state capitol in Raleigh, his hometown; all the capital city's businesses were closed for the occasion. Shipp was buried in Lincolnton, and thousands attended his funeral. Two native Tar Heels, Navy Seaman David D. Barrow of Reelsboro and Marine Corps Private Pomeroy Parker of Gates County, each received a Medal of Honor for displaying "extraordinary bravery and coolness" while under fire on the gunboat USS *Nashville* near Cienfuegos, Cuba, during the operation of May 11, 1898.[23]

13. The World Wars

THE GREAT WAR BEGINS

On June 28, 1914, a nineteen-year-old Serbian nationalist named Gavrilo Princip assassinated the Archduke Franz Ferdinand, heir to the Austro-Hungarian throne, and his wife Sophie, as they rode in an open car through the streets of Sarajevo, Bosnia. After an investigation revealed that Princip and two of his coconspirators had received training and weapons in Belgrade, Serbia, the Austrian government issued an ultimatum to the Serbian government on July 23, with the intention of provoking a war with its smaller neighbor. Five days later, the Austro-Hungarian Empire declared war on Serbia. Russia immediately sided with the Serbs, while Germany declared war on Russia and France, and Britain declared war on Germany.[1]

On August 4, President Woodrow Wilson announced that the United States would "maintain a strict and impartial neutrality." Of far greater concern to the US government than the impending war in Europe was the unrest in Mexico stemming from a series of revolutions. The US Army maintained a strong presence along the border; by April 1914, relations between the two nations had so deteriorated that following the arrest of nine US sailors by Mexican authorities, Wilson ordered a punitive expedition that culminated in the Battle of Vera Cruz and the occupation of the Mexican port. During the action of April 22, three naval officers from North Carolina—Captain Edwin A. Anderson, Lieutenant Commander Rufus Z. Johnston, and Lieutenant Adolphus Staton—displayed exceptional courage and skill in leading their men while under a heavy small-arms, machine-gun, and artillery fire, for which each of them received the Medal of Honor.[2]

While the US military contended with Mexico, Germany swept through Luxembourg and Belgium and, by early September, drove to the outskirts of Paris. In the First Battle of the Marne, French and British forces pushed back the Germans about thirty miles. After the two sides failed to outmaneuver each other, they dug elaborate fortifications and settled into a stalemate. Most North Carolinians

Madelon B. Hancock. (*North Carolina Collection, Pack Memorial Library, Asheville*)

Kiffin Y. Rockwell. (*North Carolina Museum of History*)

were content to follow the distant war through the newspapers, but a handful of Tar Heels volunteered for service. Among the first to step forward were Madelon B. Hancock and Paul A. and Kiffin Y. Rockwell, all three hailing from Asheville. In August 1914, Hancock became a nurse in a British hospital at Antwerp, Belgium, and served at the front for the duration of the war. Her untiring cheerfulness earned her the sobriquet of "Morning Glory," which was soon shortened to "Glory." The Rockwell brothers enlisted in the French Foreign Legion. By late 1914, a severe wound had taken Paul Rockwell from active duty. Upon recovery, he found a new calling in the French information and propaganda service. In May 1915, Kiffin Rockwell was shot in the thigh, likewise ending his career as an infantryman[3]

Despite a lack of aviation experience, Kiffin obtained a transfer to the French Lafayette Flying Corps. He became one of the seven founding members of the Lafayette Escadrille, an elite squadron consisting mostly of American fighter pilots. On May 18, 1916, Kiffin shot down a German plane on his first combat mission; during his brief career, he was credited with downing four enemy aircraft. On September 23, 1916, he was shot and killed during a dogfight with a two-man German reconnaissance plane. Kiffin Rockwell was buried in France with full military honors.[4]

A second Tar Heel, James R. McConnell of Carthage, was also among the famed squadron's original seven pilots. McConnell had volunteered as an ambulance driver in January 1915 and served in the American Ambulance Field Service for about a year before becoming an aviator. On March 19, 1917, McConnell and a comrade in another plane engaged three enemy planes, and though the latter managed to elude his German pursuers, Mc-

Connell was killed. Both he and Kiffin Rockwell lie beneath the Lafayette Escadrille Memorial near Paris. Two other North Carolina-born pilots, Arthur Bluethenthal and James Baugham, were killed in 1918 while serving in the Lafayette Flying Corps.[5]

THE UNITED STATES ENTERS THE WAR

On the afternoon of May 7, 1915, the German U-boat SM *U-20* torpedoed the British passenger liner RMS *Lusitania* about a dozen miles off the Irish coast. A second explosion that may have been caused by the detonation of ammunition on board sank the vessel in just eighteen minutes. Regardless of its military cargo, the sinking of the *Lusitania* infuriated Americans because 128 of their countrymen were among the dead. The incident set the United States on a path that culminated in a formal declaration of war on Germany less than two years later.[6]

The *Lusitania* sinking led prominent interventionists such as former president Theodore Roosevelt and ex-army chief of staff Leonard Wood to urge President Wilson to place the armed forces on a war footing, but Wilson had maintained a firm neutrality in hopes of brokering a negotiated settlement among the European belligerents. Attacks by German U-boats (derived from the German Unterseeboot) on Allied shipping induced Wilson to reconsider his options. In July 1915, he sent letters to the secretary of war and the secretary of the navy directing them to take steps to bolster the national defense. The president appeared to have aligned himself with the burgeoning Preparedness Movement.[7]

News of Wilson's policy shift soon reached the House majority leader, Claude Kitchin. The North Carolina Democrat was the leading opponent of the Preparedness Movement. He argued that the force buildup would be costly and that American taxpayers would have to bear the burden rather than the industrialists who stood to profit most. Kitchin drew widespread criticism for his opposition to preparedness. The Tar Heel congressional leader once noted that he "would have nothing to lose . . . if I went with the crowd, . . . but I choose, as a matter of conscientious belief, to go against the crowd." In any event, Kitchin received considerable support from many home-state newspapers; if nothing else, they praised him for adhering to his principles.

Despite Kitchin's vociferous opposition to preparedness legislation, the House passed the National Defense Act and numerous other bills in 1916, beefing up the army, the navy, the National Guard, and the merchant marine. As Kitchin had predicted, the arms industry balked at being taxed to pay the $700 million price tag that the buildup cost, and while the industrialists constituted a powerful lobby, the taxation bill he sponsored as the chairman of the Ways and Means Committee passed with few compromises.[8]

Perhaps second only to Claude Kitchin among influential North Carolinians during the Great War was Josephus Daniels, owner of the *Raleigh News and Observer*. During the presidential campaign of 1912, Daniels used his newspaper to endorse the Democratic candidate, Woodrow Wilson. A grateful Wilson appointed

Josephus Daniels.

Walter Hines Page.

Daniels secretary of the navy. In 1915, concern over the U-boat threat led Secretary Daniels to establish the Navy Consulting Board, headed by the famed inventor Thomas A. Edison. The board studied such matters as submarine design and construction. In response to Wilson's directive on naval preparedness, Daniels drew up a plan of action that evolved into the Naval Bill of 1916, which mandated the construction of 156 ships over five years.[9]

To fill vacancies in the Department of the Navy offices, Daniels ordered subordinates to begin enlisting women as yeomen in the naval reserve, and he insisted they receive the same pay as their male counterparts. His ban on alcohol on all naval vessels and installations proved as unpopular among personnel as it was memorable. The phrase "a cup of Joe" reportedly stemmed from the fact that coffee was the strongest drink a sailor could imbibe on shipboard. Prominent among Daniels's appointees was his talented young assistant secretary, Franklin D. Roosevelt, who went on to become the thirty-second US president.[10]

Like Daniels, North Carolina native Walter Hines Page was an enthusiastic supporter of his longtime friend, Woodrow Wilson, during the 1912 presidential campaign, and Wilson repaid his loyalty by appointing Page US ambassador to Great Britain. With a pang of regret, Page left his position as vice president of the Doubleday, Page & Co. publishing house and headed overseas. The start of war in summer 1914 drove a wedge between the president and his ambassador in London, for Page was an ardent interventionist who sought to persuade a reluctant Wilson to increase his support of the Allies. By 1916, Page had become so discouraged that he tendered his resignation following Wilson's reelection.

When Page received the president's tardy reply in February 1917 asking him to remain at his posting, Wilson had just severed diplomatic ties with Germany, which had warned the US government that it would renew unrestricted submarine warfare against neutrals and belligerents in the shipping lanes of Great Britain and France. Page remained as ambassador to Great Britain, and his efforts contributed substantially to cementing that nation's alliance with the United States. But the strain took a heavy toll on his health, and Page was compelled to resign in August 1918. He died at his home in Pinehurst, North Carolina, just four months later.[11]

Camp Greene. (*North Carolina Collection, UNC-Chapel Hill*)

In April 1917, Wilson urged Congress to issue a formal declaration of war on Germany. After an impassioned speech by Tar Heel congressman Claude Kitchin urging his colleagues to reject war, the House voted 373-50 to carry the resolution. Like the rest of the country, patriotic fervor gripped North Carolina, as men flocked to recruiting offices to volunteer for military service and women formed chapters of the American Red Cross and other relief organizations. Even Kitchin set aside his personal convictions and became a Wilson supporter.[12]

Like all other states, North Carolina received the War Department's injunction to fill the ranks of its National Guard units to full wartime strength. (Fourteen years earlier, the General Assembly had voted to rename the State Guard the National Guard in compliance with the Militia Act of 1903, which mandated the federalization of the state militia.) To meet its quota, the Tar Heel State had to recruit a total of five thousand troops for its three infantry regiments, as well as its cavalry, coastal artillery, engineer, and sanitary units. Although North Carolina exceeded the quotas for the National Guard and the regular army, it soon became clear that the US armed forces could not rely solely on volunteers to meet their manpower goals. As Congress began to debate a conscription law, North Carolina Gov. Thomas W. Bickett sent a message to President Wilson arguing that failure to pass the bill would be "a colossal blunder." On May 18, 1917, Wilson signed the Selective Service Act into law, and ultimately, four hundred eighty thousand Tar Heel males registered, with 60,822 of them being called into service. Over 1,600 North Carolinians refused to heed the call and were condemned as "slackers." The draftees soon joined the volunteers at training camps scattered across the country, mainly in the South.[13]

The War Department built thirty-two training camps; Camp Greene, near Charlotte, was the largest such facility in North Carolina. Named in honor of the Revolutionary War general Nathanael Greene, the cantonment opened in September 1917, while construction was still in progress. Typical of these bases, the wooden buildings were spartan and temporary. At its peak in February 1918, Camp Greene housed roughly forty thousand trainees. Camp Bragg was named after Braxton Bragg, the Tar Heel State's highest-ranking Confederate general. Located at Fayetteville, the base opened in September 1918 and served as an artillery school, its one hundred eighteen thousand acres providing ample space for firing ranges. Much to the local merchants' delight, the War Department retained the facility after the war and added Pope Field, which would rank as one of the air force's oldest bases. Three miles west of Raleigh, Camp Polk opened at the site of the State Fair Grounds about the same time as Camp Bragg. Named for the Revolutionary War colonel William Polk, the cantonment served as a training ground for seven tank battalions before the army shut it down in February 1919.[14]

Most Tar Heel draftees trained outside their home state. The North Carolina National Guard traveled to Camp Sevier near Greenville, South Carolina, where it joined guard units from South Carolina and Tennessee to form the 30th, or "Old Hickory," Division. The unit was nicknamed in honor of Andrew Jackson, the seventh US president, who was associated with all three states. Camp Jackson, South Carolina, was the home of the 81st, or "Wildcat," Division, which consisted of trainees from North Carolina, South Carolina, and Florida. Most black soldiers from the Carolinas trained at Camp Jackson and later served in the 371st Infantry Regiment of the 93rd Infantry Division. Unwanted by the US or British armies, the two all-black divisions, the 92nd and the 93rd, were welcome additions to the French army and served with distinction. The 92nd trained at Camp Funston, Kansas, and included African American soldiers from every state. Their unit flag featured a buffalo in honor of the Buffalo Soldiers.[15]

Trainees at the two South Carolina cantonments were often issued a pick or a shovel before they received a rifle, for it was up to them to make their camp habitable. After felling trees and clearing brush for drill grounds, the men began their training for trench warfare. Courses included rifle and bayonet, machine gun, automatic rifle, hand grenade, gas-attack defense, sniping, map reading, reconnaissance, radio and telephone, patrolling, and cooking.[16]

On completing their training, North Carolina doughboys traveled by rail to New York, Boston, and other port cities on the East Coast to begin the long transatlantic journey on troop ships that often had been used to transport livestock. The passengers spent much of the tedious trip attempting to remove the filth left on shipboard by their predecessors. Thanks largely to the convoy system implemented by Secretary of the Navy Daniels, every troop transport was well guarded while on the open sea, and all arrived safely at English and French ports. According to Daniels, the US Navy escorted over 80 percent of the troop ships.[17]

Although most Americans who entered the military served in the US Army, the personnel of the navy, marines, and Coast Guard also played important roles in the First World War. One such duty involved defending the shores of the United States from Ger-

Postwar Photo of the U-Boat U-117. (*Naval History and Heritage Command*)

David Worth Bagley. (*Naval History and Heritage Command*)

man U-boats. Two military installations on the North Carolina coast contributed to the effort. Camp Glenn, constructed in 1906 as the state's main National Guard training camp, stood near Morehead City. Named after Gov. Robert B. Glenn (1905–1909), it became a US Navy air base in September 1918. Fort Caswell, located on Oak Island south of Wilmington, was originally a masonry structure completed in 1836 and was periodically improved and strengthened since. During the Great War, the fort—named for the first and fifth governor of North Carolina, Richard Caswell—contained rifled guns and mortars and observation posts to scan the sea for U-boats. The military abandoned both installations in the immediate postwar years.[18]

A total of seven U-boats menaced Allied shipping along the Atlantic Seaboard; between June 5 and August 18, 1918, three enemy underwater vessels—the *U-151*, *U-140*, and *U-117*—sank a total of eleven ships off the North Carolina coast, the first such attacks by enemy warships since the War of 1812. At least twelve men and a large quantity of sugar, copper, animal hides, wool, linseed oil, gasoline, coal, and oil were lost. This was not the last time U-boats haunted the waters off North Carolina. Much larger, faster, and more lethal versions made their appearance during the Second World War.[19]

Among other duties, the US Navy carried men and supplies to Europe and, on the return voyage, brought back wounded soldiers and the remains of those killed. Two naval officers from North Carolina, David Worth Bagley and Percy W. Foote, commanded ships that were sunk by U-boat torpedoes. Both men received the Distinguished Service Medal and later rose to high rank, Bagley retiring as a vice admiral and Foote as a rear admiral.[20]

OVER THERE

On arriving overseas, the doughboys joining General John J. Pershing's American Expeditionary Forces did not immediately go into battle. First, they traveled to British or French training camps to receive advanced instruction in soldiering, followed by observation of veteran troops in action at the front. Next, they occupied a quiet sector of the line to get the feel of life in the trenches. Only after these careful preparations did they receive their baptism of fire, which for some North Carolinians came in spring 1918. At that time, the Germans launched an offensive to capture Paris. Replying to a plea for reinforcements from the French near Chateau-Thierry, eight thousand Allied soldiers arrived to prevent a German breakthrough at the Belleau Wood. Among the reinforcements was the 4th Marine Brigade, commanded by army Brigadier General James G. Harbord and including several hundred North Carolinians. Casualties piled up over the next three weeks as the two sides repeatedly attacked and counterattacked without gaining much ground. But the Leathernecks ultimately prevailed. By June 26, the marines had driven the Germans out of the woods, stopping what proved to be the enemy's final drive on Paris. The victory carried a steep price, however, as more than half of the marines—many of them North Carolinians—were casualties of the Battle of Belleau Wood.[21]

Numerous Tar Heels on the front lines were soldiers in the 30th Infantry Division, and the unit compiled an impressive combat record. The 30th served with British forces along the French-Belgian border before being transferred to the front near the German-held villages of Bellicourt and Nauroy. The enemy had fortified this sector with three rows of entrenchments, barbed wire, and concrete bunkers. Dubbed the Hindenburg Line, the fortifications were said to be impregnable.

On September 29, 1918, following a fifty-six-hour artillery barrage, the North Carolinians of the 119th and 120th Infantry Regiments (30th Division), attacked the Bellicourt-Nauroy sector of the Hindenburg Line. "The Infantry went over the top," recalled a soldier who participated in the assault. "The earth seemed to rock under the veritable rain of lead, iron, and steel. The Heavens were aflame with the flash of guns." The two regiments succeeded in punching through the line, shifting the momentum decidedly in the Allies' favor. But their success cost them dearly, for the 119th and 120th Regiments suffered roughly three-fourths of the 30th Division's 2,494 casualties, making September 29, 1918, the bloodiest day of the war for North Carolina's doughboys.[22]

The breakthrough at Bellicourt and Nauroy marked the start of the Meuse-Argonne Offensive, the final major campaign of the Great War. General Pershing's relentless assaults on the Germans denied them the opportunity to recover from their fatigue and confusion. Units with North Carolinians who served in the campaign included the 3rd Infantry Division, the 4th Infantry Division, the 117th Engineers (42nd or "Rainbow" Division), the 81st Division, and the 82nd Infantry or "All American" Division, which included the famed war hero, Sergeant Alvin York of Tennessee. Soldiers of the 81st Division received orders to deploy on the front line near Verdun, having been held in reserve since their arrival three months earlier. What the men found in that battle-scarred sector shocked them. The bones of French and German soldiers who had fought there were scattered everywhere. "Nothing was left standing," recalled Asheville resident Clarence Johnson of the 321st Infantry Regiment, "not a tree, nor even a bush. The sight was oppressive."[23]

On the morning of November 9, the 81st Division's 322nd and 324th Infantry Regiments received orders to attack the German line northeast of Verdun. It was their first assault. The no-man's-land fronting the German position bristled with barbed wire, and the line itself was heavily fortified, containing concrete pillboxes, machine guns, and three divisions of veteran soldiers. Following an Allied artillery barrage that hammered the German line for ninety minutes, the signal whistles blew, and the doughboys went over the top. "[I]t was then that I realized what war was," recalled Walter Davis of the 324th Infantry. He noted that the shells "were bursting all around us, . . . and the bullets coming by faster than the snowflakes fall." The two regiments advanced slowly, their progress intermittently halted by a German artillery barrage. At four the next morning, the 321st and 323rd Infantry Regiments replaced the 322nd and 324th on the front line. That night, the troops shivered in cold, muddy shell craters and tried to snatch some shut-eye amid the unnerving battlefield cacophony.[24]

Early on the morning of November 11, 1918, officers awakened their men for the impending assault. They were drowsy, hungry, and frightened. Forming ranks, the soldiers began their deadly advance across the hellish landscape at 6:00 AM. They moved through a thick fog amid German artillery and machine-gun fire. One North Carolina soldier later claimed that had it "been a clear day, we would have been slaughtered." As the morning wore on, the fog began to lift. At precisely 11:00 AM, the big guns fell silent. At first, the Americans—some of whom had crept to within a few hundred yards of the German line—refused to budge for fear of being shot. Then word of the armistice passed down the line, and cheering erupted along the German fortifications. Jubilant German soldiers threw aside their weapons and raced across what had been no-man's-land to meet their former enemy. The first assault of the 81st Division proved to be the final charge of the war.

Amid the celebrations there was much mourning, as soldiers on both sides reflected on the friends who had died just before the armistice. During the last three days of the war, the 81st Division lost 178 killed, nearly 800 wounded, 57 captured, and 6 missing, for a total of more than one thousand casualties. After seeing to the wounded, the survivors had to bury their fallen comrades, most of whom were hastily covered in a common grave. They were later reinterred in the Meuse-Argonne American Cemetery about thirty miles northwest of Verdun. The 130-acre site contains 14,246 burials, making it the largest American military cemetery in Europe. The US armed forces lost fifty thousand men killed in action or died of wounds, while seventy thousand perished from

William Henry Johnson. (*U.S. Army*)

disease or other causes. Of the one hundred twenty thousand American World War I dead, 2,375 were North Carolinians.[25]

Three North Carolina natives received the Medal of Honor during the First World War. The first recipient, Private Robert L. Blackwell of Person County, volunteered to carry a message requesting reinforcements after the Germans had surrounded his unit, Company K of the 119th Infantry Regiment. The fateful day was October 11, 1918. Blackwell was killed by enemy fire while trying to deliver the message. Blackwell's father, a Confederate veteran, received the medal for his late son in a ceremony at the state capitol on May 6, 1919. The second recipient, Monroe native Lieutenant Samuel I. Parker, led two attacks on July 18–19, 1918, involving elements of the 28th Infantry Regiment, to close dangerous gaps that had formed in the Allied line. During the second attack, Parker suffered a painful foot wound but refused to be evacuated. He received his medal from President Franklin Roosevelt in a ceremony at the White House on May 7, 1936. The third recipient, Winston-Salem native Sergeant William Henry Johnson, was on sentry duty with another soldier on May 15, 1918, when a German raiding party launched a surprise attack. Though heavily outnumbered and severely wounded himself, Johnson defended his gravely injured comrade by striking back at the Germans and inflicting several casualties. Johnson was armed with only a bolo knife, but he managed to drive off the attackers. The sergeant served with the 369th Infantry Regiment of the all-black 93rd Infantry Division. Although the French government bestowed its highest military honor, the Croix de Guerre, on Johnson soon afterward, he did not receive the Medal of Honor until June 2, 2015, when President Barack H. Obama presented it posthumously to members of his former unit in a ceremony at the White House.[26]

THE SECOND WORLD WAR BEGINS

On September 1, 1939, Nazi Germany invaded Poland on the false pretext that it was acting in self-defense. Great Britain and France called on the German leader, Adolf Hitler, to suspend military operations at once. Hitler ignored the ultimatum, so the two nations declared war on Germany. World War II in Europe had begun. The United States remained uncommitted, however. On September 3, President Franklin D. Roosevelt issued a neutrality proclamation in a fireside chat, or radio broadcast, to the American people. In effect, he was reaffirming the Neutrality Acts passed by Congress in the mid-1930s. But the president also conceded that he could not "ask that every American remain neutral in thought as well."[27]

By late September, the German war machine had defeated the Polish army, and Hitler divided Poland's territory with the Soviet Union after signing a nonaggression treaty with that nation. The German armed forces had developed a new operational mode of warfare known as *Blitzkrieg* (lightning war). Massed tanks and other armor spearheaded the attack, supported by columns of mechanized and foot infantry as well as close air support. By means of speed and shock, the German assault force sought to outrun, envelop, and annihilate the enemy. Germany resumed the offensive in April 1940, invading Denmark and Norway, and both fell soon afterward. One month later, Germany overran the Netherlands, Belgium, and Luxembourg before invading France, which capitulated on June 22, following the evacuation across the English Channel of more than three hundred thousand French and British troops at Dunkirk.

Great Britain now stood alone against the Axis powers, which consisted of Germany, Italy, and Japan. Hitler hoped to persuade the British government to accept a negotiated peace, but the newly appointed prime minister, Winston Churchill, rejected the German ultimatum. In response, Hitler launched a massive bombing campaign that became known as the Battle of Britain. Lasting from July to October 1940, the German Luftwaffe's aerial bombardment inflicted numerous casualties and severely damaged British resources, but it failed to defeat the Royal Air Force or break the will of the British people. Hitler therefore decided to postpone his invasion of Britain indefinitely, and Roosevelt urged Congress to pass a lend-lease bill to send the British American supplies without expectation of immediate payment.

The new bill provoked fiery debate in Congress, with opponents arguing that it would push the United States into the war while proponents maintained that the very survival of Britain—and even of democracy itself—hung in the balance. Most North Carolinians favored lend-lease. "It is safer to sell supplies than to send men," declared Gov. Clyde R. Hoey, "and if England and France can win this war, that is our best security for peace." Neither the United States nor Britain was willing to make that assumption, however; starting in January 1941, the two nations began holding secret strategic conferences in the increasing likelihood that America would enter the war. Congress, meanwhile, passed the Lend-Lease Act on March 11, 1941.[28]

American involvement in the war continued to escalate, as US Navy destroyers began to escort supply convoys part of the way across the U-boat-infested Atlantic Ocean to lighten the burden of British destroyers. American spotter planes also flew over transatlantic shipping lanes to warn British vessels of the presence of U-boats. In April, the United States occupied Greenland to prevent it from falling into German hands. One month later, the US government froze all Axis assets and seized all Axis shipping within its boundaries, and it imprisoned a thousand sailors suspected of sabotage. Germany, meanwhile, conquered Romania, Yugoslavia, Greece, and Crete, and occupied much of North Africa. On June 22, 1941, Hitler launched Operation Barbarossa, the German invasion of Russia.[29]

The United States had long viewed the Soviet Union with suspicion but regarded the Communist state more favorably now that it was at war with Nazi Germany. Russia, one Tar Heel newspaper editor wrote, "is now on the side of the democracies and whatever the former relations between the United States and Russia, [it] would seem to have placed itself in a position to expect and receive our help." The United States provided the Soviet Union with assistance under the Lend-Lease Act, and in July 1941, American forces occupied Iceland. In August, Roosevelt and Churchill signed the Atlantic Charter, pledging to bring about "the final destruction of Nazi tyranny" and to foster a postwar world in which "all peoples" would be free "to choose the form of Government under which they will live." Although Roosevelt hoped to coax the American people into entering the war, he was disappointed to learn that the consensus was to remain neutral.[30]

In fall 1941, the army conducted the Carolinas Maneuvers in what proved to be its last peacetime training exercise before the United States entered the conflict. The war games occurred east of Charlotte along the North Carolina-South Carolina border and indicated that army combat units had considerable room for improvement—but time had run out. Barely a week after the games had ended, the nation was at war.[31]

Since early 1941, the United States had been negotiating with imperial Japan to improve relations and persuade its government to end its war with China. But when Japan invaded southern Indochina, the United States and other Western nations froze Japanese assets and placed an embargo on oil imports. The Japanese government regarded the oil embargo as an act of war. As negotiations broke down, Japan prepared to strike: the objective was to cripple the US Pacific Fleet with a knockout blow. On Sunday, December 7, 1941, Japanese forces launched a surprise attack on American bases in the Pacific. Within two hours, Japanese aircraft destroyed or damaged 8 battleships, 3 cruisers, 3 destroyers, and 328 airplanes at the Pearl Harbor naval base in Hawaii. Luckily, the aircraft carriers were at sea and therefore escaped unscathed. The assault on Pearl Harbor resulted in 2,403 Americans killed and 1,178 wounded at a cost of 29 Japanese planes and 5 midget submarines destroyed and 129 Japanese personnel killed. At least six of the men who died on the battleship USS *Arizona* were North Carolinians.[32]

In his speech before Congress on December 8, President Roosevelt referred to the previous day as "a date which will live in infamy" and called for a declaration of war against Japan. The Senate voted unanimously for war, and the House approved it 388 to 1. The United States had formally entered the Second World War. Germany and Italy declared war on the United States three days later, and America reciprocated by a unanimous vote, entering a full-scale, two-front war for the first time in its history. On January 1, 1942, the Big

Two views of amphibious training at Fort Bragg, 1942. (*U.S. Army*)

Four allies—Britain, China, the Soviet Union, and the United States—joined with twenty-two other governments in issuing the Declaration by United Nations, affirming the Atlantic Charter and pledging not to sign a separate peace with the Axis powers.[33]

GEARING UP FOR WAR

Long before Pearl Harbor, the United States had been preparing for war. In September 1940, Congress passed the first peacetime military draft in US history. By mid-1941, a total of two hundred fifty-eight thousand North Carolinians served in the army, ninety thousand in the navy, and thirteen thousand in the marines. During the war, North Carolina was home to more than one hundred military bases, where roughly two million soldiers, sailors, marines, and coast guardsmen received their training—more than in any other state. The three largest military bases in North Carolina were Fort Bragg, an army base, and two new Marine Corps bases: Cherry Point and Camp Lejeune.[34]

Fort Bragg had been a training camp during World War I and later became the largest artillery post in the world during the Second World War. The adjoining Pope Field was named after pilot Lieutenant Harley H. Pope, who was killed when his aircraft crashed into the Cape Fear River. Later renamed Pope Air Force Base, it was one of the world's largest such installations. Cherry Point became the largest marine airfield in the world and was the home of the 3rd and later the 9th Marine Aircraft Wings, both of which trained aviation personnel headed to the Pacific theater. Camp Lejeune, named for former Marine Corps Commandant John A. Lejeune, was a marine training base situated on more than one hundred thousand rural acres near Jacksonville, North Carolina. Medics, Seabees (naval construction battalions), coast guardsmen, female marines, and marine infantry received their training there. The Montford Point section served as a segregated training area for twenty thousand black marines. Marine Corps working dogs also trained at Lejeune as messengers, sentries, and scouts. Among other bases in North Carolina, Camp Mackall—named after Private John T. "Tommy"

Gilbert "Hashmark" Johnson inspecting new recruits at Montford Point, 1943. Johnson was one of the first African American drill instructors in the Marine Corps. He served in the army and the navy for a total of fifteen years before joining the corps, receiving his nickname because he had more service stripes, or "hashmarks," than did many of his instructors. On April 19, 1974, the corps dedicated the Montford Point facility as Camp Gilbert H. Johnson. (*U.S. Marine Corps*)

Top: Wilmington Shipyard, North Carolina Shipbuilding Company. (*New Hanover County Public Library, Wilmington*) Bottom: Sinking of the *Dixie Arrow*. The American tanker was torpedoed by the U-71 off the Outer Banks on March 26, 1942. (*National Archives*)

Mackall, a paratrooper who was killed during the invasion of North Africa—was the army's second-largest training facility for paratroopers. In addition, Camp Butner, named in honor of army General Henry W. Butner, served as a training ground for army infantry, while Camp Davis—named after Statesville native and army General Richmond P. Davis—was the first antiaircraft base in the United States, housing as many as sixty thousand trainees.[35]

On June 12, 1942, the War Department activated the Headquarters, Technical School, Army Air Forces Technical Training Command near Goldsboro. Four months later, US Rep. Graham A. Barden of North Carolina announced that the air base was renamed Seymour Johnson Field, in honor of Lieutenant Seymour A. Johnson, a navy test pilot from Goldsboro who died in an airplane crash on March 5, 1941. In October 1943, the air base assumed responsibility for training army air forces personnel for overseas deployment; it also became the home of the 75th Flying Training Wing, which operated a pretraining school for aviation cadets. In 1944, the 326th Fighter Group began conducting basic training for P-47 Thunderbolt pilots.[36]

As the only major industrialized Allied nation not subject to enemy aerial bombing raids, the United States became the Second World War's "Great Arsenal of Democracy"—a slogan coined by President Franklin Roosevelt. The US government spent over $2 billion for manufactured goods in North Carolina alone, made by almost one million men and women. Products manufactured in the Tar Heel State included rockets, bombs, airplane assemblies, radar components, tent fabric, blankets, towels, clothing, and ships. With its many inlets, rivers, and sheltered harbors, North Carolina was well suited for shipbuilding. Shipyards at Elizabeth City built submarine chasers, while facilities at New Bern made minesweepers, and ship-repair centers sprang up at Morehead City and Southport. Wilmington boasted a thriving wartime shipbuilding industry that employed over twenty thousand workers. A total of 243 "Liberty Ships"—the nickname for cargo vessels and troop transports—were built at Wilmington during the war.[37]

TAR HEELS ON THE FRONT LINES

On the morning of January 18, 1942, just over a month after the United States had officially entered World War II, a German U-boat sank the American tanker *Allan Jackson* about sixty miles off the coast of Cape Hatteras. The vessel was carrying seventy-two thousand barrels of crude oil; of the thirty-five men on board, only three officers and ten crew members survived. Just after two the next morning, a thunderous explosion rocked the Outer Banks village of Avon, rattling furniture and glass and knocking books from their shelves. Residents looked east at the ocean and beheld an orange fireball erupting on the horizon, followed by a huge canopy of black smoke that blotted out the stars above. Just seven miles away, a German U-boat had torpedoed the *City of Atlanta*, a 337-foot-long American freighter, killing all but three of the forty-seven men on board.[38]

The two sinkings were part of Operation Drumbeat, the Germans' attempt to disrupt Allied shipping along the US East Coast. Of the five large U-boats that launched the first wave of the operation, the *U-66* sank five ships off the coast of the Tar Heel State, including the Canadian passenger liner *Lady Hawkins*, with the loss of its 250 crew and passengers. U-boats sank a total of ten ships within two hundred miles of the North Carolina coast in January 1942 and eight more the following month. An increased U-boat force struck in March, sinking or damaging twenty-five ships, with the *U-124* alone destroying five vessels. The worst night of the war for Allied shipping occurred on March 18, when U-boats sank five ships. April saw seventeen U-boats destroy a total of twenty-seven ships; during the first four months of 1942, German torpedoes sent almost seventy Allied vessels to the bottom of the ocean. These U-boat attacks were so devastating that the Cape Hatteras region earned the nickname, "Torpedo Junction." Operation Drumbeat added to the reputation of the North Carolina coastal waters as "the Graveyard of the Atlantic."[39]

Most of the ships sunk at Torpedo Junction went down between January

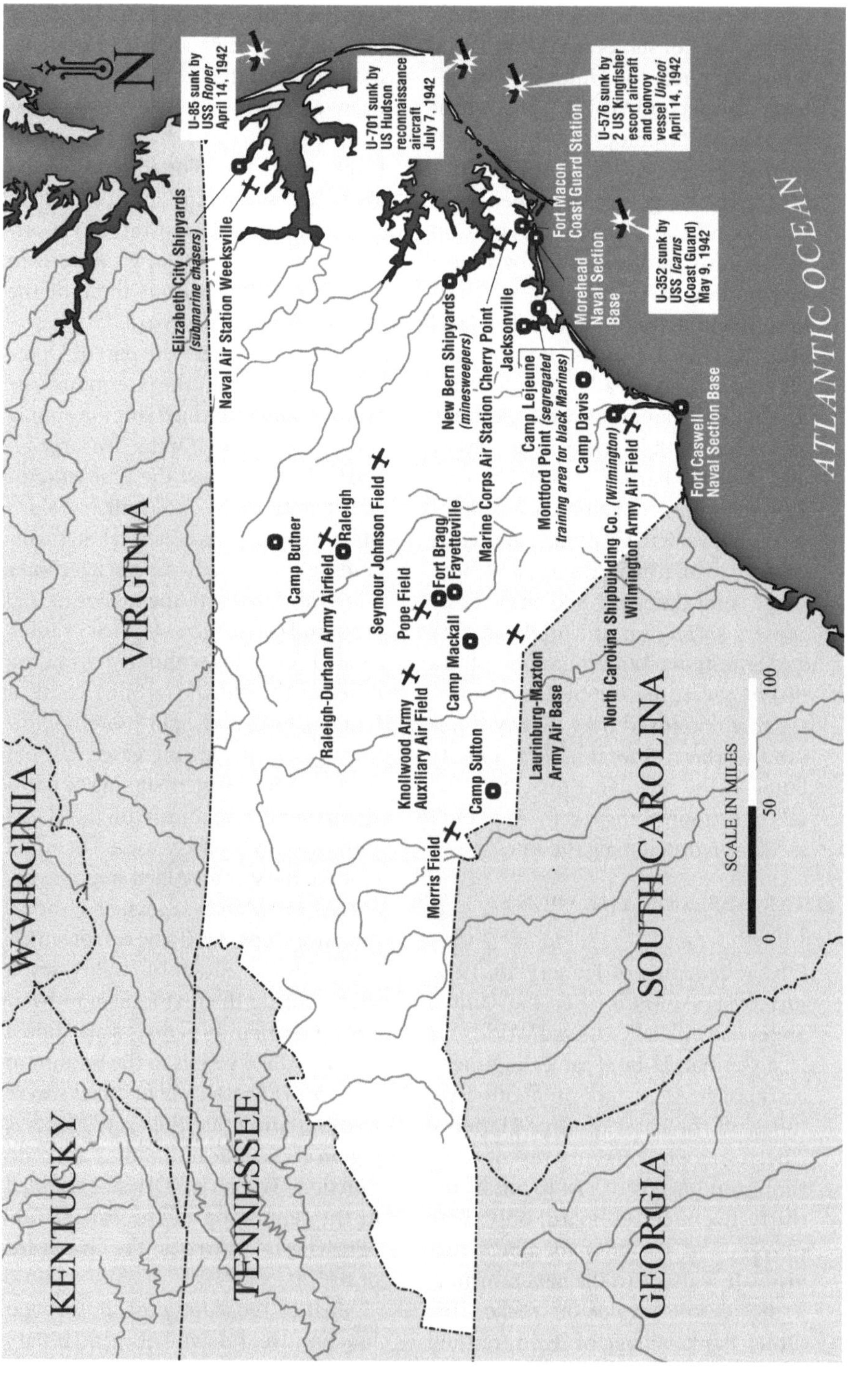

N
KENTUCKY
W. VIRGINIA
VIRGINIA
TENNESSEE
SOUTH CAROLINA
GEORGIA
ATLANTIC OCEAN
U-85 sunk by USS *Roper* April 14, 1942
U-701 sunk by US Hudson reconnaissance aircraft July 7, 1942
U-576 sunk by 2 US Kingfisher escort aircraft and convoy vessel *Unicoi* April 14, 1942
U-352 sunk by USS *Icarus* (Coast Guard) May 9, 1942
Elizabeth City Shipyards *(submarine chasers)*
Naval Air Station Weeksville
Fort Macon Coast Guard Station
Morehead Naval Section Base
New Bern Shipyards *(minesweepers)*
Marine Corps Air Station Cherry Point
Jacksonville
Camp Lejeune
Montford Point *(segregated training area for black Marines)*
Camp Davis
North Carolina Shipbuilding Co. *(Wilmington)*
Wilmington Army Air Field
Fort Caswell Naval Section Base
Camp Butner
Raleigh
Raleigh-Durham Army Airfield
Seymour Johnson Field
Pope Field
Fort Bragg
Fayetteville
Camp Mackall
Knollwood Army Auxiliary Air Field
Laurinburg-Maxton Army Air Base
Camp Sutton
Morris Field
SCALE IN MILES
0
50
100

and July 1942. The tide in the U-boat campaign began to turn that spring, as the US Navy and US Coast Guard bolstered their force of antisubmarine vessels and aircraft. This action was prompted in part by a report from Gov. J. Melville Broughton to Secretary of the Navy Frank Knox. On March 26, Broughton wrote that "the defenses against submarine depredations certainly in the North Carolina coastal areas are wholly inadequate and frequently inept." He noted that U-boats were "menacing our coastal waters with impunity, causing tremendous tanker losses and overrunning the hospital and medical facilities on the eastern coast of North Carolina."[40]

On April 14, 1942, the destroyer USS *Roper* sank the *U-85* sixteen miles southeast of Nag's Head. It was the first U-boat sunk by the US Navy. In May, the navy began to escort merchant vessels in large convoys, resulting in a sharp drop-off in losses. Although the Germans sank two American warships that month, a U-boat—the *U-352*—went down off Cape Lookout on May 9, sunk by the US Coast Guard cutter *Icarus*. In June, ten Allied vessels were torpedoed, followed by just three in July. In the meantime, two more U-boats—the *U-701* and the *U-576*—were sunk, and a third was severely damaged by air assault. At this point, the Germans withdrew their U-boats from the East Coast because of the difficulty in penetrating the Allied defenses. Subsequent attacks were sporadic and usually involved a lone wolf U-boat. In 1943, just one naval warship and two merchant vessels were sunk off North Carolina, while only one ship sustained damage in 1944. In April 1945, German U-boats mounted a last-ditch offensive against the East Coast, sinking one ship and damaging another, while losing the *U-548*.[41]

A total of forty-one American ships were named for North Carolina people or places, including the battleship USS *North Carolina*, which participated in every major naval campaign in the Pacific theater. Its fifteen battle stars made the "Showboat"—as it was called—the most decorated American battleship of World War II. Armed with nine 16-inch, .45-caliber guns mounted in three turrets plus 128 smaller guns, the *North Carolina* measured 728 feet long and 108 feet maximum width. The wartime crew consisted of 144 officers and 2,195 enlisted men. By the end of the war, the battleship had logged three hundred thousand miles and had lost just ten men killed and sixty-seven wounded. The *North Carolina* was decommissioned in 1947 and then slated to be scrapped in 1958. A "Save Our Ship" (SOS) campaign led by the Tar Heel State's schoolchildren raised the $330,000 needed to purchase and relocate the battleship. Arriving at its current berth on the Cape Fear River opposite downtown Wilmington in 1961, it was dedicated on April 29, 1962, as a museum and the state's memorial to its World War II veterans.[42]

Probably the most famous airplane piloted by a North Carolinian in the Second World War was the *Memphis Belle*, a B-17 Flying Fortress commanded by Captain Robert K. Morgan of Asheville. Named for Morgan's girlfriend, the *Memphis Belle* earned the official distinction of being the first heavy bomber to complete twenty-five

The deck of the USS *North Carolina*, taken off the coast of Japan in July 1945. (*NavSource Online: Battleship Photo Archive*)

successful missions in the European theater. To bolster morale, in early 1943, the US Army Air Forces had announced that air crews completing twenty-five missions would be sent home. The *Memphis Belle* crew flew its twenty-fifth and final mission—an attack on U-boat pens at Lorient, France—on May 17, 1943. All twenty-four of the bombers that left the air station at Bassingbourn, England, that morning returned safely. "It was like we'd had an angel covering us that day," Morgan later recalled. The movie director William Wyler, who was a major in the US Army Air Forces, and a film crew recorded the *Memphis Belle's* final mission for posterity. Wyler's documentary, *The* Memphis Belle: *A Story of a Flying Fortress*, appeared in movie theaters across America the following April. In June 1943, Morgan, who had been promoted to major, and his crew flew the *Memphis Belle* back to the United States and then led a thirty-one-city war bond tour.[43]

Greensboro native Major George E. Preddy was the state's leading World War II fighter ace. A P-51 Mustang pilot, Preddy was credited by the Army Air Forces with shooting down thirty-two enemy aircraft before he was killed by friendly fire on Christmas Day 1944. He was the seventh-ranking ace among American pilots.[44]

An early proponent of airborne infantry, Dunn native Major General William C. Lee was appointed the first commander of the US Army's jump school at Fort Benning, Georgia, and he became the first commander of the

Robert K. Morgan in front of *Memphis Belle.* (*U.S. Air Force*)

William C. Lee, the "Father of the Airborne," receiving an honorary degree from North Carolina State College in 1945. (*NCSU Libraries*)

101st Airborne Division, which was stationed at Fort Bragg in 1942. In 1944, Lee planned the airborne phase of the Normandy invasion and trained for the jump alongside his men. But he suffered a heart attack on February 5, 1944, and had to miss the D-Day operation. As a tribute to their stricken leader, the men of the 101st yelled "Bill Lee!" as they parachuted into Normandy. Lee retired from the army in 1944 and died in 1948. His home in Dunn now serves as the General William C. Lee Airborne Museum.[45]

The army unit with the most Tar Heel soldiers was the 30th Infantry Division. The "Old Hickory" Division had served in World War I and later became a National Guard unit between the wars. Recalled to service on September 16, 1940, the 30th landed on Omaha Beach in Normandy on June 11, 1944, five days after D-Day. Dubbed "the workhorse of the western front," the division saw action in nearly every major operation in that theater. Commanded by Major General Leland S. Hobbs, the 30th led the breakthrough at St. Lo, smashed through the Siegfried Line, raced 180 miles into Belgium in just three days during the Battle of the Bulge, and pushed into Germany, where it met the Soviet advance along the Elbe River on May 8, 1945.[46]

Like the Old Hickory Division, the 4th Infantry Division had a large Tar Heel contingent and its service dated back to World War I. It was reactivated at Fort Benning on June 1, 1940. The 4th Division landed at Utah Beach on D-Day, with the 8th Infantry of the 4th being the first Allied ground unit to hit the Normandy beaches. After clearing the Cotentin Peninsula, the 4th Division participated in the capture of Cherbourg on June 25. The division then broke through the left flank of the German Seventh Army and was the first American unit to enter Paris on August 25, 1944, having yielded the liberation of the city to French forces. Passing through Belgium, the 4th encountered stiff German resistance in the Battle of the Hürtgen Forest. In December, the division opposed the German Ardennes Offensive and was back on the attack in early 1945, crossing the Rhine in late March and moving through Bavaria when the Germans surrendered in May. Soon afterward, the 4th Division moved to Camp Butner to prepare for redeployment to the Pacific theater, but the Japanese surrendered before the 4th shipped out.

The origins of the 80th Infantry Division likewise dated back to World War I, and it also contained many North Carolina soldiers. Nicknamed the "Blue Ridge" Division because most of its personnel hailed from the mid-Atlantic states, it sailed for England on July 4, 1944, aboard the *Queen Mary*. The 80th landed on Utah Beach on August 7, 1944, and became a fixture in General George S. Patton Jr.'s Third Army for the rest of the war. After sweeping across France, the division moved north into Luxembourg to relieve the 101st Airborne Division trapped in Bastogne during the Battle of the Bulge. In February 1945, the Blue Ridge Division broke through the Siegfried Line and then crossed the Rhine River on March 27–28. During its advance through Germany, the 80th liberated prisoners in Buchenwald and other concentration camps. Pushing through southern Germany, Austria, and Czechoslovakia, the Blue Ridge Division reportedly fired the last shot in the European theater as General Patton issued his cease-fire order on May 8.[47]

North Carolina soldiers also fought in the Pacific theater. Many served in the 81st Infantry Division, yet another army unit that traced its lineage back to the Great War. The 81st was reactivated at Fort Rucker, Alabama, on June 15, 1942, and trained on bases in Tennessee, Arizona, and California before shipping out to Hawaii in June 1944. From September 1944 to January 1945, the Wildcat Division fought in the western Pacific in the Palau Islands Campaign, capturing Angaur and Peleliu. The 11th Airborne Division served on Leyte and Luzon in the Philippines. When Tar Heel paratroopers liberated their comrades from an internment camp on Luzon, one grateful North Carolina inmate—a former employee of Liggett and Myers— accepted a Camel cigarette with the comment, "I hope the boss will not take this as an act of disloyalty." The 2nd Marine Division fought at Guadalcanal, Tarawa, Saipan, Tinian, and Okinawa. After a brief occupation stint in Japan, the 2nd returned to the United States and made Camp Lejeune its permanent home.[48]

Most Tar Heel marines served in the Pacific. Of the 464 Medals of Honor presented to military personnel during World War II, two went to marines from North Carolina—Pharmacist's Mate Second Class William D. Halyburton Jr. and Private Jaclyn H. "Jack" Lucas. Halyburton was a medic in the 2nd Battalion, 5th Marines, 1st Marine Division. During the Battle of Okinawa, on May 10, 1945, Halyburton received a mortal wound while attempting to give first aid to a severely wounded comrade. Lucas served with the 1st Battalion, 26th Marines, 5th Marine Division. During the Battle of Iwo Jima, on February 20, 1945, a Japanese squad ambushed Lucas and three other marines. To save his comrades, Lucas fell on an enemy grenade and grabbed a second one to absorb the force of both blasts; only the first one exploded, severely wounding him. His self-sacrifice shielded his fellow marines and enabled them to kill the enemy soldiers. Barely seventeen at the time, Lucas recovered from his wounds and lived until 2008.[49]

Jaclyn H. "Jack" Lucas. (*U.S. Marine Corps*)

One Medal of Honor recipient from North Carolina was a member of the US Navy. Roseboro native Lieutenant Junior Grade Rufus G. Herring was the commander of LCI (Landing Craft, Infantry) 449 during the assault on Iwo Jima. On February 17, 1945, the vessel came under the devastating fire of Japanese coastal defense guns as it approached the beach and sustained heavy damage. Despite being severely wounded, Herring remained in command even when loss of blood compelled him to prop himself up against empty shell cases. He piloted his crippled landing craft to safety and saw to his wounded men before receiving medical care for himself.[50]

The remaining Tar Heel Medal of Honor recipients served in the US Army. On July 23, 1944, Sergeant Ray E. Eubanks of Snow Hill led his squad in an attack on a Japanese position on Noemfoor Island, Dutch New Guinea. Advancing to within fifteen yards of the enemy, Eubanks was gravely wounded, and a bullet rendered his automatic rifle useless. Using his disabled weapon as a club, he killed four of the enemy before receiving his death wound. Eubanks's example so inspired his men that they continued the assault, killing forty-five Japanese and driving the remainder from their position. Lieutenant Charles P. "Chuck" Murray Jr. of Wilmington was severely wounded while singlehandedly overcoming two hundred German soldiers on December 16, 1944, near Keysersberg, France. During the assault, Murray killed twenty of the enemy, wounded many others, and captured ten. On October 18, 1944, Bethel native Sergeant Max Thompson of the 18th Infantry was severely wounded while single-handedly repulsing an enemy assault supported by tanks near Haaren, Germany. Corporal Henry F. Warner of Troy was an antitank gunner with the 2nd Battalion, 26th Infantry. During the fighting near Dom Butgenbach, Belgium, on December 20–21, 1944, Warner knocked four German tanks out of commission, at one point killing an enemy tank commander in a close-range pistol duel.

Margaret D. Craighill. (*U.S. National Library of Medicine*)

Wounded several times, Warner was killed by an enemy machine-gun burst.[51]

The Tar Heel State had many more heroes who never returned home. Of the roughly four hundred five thousand US military personnel who died, eighty-five hundred North Carolinians made the ultimate sacrifice.[52]

TAR HEELS ON THE HOME FRONT

During the Second World War, thousands of women served as nurses, and in 1943, Southport native Major Margaret D. Craighill became the first female physician to receive a commission in the US Army. Over three hundred fifty thousand women served in the Women's Army Corps (WACs), the Women's Air Force Service Pilots (WASPs), the navy's Women Accepted for Volunteer Emergency Service (WAVES), the Marine Corps Women's Reserve, and the Coast Guard's SPARS. With so many men in the military, women entered the workforce in unprecedented numbers. The iconic figure of Rosie the Riveter—popularized by the 1942 song and the 1943 "We Can Do It!" poster by J. Howard Miller—symbolized the millions of women who worked vital jobs in factories and shipyards.[53]

The Office of Civilian Defense presided over local vigilance and support efforts. Taxes covered less than half of the war's cost, so the US government had to rely on banks and private citizens to finance the remainder. These loans came in the form of stamps and war bonds sold by banks, civic groups, and other volunteers. North Carolina public schools alone raised over $43 million during eight war bond drives, earning them national recognition.[54]

The high demand for war materiel, combined with the interruption of regular shipping schedules, led to the formation of the Office of Price Administration. Local rationing boards oversaw the allotment and pricing of items such as gasoline, rubber, sugar, coffee, meat, firewood, coal, and building materials. Starting May 4, 1942, civilians received ration books with stamps needed to purchase items in limited supply. The North Carolina Salvage Committee handled the recycling of materials such as metal, rubber, nylon, silk, and paper under the slogan "Get in the Scrap!" Most rationing restrictions ended in August 1945, following the surrender of Nazi Germany on May 8 (V-E Day) and imperial Japan on August 15 (V-J Day), after the Americans had dropped atomic bombs on the Japanese cities of Hiroshima and Nagasaki.[55]

Few North Carolinians were aware of it at the time, but for much of the Second World War, thousands of prisoners of war (POWs) lived and worked in their state. Italian POWs were among the first to arrive. When the Fascist regime under Benito Mussolini collapsed in September 1943, the new Italian government allied itself with the United States. In March 1944, the U.S. Army formed Italian Service Units composed of Italian POWs who took an oath of allegiance to their new government and served as noncombatant auxiliaries to American forces. They received American uniforms and were even permitted to leave their bases. In May 1945, eighteen North Carolina prison camps held about 10,000 German POWs. By far the largest camps were at Fort Bragg and Camp Butner, which each held up to 3,000 prisoners. POWs worked mainly on military bases and farms; their contribution to the American war effort was considerable. According to the state director of the War Manpower Commission, POWs had performed nearly two million man-days of agricultural labor.[56]

14. From the Cold War to the War on Terror

Following the defeat of the Axis powers in 1945, the Soviet Union emerged as the chief adversary of the United States in what became a decades-long struggle for global dominance known as the Cold War. Initially political in nature, the Cold War became increasingly militarized. In rapid succession, the US government set forth its resolve to oppose the spread of communism with the Truman Doctrine and the policy of containment; rival alliances formed under the banners of the US-led North Atlantic Treaty Organization (NATO) and the Soviet bloc; the Soviets developed the atomic bomb, triggering the nuclear arms race; and the Chinese Communist leader Mao Zedong declared the creation of the People's Republic of China, which signed a treaty of mutual assistance with the Soviet Union. The United States sought to contain Communist aggression while avoiding a full-scale war—a policy that was soon tested.[1]

THE KOREAN WAR

When Communist North Korea invaded South Korea on June 25, 1950, the United Nations—with the United States as the main force—came to the assistance of the South Korean government, while China—and to a lesser extent the Soviet Union—supported the North Koreans. The entire North Carolina congressional delegation approved President Harry S. Truman's decision to block the Communist aggressors. In early July, the Tar Heel State sent several National Guard units to Fort Jackson, South Carolina, for combat training, while the Air National Guard began mobilizing. When the federal government directed the state to open 101 draft boards at once and induct 610 recruits by September, Raleigh vaulted from nineteenth to first place among southern induction centers in monthly recruitment. The Wilmington shipyard also reopened with a capacity for twenty-one thousand workers.[2]

The war, meanwhile, was going badly for the UN alliance. Within two months, the Communists had driven the South Korean and American troops into a small pocket in the south known as the Pusan Perimeter. In September 1950, the UN forces launched an amphibious counteroffensive at Incheon, capturing thousands of North Korean soldiers. As the remainder fled north, the UN troops advanced to the Yalu River, on the border with China. The Chinese then launched a massive counterattack; this sudden and overwhelming intervention precipitated a retreat of the UN forces that lasted until mid-1951. What followed was a bloody war of attrition, culminating in a stalemate with the two forces dug in on opposite sides of the 38th parallel. On July 27, 1953, the belligerents signed an armistice that established the Korean Demilitarized Zone separating North Korea and South Korea. The two sides are technically still at war—though war had never been declared.[3]

Over one hundred seventy-seven thousand North Carolinians served in the Korean War, with 784 killed and 201 either captured or missing in action. Three Tar Heels received the Medal of Honor for exceptional bravery and selflessness in Korea: Corporal Jerry K. Crump of Charlotte, Private Charles George of Cherokee, and Private Bryant H. Womack of Mill Spring. Crump was severely wounded, and both George and Womack were mortally wounded while saving the lives of their comrades.[4]

Jerry K. Crump. (*U.S. Army*)

NUCLEAR CATASTROPHE AVERTED

On November 1, 1952, the United States regained the edge in the nuclear arms race when it detonated a hydrogen bomb on Eniwetok Atoll in the Pacific Ocean, but the Soviet Union responded quickly, exploding a similar thermonuclear device in August 1953. To achieve a credible deterrence, the two superpowers each developed a strategic nuclear triad consisting of bomber aircraft, land-based missiles, and ship- or submarine-based missiles. By the early 1960s, they possessed sufficient nuclear firepower to annihilate each other, resulting in a policy known as mutual assured destruction, in which each nation had the capacity to launch a devastating second strike even after sustaining a full-scale nuclear assault.[5]

In the late 1950s, the US Air Force's Strategic Air Command dispersed its nuclear-armed B-52 Stratofortress bombers to prevent the Soviet Union from knocking out the entire fleet with a surprise first strike. From 1959 to 1963, Seymour Johnson Air Force Base near Goldsboro served as the base for the 4241st Bomb Wing and its B-52G bombers. At the time, it was US strategy to keep nuclear-armed bombers in the air twenty-four hours a day in the event of a sudden attack. On the night of January 23, 1961, one such bomber

Close call: This MK39 nuclear bomb nearly detonated. (*U.S. Air Force*)

developed a fuel leak while refueling over South Carolina. The B-52 assumed an offshore holding pattern east of Wilmington for two hours to drain its tanks, but with a sudden increase in fuel loss, ground control ordered the pilot to return at once to Seymour Johnson. During the descent, the pilot lost control of the aircraft and ordered the crew to bail out. Three members of the eight-man crew—Major Eugene H. Richards, Major Eugene Shelton, and Sergeant Francis R. Barnish—were killed. The B-52 broke up in midair shortly after midnight on January 24. The debris covered a two-square-mile area of farmland near Faro about twelve miles north of Goldsboro. According to one of the survivors, copilot Major Richard Rardin, "My biggest difficulty getting back [to base] was the various and sundry dogs I encountered on the road."[6]

Rardin was unaware of the condition and location of the two MK39 thermonuclear devices that had constituted the B-52's payload. Each bomb measured roughly twelve feet long and weighed up to five tons. They landed about one mile from the B-52's wreckage. Because the parachute had deployed on one of the bombs, it sustained minimal damage on landing. However, all but one of the firing, fusing, and arming switches had activated—only a crew-controlled switch that remained in the "safe" position had prevented a nuclear catastrophe. The other device crashed in freefall, breaking apart on impact and leaving a deep impact crater, which made retrieving parts of the bomb that contained uranium impractical. The federal government bought a portion of the site and still maintains an easement to prevent digging there. The state conducts periodic groundwater tests and thus far has detected no radioactive contamination.[7]

The potential yield of the two MK39 thermonuclear devices was 2.4 megatons each, making them roughly two hundred times more powerful than the atomic bombs dropped on Hiroshima and Nagasaki. The weapons were capable of leveling homes within a five-mile radius and causing third-degree burns and starting fires within nine miles. The Goldsboro "broken arrow" (the term for an incident involving the loss of control of a nuclear device) is believed to be one of the United States' nearest brushes with nuclear disaster during the Cold War. This incident and several other close calls induced President John F. Kennedy to relax the around-the-clock deployment of nuclear-armed B-52 bombers to reduce the likelihood of further such incidents.[8]

THE CUBAN MISSILE CRISIS

On August 10, 1962, Central Intelligence Agency Director John A. McCone informed President Kennedy that U-2 reconnaissance aircraft had spotted eight surface-to-air missile sites in Cuba. McCone reasoned that the Soviet Union would deploy them only if they planned to defend ballistic missiles with nuclear warheads aimed at the United States. By mid-September, intelligence reports indicated that the Soviets were building nine launch sites for medium-range or intermediate-range ballistic missiles capable of reaching most of the continental United States. Additional U-2 photos confirmed the presence of medium-range ballistic missiles. After conferring with his national security advisers, Kennedy decided to impose a blockade—or "quarantine," which sounded less warlike—to prevent Soviet ships from delivering additional missiles. In a nationwide televised address on October 22, Kennedy informed the American people of the missiles and announced his intention to impose "a strict quarantine on all offensive military equipment" bound for Cuba. Among the air force units on full alert at that time was the 4241st Bomb Wing at Seymour Johnson Air Base—the same unit that had been involved in the Goldsboro broken arrow incident in January 1961.[9]

After a period of tense negotiations—during which the world teetered on the brink of full-scale thermonuclear war—Kennedy reached an agreement with Soviet Premier Nikita Khrushchev. The Soviets would dismantle their ballistic missiles in Cuba and return them to the Soviet Union subject to United Nations verification; in exchange, the United States would pledge not to invade Cuba and would remove its Jupiter nuclear missiles from Turkey, which were aimed at the Soviet Union.[10]

Throughout the Cuban Missile Crisis, US military photo reconnaissance aircraft flew over Cuba every two hours, collecting crucial intelligence on Soviet progress in building missile sites. The four RF-8A Crusaders attached to Marine Composite Squadron 2 stationed at the Marine Corps Air Station, Cherry Point, participated in the mission, code named Operation Blue Moon. At first, the pilots did not know what they were photographing. "No one [in the squadron] knew they had nukes down there," recalled Colonel Ed Love, the squadron's senior pilot. "We were aware they had missile sites that put Washington, DC, and a few other places in range."

Regardless of the presence of nuclear warheads, the reconnaissance missions were extremely hazardous. From takeoff at Key West, Florida, the pilots flew between fifty and seventy-five feet above the sea. On reaching Cuba, they climbed to about one thousand feet and maneuvered from target site to target site, often dodging antiaircraft fire. On completing their mission, the pilots headed back to Key West, where they refueled and then flew to an air base near Jacksonville, Florida, and delivered the film there. The photographs revealed that the Soviet missiles were not yet armed, convincing Kennedy that he still had time to negotiate with Khrushchev. The pilots continued to fly reconnaissance missions in November 1962 to confirm that the Soviets were fulfilling their end of the agreement. During the crisis, the four pilots—then-Captains Love, Fred Carolan, Richard Conway, and John Hudson—did not know the full story. Only after they had returned home and watched the news on television did they realize their achievement. They eventually received official recognition for their courage and skill. All four pilots received Distinguished Flying Crosses, and their squadron was the first Marine Corps unit to receive the Navy Unit Commendation during peacetime.[11]

The Cuban Missile Crisis was the closest the Cold War-era world came to nuclear Armageddon. To avert another such crisis, Kennedy and Khrushchev established a communications hotline between Moscow and Washington in 1963. What later followed was a series of talks between the leaders of the two superpowers that culminated in the Strategic Arms Limitations Treaty—or SALT I—signed by President Richard M. Nixon and Soviet General Secretary Leonid I. Brezhnev on May 26, 1972. For the first time, the United States and the Soviet Union had agreed to limit their respective nuclear missile arsenals.[12]

THE VIETNAM WAR

To contain the spread of communism in Southeast Asia, the United States supported the French in the First Indochina War, from 1950 to 1954, providing military advisers and most of the funding for the French effort against the Viet Minh. Following France's defeat in 1954 and the partitioning of Indochina into North Vietnam and South Vietnam, the United States increased its presence in Vietnam to prevent the Communist North from overrunning the non-Communist South.[13]

In August 1964, US and North Vietnamese naval vessels clashed in the Gulf of Tonkin, prompting Congress to pass the Gulf of Tonkin Resolution, authorizing President Lyndon B. Johnson to increase the US military force in Vietnam. In 1965, Johnson began sending soldiers and marines to Vietnam to prevent the collapse of South Vietnam. The enemy force consisted of North Vietnamese Army regulars and South Vietnamese Communist guerrillas or, Viet Cong. They were supported by the Soviet Union and Communist China. The US force in Vietnam increased to one hundred eighty-four thousand by the end of 1965. In addition to the South Vietnamese armed forces, Australia, New Zealand, South Korea, and Thailand contributed troops to the war effort. Through bombing of the North Vietnamese supply line along the Laotian and Cambodian border—known as the Ho Chi Minh Trail—as well as search-and-destroy missions on the ground, US forces sought to annihilate the enemy with superior firepower. But the commander of US forces in Vietnam, General William C. Westmoreland, was under strict orders from Washington not to launch cross-border operations into North Vietnam for fear of dragging the Chinese armed forces into the conflict. The insurgents proved to be elusive adversaries, rarely engaging the Americans and their allies unless at a time and place of their own choosing.[14]

From the start, North Carolina's military bases provided training, supply, and support for American soldiers, marines, sailors, and airmen who deployed to Vietnam. In 1961, the army activated the Fort Bragg-based 5th Special Forces Group (Airborne); known as the Green Berets, this unit was trained in counterinsurgency warfare, and many served as advisers in Vietnam. From December 1961 to mid-1963, the 464th Troop Carrier Wing shuttled troops and aircraft from Pope Air Force Base to Tan Son Nhut Air Base in Vietnam. Pope also became a training base for aircrews flying C-130 transport aircraft on low-altitude airdrop missions.

Camp Lejeune trained and deployed marines for service in South Vietnam, and Cherry Point sent three A-6 Intruder squadrons as well as numerous aviation personnel to Southeast Asia. The 145th Air Transport Group (Heavy) of the North Carolina Air Force National Guard flew missions in Vietnam from 1966 to 1971, logging a remarkable eleven million miles without an accident. The 312th Evacuation Hospital, a North Carolina-based army reserve unit, served in Vietnam from September 1968 to August 1969.[15]

Before deploying to Vietnam, General Westmoreland had been commandant of Fort Bragg in 1963. More than two hundred thousand men underwent basic training there during the Vietnam War; at its peak, the base's population was almost sixty thousand. The largest unit based at Bragg that deployed to Vietnam in 1968 was the 3rd Brigade, 82nd Airborne Division. Among other missions, the 82nd had intervened in the Dominican Republic's civil war in 1965 and was deployed to suppress the Detroit riots in 1967.[16]

In early 1968, the Communists launched the Tet Offensive across South Vietnam. Although the general assault failed to topple the South Vietnamese government and resulted in heavy insurgent losses, it convinced a large segment of the American people that the government's claims of military success were exaggerated, despite a massive investment of manpower and money. In 1969, President Nixon began his "Vietnamization" program involving the gradual withdrawal of US forces while placing the burden of fighting the Communists on the South Vietnamese. Nixon began the withdrawal as the US forces in Vietnam peaked at five hundred forty-nine thousand personnel. Despite the signing of the Paris Peace Accords in January 1973 by all parties, the war continued. It ended in April 1975 with the North Vietnamese Army's conquest of South Vietnam, culminating in the fall of Saigon. The North and the South were officially reunified the following year.[17]

A total of 58,220 American military personnel were killed in the Vietnam War, and 1,626 others remain missing in action. Of the 216,348 personnel from North Carolina who served in the war, 1,302 were killed in action and about 300 died of other causes.[18]

Two North Carolinians, and four others who were born in the Tar Heel State but enlisted elsewhere, received the Medal of Honor:

Sergeant First Class Eugene Ashley Jr., Wilmington. On February 7, 1968, Ashley was mortally wounded while leading an assault to rescue Special Forces advisers at Camp Lang Vei.

Specialist Lawrence Joel receiving his Medal of Honor from President Lyndon B. Johnson. (*U.S. Army*)

Lieutenant Harold B. Durham Jr., Rocky Mount. On October 17, 1967, Durham was killed while aiding wounded comrades and serving as a forward observer for his artillery battalion.

Specialist Fifth Class Lawrence Joel, Winston-Salem. On November 8, 1965, Joel, a medic, was shot twice while treating wounded comrades under an intense fire, all the while disregarding his commander's orders to hug the ground. He was the first living African American to receive the Medal of Honor since the Spanish-American War in 1898. On April 8, 1967, Joel's hometown of Winston-Salem held a parade for him, the first time it had done so for an individual. The Joel Coliseum in Winston-Salem was named in his honor.

Staff Sergeant Franklin D. Miller, Elizabeth City. On January 5, 1970, Miller single-handedly defended his men from several assaults of the enemy in complete disregard for his own safety, despite being severely wounded.

Sergeant Robert M. Patterson, Durham. On May 6, 1968, Patterson single-handedly destroyed five enemy bunkers, killed eight enemy soldiers, and captured seven enemy weapons, inspiring his men to follow his brave example.

Sergeant Mitchell W. Stout, Raleigh. On March 12, 1970, Stout grabbed an enemy grenade thrown into the bunker where he and his men were waiting out a mortar barrage, and he ran outside while holding the grenade close to his body. In doing so, he shielded them from the blast at the cost of his own life.[19]

POST-VIETNAM MILITARY OPERATIONS AND HUMANITARIAN MISSIONS

The US military spent much of the decade after its withdrawal from Vietnam rebuilding itself into a capable all-volunteer force, thanks to new doctrine and equipment and capable leadership at all levels. Focused on countering the Soviet/Warsaw Pact threat to central Europe, the US Army prepared for large-scale conventional operations, but its first test in the post-Vietnam era occurred on Grenada, a small island in the Caribbean. In October 1983, an internal power struggle erupted between rival Communist leaders, culminating in the death of the prime minister of Grenada, Maurice Bishop, who was shot by a firing squad. The bloody coup led to a short but intense contingency operation for the US Army.

Elements of the 82nd Airborne Division stationed at Fort Bragg participated in Operation Urgent Fury, code name for the invasion of Grenada. At nearby Pope Air Force Base, the paratroopers boarded C-141 Starlifter transport aircraft at midmorning on October 25 and began arriving at Pearls Airport on Grenada about four hours later. Despite unexpectedly stubborn resistance by Grenadian and Cuban defenders, the joint American forces accomplished their objectives within three days of their deployment. The Navy SEALs and their Army Special Forces counterparts rescued Sir Paul Scoon, the official governor-general of the island, while the 82nd Airborne evacuated several hundred American medical students at St. George's University School of Medicine. US forces rescued 581 Americans and over 100 foreign nationals during the operation. After the collapse of Communist opposition on October 28, it became apparent that there would be no need for troops to suppress local guerrillas, enabling the last of the 82nd Airborne to return to Fort Bragg by mid-December. Nineteen US soldiers were killed and 116 were wounded on Grenada.[20]

Soldiers of the 82nd Airborne Division boarding a C-141B Starlifter Aircraft in Grenada. (*U.S. Army*)

Although Operation Urgent Fury had ended in victory, the Senate Armed Services Committee found much to criticize. Its report cited "serious problems in the ability of the Services to operate jointly" and proposed major changes. The resulting Goldwater-Nichols Defense Reorganization Act, signed into law by President Ronald Reagan on October 1, 1986, sought to ensure that in future operations, senior officers would have a joint, as opposed to a single-service, viewpoint. This far-reaching legislation ensured that the brief combat of Operation Urgent Fury would exert an impact on subsequent military operations out of proportion to its size, duration, or immediate outcome.[21]

Six years after the invasion of Grenada, the 82nd Airborne Division took part in Operation Just Cause—the invasion of Panama. President George H. W. Bush justified the operation by noting that a state of war existed between the United States and Panama, endangering the lives of thirty-five thousand Americans who resided there. Bush also sought to defend democracy and human rights in Panama, which were threatened by the dictator General Manuel Noriega. The president also cited his determination to combat drug trafficking in the country and to protect the neutrality of the Panama Canal. He later ordered that Noriega be apprehended and extradited to the United States.

On December 20, 1989, the 82nd Airborne Division conducted its first combat jump since World War II by dropping into Omar Torrijos International Airport near Panama City. Within a matter of days, the American force had defeated the Panamanian army and deposed Noriega, who surrendered on January 3, 1990. The former dictator was arrested and brought to America, where he was tried and convicted on eight counts of drug trafficking, racketeering, and money laundering. Noriega was sentenced to forty years in federal prison. The 82nd had sustained six of the twenty-three American fatalities in Just Cause. The paratroopers began redeploying to Fort Bragg on January 12, 1990. The operation closed on January 31, having demonstrated that the US Army had profited from the lessons learned in the Grenada operation. Just Cause was a precursor to other interventions in the coming decade.[22]

Iraq's invasion of Kuwait in August 1990 provoked a swift response from the United States, starting with the transfer of the 82nd Airborne Division from Fort Bragg to Saudi Arabia. And thus began Operation Desert Shield, the US military's largest troop deployment since the Vietnam War. Despite the army's efforts to shroud the 82nd's movement in secrecy, the sudden departure of the entire division could not be concealed. The paratroopers' absence soon triggered a sharp downturn in the local economy, forcing some Fayetteville businesses to shut their doors. In addition, the mobilization of reserve and National Guard units left hospitals, fire departments, and other essential services shorthanded. Also deploying to Saudi Arabia from Fort Bragg was the XVIII Airborne Corps, which served as the army's command-and-control element.[23]

Camp Lejeune contributed the 2nd Marine Division and its support units to the US joint force deploying to Saudi Arabia. The infantry division was joined by the 26th and 29th Marine Aircraft Groups from Cherry Point. Just before its deployment, the 2nd Division assembled on W. P. T. Hill Field for a final review. Numbering over twenty-four thousand officers and men, it was the largest formation in Marine Corps history. Camp Lejeune also served as a processing and training center for roughly twenty-five thousand Marine Corps reservists. Like Fayetteville, the town of Jacksonville felt the economic pinch caused by the departure of 20 percent of its population.[24]

The combat phase of the Persian Gulf War—code named Operation Desert Storm—began on January 17, 1991. For over a month, US-led coalition forces subjected Iraqi military targets to one of the most intensive aerial bombing campaigns in history. On February 24, the ground campaign began with the assault of coalition forces, including the 82nd Airborne Division and the 2nd Marine Division, to liberate Kuwait and defeat the Iraqi Republican Guard. The brief conflict included three of the largest tank battles in American history. Then-Colonel Ronald G. Richard of the 2nd Marine Division likened the breakthrough on his front to a mechanized tidal wave. "As the Marines, Sailors and Soldiers started pouring through," he recalled, "flags started appearing. US flags and

Marine Corps flags started to appear, latched to the vehicles. You could look to the left and look to the right, and you could see all these flags waving in the air. You could see for great distances." Barely one hundred hours later, President Bush declared a cease-fire and announced that Kuwait had been liberated. By mid-March, some of the 82nd Airborne's paratroopers were back at Fort Bragg, and by the end of May, most of the 2nd Marine Division as well as North Carolina's reserve and National Guard units had returned home. Roughly twenty-five thousand North Carolinians served in the Gulf War, 17 of whom were killed out of 383 American in-theater fatalities.[25]

The 82nd Airborne Division and other XVIII Airborne Corps units provided humanitarian assistance in southern Florida after Hurricane Andrew in August 1992. (The 82nd's later hurricane relief efforts included New Orleans in September 2005 following Katrina and post-Irma assistance in Florida during September 2017). On September 19, 1994, the 82nd Airborne received orders to deploy to Port-au-Prince, Haiti, as part of a US-led multinational force to reinstate Jean-Bertrand Aristide as president. The operation was code named Uphold Democracy. The leader of the 1991 military junta that deposed Aristide, Lieutenant General Joseph Raoul Cédras, had refused to yield to an American delegation until he was shown footage of the 82nd Airborne boarding aircraft at Pope Air Force Base bound for Haiti. Convinced that his position was hopeless, Cédras surrendered. On learning of the dictator's capitulation, the 82nd Airborne, which was in midflight, immediately changed course and returned to base. In the meantime, a twenty-three-thousand-man security force deployed to Haiti to ensure a peaceful transfer of power. The American contingent from Fort Bragg included the 3rd Special Forces Group (Airborne) and elements of the 16th Military Police Brigade.[26]

In December 1992, during the final weeks of his administration, President George H. W. Bush sent American troops to the war-torn African nation of Somalia in Operation Restore Hope. The objective was to lead a joint UN effort to restore order and distribute food to a starving people. Upon taking office, President Bill Clinton continued the humanitarian mission. On October 3, 1993, Task Force Ranger, an elite unit consisting of 160 Fort Bragg-based Delta Force operators and army rangers sent into Mogadishu to apprehend two key lieutenants of the recalcitrant warlord, Mohamed Farrah Aidid, ran into unexpectedly fierce resistance.

During the close-quarters street battle—the deadliest since the Vietnam War—Somali militants shot down two MH-60 Black Hawk helicopters. Two Fort Bragg-based Delta Force snipers, Master Sergeant Gary Gordon and Sergeant First Class Randall Shughart, volunteered to secure the second crash site. Gordon and Shughart were killed while defending the downed Black Hawk, and each man later received a posthumous Medal of Honor. In executing its mission, Task Force Ranger lost seventeen men killed and sixty-nine wounded. The UN relief effort saved thousands of Somalians from starving but could not prevent the

Randall Shughart (left) and Gary Gordon. (*U.S. Army*)

country from sliding into violence and anarchy.[27]

During the post-Vietnam era, the US armed forces relied heavily on training exercises to maintain a high state of readiness. Accidents sometimes happened, and the Green Ramp Disaster ranks among the worst. On March 23, 1994, personnel from the 82nd Airborne Division stationed at Fort Bragg were preparing to make a jump at neighboring Pope Air Force Base. About five hundred paratroopers were assembled at the staging area known as Green Ramp near the southern end of Pope's main runway.[28]

About 2:10 that afternoon, an F-16D Fighting Falcon collided with a C-130 Hercules transport as the two aircraft were attempting to land. Although the crippled C-130 landed safely, the F-16 crashed just after the two pilots had ejected. The fighter jet careened across the tarmac and slammed into a parked C-141 Starlifter transport. The two aircraft burst into flames, hurling searing-hot metal into the air and spraying fifty-five thousand gallons of fuel onto Green Ramp. A massive fireball swept through the staging area where the paratroopers were making their pre-jump preparations. The deadly inferno claimed 130 casualties. Those who managed to escape the flames helped injured comrades, many of whom were on fire. Some received wounds caused by flying metal or ammunition that cooked off in the heat generated by the fireball. Medics who arrived on the scene administered first aid, and soldiers rushed the wounded to Womack Army Medical Center at Fort Bragg, using privately owned cars as well as military vehicles. The number of injured was so great that doctors and nurses established a triage area on the grass outside the emergency room. Of the 130 casualties, 24 were either killed or died of their wounds. The Green Ramp Disaster is one of the deadliest accidents in the history of Fort Bragg and the greatest single-day loss of life suffered by the 82nd Airborne Division since the Battle of the Bulge in December 1944.[29]

In summer 1995, a bloody civil war in Bosnia-Herzegovina between Bosnian Serb and Bosnian Muslim forces escalated into a brutal campaign of so-called ethnic cleansing, in which the Serbs invaded the UN-protected area of Srebrenica in eastern Bosnia and massacred eight thousand Muslim men and boys. Two international courts declared the mass killing genocide—the worst such incident in Europe since World War II. One month later, Bosnian Serb forces bombed a market in Sarajevo, killing forty-one people. US-led NATO forces retaliated, launching airstrikes on Serb troop positions. This action induced the Serbs to open peace talks. On November 21, 1995, after three weeks of negotiations in Dayton, Ohio, the leaders of Bosnia, Croatia, and Serbia agreed to a peace treaty—the Dayton Accords—ending the Bosnian War, in which one hundred forty thousand to two hundred fifty thousand people were killed and over one million became refugees.[30]

In December 1995, a fifty-seven-thousand-troop NATO Implementation Force deployed to Bosnia in Operation Joint Endeavor. Signed in Paris, France, on December 14, the Dayton Accords divided Bosnia into a Muslim-Croat federation and the Republika Srpska, or Serb Republic. American soldiers made up about one-third of the peacekeepers. Units from Fort Bragg or Pope Air Force Base included the 23rd Aeromedical Evacuation Squadron, the 65th Military Police Company (Airborne), the 3rd Battalion, 229th Attack Helicopter Regiment ("Flying Tigers"), and the 96th Civil Affairs Battalion.[31]

In the late 1990s, another ethnic conflict erupted in the Balkans, this time in the Serbian province of Kosovo. The ethnic Albanians of Kosovo—known as Kosovar Albanians—sought to regain their independence, which the Serbian leader, Slobodan Milosevic, had taken from them. By early 1999, Serbian forces had driven about a half-million Kosovar Albanians from their homes. In a wave of ethnic cleansing that shocked the world, the Serbs murdered thousands of Kosovar Albanians. Working once more with European allies, US forces entered Kosovo in June 1999 with the intention of bringing peace to the war-torn land. The operation, code named Joint Guardian, proved extremely difficult. Ethnic hatred between Kosovar Albanians and Serbians continued to fuel the conflict, and the fighting continued for many months. Among the units sent to Kosovo from North Carolina were the 2nd Battalion, 505th Infantry and the 3rd Battalion, 504th Infantry of the 82nd Airborne Division from Fort Bragg, plus the 26th Marine Expeditionary Unit from Camp Lejeune. Organized as the Kosovo Forces, the Allies finally managed to enforce a tentative peace by October 1999. Over two hundred paratroopers serving with the 3rd Battalion, 319th Field Artillery Regiment of the 82nd Airborne Division deployed to Kosovo as recently as June 2017. As of 2018, the conflict remains unresolved. Although Kosovo declared its independence in 2008, the United Nations continues to administer the troubled province.[32]

THE WAR ON TERROR

Tuesday, September 11, 2001, began as a beautiful prelude to autumn across much of the northeastern United States but soon warped into a waking nightmare. At 8:46 AM, American Airlines Flight 11 slammed into the 96th floor of the 110-story North Tower of New York's World Trade Center. As millions of Americans watched in horror on television, United Airlines Flight 175 roared into the 80th floor of the South Tower sixteen minutes later. Firefighters and police rushed to the scene while thousands fled the Twin Towers. At 9:59 AM, the overheated steel framework of the South Tower

Troops of the 82nd Airborne Division patrolling the streets of Mosul, Iraq, in January 2005. (*U.S. Army*)

gave way, and in seconds, the 110-story building disintegrated into a mammoth pile of rubble. Within a half hour, the North Tower collapsed as well. Twenty-one minutes earlier, American Airlines Flight 77 had smashed into the western facade of the Pentagon just south of Washington, DC. A fourth passenger jet, United Airlines Flight 93, mysteriously crashed into a field near Shanksville, Pennsylvania.

Nineteen terrorists working in four teams had hijacked the planes. They succeeded in seizing and rerouting three of the aircraft to their targets, while the passengers aboard Flight 93—having learned via cell phone the fate of the earlier flights—attempted to regain control of the airliner and caused it to crash before reaching its destination, probably either the White House or the US Capitol. A total of 2,977 workers, passengers, and first responders plus all 19 of the hijackers died in the attacks. The American people had their first heroes and martyrs in what President George W. Bush would call the Global War on Terrorism. Like December 7, 1941, that day—known thereafter as "9/11"—would live in infamy.[33]

Following the 9/11 attacks, the United States uncovered the identity of the perpetrators and the terrorist organization they were affiliated with: al-Qaeda. But finding the terrorists and their enigmatic leader, Osama bin Laden, would be difficult. Al-Qaeda was based in Afghanistan, a vast, undeveloped country with massive mountain ranges and remote valleys in the north and east and arid plains in the south and west. Worse yet, the Taliban—a brutal, Muslim fundamentalist regime—controlled most of the country and provided a safe haven to al-Qaeda and other terrorist groups.

Army Special Forces units began combat operations, code named Operation Enduring Freedom, in October 2001. Their mission was to land by helicopter deep in enemy territory, link up with Northern Alliance opposition forces, launch a series of offensives against the Taliban and al-Qaeda with the aid of US air power, and overthrow the pro-terrorist regime in Afghanistan. Wasting no time, the American and Afghan allies—sometimes maneuvering on horseback due to the rugged terrain—accomplished their mission within a few months. Deploying to Afghanistan in early 2002, elements of the Fort Bragg-based 3rd Special Forces Group participated in the operation. In June 2002, elements of the 82nd Airborne Division departed Fort Bragg for Afghanistan, where they served as Task Force Panther.[34]

Though the terrorists were crushed by US-led allied forces in March 2002, remnants of al-Qaeda and the Taliban continued to resist. In January 2003, a second contingent of the 82nd Airborne deployed to Afghanistan as Task Force Devil, relieving Task Force Panther. Since then, elements of the 82nd Airborne have periodically deployed to Afghanistan, the most recent tours occurring in 2012, 2014, and 2017. The 3rd Special Forces Group, meanwhile, has maintained an ongoing presence in Afghanistan, with two battalions serving there for six months of every twelve. In 2010, a twenty-four-year-old soldier in the 3rd, Staff Sergeant Robert J. Miller, received a posthumous Medal of Honor for moving his wounded commander out of danger and enabling his men to escape an ambush in Kunar Province near the Pakistani border. Though severely wounded himself, Miller laid down a suppressive fire to protect the rest of the patrol until he succumbed to his wounds.[35]

Robert J. Miller. (*U.S. Army*)

Following the defeat of Iraq in Desert Storm, the US government viewed Saddam Hussein's ongoing threat to Middle Eastern stability with increasing concern, but it was the 9/11 attacks that spurred President Bush to set in motion the events that culminated in Operation Iraqi Freedom. On March 20, 2003, a US-led coalition invaded Iraq and captured the capital of Baghdad three weeks later, overthrowing the Ba'athist government led by Hussein. Two major North Carolina-based units participated in Iraqi Free-

Michael Erik Kurilla. (*U.S. Army*)

dom: the 2nd Marine Expeditionary Brigade—designated Task Force Tarawa—from Camp Lejeune, and the 82nd Airborne Division from Fort Bragg. Both units were engaged in heavy fighting—the marines at An Nasiriyah and the paratroopers at As Samawah. The total combat casualties up to that time were 42 killed and 133 wounded for the army, and 41 killed and 151 wounded for the marines.[36]

Following Saddam's downfall, a collection of terrorist groups that included al-Qaeda in Iraq initiated a war against the Americans and their allies. In 2007–2008, elements of the 82nd Airborne took part in the so-called surge—a temporary increase of American troop strength to suppress insurgent violence and establish security. In 2009, the 2nd Marine Expeditionary Brigade deployed to Afghanistan and became Task Force Leatherneck. The marine task force spearheaded the 2010 Battle of Marjah, the largest operation of the Afghan war to that time.[37]

It briefly appeared that the US military might disentangle itself from two of its lengthiest overseas commitments. On May 2, 2011, a Navy SEALs team killed Osama bin Laden, cutting off the head of al-Qaeda; seven months later, the last contingent of US troops withdrew from Iraq; and on December 31, 2014, President Barack Obama ended Operation Enduring Freedom. But the rise of the Islamic State group, also known as ISIS, and the resurgence of the Taliban led the United States to send troops—including paratroopers of the 82nd Airborne Division—back to Afghanistan and Iraq. In the words of Major General Erik Kurilla, commander of the 82nd Airborne Division in 2017, "We stand prepared to provide combat power on short notice while continually maintaining readiness for other contingencies should those emerge. We are the 82nd Airborne Division; this is who we are and the business we are in." Given the current global situation—in which a seemingly endless succession of threats looms on the horizon—perpetual readiness has become the byword for the entire US armed forces.[38]

Notes

INTRODUCTION

1. Mark Anderson Moore, Jessica A. Bandel, and Michael Hill, *The Old North State at War: The North Carolina Civil War Atlas* (Raleigh: North Carolina Department of Cultural Resources, 2015), 64-65.

CHAPTER ONE: THE EARLY COLONIAL PERIOD

1. David J. Weber, *The Spanish Frontier in North America* (New Haven, CT: Yale University Press, 1994), 30-38.
2. Paul E. Hoffman, "Lucas Vazquez de Ayllon's Discovery and Colony," in *The Forgotten Centuries: Indians and Europeans in the American South, 1521-1704,* ed. Charles Hudson and Carmen Chaves Tesser (Athens: University of Georgia Press, 1994), 36; Paul E. Hoffman, *Spain and the Roanoke Voyages* (Raleigh: North Carolina Department of Cultural Resources, 1987), 2.
3. Hoffman, "Lucas Vazquez," 45. Hoffman convincingly refutes several older hypotheses about the location of San Miguel de Guadalupe, including one suggestion that it was at Cape Fear.
4. Hugh Lefler and Albert R. Newsome, *North Carolina: The History of a Southern State* (Chapel Hill: University of North Carolina Press, 1954), 4; "Spain in the New World to 1600," National Park Service, accessed October 3, 2019, http://www.nps.gov/fora/forteachers/unit-1-spain-in-the-new-world-to-1600.htm.
5. Charles Hudson, *The Juan Pardo Expeditions: Exploration of the Carolinas and Tennessee, 1566-1568* (Tuscaloosa: University of Alabama Press, 2009), 12.
6. Hoffman, *Spain*, 11.
7. Charles Hudson, "The Hernando de Soto Expedition, 1539–1543," in *Forgotten Centuries,* ed. Hudson and Tesser, 74.
8. Weber, *Spanish Frontier*, 41-55; David Lavender, *De Soto, Coronado, Cabrillo: Explorers of the Northern Mystery* (Washington, DC: National Park Service, 1992), 39-51; Hugh T. Lefler and William S. Powell, *Colonial North Carolina: A History* (New York: Scribner, 1973), 4; "De Soto Expedition," *Encyclopedia of North Carolina,* ed. William S. Powell (Chapel Hill: University of North Carolina Press, 2006), 340.
9. Lefler and Powell, *Colonial North Carolina*, 4; L. A. Vigneras, "A Spanish Discovery of North Carolina in 1655," *North Carolina Historical Review* (hereafter cited as *NCHR*) 46 (1969): 398-407; David Beers Quinn, *Set Fair for Roanoke: Voyages and Colonies, 1584-1606* (Chapel Hill: University of North Carolina Press, 1986), 13; Weber, *Spanish Frontier*, 35-36.
10. Weber, *Spanish Frontier*, 60.
11. Ibid., 65.
12. Ibid., 70; Hudson, *Juan Pardo*, 3, 5; "Fort San Felipe," *South Carolina Encyclopedia*, accessed November 2, 2019, http://www.scencyclopedia.org/sce/entries/fort-san-felipe/.
13. "Account of Florida, 1566-1568," Wisconsin Historical Society, accessed November 2, 2019, http://content.wisconsinhistory.org/cdm4/document.php?CISOROOT=/aj&CISOPTR=8687.

14. Hudson, *Juan Pardo*, 23-46.
15. "Pardo Expeditions," Powell, *Encyclopedia of North Carolina*, 866-67; Robin A. Beck Jr., et al., "Identifying Fort San Juan," *Southeastern Archaeology* 25, no. 1 (Summer 2006): 65-77; Hudson, *Juan Pardo*, 3-5, 18, 23; Constance E. Richards, "Contact and Conflict," *American Archaeology* 12, no. 1 (Spring 2008): 12-18; Robin A. Beck Jr., "From Joara to Chiaha: Spanish Exploration of the Appalachian Summit Area, 1540–1568," *Southeastern Archaeology* 16 (1997):162–169.
16. "Moyano's Foray, 1567," North Carolina History Project, accessed November 2, 2019, http://www.northcarolinahistory. org/encyclopedia/166/entry; "Warren Wilson Archaeology," Warren Wilson College, accessed November 2, 2019, https://www. warrenwilson.edu/programs/archaeology/.
17. Hudson, *Juan Pardo*, 23-46; "Juan Pardo Expeditions," North Carolina History Project, accessed November 2, 2019, http://www.northcarolinahistory.org/encyclopedia/165/entry.
18. "Pardo Expeditions," Powell, *Encyclopedia of North Carolina*, 866-67; Beck, "Identifying Fort San Juan," 65-77; Hudson, *Juan Pardo*, 3-5, 18, 23; "Juan Pardo Expeditions," North Carolina History Project.
19. Richards, "Contact," 12-18; David G. Moore, "Finding a Lost Spanish Fort (North Carolina's Real First Colony)", *Tar Heel Junior Historian* 47, no. 1 (Fall 2007): 12-14.
20. Beck, "Identifying Fort San Juan," 65-77.
21. Quinn, *Set Fair for Roanoke*, 12.
22. Lefler and Newsome, *North Carolina*, 3; Richards, "Contact," 12-18.
23. Quinn, *Set Fair for Roanoke*, 13. See also John Patrick Montaño, *The Roots of English Colonialism in Ireland* (New York: Cambridge University Press, 2011), and Brian Mac Cuarta, *Reshaping Ireland, 1550-1700: Colonization and Its Consequences* (Dublin: Four Courts Press, 2011).
24. Lefler and Powell, *Colonial North Carolina*, 5.
25. Quinn, *Set Fair for Roanoke*, 14-15; Kenneth O. Morgan, ed., *The Oxford Illustrated History of Britain* (New York: Oxford University Press, 1986), 266-68; Mark Charles Fissel, *English Warfare, 1511-1642* (London: Routledge, 2001), 137; Karen Ordahl Kupperman, *Roanoke: The Abandoned Colony* (Lanham, MD: Rowman and Littlefield, 2007), 3-4; James Horn, *A Kingdom Strange: The Brief and Tragic History of the Lost Colony of Roanoke* (New York: Basic Books, 2011) 12, 56-57.
26. John Barratt, *Armada 1588: The Spanish Assault on England* (S. Yorkshire, England: Penn & Sword Books, 2005), 1-2, 5; Morgan, *Oxford Illustrated History*, 260-269; Horn, *A Kingdom Strange*, 59.
27. William S. Powell, *North Carolina Through Four Centuries* (Chapel Hill: University of North Carolina Press, 1990), 35-36; Kupperman, *Roanoke*, 5-6; Karen O. Kupperman, "Roanoke's Achievement," 3; David Stick, *Roanoke Island: The Beginnings of English America* (Chapel Hill: University of North Carolina Press, 1983), 29.
28. Powell, *North Carolina*, 35; Lefler and Powell, *Colonial North Carolina*, 5; Kupperman, "Roanoke's Achievement," 3; Stick, *Roanoke Island*, 56; Horn, *A Kingdom Strange*, 34.
29. Powell, *North Carolina*, 37; Stick, *Roanoke Island*, 29; Horn, *A Kingdom Strange*, 17.
30. Powell, *North Carolina*, 37; Quinn, *Set Fair for Roanoke*, 5-14; Kupperman, *Roanoke*, 11; Eric Hinderaker and Peter C. Mancall, *At the Edge of Empire: The Backcountry in British North America* (Baltimore: Johns Hopkins University Press, 2003), 4.
31. Horn, *A Kingdom Strange*, 34.
32. Ibid., 55.
33. Ibid., 46-47.
34. Quinn, *Set Fair for Roanoke*, 31-38, 44; Stick, *Roanoke Island*, 51.
35. Powell, *North Carolina*, 18.
36. Ibid., 38-39; Lefler and Newsome, *North Carolina*, 5; Quinn, *Set Fair for*

Roanoke, 9; Kupperman, *Roanoke*, 13, 16, 18, 22, 69-73; Stick, *Roanoke Island*, 50, 131; Michael L. Oberg, "Lost Colonists and Lost Tribes," in *European Visions: American Voices*, ed. Kim Sloan, British Museum Research Publication 172 (London: British Museum, 2009), 101-105, http://www.britishmuseum.org/pdf/4-Oberg-Lost%20Colonists%20and%20Lost%20Tribes.pdf.

37. Horn, *A Kingdom Strange*, 54.

38. Quinn, *Set Fair for Roanoke*, 46.

39. Ibid., 53; Stick, *Roanoke Island*, 63.

40. Quinn, *Set Fair for Roanoke*, 52; Kupperman, *Roanoke*, 18.

41. Lefler and Powell, *Colonial North Carolina*, 9; Quinn, *Set Fair for Roanoke*, 56.

42. Quinn, *Set Fair for Roanoke*, 56.

43. Kupperman, *Roanoke*, 22-23; Oberg, "Lost Colonists," 102; Powell, *North Carolina*, 40-41, 44; Lefler and Newsome, *North Carolina*, 7.

44. Quinn, *Set Fair for Roanoke*, 75-77; Kupperman, *Roanoke*, 22-25; Stick, *Roanoke Island*, 90-92.

45. Kupperman, *Roanoke*, 22-23.

46. Kupperman, *Roanoke*, 73-74; Lefler and Powell, *Colonial North Carolina*, 10; Quinn, *Set Fair for Roanoke*, 67-70, 72; Stick, *Roanoke Island*, 83-84; Thomas Hariot, *A Briefe and True Report of the New Found Land of Virginia* (Frankfort, Germany: Theodore De Bry, 1590), 59.

47. Kupperman, *Roanoke*,22-27.

48. Powell, *North Carolina*, 41-42; "Spain in the New World to 1600," National Park Service, accessed November 2, 2019, http://www.nps.gov/fora/forteachers/unit-1-spain-in-the-new-world-to-1600.htm; Lefler and Newsome, *North Carolina*, 7; Lefler and Powell, *Colonial North Carolina*, 10-11, 14; Quinn, *Set Fair for Roanoke*, 85; Kupperman, *Roanoke*, 64, 73-76; Oberg, "Lost Colonists," 102.

49. Kupperman, *Roanoke*, 76-78.

50. Kupperman, *Roanoke*, 77, 79-80; Stick, *Roanoke Island*, 126-27, 137.

51. Kupperman, *Roanoke*, 80-81; Stick, *Roanoke Island*, 126-27; Lane's account is at Ralph Lane, "Raleigh's First Roanoke Colony," Documenting the American South, accessed November 2, 2019, http://docsouth.unc.edu/nc/lane/lane.html.

52. Kupperman, *Roanoke*, 81-85; Oberg, "Lost Colonists" 102; Stick, *Roanoke Island*, 138; Lane, "Raleigh's First Roanoke Colony."

53. Kupperman, *Roanoke*, 86-87.

54. Ibid., 26.

55. Ibid., 88-91.

56. Ibid., 92-94; Powell, *North Carolina*, 42-43; Lefler and Powell, *Colonial North Carolina*, 10-11, 15; Lefler and Newsome, *North Carolina*, 9.

57. Kupperman, *Roanoke*, 106-108, 114; Kupperman, "Roanoke's Achievement," 10.

58. Kupperman, *Roanoke*, 109-114.

59. John Pinkerton, *A General Collection of the Best and Most Interesting Voyages and Travels in All Parts of the World . . .* (London: Cadell and Davies, 1812), 12:613.

60. Kupperman, *Roanoke*, 114-117; Powell, *North Carolina*, 44-46; Lefler and Newsome, *North Carolina*, 9; Oberg, "Lost Colonists," 102;

61. Kupperman, *Roanoke*, 117, 119-122.

62. For the English defeat of the Spanish Armada, see Neil Hanson, *The Confident Hope of a Miracle: The True History of the Spanish Armada* (New York: Knopf, 2003), and Garrett Mattingly, *The Armada* (Boston: Houghton Mifflin, 1959).

63. "The Lost Colony of 1587," National Park Service, accessed November 2, 2019, http://www.nps.gov/fora/forteachers/teachers-handbook-part-2.htm.

64. Kupperman, *Roanoke*, 122-132; Powell, *North Carolina*, 46-48; Lefler and Newsome, *North Carolina*, 9-11; "Lost Colony," National Park Service."

65. Kupperman, *Roanoke*, 96-97, 105, 142-146.

66. Oberg, "Lost Colonists," 101.

CHAPTER TWO: A SPIRIT OF DISOBEDIENCE

1. Jonathan Barth, "'The Sinke of America': Society in the Albemarle Borderlands of North Carolina, 1663-1729," *NCHR* 87, no. 1 (January 2010): 15-20.

2. Kirsten Fischer, *Suspect Relations: Sex, Race, and Resistance in Colonial North Carolina* (Ithaca, NY: Cornell University Press, 2002), 24; Barth, "'Sinke of America,'" 21; Noeleen McIlvenna, *A Very Mutinous People: The Struggle for North Carolina, 1660-1713* (Chapel Hill: University of North Carolina Press, 2009), 15-27.

3. Hugh F. Rankin, *Upheaval in Albemarle: The Story of Culpeper's Rebellion, 1675-1689* (Raleigh: Carolina Charter Tercentenary Commission, 1962), 11.

4. "Charter of Carolina," Avalon Project, Yale Law School, accessed November 2, 2019, http://avalon.law.yale.edu/17th_century/nc01.asp.

5. Ibid.

6. Barth, "'Sinke of America,'" 20-22.

7. Lindley S. Butler, "The Governors of Albemarle County," *NCHR* 46 (July 1969): 280-299; Rankin, *Upheaval,* 18; Powell, *North Carolina,* 63.

8. Mattie Erma E. Parker, "Legal Aspects of 'Culpeper's Rebellion,'" *NCHR* 45, no. 2 (Apr 1968): 111-127; Butler, "Governors"285; Rankin, *Upheaval,* 19-21.

9. Charles M. Andrews, ed., *Original Narratives of Early American History: Narratives of the Insurrections, 1675-1690* (New York: Charles Scribner's Sons, 1915), 147, 159; Parker, "Legal Aspects," 118-123; Butler, "Governors"; "Commission to appoint Thomas Eastchurch as Governor of Albemarle County," in Walter Clark, ed,, *Colonial and State Records of North Carolina* (hereafter cited as *CSRNC*), 30 vols. (Winston, NC: M.I. and J.C. Stewart, 1896), 1:232; "Representation concerning the rebellion in Albemarle County," *CSRNC,* 1:256-61; "Affidavit of Solomon Summers concerning rebellion in Albemarle County," January 31, 1680, *CSRNC,* 1:296-98; Rankin, *Upheaval,* 30, 32; William S. Smith Jr., "Culpeper's Rebellion: New Data and Old Problems" (master's thesis, North Carolina State University, 1990).

10. Andrews, *Original Narratives,* 152.

11. "Petition of Thomas Miller concerning the case against John Culpeper and Zachariah Gillam," *CSRNC,* 1:264.

12. "Account of tobacco shipped by Zachariah Gillam from Carolina from 1676 to 1679," 1680, *CSRNC,* 1:322-323; Butler, "Governors," 290; Powell, *North Carolina,* 64-66; McIlvenna, *Very Mutinous People,* 56.

13. Parker, "Legal Aspects," 123-124; Rankin, *Upheaval,* 36. The revolt was not referred to as "Culpeper's rebellion" until the late eighteenth century, as John Culpeper was not the leader of the rebels. "Affidavit of Solomon Summers," *CSRNC,* 1:296-98; Andrews, *Original Narratives,* 153.

14. Andrews, *Original Narratives,* 154-155; McIlvenna, *Very Mutinous People,* 56-60.

15. Andrews, *Original Narratives,* 155; Rankin, *Upheaval,* 28; McIlvenna, *Very Mutinous People,* 59.

16. "Affidavit of Henry Hudson concerning the cases of Thomas Miller and John Culpeper," January 31, 1680, *CSRNC,* 1:272-274; Rankin, *Upheaval,* 38, 40.

17. "Representation concerning the rebellion," *CSRNC,* 1:256-261.

18. Barth, "'Sinke of America,'" 1-27.

19. "Deposition of Timothy Biggs concerning rebellion in Albemarle County," 1678, CSRNC, 1:309-311.

20. "Affidavit of Henry Hudson," *CSRNC,* 1:272-274; Andrews, *Original Narratives::,* 156; Butler, "Governors," 288.

21. Andrews, *Original Narratives,* 160.

22. Parker, "Legal Aspects," 126-127; Butler, "Governors," 280-299.

23. "Affidavit of Solomon Summers," *CSRNC,* 1:296-98; "Petition of Thomas Miller," *CSRNC,* 1: 264.

24. Butler, "Governors," 280-299; Rankin, *Upheaval,* 50-54; McIlvenna, *Very Mutinous People,* 66-70.

25. McIlveena, *Very Mutinous People*, 82-83; Powell, *North Carolina*, 68; "Commission to appoint Philip Ludwell as Governor of North Carolina," December 5, 1689, *CSRNC*, 1:360-61.
26. Powell, *North Carolina*, 75; McIlveena, *Very Mutinous People*, 127-48; "Description by Thomas Pollock concerning Cary's Rebellion [Extract]," October 11, 1708, *CSRNC*, 1:696-99.
27. McIlveena, *Very Mutinous People*, 137-39.
28. Powell, *North Carolina*, 75; McIlveena, *Very Mutinous People*, 139.
29. McIlveena, *Very Mutinous People*, 140; Alexander Spotswood to Thomas Cary and Edward Hyde, June 20, 1711, *CSRNC*, 1-758.
30. "North Carolina's First Town," North Carolina Historic Sites, accessed November 2, 2019, https://historicsites.nc.gov/all-sites/historic-bath/history.
31. McIlveena, *Very Mutinous People*, 140.
32. Ibid., 142-43; North Carolina Governor's Council to Alexander Spotswood, June 29, 1711, *CSRNC*, 1:760-61; "Alexander Spotswood," *Encyclopedia Virginia*, accessed October 23, 2019, http://encyclopediavirginia.org/media_player?mets_filename=evm00002441mets.xml.
33. Letter from Alexander Spotswood to Thomas Cary, June 21, 1711, *CSRNC*, 1:759.
34. McIlveena, *Very Mutinous People*, 143-47.
35. Ibid., 113-115; Lefler and Newsome, *North Carolina*, 29-40.
36. Lawrence E. Lee, *Indian Wars in North Carolina, 1663-1763* (Raleigh: Carolina Charter Tercentenary Commission, 1963), 14-15, 16, 18-20; Lefler and Powell, *Colonial North Carolina*, 65-68; Perdue and Oakley, *Native Carolinians*, 31-32; Alan Gallay, *The Indian Slave Trade: The Rise of the English Empire in the American South, 1670-1717* (New Haven, CT: Yale University Press, 2003), 262-66; "Tuscarora War," North Carolina History Project, accessed November 2, 2019, https://northcarolinahistory.org/encyclopedia/tuscarora-war/s; David La Vere, *The Tuscarora War: Indians, Settlers, and the Fight for the Carolina Colonies* (Chapel Hill: University of North Carolina Press, 2013), 58-59.
37. La Vere, *Tuscarora War*, 3-17, 39-60.
38. Lee, *Indian Wars*, 21-23; McIlveena, *Very Mutinous People*, 148-49; Wayne E. Lee, "Fortify, Fight, or Flee: Tuscarora and Cherokee Defensive Warfare and Military Culture Adaptation," *Journal of Military History* 68 (July 2004): 732; La Vere, *Tuscarora War*, 27-28, 69-71.
39. Alexander Spotswood to the Board of Trade of Great Britain, October 15, 1711, *CSRNC*,1:810-813.
40. Lefler and Newsome, *North Carolina*, 58-59; Spotswood to the Board of Trade, October 15, 1711, *CSRNC*, 1:810-813; La Vere, *Tuscarora War*, 72-73.
41. Lee, "Fortify, Fight, or Flee," 732-33; La Vere, *Tuscarora War*, 69-74.
42. "Tuscarora War," North Carolina History Project; Jerry Keenan, *Encyclopedia of American Indian Wars, 1492-1890* (Santa Barbara, CA: ABC-CLIO, 1997), 236; Lee, *Indian Wars*, 23-27.
43. Spotswood to the Board of Trade, October 15, 1711, *CSRNC*, 1:810-813.
44. "Tuscarora War," North Carolina History Project; Lee, "Fortify, Fight, or Flee," 733-34; Spotswood to the Board of Trade, October 15, 1711, *CSRNC*, 1:810-813; Christopher Gale to his sibling, November 2, 1711, *CSRNC*, 1:825-29; La Vere, *Tuscarora War*, 84-85, 88-89.
45. Lee, *Indian Wars*, 26; Lefler and Newsome, *North Carolina*, 59; Keenan, *Encyclopedia of American Indian Wars, 1492-1890*; Gallay, *Indian Slave Trade*, 259; Spotswood to the Board of Trade, October 15, 1711, *CSRNC*, 1:810-813; Alexander Spotswood to the Board of Trade of Great Britain, November 7, 1711, *CSRNC*, 1:816-818.
46. McIlveena, *Very Mutinous People*, 150-51; Gallay, *Indian Slave Trade*, 260, 267; La Vere, *Tuscarora War*, 103.
47. Lee, *Indian Wars*, 28; Lee, "Fortify, Fight, or Flee," 734-35; Gallay, *Indian Slave Trade*, 269; La Vere, *Tuscarora War*, 106-07.

48. La Vere, *Tuscarora War*, 120-25; Lee, *Indian Wars*, 28-29; Lee, "Fortify, Fight, or Flee," 735-36.
49. Lee, *Indian Wars*, 29; Lee, "Fortify, Fight, or Flee," 736-37.
50. Gallay, *Indian Slave Trade*, 272.
51. Lee, "Fortify, Fight, or Flee," 737-39; Lee, *Indian Wars*, 30-31.
52. Lefler and Newsome, *North Carolina*, 60; Lee, *Indian Wars*, 32-33.
53. Lee, *Indian Wars*, 36; Lee, "Fortify, Fight, or Flee," 739-41; Thomas Pollock to Alexander Spotswood, October 5, 1712, *CSRNC*, 1:880.
54. Lee, "Fortify, Fight, or Flee," 743-44; Lee, *Indian Wars*, 36-37; James Moore to unknown, March 27, 1713, *CSRNC*, 2:37; Thomas Pollock to Alexander Spotswood, April 2, 1713, *CSRNC*, 2:29-31.
55. Thomas Pollock to Alexander Spotswood, November 16, 1713, *CSRNC*, 2:73-75.
56. Thomas Pollock to James Moore, March 31, 1713, *CSRNC*, 2:27-29; Lee, *Indian Wars*, 37-38.
57. Lefler and Newsome, *North Carolina*, 60-61; Thomas C. Parramore, "The Tuscarora Ascendancy," *NCHR* 59, no. 4 (Oct 1982): 307-326.
58. Lefler and Newsome, *North Carolina*, 62; Hugh F. Rankin, *The Pirates of Colonial North Carolina* (Raleigh: North Carolina Division of Archives & History, 1960), 17; Lindley S. Butler, *Pirates, Privateers, and Rebel Raiders of the Carolina Coast* (Chapel Hill: University of North Carolina Press, 2000), 12; Angus Konstam, *Blackbeard's Last Fight: Pirate Hunting in North Carolina 1718* (Oxford, UK: Osprey, 2013), 4-5.
59. Butler, *Pirates*, 6; Instructions to the Lords Proprietors of Carolina concerning pirates, William III, King of England, 1650-1702, February 10, 1700, *CSRNC*, 1:526-527.
60. Butler, *Pirates*, 4-5, 7.
61. Lefler and Newsome, *North Carolina*, 64; Butler, *Pirates*, 51-72; Christopher B. Downey, *Stede Bonnet: Charleston's Gentleman Pirate* (Charleston, SC: History Press, 2012), 64-65; Ruth M. Miller and Ann Taylor Andrus, *Charleston's Old Exchange Building* (Charleston, SC: History Press, 2006), 16; Konstam, *Blackbeard's Last Fight*, 13.
62. Lefler and Newsome, *North Carolina*, 64; Konstam, *Blackbeard's Last Fight*, 13; Minutes of the General Court of North Carolina, July 28, 1719 to August 01, 1719, *CSRNC*, 2:359.
63. Konstam, *Blackbeard's Last Fight*, 26.
64. Gov. Alexander Spotswood to John Carteret, Earl Granville, February 14, 1719, *CSRNC*, 2:324-27.
65. Butler, *Pirates*, 43-47; Spotswood to Carteret, *CSRNC*, 2:324-27. The most detailed description of Blackbeard's last fight and death is in Konstam, *Blackbeard's Last Fight*, 37-62.

CHAPTER THREE: WARS OF EMPIRE

1. Powell, *North Carolina*, 84-86. Only Sir George Carteret, later Earl Granville, retained his shares and land, although not his "voice in the government." Ibid.
2. Lefler and Newsome, *North Carolina*, 138; Powell, *North Carolina*, 87; Blackwell P. Robinson, *The Five Royal Governors of North Carolina, 1729-1775* (Raleigh: Carolina Charter Tercentenary Commission, 1963), viii; Lefler and Powell, *Colonial North Carolina*, 113.
3. Lefler and Powell, *Colonial North Carolina*, 113-115. See also Jack P. Greene, *The Quest for Power: The Lower Houses of Assembly in the Southern Royal Colonies* (Chapel Hill, NC: Published for the Institute of Early American History and Culture at Williamsburg, VA, by the University of North Carolina Press, 1963)
4. Lefler and Powell, *Colonial North Carolina*, 129; Powell, *North Carolina*, 96-103; Lefler and Newsome, North Carolina, 152-159; John R. Maass, "'All This Poor Province Could Do': North Carolina and the Seven Years' War, 1757-1762," *NCHR* 79 (January 2002): 50-89.

5. Lefler and Newsome, North Carolina, 153; Howard Peckham, *The Colonial Wars, 1689–1762* (Chicago: University of Chicago Press, 1964), 57-76; John Ferling, *Struggle for a Continent: The Wars of Early America* (Arlington Heights, IL: Harlan Davidson, 1993), 79-100.

6. George II, King of Great Britain, to Gov. Gabriel Johnston, June 1739, *CSRNC*, 4:338-339; J. Revell Carr, *Seeds of Discontent: The Deep Roots of the American Revolution 1650-1750* (New York: Walker Books, 2008), 143-45.

7. Peckham, *Colonial Wars*, 91; Rene Chartrand, *Colonial American Troops 1610-1774*, 3 vols. (Oxford, UK: Osprey, 2002), 1:18-19; Douglas Edward Leach, *Roots of Conflict: British Armed Forces and Colonial Americans, 1677-1763* (Chapel Hill: University of North Carolina Press, 1986), 49-50; Minutes of the Lower House of the North Carolina General Assembly, July 31, 1740–August 22, 1740, *CSRNC*, 4:553; E. Alfred Jones, "The American Regiment in the Cartagena Expedition," *Virginia Magazine of History and Biography* 30, no.1 (January 1922): 1-20; Leach, *Arms for Empire*, 217-219; Carr, *Seeds*, 150.

8. Ferling, *Struggle*, 115-116; Chartrand, *Colonial American Troops*, 1:18-19; Lee Offen, *Gooch's American Regiment, 1740-1742: America's First Marines* (Jacksonville, FL: Fortis, 2010), 2-4, 8, 31; Leach, *Roots*, 51; Gabriel Johnston to Thomas Pelham-Holles, Duke of Newcastle, November 5, 1740, *CSRNC*, 4:421; Charles H. McBarron et al., "The American Regiment, 1740-1746," *Military Collector and Historian* 21 (1969): 84-86; Carr, *Seeds*, 152.

9. Leach, *Roots*, 53-54; Ferling, *Struggle*, 115-117; Offen, *America's First Marines*, 31, 37-38, 52; Gabriel Johnston to Thomas Pelham-Holles, Duke of Newcastle, November 5, 1740, *CSRNC*, 4:421; McBarron, "American Regiment," 84-86; Carr, *Seeds*, 157-158.

10. Return of William Gooch's Regiment (extract), April 25, 1741, *CSRNC*, 15:756; Carr, *Seeds*, 172-173.

11. Ferling, *Struggle*, 115-117; Carr, *Seeds*, 155-169.

12. Chartrand, *Colonial American Troops* 18-20; Offen, *America's First Marines*, 63-69, 72, 77, 85, 94-95; Return of William Gooch's Regiment (extract), December 7, 1741, *CSRNC*, 15:759; Lefler and Newsome, *North Carolina*, 154; McBarron, "American Regiment," 84-86.

13. Acts of the North Carolina General Assembly, April 8, 1745–April 20, 1745, *CSRNC*, 23:229; Powell, *North Carolina*, 99.

14. Minutes of the Lower House of the North Carolina General Assembly, September 29, 1747–October 9, 1747, *CSRNC*, 4:863.

15. Gabriel Johnston to the Board of Trade of Great Britain, April 4, 1749, *CSRNC*, 4:919-923. The governor's assertion that Fort Johnston was finished was incorrect.

16. *Boston Gazette or Weekly Journal*, October 16, 1748, accessed November 3, 2019, http://www.nchistoricsites.org/brunswic/boston-gazette-clipped-out.jpg.

17. Ibid.; Powell, *North Carolina*, 99.

18. The most recent studies of North Carolina's participation in the Seven Years' War are John R. Maass, *The French and Indian War in North Carolina: The Spreading Flames of War* (Charleston, SC: History Press, 2013); Maass, "'All This Poor Province Could Do,'" 50-89; and John R. Maass, "North Carolina and the Seven Years' War, 1754-1758, *Military Collector and Historian* 55, no. 3 (Fall 2003): 155-160. All provide the basis for this section on the war.

19. Lefler and Powell, *Colonial North Carolina*, 140; Maass, "North Carolina," 155; Samuel A. Ashe, *History of North Carolina*, 2 vols. (Greensboro, NC: Charles L. Van Noppen, 1925), 1:283-84; Matthew Rowan to the Board of Trade, March 19, 1754, *CSRNC*, 5:108-109.

20. Maass, "North Carolina," 156; Lawrence Henry Gipson, *The Great War for Empire: The Years of Defeat, 1754-1757* (New York: Alfred A. Knopf, 1946), 6:32; Powell, *North Carolina*, 100; Edward G. Lengel, *General*

George Washington: A Military Life (New York: Random House, 2005), 30-48; Matthew Rowan to the Board of Trade of Great Britain, October 22, 1754, *CSRNC*, 5: 144c-144d.

21. Lengel, *General George Washington*, 49-62; Albert W. Haarmann, "American Uniforms during the French and Indian War, *Military Collector and Historian* 32, no. 2 (Summer 1980): 61.

22. Maass, "North Carolina," 156; Peckham, *Colonial Wars*, 143-147.

23. Robert Dinwiddie to Arthur Dobbs, August 7, 1756, *CSRNC*, 5:608-609; Arthur Dobbs to John Campbell, Earl of Loudoun, July 10, 1756, *CSRNC*, 5:599-600; Memorandum from Arthur Dobbs to the Board of Trade, 1760, *CSRNC*, 6: 280-310.

24. Maass, "North Carolina," 157; Stanley Pargellis, ed., *Military Affairs in North America, 1748-1765* (New York: Appleton-Century, 1936), 223, 226, 267; Maass, *French and Indian War in North Carolina*, 46-49.

25. Gertrude Kimball, ed., *The Correspondence of William Pitt while Secretary of State . . .*, 2 vols. (New York: Macmillan, 1906), 1:xxix; Maass, "North Carolina," 157; Peckham, *Colonial Wars*, 155-160; Arthur Dobbs to the Board of Trade, March 22, 1757, *NCHR* 5:753; Maass, "'All This Poor Province Could Do,'" 50-51.

26. Lefler and Newsome, *North Carolina*, 157; Minutes of the Lower House of the North Carolina General Assembly, May 16, 1757–May 28, 1757, *CSRNC*, 5:860; Arthur Dobbs to the Board of Trade, May 30, 1757, *CSRNC* 5: 761-764.

27. Maass, "North Carolina," 158; Kimball, *Correspondence*, 1:27.

28. Maass, "North Carolina," 158; Arthur Dobbs to William Pitt, December 30, 1757, *CSRNC*, 5:792-793.

29. Fred Anderson, *Crucible of War: the Seven Years' War and the Fate of Empire in British North America, 1754-1766* (New York: Alfred A. Knopf, 2000), 283-284. See also Douglas R. Cubbison, *The British Defeat of the French in Pennsylvania, 1758: A Military History of the Forbes Campaign against Fort Duquesne* (Jefferson, NC: McFarland, 2010).

30. John Forbes to Arthur Dobbs, March 21, 1758, *CSRNC*, 5:926-27; Kimball, *Correspondence*, 1:240.

31. Maass, "North Carolina," 158-159; Alfred M. Waddell, *A Colonial Officer and his Times, 1754-1773* (Raleigh, NC: Edwards & Broughton, 1890), 57; S. K. Stevens et al., eds., *The Papers of Henry Bouquet*, 6 vols. (Harrisburg: Pennsylvania Historical and Museum Commission, 1951), 2:130, 209, 210, 256, 292, 313, 473; Maass, "'All This Poor Province Could Do,'" 58-59.

32. Maass, "North Carolina," 159; Stevens, *Bouquet Papers*, 2:552, 566-67; Gipson, *Great War*, 7:282-83; Memorandum from Arthur Dobbs to the Board of Trade, 1760, *CSRNC*, 6: 280-310.

33. Arthur Dobbs to the Board of Trade of Great Britain, October 28, 1755, *CSRNC*, 5: 439-441; Maass, "'All This Poor Province Could Do,'" 54.

34. Maass, "'All This Poor Province Could Do,'" 61-63; Roger Ekirch, *"Poor Carolina": Politics and Society in Colonial North Carolina, 1729-1776* (Chapel Hill: University of North Carolina Press, 1981), 123-124.

35. Maass, "'All This Poor Province Could Do,'" 66; Minutes of the Upper House of the North Carolina General Assembly, May 1759, *CSRNC*, 6:85-95.

36. Lefler and Powell, *Colonial North Carolina*, 142; Arthur Dobbs to the Earl of Loudoun, July 10, 1756, *CSRNC*, 5:595-596; Arthur Dobbs to the Board of Trade of Great Britain, October 28, 1755, *CSRNC*, 5: 439-441.

37. Tom Hatley, *The Dividing Paths: Cherokees and South Carolinians through the Revolutionary Era* (New York: Oxford University Press, 1995), 100-101, 105-115; John Oliphant, *Peace and War on the Anglo-Cherokee Frontier, 1756-63* (Baton Rouge: Louisiana State University Press, 2001), 31-69; Peckham, *Colonial Wars*, 201-205.

38. Maass, "'All This Poor Province Could Do,'" 67.
39. Ibid., 69; Oliphant, *Peace and War*, 69-70, 104-112; Arthur Dobbs to William Pitt, October 14, 1759, *CSRNC*, 6:60-62.
40. Arthur Dobbs to William Pitt, January 21, 1760, *CSRNC*, 6:220-221; Oliphant, *Peace and War*, 109-110; Arthur Dobbs to Board of Trade, January 19, 1760, *CSRNC*, 6:216-220.
41. Hugh Waddell to Arthur Dobbs, February 29, 1760, *CSRNC*, 6:229-230.
42. Maass, "'All This Poor Province Could Do,'" 71; Lefler and Powell, *Colonial North Carolina*, 145; Douglas L. Rights, *The American Indian in North Carolina* (Winston-Salem, NC: John F. Blair, 1957), 166-168.
43. Arthur Dobbs to Board of Trade, May 28, 1760, *CSRNC*, 6:243-251; Arthur Dobbs to William Pitt, May 29, 1760, *CSRNC*, 6:257-259; Maass, "'All This Poor Province Could Do,'" 72-74.
44. Maass, "'All This Poor Province Could Do,'" 75-76.
45. Leach, *Arms*, 487; Anderson, *Crucible*, 765; Peckham, *Colonial Wars*, 203; Oliphant, *Peace and War*, 113-139; Maass, *Spreading Flames*, 98-101.
46. Jeffrey Amherst to Arthur Dobbs, January 19, 1761, in *The Official Papers of Francis Fauquier*, ed. George Reese, 3 vols. (Charlottesville: University Press of Virginia, 1981), 2:466-467.
47. Maass, "'All This Poor Province Could Do,'" 78-79; James Grant, "Journal of Lieutenant-Colonel James Grant, Commanding an Expedition against the Cherokee Indians, June-July, 1761," *Florida Historical Society Quarterly* 12, no. 1 (July 1933): 25-36.
48. Maass, "'All This Poor Province Could Do,'" 79-80; Lefler and Newsome, *North Carolina*, 148; Oliphant, *Peace and War*, 140-186; Hatley, *Dividing Paths*, 135-139.
49. Maass, "'All This Poor Province Could Do,'" 81-85; George Reese, ed., *The Official Papers of Francis Fauquier, Lieutenant Governor of Virginia, 1758–1768*, 3 vols. (Charlottesville: University Press of Virginia, 1980–83) 2:654; Lee, *Indian Wars*. 87-88; Arthur Dobbs to Lord Egremont, December 1761, *CSRNC*, 6:595-596; Arthur Dobbs to Board of Trade, December 1761, CSRNC, 6:596-600.
50. Harry M. Ward, *"Unite or Die": Intercolony Relations 1690–1763* (Port Washington, NY: Kennikat Press, 1971), 120; Maass, *Spreading Flames*, 121.

CHAPTER FOUR: THE REGULATOR MOVEMENT AND THE BATTLE OF ALAMANCE, 1771

1. William Edward Fitch, *Some Neglected History of North Carolina; Being an Account of the Revolution of the Regulators and of the Battle of Alamance, the First Battle of the American Revolution* (New York: Neale, 1905), 262.
2. Alamance Battleground, North Carolina Historic Sites, accessed November 3, 2019, http://www.northcarolinahistory.org/commentary/687/entry.
3. Ekirch, *"Poor Carolina,"*166.
4. William S. Powell, *The War of the Regulation and The Battle of Alamance, May 16, 1771* (Raleigh Division of Archives and History, North Carolina Department of Cultural Resources, 1975), 26.
5. Marjoleine Kars, *Breaking Loose Together: The Regulator Rebellion in Pre-Revolutionary North Carolina* (Chapel Hill: University of North Carolina Press 2002), 3.
6. Elisha P. Douglass, *Rebels and Democrats: The Struggle for Equal Political Rights and Majority Rule during the American Revolution* (Chapel Hill: University of North Carolina Press, 1955), 71.
7. John S. Bassett, *The Regulators of North Carolina*, Documenting the American South, accessed November 2, 2019, http://docsouth.unc.edu/nc/bassett95/bassett95.html.
8. Powell, *North Carolina*, 146-150; *Powell, War of the Regulation, 26.*
9. Kars, *Breaking Loose*, 3-6, Wayne E. Lee, *Crowds and Soldiers in Revolutionary North Carolina: The Culture of Violence in Riot*

and War (Gainesville: University Press of Florida, 2001), 47-49; Marvin L. Michael Kay, "The North Carolina Regulation, 1766-1771: A Class Conflict," in *The American Revolution: Explorations in the History of American Radicalism,* Alfred Young, ed. (DeKalb: Northern Illinois University Press, 1976), 71-123; Douglass, *Rebels and Democrats,* 71-100.

10. Kars, *Breaking Loose,* 2.

11. Ibid., 2-5; Powell, *War of the Regulation,* 8-9.

12. Carole Watterson Troxler, *Farming Dissenters: The Regulator Movement in Piedmont North Carolina* (Raleigh: North Carolina Office of Archives and History, 2011), 117-124; Powell, *North Carolina,* 147-159; Kars, *Breaking Loose,* 206-214; Powell, *War of the Regulation,* 10-11.

13. Edmund Fanning to William Tryon, April 23, 1768, *CSRNC,* 7: 713-716.

14. *Virginia Gazette* (Williamsburg), October 25, 1770, accessed November 3, 2019, https://www.ncpedia.org/anchor/chaos-hillsborough-1770; "The Hillsborough Riots," *CSRNC,* 8:239-260; Lee, *Crowds and Soldiers,* 66-70.

15. William Tryon to Richard Henderson, October 07, 1770, *CSRNC,* 8:678; Lee, *Crowds and Soldiers,* 66-70.

16. William Tryon to Wills Hill, Marquis of Downshire, April 12, 1771, *CSRNC,* 8:546-549; Lee, *Crowds and Soldiers,* 71; Paul David Nelson, *William Tryon and the Course of Empire* (Chapel Hill: University of North Carolina Press, 1990), 81.

17. North Carolina General Assembly, January 15, 1771, *CSRNC,* 8:481-486; Powell, *War of the Regulation,* 19; Nelson, *William Tryon,* 80.

18. William Tryon to Wills Hill, Marquis of Downshire, January 31, 1771, *CSRNC,* 8:494-495; Nelson, *William Tryon,* 9-10; Robinson, *Five Royal Governors,* 47.

19. Circular Letter from William Tryon to Commanding Officers of the North Carolina Militia, March 19, 1771, *CSRNC,* 8:540-542; Powell, *War of the Regulation,* 19-20.

20. Tryon to Hill, April 12, 1771, *CSRNC,* 8:546-549.

21. Ibid., 8:546-549; Circular letter from William Tryon to colonels of the North Carolina militia, March 30, 1771, *CSRNC,* 8:700-701; Powell, *War of the Regulation,* 19.

22. "Order Book for the Carteret Regiment in the military campaign against the Regulators," April 23, 1771–June 23, 1771, *CSRNC,* 8:574-600; Powell, *War of the Regulation,* 19-20.

23. William Tryon to Hugh Waddell, May 10, 1771, *NCHR* 8:714.

24. "Order Book for the Carteret Regiment," *CSRNC,* 8:574-600.

25. Troxler, *Farming Dissenters,* 101.

26. "Order Book for the Carteret Regiment," *CSRNC,* 8:574-600.

27. William Tryon to Wills Hill, Marquis of Downshire, May 18, 1771, *CSRNC,* 8:609-10; "Order Book for the Carteret Regiment," *CSRNC,* 8:574-600; Powell, *War of the Regulation,* 20; Troxler, *Farming Dissenters,* 99; Lee, *Crowds and Soldiers,* 83.

28. "Order Book for the Carteret Regiment" *CSRNC,* 8:574-600; William Tryon to Wills Hill, Marquis of Downshire, May 18, 1771, *CSRNC,* 8:609-10.

29. "Extract of a Letter from Brunswick county, dated the 1st Instant, June 6, 1771," *Virginia Gazette* (Purdie & Dixon), accessed November 3, 2019, https://www.accessible-archives.com/collections/the-virginia-gazette/; *Pennsylvania Gazette,* June 20, 1771, accessed October 23, 2019, https://www.newspapers.com/newspage/39405283/; Powell, *War of the Regulation,* 21; "Order Book for the Carteret Regiment, *CSRNC,* 8:574-600; Tryon to Hill, May 18, 1771, *CSRNC,* 8:609-10.

30. Troxler, *Farming Dissenters,* 104, 112.

31. Tryon to Hill, May 18, 1771, *CSRNC,* 8:609-10; Troxler, *Farming Dissenters,* 109; *Pennsylvania Gazette,* June 20, 1771, accesed October 23, 2019, https://www.newspapers.com/newspage/39405283/.

32. Tryon to Hill, May 18, 1771, *CSRNC,* 8:609-10; *Pennsylvania Gazette,* June 20, 1771.

33. Powell, *War of the Regulation*, 23; Tryon to Hill, May 18, 1771, *CSRNC*, 8:609-10 "Order Book for the Carteret Regiment," *CSRNC*, 8:574-600; Tryon to Hill, May 18, 1771, *CSRNC*, 8:609-10; William Tryon to Hugh Waddell, May 18, 1771, *CSRNC*, 8:712-713.
34. Order Book for William Tryon's regiment in the military campaign against the Regulators, May 1, 1771-June 20, 1771, *NCHR* 8:659-676.
35. "Order Book for the Carteret Regiment," *CSRNC*, 8:574-600.
36. Proclamation by William Tryon, May 17, 1771, *CSRNC*, 8:608-29.
37. William Tryon to Hugh Waddell, June 7, 1771, *CSRNC*, 8:717; Powell, *War of the Regulation*, 24; Troxler, *Farming Dissenters*, 115.
38. "Order Book for the Carteret Regiment," *CSRNC*, 8:574-600; Powell, *War of the Regulation*, 24.
39. William Tryon to Wills Hill, Marquis of Downshire, June 29, 1771, *CSRNC*, 8:627.
40. Description by Morgan Edwards of the North Carolina Baptists in the Battle of Alamance, *CSRNC*, 8:654-657.
41. Powell, *War of the Regulation*, 24-26, 28; Lee, *Crowds and Soldiers*, 90.
42. Joseph Hewes to Reverend Elihu Spencer, 8 December 1775, reel # 3, Samuel Johnston Papers, Hayes Collection, Wilson Library, University of North Carolina-Chapel Hill; John S. Bassett, "The Regulators of North Carolina, 1765-1771," *Annual Report of the American Historical Association for the Year 1894* (Washington: Government Printing Office, 1895), 209-242; Hugh T. Lefler, "Orange County and the War of Regulation," in *Orange County, 1752-1952*, ed. Hugh T. Lefler and Paul Wager (Chapel Hill: University of North Carolina Press, 1953), 22-40.

CHAPTER FIVE: REVOLUTION AND WAR, 1775–1776

1. Collin G. Calloway, *The Scratch of a Pen: 1763 and the Transformation of North America* (New York: Oxford University Press, 2006), 92-100.
2. Lindley S. Butler, *North Carolina and the Coming of the Revolution, 1763-1776* (Raleigh: North Carolina Department of Cultural Resources, Division of Archives and History, 1976), 23.
3. Josiah Martin to Lord George Germain, 21 March 1776, in *Documents of the American Revolution (Colonial Office Series)*, 21 vols., ed. K. G. Davies (Dublin: Irish University Press, 1976), 12:85, 89; Robinson, *Five Royal Governors*, 55. See also Vernon O. Stumpf, "Josiah Martin and His Search for Success: The Road to North Carolina," *North Carolina Historical Review* 53 (1976): 55-79.
4. Butler, *North Carolina*, 54; Minutes of the Provincial Congress of North Carolina, August 25–August 27, 1774, *CSRNC*, 9: 1041-49.
5. Minutes of the Provincial Congress of North Carolina, April 3, 1775–April 7, 1775, *CSRNC*, 9:1178-85; Josiah Martin to William Legge, Earl of Dartmouth, April 20, 1775, *CSRNC*,9:1223-28.
6. Josiah Martin to William Legge, Earl of Dartmouth, May 18, 1775, *CSRNC*, 9:1255-57.
7. Josiah Martin to William Legge, Earl of Dartmouth, June 30, 1775, *CSRNC*, 10:41-50; Butler, *North Carolina*, 58.
8. Butler, *North Carolina*, 58.
9. Jeffrey J. Crow, *A Chronicle of North Carolina during the American Revolution, 1763-1789* (Raleigh: North Carolina Division of Archives and History, 1975), 23; Butler, *North Carolina*, 59-60; Hugh F. Rankin, *North Carolina in the American Revolution* (Raleigh: Department of Cultural Resources, Division of Archives and History, 1977), 8.
10. Crow, *Chronicle*, 24-25; Butler, *North Carolina*, 60-62; J. D. Lewis, *NC Patriots, 1775-1783: Their Own Words*, 3 vols. (e-book published by author, 2012), 1:2.
11. Edward McCrady, *The History of South Carolina in the Revolution, 1775-1780* (New York: Macmillan, 1901), 3:97; Richard

Richardson to Henry Laurens, 12 December 1775, in Robert W. Gibbes, *Documentary History of the American Revolution* (New York: Appleton, 1855), 1:240.

12. David K.Wilson, *The Southern Strategy: Britain's Conquest of South Carolina and Georgia, 1775-1780* (Columbia: University of South Carolina Press, 2005), 5-18; Charles E. Bennett, *Quest for Glory: Major General Robert Howe and the American Revolution* (Chapel Hill: University of North Carolina Press, 1991), 29-33; William Woodford to Edmund Pendleton, 5 December 1775, John Rhodehamel, comp., *The American Revolution: Writings from the War of Independence* (New York: Library of America, 2001), 87-89.

13. Wilson, *Southern Strategy*, 5-18; Lewis, *NC Patriots*, 1:4; Bennett, *Quest*, 29-33; Extract of "Letter from a midshipman on the *Otter*," December 9, 1775, *CSRNC*, 10:394-95.

14. Henry Steele Commager and Richard B. Morris, *The Spirit of Seventy-Six* (New York: Harper & Row, 1975 repr.), 113; Hugh F. Rankin, *The North Carolina Continentals* (Chapel Hill: University of North Carolina Press, 1971), 23-25.

15. David L. Russell, *The American Revolution in the Southern Colonies* (Jefferson, NC: McFarland, 2000), 73-76; Bennett, *Quest*, 32-33; "Resolutions of the Virginia Convention concerning military aid from North Carolina," 22 December 1775, *CSRNC*, 10:364.

16. Wilson, *Southern Strategy*, 19-22; Josiah Martin to The Earl of Dartmouth, 12 November 1775, *CSRNC*, 10:321-328; Henry Clinton, *The American Rebellion:* William B. Willcox, *The American Rebellion: Sir Henry Clinton's Narrative of his Campaigns, 1775-1782* (New Haven, CT: Yale University Press, 1954), 23.

17. "Proclamation by Josiah Martin," January 10, 1776, *CSRNC*, 10:396-97.

18. Butler, *North Carolina*, 63; Rankin, *North Carolina in the American Revolution*, 11-12; "Manifesto by Donald MacDonald," undated [1776], *CSRNC*, 10:429-30; Wilson, *Southern Strategy*, 19-25.

19. Crow, *Chronicle*, 26-27.

20. Wilson, *Southern Strategy*, 24-26; William Purviance to the North Carolina Provincial Council, 23 February 1776, *CSRNC*, 10:465-68.

21. Wilson, *Southern Strategy*, 26-27; Commager and Morris, *Spirit*, 1:115.

22. Wilson, *Southern Strategy*, 27-28.

23. Crow, *Chronicle*, 27; Wilson, *Southern Strategy*, 28-30; Richard Caswell to President Harnett, 29 February 1776, *CSRNC*, 10:482; Commager and Morris, *Spirit*, 1:115.

24. Commager and Morris, *Spirit*, 1:115. Several accounts of the campaign from Loyalist officers can be found in Rassie Wicker, *Miscellaneous Ancient Records of Moore County, N.C.* (Moore County Historical Association, 1971), 370-373, 391-394, 397, 414. An account of the campaign from the Patriot side is in the letter of James Moore to Cornelius Harnett, 2 March 1776, which is given in an appendix in *Revolutionary History of North Carolina in Three Lectures*, comp. William D. Cooke (Raleigh: William D. Cooke, 1853), 218-220.

25. William B. Willcox, *Portrait of a General: Sir Henry Clinton in the War of Independence* (New York: Knopf, 1964), 86-93; Piers Mackesy, *The War for America, 1775-1783* (London: Longmans, 1964), 86; *Pennsylvania Evening Post*, March 26, 1776, 147-149; Clinton, *American Rebellion*, 25-26.

26. Clinton, *American Rebellion*, 28; Rankin, *North Carolina Continentals*, 59.

27. Hugh F. Rankin, *Moore's Creek Bridge Campaign* (Conshohocken, PA: Eastern National Park and Monument Association, 1986), 37-42; Ira D. Gruber, "Britain's Southern Strategy," in *The Revolutionary War in the South: Power, Conflict, and Leadership*, ed. W. Robert Higgins (Durham, NC: Duke University Press, 1979), 215; Vernon O. Stumpf, *Josiah Martin: The Last Royal Governor of North Car-*

olina (Raleigh: Carolina Academic Press, 1986), 172-173; Carole Watterson Troxler, *The Loyalist Experience in North Carolina* (Raleigh: North Carolina Division of Archives and History, 1975), 7.
28. Crow, *Chronicle*, 28; Butler, *North Carolina*, 65; Minutes of the Provincial Congress of North Carolina, April 4, 1776–May 14, 1776, *CSRNC*, 10:499-590.
29. Minutes of the Provincial Congress of North Carolina, April 4, 1776–May 14, 1776, *CSRNC*, 10:499-590.
30. Crow, *Chronicle*, 30; Robert K. Wright, *The Continental Army* (Washington, DC: Army Center of Military History, 1989), 75.
31. Rankin, *North Carolina Continentals*, 57.
32. Charles Lee to Edmund Pendleton, 29 June 1776, *CSRNC*, 10:618-618a; Bennett, *Quest*, 41-44; John Buchanan, *The Road to Guilford Courthouse* (New York: John Wiley, 1999), 11-16; Wilson, *Southern Strategy*, 58.
33. Clinton, *American Rebellion*, 37; Rankin, *North Carolina Continentals*, 70-76.
34. Colin Calloway, *The American Revolution in Indian Country* (Cambridge: Cambridge University Press, 1995), 182, 189-190, 198-197; Griffith Rutherford to the North Carolina Council of Safety, 14 July 1776, *CSRNC*, 10:669; James H. O'-Donnell, *The Cherokees of North Carolina in the American Revolution* (Raleigh: North Carolina Department of Cultural Resources, 1976), 13-22; James H. O'Donnell, *Southern Indians in the American Revolution* (Knoxville: University of Tennessee Press, 1990), 34-53.
35. William Hooper, Joseph Hewes, and John Penn to Cornelius Harnett, July 29, 1776, *CSRNC*, 10:679-80; Virginia Council of State to the North Carolina Council of Safety, August 8, 1776, *CSRNC*, 10:736; William Christian to Andrew Williamson, August 15, 1776, *CSRNC*, 10:748-49. See also "Arthur Fairies' Journal of Expedition Against the Cherokee Indians from July 18th, to October 11th, 1776," transcribed and annotated by Will Graves, *Southern Campaigns of the American Revolution* 2, no. 10 (October 2005): 20-34.
36. Richard Blackmon, *Dark and Bloody Ground: The American Revolution on the Southern Frontier* (Yardley, PA: Westholme Publishing, 2014), 62; William Hooper, Joseph Hewes, and John Penn to the North Carolina Council of Safety, August 7, 1776, *CSRNC*, 10: 730-732.
37. Calloway, *American Revolution*, 199-200; Crow, *Chronicle*, 35; Blackmon, *Dark and Bloody Ground*, 75-87.
38. Blackmon, *Dark and Bloody Ground*, 81-82.
39. Calloway, *American Revolution*, 199-200; Crow, *Chronicle*, 35; Blackmon, *Dark and Bloody Ground*, 75-87; Pension Application of Samuel Castle, 1839 (S8144), Carolana, accessed November 16, 2019, http://www.carolana.com/NC/Revolution/Cherokee_Expedition_1776_TN.pdf.
40. Rankin, *North Carolina Continentals*, 76-82; Robert Howe Orderly Book, 1776-1778, Manuscripts Division, William L. Clements Library, University of Michigan, 20-35; John Rutledge to Cornelius Harnett, August 21, 1776, *CSRNC*, 10:758-59; Bennett, *Quest*, 49-51.
41. William Hooper to Jonathan Trumbull Jr., 29 August 1776, in *Letters to Delegates to Congress, 1774-1789*, 25 vols., ed. Paul H. Smith (Washington, DC: Library of Congress, 1979), 5:79-80.
42. Crow, *Chronicle*, 34; Minutes of the Provincial Congress of North Carolina, November 12–December 23, 1776, *CSRNC*, 10:913-1003; Ordinances of the Provincial Congress of North Carolina Concerning a Temporary Government, December 20, 1776, *CSRNC*, 10:1013.
43. Minutes of the Provincial Congress of North Carolina, November 12–December 23, 1776, *CSRNC*, 10:913-1003.

CHAPTER SIX: FIGHTING REDCOATS AND TORIES

1. William Hooper to James Iredell, February 13, 1781, *The Papers of James Iredell*, ed. Don Higginbotham, 3 vols. (Raleigh, NC:

Division of Archives and History, Department of Cultural Resources, 1976), 2:209.
2. Wright, *Continental Army*, 301-03; Rankin, *North Carolina Continentals*, 87; Johnston to Thomas Burke, April 19, 1777, *CSRNC,* 11:453.
3. Thomas Burke to Richard Caswell, February 4, 1777, in *Letters of Delegates to Congress, 1774–1789,* ed. Paul H. Smith (Washington, DC: Library of Congress, 1979), 6:208-09; William Hooper to Joseph Hewes, February 15, 1777, *Letters of Delegates to Congress*, 6:288.
4. Rankin, *North Carolina Continentals*, 90-92; Thomas Burke to Richard Caswell, July 5, 1777, *CSRNC,* 11:511-13; James Duane to Robert R. Livingston, June 28, 1777, *Letters of Delegates to Congress*, 7:261.
5. Steven Siry, *Liberty's Fallen Generals: Leadership and Sacrifice in the American War of Independence* (Dulles, VA: Potomac Books, 2014), 77; Stephen Taaffe, *The Philadelphia Campaign, 1777-1778* (Lawrence: University Press of Kansas, 2003), 68; Wright, *Continental Army*, 108; Francis S. Drake, *Life and Correspondence of Henry Knox, Major-general in the American Revolutionary Army* (Boston: Samuel G. Drake, 1873), 48-49; Alexander Martin to Richard Caswell, November 4, 1777, *CSRNC,* 13:262-64. The second quote is from Thomas Burke, John Penn, and Cornelius Harnett to Richard Caswell, September 17, 1777, *CSRNC,* 11:625-26, writing from Philadelphia.
6. Taaffe, *Philadelphia Campaign*, 90-107; Cosimo de Medici to Richard Caswell, October 21, 1777, *CSRNC,* 11:661.
7. McGuire, *Philadelphia Campaign*, 2:84-85; Siry, *Liberty's Fallen Generals*, 79; Cornelius Harnett to Richard Caswell, October 10, 1777, *CSRNC,* 11:647-48; Rankin, *North Carolina Continentals*, 115-18; Orders from George Washington concerning the burial of Francis Nash, October 9, 1777, *NCHR* 11:651; Henry Laurens to Richard Caswell, November 5, 1777, *CSRNC,* 11:669-670.
8. Rankin, *North Carolina Continentals,* 122, 139; Washington's General Orders, December 20, 1777, John Fitzpatrick, ed., *The Writings of George Washington from the Original Manuscript Sources, 1745-1799* (Washington, DC: US Government Printing Office, 1931-44), 10:180-81.
9. Lachlan McIntosh to Richard Caswell, March 1778, *CSRNC,* 13:67-68.
10. Washington to Nash, January 5, 1778, Fitzpatrick, *Writings of Washington*, 10:268; General Orders, May 15, 1778, ibid., 11:388.
11. Clinton, *American Rebellion*, 87-88.
12. Rankin, *North Carolina Continentals,* 149-163.
13. Edward G. Lengel, "Bayonets at Midnight: The Battle of Stony Point" *Military History* 26 (Jan 2010): 36-43; Rankin, *North Carolina Continentals*, 171-76; Anthony Wayne to George Washington, July 17, 1779, *CSRNC* 14:327-330; Anthony Wayne to John Jay, August 10, 1779, *CSRNC* 14:337.
14. Jim Piecuch, *Three Peoples, One King: Loyalists, Indians, and Slaves in the Revolutionary South, 1775-1782* (Columbia: University of South Carolina Press, 2013), 36-76.
15. Rankin, *North Carolina Continentals*, 188.
16. Wilson, *Southern Strategy*, 81-99; Piecuch, *Three Peoples*, 142.
17. John Rutledge to Richard Caswell, June 9, 1779, *CSRNC,* 14:113; Terry W. Lipscomb and George Fenwick Jones, "A Hessian Map of the Stono Battlefield," *South Carolina Historical Magazine* 82, no. 4 (Oct, 1981): 371-381; Wilson, *Southern Strategy*, 116-31; Rankin, *North Carolina Continentals*, 198-214; John Butler to Richard Caswell, June 1779, *CSRNC,* 14:129-30; John F. Grimke to John Kean, June 21, 1779, *CSRNC* 14:311-13.
18. James Thackston to Jethro Sumner, August 24, 1779, *CSRNC,* 15:745-46.
19. Rankin, *North Carolina Continentals,* 175-176; Wilson, *Southern Strategy*, 133-192; James Swisher, *The Revolutionary War in the Southern Backcountry* (Gretna, LA:

Pelican Publishing, 2007), 85-110; Resolution by the Continental Congress concerning the defense of South Carolina, September 20–21, 1779, *CSRNC* 14:343; General Return of the North Carolina Continental Army Troops, West Point, New York, November 13, 1779, *CSRNC* 14:374-75.

20. Rankin, *North Carolina Continentals*, 215-34; Rankin, *North Carolina in the American Revolution*, 31-32; Wilson, *Southern Strategy*, 193-241. The most authoritative recent study of the siege of Charles Town is Carl P. Borick, *A Gallant Defense: The Siege of Charleston, 1780* (Columbia: University of South Carolina Press, 2003).

21. Samuel Huntington to Horatio Gates, June 13, 1780, *Letters to Delegates to Congress*, 15:312; Ezekiel Cornell to William Greene, June 18, 1780, *Letters to Delegates to Congress*, 15:340-42.

22. Richard Caswell to Horatio Gates, July 30, 1780, *CSRNC*, 14:515-16.

23. Buchanan, *Road to Guilford Courthouse*, 151-56; Rankin, *North Carolina Continentals*, 239-43.

24. Henry Lumpkin, *Savannah to Yorktown: The American Revolution in the South* (New York: Paragon House, 1981), 58-63.

25. Otho Holland Williams, "A Narrative of the Campaign of 1780," in *Sketches of the Life and Correspondence of Nathanael Greene*, comp. William Johnson (Charleston, SC: A. E. Miller, 1822), 1:485-510; John R. Maass, *Horatio Gates and the Battle of Camden: That Unhappy Affair* (Camden, SC: Kershaw County Historical Society, 2001), 46-47.

26. [Charles Magill] to Magill (his father), August 1780, *CSRNC*, 14:584-585; Maass, *Gates*, 44-45.

27. John Pancake, *This Destructive War: The British Campaign in the Carolinas, 1780-1782* (Tuscaloosa: University of Alabama Press, 1984), 95, 162; Lumpkin, *Savannah to Yorktown*, 163.

28. Pancake, *This Destructive War*, 112-16.

29. Ibid., 117-18.

30. Lumpkin, *Savannah to Yorktown*, 99-104; Buchanan, *Road to Guilford Courthouse*, 235.

31. Clinton, *American Rebellion*, 226; Thomas Jefferson to John Campbell, November 10, 1822, Campbell Papers, microfilm reel no.1, Tennessee State Library, http://philnorf.tripod.com/letterof.htm.

32. Nathanael Greene to William H. Harrington, 4 December 1780, Richard Showman and Dennis Conrad, eds., *The Papers of General Nathanael Greene*, 13 vols. (Chapel Hill: University of North Carolina Press, 1976-2005), 6:519.

33. Greene to Abner Nash, 6 December 1780, ibid., 6:533-534; Greene to Henry Knox, 7 December 1780, ibid., 6:547.

34. Buchanan, *Road to Guilford Courthouse*, 288-95.

35. For the most detailed look at the battle of Cowpens, see Lawrence E. Babits, *A Devil of a Whipping: The Battle of Cowpens* (Chapel Hill: University of North Carolina Press, 1998); Buchanan, *Road to Guilford Courthouse*, 319-33.

36. Daniel Morgan to Nathanael Greene, January 19, 1781, *Papers of Nathanael Greene*, 7:152-155.

37. Thomas E. Baker, *Another Such Victory: The Story of the American Defeat at Guilford Courthouse That Helped Win the War for Independence* (New York: Eastern Acorn Press, 1981), 23-27; Lawrence E. Babits and Joshua B. Howard, *Long, Obstinate, and Bloody: The Battle of Guilford Courthouse* (Chapel Hill: University of North Carolina Press, 2009), 13-36.

38. Baker, *Another Such Victory*, 28-32; Babits and Howard, *Long*, 37-51; 58-59.

39. Babits and Howard, *Long*, 51-55.

40. Baker, *Another Such Victory*, 46-47; Babits and Howard, *Long*, 66.

41. Babits and Howard, *Long*, 94-113; Mark Urban, *Fusiliers: The Saga of a British Regiment in the American Revolution* (New York: Walker, 2007), 240-48; Nathanael Greene to Samuel Huntington, March 16, 1781, *Papers of Nathanael Greene*, 7:433-35.

42. Nathanael Greene to Samuel Huntington, March 16, 1781, *Papers of Nathanael Greene*, 7:433-35; Baker, *Another Such Victory*, 57-61; Babits and Howard, *Long,* 117-128.
43. For this separate action, see Babits and Howard, *Long,* 129-141.
44. Nathanael Greene to Samuel Huntington, March 16, 1781, *Papers of Nathanael Greene*, 7:433-35; Babits and Howard, *Long,* 142-69, 221; Baker, *Another Such Victory*, 69-70. The story that Cornwallis intentionally ordered his artillery to fire grapeshot into the thick of the fighting, although it would cut down some of his own men, has been shown by Babits and Howard to be based on little credible evidence (see their analysis on 161-62.)
45. Baker, *Another Such Victory*, 70-73; Lindley S. Butler, "Speedwell Furnace: The Ironworks on Troublesome Creek," Rockingham County Historical Society pamphlet, 1972; Babits and Howard, *Long,* 223-24; Nathanael Greene to Samuel Huntington, March 16, 1781, *Papers of Nathanael Greene*, 7:433-35; Nathanael Greene to Samuel Huntington, March 30, 1781, ibid., 8:7-9; Nathanael Greene to Thomas Sumter, March 16, 1781, ibid., 7:442-43; Banastre Tarleton, *A History of the Campaigns of 1780 and 1781 in the Southern Provinces of North America* (London: T. Cadell, 1787), 277.
46. Lord Cornwallis to Lord Germain, March 17, 1781, in Tarleton, *Campaigns*, 303-310.
47. Spencer Tucker, *Rise and Fight Again: The Life of Nathanael Greene* (Wilmington, DE: Intercollegiate Studies Institute, 2008), 168.
48. North Carolina Assembly Records, April 1782, *CSRNC,* 24:384-387, 395-396, 404-405.
49. Abner Nash to the General Assembly, 25 August 1780, Joint Papers, General Assembly Session Records, August–September 1780, Box 1, North Carolina State Archives, Raleigh; Thomas Burke to Nathanael Greene, 28 March 1782, *Papers of Nathanael Greene*, 10:549-550.
50. Nathanael Greene to Robert Howe, 29 December 1780, *Papers of Nathanael Greene*, 7:17.
51. Algie Newlin, *The Battle of Lindley's Mill* (Burlington, NC: Alamance Historical Association, 1975), 3; *NCHR* 17:913; Robert O. DeMond, The *Loyalists in North Carolina during the Revolution* (Durham, NC: Duke University Press, 1940), 146; McCrady, *The History of South Carolina in the Revolution, 1780-1783* (New York: Macmillan, 1902), 4:466.
52. David Fanning to Thomas Burke, 29 February 1782, *CSRNC,* 16:205-208; Thomas Burke to the General Assembly, 7 July 1781, Governor's Messages, General Assembly Session Records, June-July 1781, Box 1, North Carolina State Archives.

CHAPTER SEVEN: WAR AND THE NEW NATION

1. Wiley Sword, *George Washington's Indian War: The Struggle for the Old Northwest, 1790–1795* (Norman: University of Oklahoma Press, 1993), 7-10.
2. John R. Maass, *Defending a New Nation, 1783-1811* (Washington, DC: US Army Center of Military History, 2013), 10, 13-15, 17.
3. Ibid., 18-27.
4. *The North Carolina Booklet*, vol. 12, no. 1, July (Raleigh: North Carolina Society of the Daughters of the American Revolution, 1912), 32; Revolutionary War Pension File, Joseph Montfort, BLWt1531-300, fn4NC, www.revwarapps.org/blwt1531-300.pdf; *Roster of Soldiers from North Carolina in the American Revolution* (Durham: North Carolina Daughters of the American Revolution, 1932), 295; Joseph Howell to John Davies, June 7, 1790, Papers of the War Department 1784-1800, http://wardepartmentpapers.org/s/home/item/40736.
5. Henry Knox to William Blount, August 27, 1790, Papers of the War Department, accessed November 17, 2019, http://wardepartmentpapers.org/s/home/item/78956.

6. "To George Washington from Henry Knox, 22 January 1791," Founders Online, National Archives, accessed November 17, 2019, https://www.founders.archives.gov/?q=Author%3A%22Knox%2C%20Henry%22%20Recipient%3A%22Washington%2C%20George%22%20Period%3A%22Washington%20Presidency%22&s=1111311111&r=42; "To George Washington from Henry Knox, 18 February 1793," Founders Online, National Archives, accessed November 17, 2019, https://www.founders.archives.gov/?q=Author%3A%22Knox%2C%20Henry%22%20Recipient%3A%22Washington%2C%20George%22%20Period%3A%22Washington%20Presidency%22&s=1111311111&r=146.
7. "Schedule of Troops to March for Fort Pitt," May 28, 1791, Papers of the War Department, accessed November 17, 2019, http://wardepartmentpapers.org/document.php?id=5247.
8. Richard M. Lytle, *The Soldiers of the First Army, 1791* (Lanham, MD: Scarecrow Press, 2004), 24, 39, 43, 56; Henry Knox to Richard Butler, May 19, 1791, Papers of the War Department, http://wardepartmentpapers.org/s/home/item/41396.
9. Lytle, *Soldiers*, 51, 64
10. Maass, *Defending*, 24-25; John F. Winkler, *Wabash 1791: St. Clair's Defeat* (Oxford: Osprey, 2011), 41-49.
11. Lytle, *Soldiers*, 112.
12. Maass, *Defending*, 26-27; Winkler, *Wabash 1791*, 53-85; Sword, *George Washington's Indian War*, 176-89.
13. Lytle, *Soldiers*, 112-15.
14. Andrew J. Birtle, "The Origins of the Legion of the United States," *Journal of Military History* 67, no. 4 (Oct 2003): 1249-61.
15. Lytle, *Soldiers*, 161-62; Henry Knox to Cornelius Sedan, March 1, 1793, Papers of the War Department, accessed November 17, 2019, http://wardepartmentpapers.org/s/home/item/41200; Alan D. Gaff, *Bayonets in the Wilderness: Anthony Wayne's Legion in the Old Northwest* (Norman: University of Oklahoma Press, 2004), 12.
16. Henry Knox to Winthrop Sargent, July 23, 1792, Papers of the War Department, accessed November 17, 2019, http://wardepartmentpapers.org/s/home/item/41283.
17. Gregory Urwin, *The United States Infantry: An Illustrated History, 1775–1918* (Norman: University of Oklahoma Press, 1988), 33-37.
18. Maass, *Defending*, 5, 57; Jeremy Black, *The War of 1812 in the Age of Napoleon* (Norman: University of Oklahoma Press, 2009), 10-43; Donald R. Hickey, *The War of 1812: A Forgotten Conflict* (Urbana and Chicago: University of Illinois Press, 1989), 5-28.
19. Sarah M. Lemmon, *North Carolina and the War of 1812* (Raleigh, NC: Division of Archives and History, North Carolina Department of Cultural Resources, 1971), 5-8, 14; Sarah M. Lemmon, *Frustrated Patriots: North Carolina and the War of 1812* (Chapel Hill: University of North Carolina Press, 1973), 18-19.
20. Maass, *Defending*, 50-51; John Charles Anderson Stagg, *Mr. Madison's War: Politics, Diplomacy and Warfare in the Early American Republic, 1783-1830* (Princeton, NJ: Princeton University Press, 1983), 143-47.
21. John C. Fredericksen, *The United States Army in the War of 1812* (Jefferson, NC: McFarland, 2009), 215-216, 275; William A. Gordon, comp., *A Compilation of Registers of the Army of the United States, 1815–1837* (Washington, DC: James C. Dunn, 1837), 9-10, 23-24; Lemmon, *North Carolina*, 10; Lemmon, *Frustrated Patriots*, 49.
22. Richard V. Barbuto, *The Canadian Theater, 1813* (Washington, DC: US Army Center of Military History, 2013), 42-45; J. Mackay Hitsman, *The Incredible War of 1812: A Military History* (Montreal: Robin Brass Studio, updated ed., 1999), 182-87.
23. Barbuto, *Canadian Theater,* 12-22; Hickey, *War of 1812*, 139-40; Lemmon, *North Carolina*, 17-20; John R. Elting, *Amateurs, to Arms!: A Military History of the War of 1812* (New York: Da Capo Press, 1995), 52.
24. "War of 1812 Records in the North Carolina State Archives," Archives Information

Circular, North Carolina Department of Cultural Resources, no. 18; John K. Mahon, "The Carolina Brigade Sent against the Creek Indians in 1814," *NCHR* 28 (1951), 421-425.

25. For details on the Creek War, see Tom Kanon, *Tennesseans at War, 1812–1815: Andrew Jackson, the Creek War, and the Battle of New Orleans* (Tuscaloosa: University of Alabama Press, 2014); Howard T. Weir III, *A Paradise of Blood: The Creek War of 1813–14* (Yardley, PA: Westholme, 2015); and Kathryn Holland Braund, ed., *Tohopeka: Rethinking the Creek War and the War of 1812* (Tuscaloosa: University of Alabama Press, 2012).

26. Mahon, "Carolina Brigade," 421-25; Lemmon, *North Carolina*, 46-49.

27. Mahon, "Carolina Brigade," 421-25; Lemmon, *North Carolina*, 48-49; Lemmon, *Frustrated Patriots*, 113-17.

28. Lemmon, *Frustrated Patriots*, 120-42.

29. Edgar S. Maclay, *A History of American Privateers* (London: Sampson, Low, Marston, 1900), 225-327.

30. Kemp P. Battle, "Otway Burns, Privateer and Legislator," *North Carolina University Magazine*, Old Series 32, no. 1 (October 1901): 1-30; Lindley S. Butler, *Pirates, Privateers, and Rebel Raiders of the Carolina Coast* (Chapel Hill: University of North Carolina Press, 2000), 73-94; J. D. Nash, "Snap Dragon," Powell, *Encyclopedia of North Carolina*, 1053.

31. J. L. Cross, "Wasp," *Encyclopedia of North Carolina*, Powell, 1181; "Blakely," *Dictionary of American Fighting Ships, Naval History and Heritage Command*, http://www.history.navy.mil/danfs/b7/blakely-blakeley-i.htm, accessed June 19, 2014; Butler, *Pirates*, 95-117.

32. Richard W. Stewart, ed., *American Military History: The United States Army and the Forging of a Nation, 1775–1917* (Washington: US Army Center of Military History, 2004), 1:171-72.

33. Stewart, *American Military History*, 1:175.

34. Urwin, *United States Infantry*, 64; Lee A. Wallace Jr., "Raising a Volunteer Regiment for Mexico, 1846–47," *NCHR* 35, no. 1 (January 1958): 20-33; *Raleigh News and Observer*, May 1, 1888; Williams S. Hoffman, *North Carolina in the Mexican War, 1846–1848* (Raleigh: State Department of Archives and History, 1959), 14-17, 20-21.

35. Hoffman, *North Carolina*, 18-21; "Mexican War," Powell, *Encyclopedia of North Carolina*, 734-35.

36. Gaston Lichtenstein, *Louis D. Wilson, Mexican War Martyr . . .* (Richmond, VA: H. T. Ezekiel, 1911), 7-8; Hoffman, *North Carolina in the Mexican War*, 25.

37. Hoffman, *North Carolina*, 25; Stewart, *American Military History*, 175; Timothy D. Johnson, *A Gallant Little Army: The Mexico City Campaign* (Lawrence: University Press of Kansas, 2007), 246-47.

38. For biographical information on Bragg's pre-Civil War career, see Grady McWhiney, *Braxton Bragg and Confederate Defeat*, vol. 1 (New York: Columbia University Press, 1969), and Steven E. Woodworth, *Jefferson Davis and His Generals: The Failure of Confederate Command in the West* (Lawrence: University Press of Kansas, 1990).

CHAPTER EIGHT: THE CIVIL WAR: OPENING BATTLES

1. William C. Harris, *North Carolina and the Coming of the Civil War* (Raleigh: North Carolina Division of Archives and History, 1988), 23-24, 26-29; Moore, Bandel, and Hill, *Old North State*, 1.

2. John S. Carbone, *The Civil War in Coastal North Carolina* (Raleigh: North Carolina Division of Archives and History, 2001), 2; Moore, Bandel, and Hill, *Old North State*, 1-2.

3. John G. Barrett, *The Civil War in North Carolina* (Chapel Hill: University of North Carolina Press, 1963), 9; Harris, *North Carolina*, 45.

4. Harris, *North Carolina*, 50-54; Barrett, *Civil War*, 10-13; Joseph Carlyle Sitterson,

The Secession Movement in North Carolina (Chapel Hill: University of North Carolina Press, 1939), 239-40; Moore, Bandel, and Hill, *Old North State*, 4.

5. Clement Dowd, *Life of Zebulon B. Vance* (Charlotte: Observer Printing and Publishing House, 1897), 441; Gordon B. McKinney, *Zeb Vance: North Carolina's Civil War Governor and Gilded Age Political Leader* (Chapel Hill: University of North Carolina Press, 2004), 76.

6. Michael C. Hardy, *North Carolina in the Civil War* (Charleston, SC: History Press, 2011), 16.

7. Barrett, *Civil War*, 20-21; Hardy, *North Carolina*, 16-17, 21; Moore, Bandel, and Hill, *Old North State*, 11.

8. Richard W. Iobst, "Henry Toole Clark," in *Dictionary of North Carolina Biography*, ed. William S. Powell, 6 vols. (Chapel Hill: University of North Carolina Press, 1979-1996); Hardy, *North Carolina*, 20.

9. Carbone, *Civil War*, 6-10; Moore, Bandel, and Hill, *Old North State*, 22-23.

10. Barrett, *Civil War*, 39-41; Carbone, *Civil War*, 10-11.

11. Barrett, *Civil War*, 43-45.

12. Carbone, *Civil War*, 13.

13. Barrett, *Civil War*, 66-73; Carbone, *Civil War*, 23-32; Moore, Bandel, and Hill, *Old North State*, 24-25.

14. Carbone, *Civil War*, 32, 34.

15. Barrett, *Civil War*, 78-80; Carbone, *Civil War*, 38-39; Hardy, *North Carolina*, 25-26.

16. Barrett, *Civil War*, 83-84; Hardy, *North Carolina*, 26; Moore, Bandel, and Hill, *Old North State*, 26-27.

17. Barrett, *Civil War*, 85-87; Hardy, *North Carolina*, 26-27; Alex Christopher Meekins, *Elizabeth City, North Carolina and the Civil War: A History of Battle and Occupation* (Charleston, SC: History Press, 2007), 29-30; Moore, Bandel, and Hill, *Old North State*, 25, 95-96.

18. Barrett, *Civil War*, 92-95; Carbone, *Civil War*, 47-48; Meekins, *Elizabeth City*, 31-32; Hardy, *North Carolina*, 27.

19. Meekins, *Elizabeth City*, 32-34.

20. Barrett, *Civil War*, 98-99; Carbone, *Civil War*, 49-51.

21. McKinney, *Zeb Vance*, 87; Barrett, *Civil War*, 96-97, 99-100; Hardy, *North Carolina*, 27-28; Moore, Bandel, and Hill, *Old North State*, 28.

22. Barrett, *Civil War*, 100-101.

23. Carbone, *Civil War*, 53.

24. Barrett, *Civil War*, 104-06; Carbone, *Civil War*, 53-54; Hardy, *North Carolina*, 28; Moore, Bandel, and Hill, *Old North State*, 28; Richard A. Sauers, *The Burnside Expedition in North Carolina: A Succession of Honorable Victories* (Dayton, OH: Morningside, 1996), 261-308.

25. Barrett, *Civil War*, 109-10; Hardy, *North Carolina*, 29.

26. Barrett, *Civil War*, 110-13; Hardy, *North Carolina*, 28-29; Moore, Bandel, and Hill, *Old North State*, 29.

27. Sauers, *Burnside Expedition*, 313-40; Hardy, *North Carolina*, 29-30; Judkin Browning, *Shifting Loyalties: The Union Occupation of Eastern North Carolina* (Chapel Hill: University of North Carolina Press, 2014), 60-62; Moore, Bandel, and Hill, *Old North State*, 30.

28. Hardy, *North Carolina*, 30; Chris E. Fonvielle Jr., *Fort Fisher 1865: The Photographs of T. H. O'Sullivan* (Carolina Beach, NC: SlapDash Publishing, 2011), 4-6; Moore, Bandel, and Hill, *Old North State*, 100-103.

29. Moore, Bandel, and Hill, *Old North State*, 6.

30. Hardy, *North Carolina*, 31.

31. Ibid., 31-32; McKinney, *Zeb Vance*, 136-37; Joe A. Mobley, *"War Governor of the South": North Carolina's Zeb Vance in the Confederacy* (Gainesville: University Press of Florida, 2005), 127.

32. McKinney, *Zeb Vance*, 106, 139; Mobley, *"War Governor,"* 128-29, 131, 136-37; Stephen R. Wise, *Lifeline of the Confederacy: Blockade Running during the Civil War* (Columbia: University of South Carolina Press, 1988), 106.

33. Barrett, *Civil War*, 122-24; Carbone, *Civil War*, 66; Moore, Bandel, and Hill, *Old North State*, 25.
34. Norman D. Brown, "Edward Stanly," in Powell, *Dictionary of North Carolina Biography*; Carbone, *Civil War*, 83-86.
35. Barrett, *Civil War*, 128-29; Sauers, *Burnside Expedition*, 443-45.
36. Barrett, *Civil War*, 133-34, 135-36; Moore, Bandel, and Hill, *Old North State*, 37.
37. Barrett, *Civil War*, 135; Carbone, *Civil War*, 70; Hardy, *North Carolina*, 36; Moore, Bandel, and Hill, *Old North State*, 37.
38. Barrett, *Civil War*, 139-40; Carbone, *Civil War*, 71-72; Moore, Bandel, and Hill, *Old North State*, 32-33, 37.
39. Barrett, *Civil War*, 140-42.
40. Ibid., 142-44; Carbone, *Civil War*, 72.
41. Barrett, *Civil War*, 144; Moore, Bandel, and Hill, *Old North State*, 33-35.
42. Barrett, *Civil War*, 144-45; Moore, Bandel, and Hill, *Old North State*, 96-97.
43. "The Life of the CSS *Neuse*: 'The Ram Is No Myth,'" https://historicsites.nc.sites.gov/all-sites/css%C2%A0neuse-and-gov-caswell-memorial/history/css-neuse-history/life-css-neuse.
44. Barrett, *Civil War*, 146-47; Moore, Bandel, and Hill, *Old North State*, 34-35.
45. US War Department, *The War of the Rebellion: A Compilation of the Official Records (OR) of the Union and Confederate Armies*, 128 vols. (Washington, DC: Government Printing Office, 1880–1901), *OR* 18:57-58, 117-18; Moore, Bandel, and Hill, *Old North State*, 34, 36-37.
46. *OR* 18:60, 86, 113-14.
47. *OR* 18:489; Moore, Bandel, and Hill, *Old North State*, 37.
48. Hardy, *North Carolina*, 37. Teams of marine archaeologists have since recovered the gun turret and numerous other artifacts from the *Monitor*, many of which are on display at The USS *Monitor* Center at The Mariners' Museum & Park, Newport News, Virginia.

CHAPTER NINE: THE CIVIL WAR GRINDS ON

1. Barrett, *Civil War*, 149-50; Carbone, *Civil War*, 107; Hardy, *North Carolina*, 41; Moore, Bandel, and Hill, *Old North State*, 50.
2. Barrett, *Civil War*, 152-55; Carbone, *Civil War*, 107; Moore, Bandel, and Hill, *Old North State*, 52.
3. Barrett, *Civil War*, 156-59; Carbone, *Civil War*, 107-08; Hardy, *North Carolina*, 41; Moore, Bandel, and Hill, *Old North State*, 55.
4. Barrett, *Civil War*, 159-60; Moore, Bandel, and Hill, *Old North State*, 55.
5. Barrett, *Civil War*, 161-62; Carbone, *Civil War*, 108.
6. *OR* 18:363-69.
7. *OR* 27, pt. 2:859-63; Moore, Bandel, and Hill, *Old North State*, 54; John W. McAden Jr. and Chris E. Fonvielle Jr., *Louis Froelich, Arms-Maker to the Confederacy* (Carolina Beach, NC: NC Starburst Press, 2008), 24-26. Froelich rebuilt his facilities and resumed business later that year.
8. David A. Norris, "'The Yankees Have Been Here!': The Story of Brig. Gen. Edward E. Potter's Raid on Greenville, Tarboro, and Rocky Mount, July 19–23, 1863," *NCHR* 73 (1996), https://web.cortland.edu/woosterk/pot_raid.html.
9. *OR* 27, pt. 2:964-65, 968-69; Norris, "'Yankees,'"; Barrett, *Civil War*, 164-65; Moore, Bandel, and Hill, *Old North State*, 53.
10. Norris, "'Yankees,'"; Barrett, *Civil War*, 166.
11. Barrett, *Civil War*, 166-68.
12. Carbone, *Civil War*, 109-10; Hardy, *North Carolina*, 47; Moore, Bandel, and Hill, *Old North State*, 56.
13. Hardy, *North Carolina*, 41-42, 45; Barrett, *Civil War*, 197.
14. John C. Inscoe and Gordon B. McKinney, *The Heart of Confederate Appalachia: Western North Carolina in the Civil War* (Chapel Hill: University of North Carolina Press, 2000), 119-20; Barrett, *Civil War*, 197-98; Philip Shaw Paludan, *Victims: A*

True Story of the Civil War (Knoxville: University of Tennessee Press, 1981), 109-15; Moore, Bandel, and Hill, *Old North State*, 58-60; Philip Gerard, *The Last Battleground: The Civil War Comes to North Carolina* (Chapel Hill: University of North Carolina Press, 2019), 90-91; Rick Beard, "Murder in the Mountains," *New York Times*, January 19, 2013, https://opinionator.blogs.nytimes.com/2013/01/19/murder-in-the-mountains/.

15. Hardy, *North Carolina*, 44-46; Barrett, *Civil War*, 185-86.

16. Inscoe and McKinney, *Heart*, 126-28; Hardy, *North Carolina*, 46-47; Moore, Bandel, and Hill, *Old North State*, 60-61.

17. *Carolina Watchman*, March 23, 1863; Mobley, "*War Governor*," 148-49; Moore, Bandel, and Hill, *Old North State*, 72.

18. Mobley, "War Governor," 106-09; McKinney, *Zeb Vance*, 185-88; Barrett, *Civil War*, 195-96; Hardy, *North Carolina*, 48-49.

19. Barrett, *Civil War*, 177; Meekins, *Elizabeth City*, 104-05; Carbone, *Civil War*, 99; Richard Reid, "Raising the African Brigade: Early Black Recruitment in Civil War North Carolina," *NCHR* 70 (1993): 292-93.

20. Moore, Bandel, and Hill, *Old North State*, 57.

21. Meekins, *Elizabeth City*, 106; Barrett, *Civil War*, 177-78.

22. Meekins, *Elizabeth City*, 107-13; Moore, Bandel, and Hill, *Old North State*, 57.

23. Meekins, *Elizabeth City*, 113-15.

24. Barrett, *Civil War*, 179; Meekins, *Elizabeth City*, 116-18; Barton A. Myers, *Executing Daniel Bright: Race, Loyalty, and Guerrilla Violence in a Coastal Carolina Community, 1861-1865* (Baton Rouge: Louisiana State University Press, 2009), 1-6; Barton A. Myers, *Rebels Against the Confederacy: North Carolina's Unionists* (New York: Cambridge University Press, 2014), 58; Barton A. Myers, "'A More Rigorous Style of Warfare': Wild's Raid, Guerrilla Violence, and Negotiated Neutrality in Northeastern North Carolina," in *North Carolinians in the Era of Civil War and Reconstruction*, ed. Paul D. Escott (Chapel Hill: University of North Carolina Press, 2008), 48-50, 57.

25. Inscoe and McKinney, *Heart*, 15-16, 110, 123; Hardy, *North Carolina*, 47; Barrett, *Civil War*, 199; Moore, Bandel, and Hill, *Old North State*, 88, 92.

26. Barrett, *Civil War*, 199-200.

27. Barrett, *Civil War*, 200-01; Moore, Bandel, and Hill, *Old North State*, 93.

28. Hampton Newsome, *The Fight for the Old North State: The Civil War in North Carolina, January-May 1864* (Lawrence: University Press of Kansas, 2019), 42; *Hardy*, *North Carolina*, 51; Barrett, *Civil War*, 202-03; Moore, Bandel, and Hill, *Old North State*, 75.

29. Barrett, *Civil War*, 203-04; Carbone, *Civil War*, 110-11; Moore, Bandel, and Hill, *Old North State*, 77-78.

30. Barrett, *Civil War*, 205-07; Moore, Bandel, and Hill, *Old North State*, 75, 77.

31. Newsome, *Fight*, 94-104; Barrett, *Civil War*, 208-12; Carbone, *Civil War*, 111-12; Moore, Bandel, and Hill, *Old North State*, 77.

32. Newsome, *Fight*, 141-51; Hardy, *North Carolina*, 51-52; Mark L. Bradley, *Bluecoats and Tar Heels: Soldiers and Civilians in Reconstruction North Carolina* (Lexington: University Press of Kentucky, 2009), 111-13.

33. Moore, Bandel, and Hill, *Old North State*, 80.

34. Weymouth T. Jordan Jr. and Gerald W. Thomas, "Massacre at Plymouth: April 20, 1864," *NCHR* 72 (April 1995): 131, 138-39; Newsome, *Fight*, 217-27.

35. Jordan and Thomas, "Massacre," 139-40; Moore, Bandel, and Hill, *Old North State*, 81; Newsome, *Fight*, 228-35.

36. Moore, Bandel, and Hill, *Old North State*, 75, 80; Newsome, *Fight*, 236-56.

37. Barrett, *Civil War*, 219-20; Carbone, *Civil War*, 115-116; Meekins, *Elizabeth City*, 125; Jordan and Thomas, "Massacre," 192; Newsome, *Fight*, 259-62.

38. Barrett, *Civil War*, 220-21; Carbone, *Civil War*, 116-17.

39. Barrett, *Civil War*, 224-25; Moore, Bandel, and Hill, *Old North State*, 76, 82; Newsome, *Fight*, 311-12.
40. Barrett, *Civil War*, 222-24; Carbone, *Civil War*, 117; Hardy, *North Carolina*, 55; Moore, Bandel, and Hill, *Old North State*, 76, 83.
41. Barrett, *Civil War*, 227-31; Carbone, *Civil War*, 117-19; Hardy, *North Carolina*, 63; Moore, Bandel, and Hill, *Old North State*, 76, 85.
42. Barrett, *Civil War*, 233-35; Hardy, *North Carolina*, 57; Moore, Bandel, and Hill, *Old North State*, 90-91.
43. Barrett, *Civil War*, 235-37; Hardy, *North Carolina*, 57; Inscoe and McKinney, *Heart*, 135-36.
44. Carbone, *Civil War*, 123.
45. McKinney, *Zeb Vance*, 225-26; Mobley, "*War Governor*," 119-25; Moore, Bandel, and Hill, *Old North State*, 70-71.
46. McKinney, *Zeb Vance*, 228-30; Mobley, "*War Governor*," 125-26; Moore, Bandel, and Hill, *Old North State*, 71.
47. Fonvielle, *Fort Fisher 1865*, 15; Carbone, *Civil War*, 134-35; Moore, Bandel, and Hill, *Old North State*, 100-02.
48. Gideon Welles, *Diary of Gideon Welles*, 3 vols. (Boston and New York: Houghton Mifflin, 1911), 2:127.
49. Fonvielle, *Fort Fisher 1865*, 10-11, 16; Moore, Bandel, and Hill, *Old North State*, 102, 106.
50. Fonvielle, *Fort Fisher 1865*, 10, 16-17; Chris E. Fonvielle Jr., *The Wilmington Campaign: Last Rays of Departing Hope* (Campbell, CA: Savas, 1997), 80-82.
51. "The Civil War at Fort Fisher: A Joint Attack upon Wilmington," North Carolina Historic Sites, https://historicsites.nc.gov/all-sites/fort-fisher/history/civil-war-fort-fisher.
52. Fonvielle, *Fort Fisher 1865*, 17; Moore, Bandel, and Hill, *Old North State*, 113-15.
53. Fonvielle, *Fort Fisher 1865*, 18.
54. Fonvielle, *Wilmington Campaign*, 121-26; Fonvielle, *Fort Fisher 1865*, 18, 20; Moore, Bandel, and Hill, *Old North State*, 114.
55. Fonvielle, *Fort Fisher 1865*, 19.
56. Ibid., 19-20; Fonvielle, *Wilmington Campaign*, 172; Moore, Bandel, and Hill, *Old North State*, 116-17.
57. Fonvielle, *Fort Fisher 1865*, 20-21; Fonvielle, *Wilmington Campaign*, 180-81.
58. Fonvielle, *Fort Fisher 1865*, 21-23; Mark L. Bradley, *Last Stand in the Carolinas: The Battle of Bentonville* (Campbell, CA: Savas Woodbury, 1996), 2-4.
59. Fonvielle, *Fort Fisher 1865*, 23-24, 31; Moore, Bandel, and Hill, *Old North State*, 119-20.
60. Fonvielle, *Fort Fisher 1865*, 24; Moore, Bandel, and Hill, *Old North State*, 119, 121.
61. Moore, Bandel, and Hill, *Old North State*, 119, 122-23.
62. Fonvielle, *Fort Fisher 1865*, 24-26; Carbone, *Civil War*, 139-41; Moore, Bandel, and Hill, *Old North State*, 119.

CHAPTER TEN: THE FINAL MONTHS OF THE CIVIL WAR

1. William T. Sherman, *Memoirs* (New York: Da Capo Press, 1984), 2:221; Bradley, *Last Stand*, 1-4, 20-21; Mark L. Bradley, *This Astounding Close: The Road to Bennett Place* (Chapel Hill: University of North Carolina Press, 2000), 1.
2. Bradley, *Last Stand*, 4-5; Moore, Bandel, and Hill, *Old North State*, 133-34; R. Scott Moore, *The Civil War on the Atlantic Coast, 1861–1865* (Washington, DC: US Army Center of Military History, 2015), 57-58.
3. Bradley, *Last Stand*, 21-23.
4. Ibid., 28-30.
5. Bradley, *This Astounding Close*, 5-6.
6. Moore, *Civil War*, 58; Chris E. Fonvielle Jr., "The Fight for Freedom at Wilmington's Battle of Fork's Road," *Wilmington Star News Online*, February 22, 2019.
7. Bradley, *Last Stand*, 24, 36.
8. Ibid., 24-26.
9. Ibid., 27-28.
10. Ibid., 28, 73-75.
11. Wade Sokolosky and Mark A. Smith, "*To Prepare for Sherman's Coming*": *The*

Battle of Wise's Forks, March 1865 (El Dorado Hills, CA: Savas Beatie, 2015), 58, 87; Bradley, *Last Stand*, 171.
12. Sokolosky and Smith, *Prepare*, 131, 195; Moore, Bandel, and Hill, *Old North State*, 139-41.
13. Bradley, *Last Stand*, 75-78.
14. Eric J. Wittenberg, *The Battle of Monroe's Crossroads and the Civil War's Final Campaign* (New York: Savas Beatie, 2006), 104; Moore, Bandel, and Hill, *Old North State*, 136; Bradley, *Last Stand*, 85-88.
15. Bradley, *Last Stand*, 86, 90-92, 102.
16. Wittenberg, *Battle of Monroe's Crossroads*, 214; Barrett, *Civil War*, 309; Moore, Bandel, and Hill, *Old North State*, 142-43; Bradley, *Last Stand*, 93-104.
17. Bradley, *Last Stand*, 107-112, 114-16.
18. Perry D. Jamieson, *Spring 1865: The Closing Campaigns of the Civil War* (Lincoln: University of Nebraska Press, 2015), 56-57; Bradley, *Last Stand*, 114-19.
19. Moore, Bandel, and Hill, *Old North State*, 144-46; Bradley, *Last Stand*, 121-32; Mark A. Smith and Wade Sokolosky, *"No Such Army Since the Days of Julius Caesar": Sherman's Carolinas Campaign from Fayetteville to Averasboro, March 1865* (El Dorado Hills, CA: Savas Beatie, 2017), 62-132.
20. Bradley, *Last Stand*, 132-33.
21. Jamieson, *Spring 1865*, 61; Bradley, *Last Stand*, 137-39, 309. In mid-March 1865, Johnston's army numbered about sixteen thousand infantry and artillery and four thousand cavalry.
22. Bradley, *Last Stand*, 141-44. For an accurate layout of the road network, see Moore, Bandel, and Hill, *Old North State*, 149.
23. Bradley, *Last Stand*, 145-46.
24. Jamieson, *Spring 1865*, 68-69; Bradley, *Last Stand*, 148-49.
25. Bradley, *Last Stand*, 144, 153-55, 233.
26. Ibid., 154.
27. Ibid., 156-59, 161-65, 176-88; Moore, Bandel, and Hill, *Old North State*, 151.
28. Bradley, *Last Stand*, 189-91.
29. Ibid., 166, 179-80.
30. Ibid., 203-04, 208-21; Moore, Bandel, and Hill, *Old North State*, 152.
31. Bradley, *Last Stand*, 222-23, 301-02.
32. Ibid., 223-60, 264-70; Moore, Bandel, and Hill, *Old North State*, 152-54.
33. Bradley, *Last Stand*, 279-95; Moore, Bandel, and Hill, *Old North State*, 154.
34. Bradley, *Last Stand*, 320-30, 338-48, 354; Moore, Bandel, and Hill, *Old North State*, 155.
35. Bradley, *Last Stand*, 343, 348; Jamieson, *Spring 1865*, 74-75.
36. Bradley, *Last Stand*, 371-95; Moore, Bandel, and Hill, *Old North State*, 156.
37. Bradley, *Last Stand*, 365, 400-01, 404.
38. Chris J. Hartley, *Stoneman's Raid 1865* (Winston-Salem, NC: John F. Blair, 2010), 21-22; Moore, Bandel, and Hill, *Old North State*, 160-61.
39. Hartley, *Stoneman's Raid*, 14-22, 32-33; Bradley, *This Astounding Close*, 133; Inscoe and McKinney, *Heart*, 243.
40. Hartley, *Stoneman's Raid*, 69, 74-77, 79-83, 86-87, 160-63.
41. Ibid., 98-103.
42. Ibid., 162, 167, 190-91, 207; Bradley, *This Astounding Close*, 132-33.
43. Hartley, *Stoneman's Raid*, 228-32; Bradley, *This Astounding Close*, 133-34.
44. Hartley, *Stoneman's Raid*, 231-52, 265; Bradley, *This Astounding Close*, 134-35.
45. Hartley, *Stoneman's Raid*, 254-58.
46. Ibid., 258-63; Bradley, *This Astounding Close*, 135.
47. Hartley, *Stoneman's Raid*, 268, 270-71, 297, 374-76, 393.
48. Bradley, *This Astounding Close*, 28-30, 40-50.
49. Ibid., 50, 69-71.
50. Ibid., 68-69, 79-80.
51. Moore, Bandel, and Hill, *Old North State*, 166-67; Bradley, *This Astounding Close*, 81-83, 88-89, 96-97, 99, 103-05.
52. Bradley, *This Astounding Close*, 114, 119.
53. Ibid., 139-43.
54. Ibid., 123, 126-27.
55. Ibid., 148-49, 155-56; Jamieson, *Spring 1865*, 184, 257-58n45.

56. Bradley, *This Astounding Close*, 157-59; Moore, Bandel, and Hill, *Old North State*, 169-71.
57. Bradley, *This Astounding Close*, 160-61.
58. Ibid., 163-65; Moore, Bandel, and Hill, *Old North State*, 168-69.
59. Bradley, *This Astounding Close*, 165-68.
60. Ibid., 170-71.
61. Ibid., 171-76; Jamieson, *Spring 1865*, 201, 261n132.
62. Bradley, *This Astounding Close*, 178-79, 206-09.
63. Bradley, *This Astounding Close*, 210-11, 213-14, 214-17, 224, 226.
64. Ibid., 221, 222, 224-25, 227, 234.
65. Ibid., 227-28, 253-55.
66. Inscoe and McKinney, *Heart*, 258-59; Kelly Agan, "North Carolina's 'Last Shot' in the Civil War: Surrender of General James Green Martin at Waynesville," 2015, NCpedia, https://www.ncpedia.org/north-carolinas-last-shot-Civil-War.

CHAPTER ELEVEN: NORTH CAROLINA TROOPS WHO FOUGHT OUTSIDE THEIR HOME STATE

1. Moore, Bandel, and Hill, *Old North State*, 17; Hardy, *North Carolina*, 81.
2. Moore, Bandel, and Hill, *Old North State*, 17; Hardy, *North Carolina*, 82.
3. Hardy, *North Carolina*, 83.
4. Stephen W. Sears, *To the Gates of Richmond: The Peninsula Campaign* (New York: Ticknor and Fields, 1992), 155-56; Seven Pines Battle Summary, American Battlefield Protection Program, National Park Service, https://www.nps.gov/abpp/battles/va014/htm; Hardy, *North Carolina*, 84-85.
5. Hardy, *North Carolina*, 85-86.
6. Moore, Bandel, and Hill, *Old North State*, 17-18.
7. George C. Rable, *Fredericksburg! Fredericksburg!* (Chapel Hill: University of North Carolina Press, 2002), 87-88.
8. Perry D. Jamieson and Bradford A. Wineman, *The Maryland and Fredericksburg Campaigns, 1862–1863* (Washington, DC: US Army Center of Military History, 2015), 53-54; Hardy, *North Carolina*, 87-88.
9. *OR* 20, pt. 1:677, 679, 681; Moore, Bandel, and Hill, *Old North State*, 18; Hardy, *North Carolina*, 88-89.
10. Rable, *Fredericksburg!*, 410-19; Stephen W. Sears, *Chancellorsville* (Boston: Houghton Mifflin, 1996), 19-22; Jamieson and Wineman, *Maryland and Fredericksburg*, 55.
11. Sears, *Chancellorsville*, 63-75, 80-82.
12. Bradford A. Wineman, *The Chancellorsville Campaign, January-May 1863* (Washington, DC: US Army Center of Military History, 2013), 9-11, 12-13, 14-18, 24-27; Sears, *Chancellorsville*, 245-47.
13. Moore, Bandel, and Hill, *Old North State*, 41; Hardy, *North Carolina*, 89-90; Wineman, *Chancellorsville*, 27-33; Sears, *Chancellorsville*, 293-97, 446-48.
14. Moore, Bandel, and Hill, *Old North State*, 40; Wineman, *Chancellorsville*, 33-43.
15. Hardy, *North Carolina*, 90; Carol Reardon and Tom Vossler, *The Gettysburg Campaign, June-July 1863* (Washington, DC: US Army Center of Military History, 2013), 8-9, 10.
16. Reardon and Vossler, *Gettysburg*, 10-11, 16-17.
17. Reardon and Vossler, *Gettysburg*, 19-23.
18. Hardy, *North Carolina*, 91; Reardon and Vossler, *Gettysburg*, 23.
19. Hardy, *North Carolina*, 91-92; "'No Man Can Take Those Colors and Live': The Epic Battle of the 24th Michigan and 26th North Carolina at Gettysburg," Civil War Trust Online, www.civilwar.org/battlefields/gettysburg/gettysburg-2011/the-battle-for-herbst-woods.html.
20. Stephen W. Sears, *Gettysburg* (Boston: Houghton Mifflin, 2003), 199-201; Gerard A. Patterson, "The Death of Iverson's Brigade," *Gettysburg Magazine* 5 (July 1, 1991), www.gdg.org/Gettysburg%20Magazine/iverson.html..
21. Patterson, "Death."
22. Larry Tagg, "The Generals of Gettysburg: The Leaders of America's Greatest

Battle," www.rocemabra.com/~roger/tagg/generals/index.html.

23. Reardon and Vossler, *Gettysburg*, 31-32, 35-44.

24. Ibid., 44-46; Hardy, *North Carolina*, 92; Moore, Bandel, and Hill, *Old North State*, 40, 42.

25. Reardon and Vossler, *Gettysburg*, 49.

26. Charles M. Cook, "Fifty-Fifth Regiment," in *Histories of the Several Regiments and Battalions from North Carolina in the Great War, 1861–1865*, ed. Walter Clark (Goldsboro, NC: Nash Brothers, 1901), 3:299-300; Earl J. Hess, *Pickett's Charge: The Last Attack at Gettysburg* (Chapel Hill: University of North Carolina Press, 2001), 252; Hardy, *North Carolina*, 92; Moore, Bandel, and Hill, *Old North State*, 40; Reardon and Vossler, *Gettysburg*, 49-51, 53-55.

27. Reardon and Vossler, *Gettysburg*, 57-59, 61; Sears, *Gettysburg*, 495-98.

28. *OR* 29(1):592-93, 623-25, 629-30; Rappahannock Station Battle Summary, American Battlefield Protection Program, National Park Service, https://www.nps.gov/abpp/battles/va023.htm.

29. Hardy, *North Carolina in the Civil War*, 94, 95.

30. Peter Cozzens, *This Terrible Sound: The Battle of Chickamauga* (Urbana: University of Illinois Press, 1992) 401-02; Theo F. Davidson, "Thirty-Ninth Regiment," in Clark, *Histories*, 2:713-19; Moore, Bandel, and Hill, *Old North State*, 39; Hardy, *North Carolina*, 95-96.

31. Hardy, *North Carolina*, 96.

32. Andrew N. Morris, *The Civil War in the West, 1863* (Washington, DC: US Army Center of Military History, 2016), 40-41.

33. Moore, Bandel, and Hill, *Old North State*, 39; Hardy, *North Carolina*, 96.

34. William A. Dobak, *Freedom by the Sword: The U.S. Colored Troops, 1862–1867* (Washington, DC: US Army Center of Military History, 2011), 63-64; Moore, Bandel, and Hill, *Old North State*, 69.

35. Hardy, *North Carolina*, 97.

36. Dobak, *Freedom*, 64-66.

37. Moore, Bandel, and Hill, *Old North State*, 69; Hardy, *North Carolina*, 98; Dobak, *Freedom*, 67-68.

38. Gordon C. Rhea, *The Battle of the Wilderness, May 5–6, 1864* (Baton Rouge: Louisiana State University Press, 1994), 168-69; David W. Hogan Jr., *The Overland Campaign, 4 May–15 June 1864* (Washington, DC: US Army Center of Military History, 2014), 18-22.

39. Hardy, *North Carolina*, 98-99; Hogan, *Overland*, 26; Moore, Bandel, and Hill, *Old North State*, 67.

40. Hogan, *Overland*, 27, 35-36; Hardy, *North Carolina*, 99-100.

41. Hardy, *North Carolina*, 100; Hogan, *Overland*, 37.

42. Hardy, *North Carolina*, 100-01; Hogan, *Overland*, 40; Thomas H. Johnson Jr., "Watson, Cyrus Barksdale," 1996, NCpedia, https://www.ncpedia.org/biography/watson-cyrus-barksdale.

43. Hardy, *North Carolina*, 100; Hogan, *Overland*, 41.

44. Hardy, *North Carolina*, 101; Hogan, *Overland*, 45-47; Bernard Fisher, "Battle at Meadow Bridge: Forcing a Crossing," Virginia Civil War Trails Historical Marker, HMdb.org, https://www.hmdb.org/marker.asp?marker=15217.

45. Hogan, *Overland*., 51-56, 61-66, 67, 70.

46. J. Britt McCarley, *The Atlanta and Savannah Campaigns, 1864* (Washington, DC: US Army Center of Military History, 2014), 14; Moore, Bandel, and Hill, *Old North State*, 67.

47. McCarley, *Atlanta*, 14-15.

48. Hardy, *North Carolina*, 102; McCarley, *Atlanta*, 16-18.

49. McCarley, *Atlanta*, 18-21; Hardy, *North Carolina*, 102.

50. McCarley, *Atlanta*, 31-33; Earl J. Hess, *Kennesaw Mountain: Sherman, Johnston, and the Atlanta Campaign* (Chapel Hill: University of North Carolina Press, 2013), 40-42.

51. Hess, *Kennesaw Mountain*, 145, 152-53; McCarley, *Atlanta*, 33-38.

52. McCarley, *Atlanta*, 39-44.
53. Ibid.,, 47-49; Billy Kurtz West Jr., "Ector's Brigade in the Civil War" (master's thesis, Texas Tech University, 1987), 50.
54. West, "Ector's Brigade," 50-51.
55. McCarley, *Atlanta*, 50-55, 59-61; West, "Ector's Brigade," 52.
56. McCarley, *Atlanta*, 64-65; Jonesborough Battle Summary, American Battlefield Protection Program, National Park Service, https://www.nps.org/abpp/battles/ga022.htm; West, "Ector's Brigade," 53.
57. Hardy, *North Carolina*, 104; McCarley, *Atlanta*, 65-66; West, "Ector's Brigade," 58-64.
58. Derek W. Frisby, *Campaigns in Mississippi and Tennessee, February–December 1864* (Washington, DC: US Army Center of Military History, 2014), 30-32.
59. Hardy, *North Carolina*, 104; Frisby, *Campaigns*, 42-46; West, "Ector's Brigade," 65.
60. Hardy, *North Carolina*, 104-05; Frisby, *Campaigns*, 46-49.
61. Hardy, *North Carolina*, 105; Jeffrey Craig Weaver, "November 1864–January 1865—Playing Hell in Tennessee," in "58th North Carolina Infantry, Confederate States Army" (unpublished manuscript, 1997), 26th North Carolina Regiment, http://www.26nc.org/History/58th-History/58th%20history.html.
62. Hardy, *North Carolina*, 105-06; West, "Ector's Brigade," 66; Frisby, *Campaigns*, 50-55.
63. Hardy, *North Carolina*, 106; Frisby, *Campaigns*, 56-60.
64. West, "Ector's Brigade," 66-68, 71-72, 74-75; Frisby, *Campaigns*, 60-63; Bradley, *This Astounding Close*, 296.
65. *Raleigh Confederate*, June 23, 1864; John R. Maass, *The Petersburg and Appomattox Campaigns, 1864–1865* (Washington, DC: US Army Center of Military History, 2015), 11-12, 15-18; Hardy, *North Carolina*, 106-07.
66. Maass, *Petersburg*, 19-23; Hardy, *North Carolina*, 107.
67. Moore, Bandel, and Hill, *Old North State*, 67; Maass, *Petersburg*, 23-25; Hardy, *North Carolina*, 107.
68. Maass, *Petersburg*, 26-28; Hardy, *North Carolina*, 108-09; Jeffrey D. Wert, "Wilcox, Cadmus Marcellus," 1996, .NCpedia, https://www.ncpedia.org/biography/wilcox-cadmus-marcellus.
69. Moore, Bandel, and Hill, *Old North State*, 69; Maass, *Petersburg*, 29; Joseph Henry Shea, Medal of Honor—Civil War, Home of Heroes, .https://homeofheroes.com/medal-of-honor-citation/civil-war-medal-of-honor-recipients/.
70. Maass, *Petersburg*, 26-28; Hardy, *North Carolina*, 109.
71. Maass, *Petersburg*, 15; Jeffrey D. Wert, "Closing the Back Door: The Shenandoah Valley Campaign of 1864," American Battlefield Trust, https://battlefields.org/learn/articles/closing-back-door.
72. Wert, "Closing the Back Door"; Hardy, *North Carolina*, 109-10.
73. Maass, *Petersburg*, 35-41; *OR* 47, pt. 2:1270-71.
74. Maass, *Petersburg*, 43-45; Hardy, *North Carolina*, 110.
75. Maass, *Petersburg*, 48-52; Hardy, *North Carolina*, 110-12.
76. Maass, *Petersburg*, 53-54; Hardy, *North Carolina*, 112-13.
77. Maass, *Petersburg*, 53; Hardy, *North Carolina*, 112.
78. Maass, *Petersburg*, 54-56.
79. Chris Calkins, "The Battles of Little Sailor's Creek," American Battlefield Trust, https://www.battlefields.org/learn/articles/battles-little-sailors-creek; Maass, *Petersburg*, 57-59.
80. *OR* 46, pt. 3:619; Hardy, *North Carolina*, 113.
81. Maass, *Petersburg*, 61-64; Hardy, *North Carolina*, 113-14.
82. Moore, Bandel, and Hill, *Old North State*, 111; Hardy, *North Carolina*, 114.
83. John R. DeTreville, "*Shenandoah*, CSS," 2006, NCpedia, https://www.ncpedia.org/shenandoah-css.

CHAPTER TWELVE: FROM RE-

CONSTRUCTION TO THE SPANISH-AMERICAN WAR

1. Moore, Bandel, and Hill, *Old North State*, 176-79; Ansley Herring Wegner, *Phantom Pain: North Carolina's Artificial Limbs Program for Confederate Veterans* (Raleigh: North Carolina Department of Cultural Resources, 2004), 26-27, 32-33.
2. Hardy, *North Carolina*, 115-16; Bradley, *Bluecoats*, 25, 39-40.
3. Much of the discussion that follows about Presidential and Military Reconstruction is based on Bradley, *Bluecoats*, 44–181, with other sources noted.
4. Hardy, *North Carolina*, 119-20.
5. Bradley, *Bluecoats*, 182-83; Hardy, *North Carolina*, 124; Mark L. Bradley, *The Army and Reconstruction* (Washington, DC: US Army Center of Military History, 2015), 47-50.
6. Bradley, *Army*, 50-51.
7. Bradley, *Bluecoats*, 190-91.
8. Bradley, *Army*, 46-47.
9. Bradley, *Bluecoats*, 200-208.
10. Ibid., 210-11, 212-13
11. Ibid., 217-19.
12. Ibid., 222-31.
13. Ibid., 229-34.
14. Hardy, *North Carolina*, 126.
15. Bradley, *Bluecoats*, 250-51.
16. Ibid., 263-64.
17. Lorenzo Dow Brown and William H. Jones, Medal of Honor—Campaigns, Conflicts and Peacetime, Home of Heroes, https://homeofheroes.com/medal-of-honor-citation/campaigns-conflicts-peacetime/campaigns-conflict-and-peace-time-1826-1875/.
18. Ansley Wegner, "William McBryar," 2006, NCpedia, https://www.ncpedia.org/william-mcbrayer; "William McBryar, First Lieutenant, United States Army," Arlington National Cemetery, www.arlingtoncemetery.net/williamm.net; William McBryar, Medal of Honor—Campaigns, Conflicts and Peacetime, Home of Heroes, .https://homeofheroes.com/medal-of-honor-citation/campaigns-conflicts-peace-time/campaigns-conflict-and-peace-time-1826-1875/.
19. Joseph F. Steelman, *North Carolina's Role in the Spanish-American War* (Raleigh: North Carolina Department of Cultural Resources, 1975), 1-2.
20. Ibid., 3, 8-11.
21. Steelman, *North Carolina's Role*, 13-15, 17-21.
22. Steelman, *North Carolina's Role*, 23-27; Willard B. Gatewood Jr., "North Carolina's Negro Regiment in the Spanish-American War," *NCHR* 48 (October 1971): 370-87; David Walbert, "The Third North Carolina Regiment," n.d., NCpedia, https://www.ncpedia.org/anchor/third-north-carolina; LeRae Sikes Umfleet, *A Day of Blood: The 1898 Wilmington Race Riot* (Raleigh: North Carolina Office of Archives and History, 2009), 35, 206n3.
23. Steelman, *North Carolina's Role*, 31-33, 36; David Walbert, "Ensign Worth Bagley," n.d., NCpedia, https://www.ncpedia.org/anchor/ensign-worth-bagley; David Duffy Barrow and Pomeroy Parker, Medal of Honor—Campaigns, Conflicts and Peacetime, Home of Heroes, https://homeofheroes.com/medal-of-honor-citation/campaigns-conflicts-peace-time/campaigns-conflicts-and-peace-time-1876-1925/.

CHAPTER THIRTEEN: THE WORLD WARS

1. Jessica A. Bandel, *North Carolina and the Great War, 1914–1918* (Raleigh: North Carolina Office of Archives and History, 2017), 4-5.
2. Sarah McCulloh Lemmon and Nancy Smith Midgette, *North Carolina and the Two World Wars* (Raleigh: North Carolina Office of Archives and History, 2013), 1-3; Edwin Alexander Anderson, Rufus Zenas Johnston, and Adolphus Staton, Medal of Honor—Campaigns, Conflicts and Peacetime, Home of Heroes, https://homeofheroes.com/medal-of-honor-citation/campaigns-conflicts-peace-time/campaigns-

conflicts-and-peace-time-1876-1925/.

3. Lemmon and Midgette, *North Carolina*, 5, 7-9; Bandel, *North Carolina*, 10-11; Charlie Knight, "Madelon 'Glory' Hancock," North Carolina Museum of History, https://www.ncmuseumofhistory.org/blog/madelon-glory-hancock.

4. Bandel, *North Carolina*, 12, 96; Lemmon and Midgette, *North Carolina*, 10-11.

5. Lemmon and Midgette, *North Carolina*, 11-13; Bandel, *North Carolina*, 96-97; Tom Belton, "Flying the Unfriendly Skies: North Carolinians in the Two World Wars," 2003, NCpedia, https://www.ncpedia.org/history/20th-Century/two-world-wars.

6. Bandel, *North Carolina*, 6-7.

7. Ibid., 8; Lemmon and Midgette, *North Carolina*, 14.

8. Bandel, *North Carolina*, 8-9; Lemmon and Midgette, *North Carolina*, 14, 18-19; Richard W. Stewart, ed., *American Military History: The United States Army in a Global Era, 1917–2008* (Washington, DC: US Army Center of Military History, 2010), 2:23.

9. Bandel, *North Carolina*, 56-57; Lemmon and Midgette, *North Carolina*, 31-34.

10. Bandel, *North Carolina*, 57.

11. Bandel, *North Carolina*, 117; Lemmon and Midgette, *North Carolina*, 34-36.

12. Bandel, *North Carolina*, 20-21; Stewart, *American Military History*, 1917-2008, 2:7.

13. Bandel, *North Carolina*, 22-23, 26-27; Stewart, *American Military History, 1917-2008*, 2:20.

14. Bandel, *North Carolina*, 28, 30; Lemmon and Midgette, *North Carolina*, 71-72.

15. Lemmon and Midgette, *North Carolina*, 63-64; Bandel, *North Carolina*, 85; Stewart, *American Military History, 1917-2008*, 2:27.

16. Bandel, *North Carolina*, 29; Lemmon and Midgette, *North Carolina*, 73-74.

17. Bandel, *North Carolina*, 76-77; Lemmon and Midgette, *North Carolina*, 80.

18. Bandel, *North Carolina*, 58-59.

19. Ibid., 64-65; Paul Branch and Daniel W. Barefoot, "Submarine Attacks," 2006, NCpedia, https://www.ncpedia.org/submarine-attacks.

20. David Worth Bagley was the brother of Worth Bagley, who was mentioned in chapter 12 as the first US Navy officer killed in action in the Spanish-American War. Lemmon and Midgette, *North Carolina*, 80-82.

21. Bandel, *North Carolina*, 78-79, 95, 98-99; Lemmon and Midgette, *North Carolina*, 103-04; Stewart, *American Military History, 1917-2008*, 2:25-26.

22. Lemmon and Midgette, *North Carolina*, 104-07; Bandel, *North Carolina*, 102-03; Stewart, *American Military History, 1917-2008*, 2:48.

23. Lemmon and Midgette, *North Carolina*, 109; Bandel, *North Carolina*, 104; Stewart, *American Military History, 1917-2008*, 2:49-50.

24. Bandel, *North Carolina*, 104-05; Lemmon and Midgette, *North Carolina*, 110.

25. Bandel, *North Carolina*, 106-08.

26. Ibid., 90-91; Henry Johnson, Medal of Honor—World War I, Home of Heroes, https://homeofheroes.com/medal-of-honor-citation/world-war-i-medal-of-honor-recipients/.

27. Lemmon and Midgette, *North Carolina*, 126, 129; Stewart, *American Military History, 1917-2008*, 2:71.

28. Lemmon and Midgette, *North Carolina*, 127-28, 130-32.

29. Ibid., 132; Anita Price Davis, *North Carolina and World War II: A Documentary Portrait* (Jefferson, NC: McFarland, 2015), 6.

30. Lemmon and Midgette, *North Carolina*, 132-33; Davis, *North Carolina*, 5-7; Stewart, *American Military History, 1917-2008*, 2:75-76; "The Atlantic Charter," North Atlantic Treaty Organization, accessed December 29, 2019, https://www.nato.int/cps/en/natohq/official_texts_16912.htm?.

31. Christopher R. Gabel, *The U.S. Army GHQ Maneuvers of 1941* (Washington, DC: US Army Center of Military History, 1992), 133-169; Lemmon and Midgette, *North Carolina*, 145.

32. Davis, *North Carolina*, 9; Stewart, *American Military History*, 1917-2008, 2:76-77; "A Pearl Harbor Fact Sheet," National World War II Museum, New Orleans, accessed December 29, 2019, https://www.census.gov/history/pdf/pearl-harbor-fact-sheet-1.pdf.

33. Lemmon and Midgette, *North Carolina*, 136; Davis, *North Carolina*, 12; Stewart, *American Military History, 1917-2008*, 2:80.

34. Davis, *North Carolina*, 177; Lemmon and Midgette, *North Carolina*, 137-38; Robert D. Billinger Jr. and Jo Ann Williford, "World War II Military Installations in the State," 2006, NCpedia, https://www. ncpedia.org/world-war-ii-part-3-world-war-ii.

35. Davis, *North Carolina*, 74-75, 80-82, 83-85, 123-25, 140-43; Lemmon and Midgette, *North Carolina*, 138-45; Billinger and Williford, "World War II Military Installations," John L. Bell, "Cherry Point Marine Corps Air Station," 2006, NCpedia, https://www. ncpedia.org/cherry-point-marine-corps-air-stati; Timothy L. Howerton, "Davis, Richmond Pearson," 1986, NCpedia, https://www.ncpedia.org/biography/davis-richmond-pearson; "History, 3rd Marine Aircraft Wing," US Marine Corps, https:// 3rdmaw.marines.mil/About/History.

36. Davis, *North Carolina*, 93-95; Eugene Price, "Seymour Johnson Air Force Base," 2006, NCpedia, https://www.ncpedia.org/ seymour-johnson-air-force-base.

37. Franklin D. Roosevelt, "The Great Arsenal of Democracy," American Rhetoric: Top 100 Speeches, https://american-rhetoric.com/speeches/fdrarsenalofdemocracy.html; Robert D. Billinger Jr. and Jo Ann Williford, "North Carolina Contributions in Battle and on the Home Front," 2006, NCpedia, https://www.ncpedia.org/ world-war-ii-part-2-north-carolina; Jim Fowlkes, "Liberty Ships," 2006, NCpedia, https://www.ncpedia.org/liberty-ships; Lemmon and Midgette, *North Carolina*, 151-54.

38. Branch and Barefoot, "Submarine Attacks"; Kelly Agan, "The *Allan Jackson*: First North Carolina Coastal Casualty in 1942 WWII U-Boat Campaign," 2014, NCpedia, https://www.ncpedia.org/allan-jackson-first-north-carolina; Kevin P. Duffus, "U-Boats off the Outer Banks," 2008, NCpedia, https://www.ncpedia.org/history/20th-Century/wwii-uboats.

39. Duffus, "U-Boats," and Branch and Barefoot, "Submarine Attacks"; Davis, *North Carolina*, 150-53.

40. Lemmon and Midgette, *North Carolina*, 191.

41. Davis, *North Carolina*, 151-52, 160-61; Duffus, "U-Boats," and Branch and Barefoot, "Submarine Attacks."

42. Lemmon and Midgette, *North Carolina*, 198-99, 200-01; Davis, *North Carolina*, 116-17; Craig M. Stinson, "*North Carolina*, USS," 2006, NCpedia, https://www.ncpedia.org/north-carolina-uss.

43. Lemmon and Midgette, *North Carolina*, 196-97; "The *Memphis Belle*: American Icon," National Museum of the United States Air Force, accessed December 29, 2019, https://www.nationalmuseum.af.mil/ Visit/Museum-Exhibits/Fact-Sheets/Display/Article/1506245/the-memphis-belle-american-icon/.

44. Davis, *North Carolina*, 70; Lemmon and Midgette, *North Carolina*, 203.

45. W. Lee Johnston, "Lee, William Carey," 1991, NCpedia, https://www.ncpedia.org/ biography/lee-william-carey; Billinger and Williford, "North Carolina Contributions."

46. Billinger and Williford. "North Carolina Contributions"; Lemmon and Midgette, *North Carolina*, 195.

47. Lemmon and Midgette, *North Carolina*, 195, 198.

48. Ibid., 199, 202; "History, 2nd Marine Division," US Marine Corps, https://www. 2ndmardiv.marines.mil/About/History/; Thomas J. Farnham, "Camp Lejeune," 2006, NCpedia, https://www.ncpedia.org/ camp-lejeune.

49. Davis, *North Carolina*, 179, 181, 182-83; William David Halyburton Jr. and Jacklyn Harold Lucas, Medal of Honor—World

War II, Home of Heroes, https://homeofheroes.com/medal-of-honor-citation/world-war-ii-medal-of-honor-recipients/.
50. Davis, *North Carolina*, 181-82; Rufus Geddie Herring, Medal of Honor—World War II, Home of Heroes, https://homeofheroes.com/medal-of-honor-citation/world-war-ii-medal-of-honor-recipients/.
51. "Retired Col. Charles P. Murray Jr., Medal of Honor Recipient, Dies at 89," *Washington Post*, August 15, 2011; Davis, *North Carolina I*, 180, 183-84, 186-87; Ray E. Eubanks, Charles Patrick "Chuck" Murray, Max Thompson, and Henry F. Warner, Medal of Honor—World War II, Home of Heroes, https://homeofheroes.com/medal-of-honor-citation/world-war-ii-medal-of-honor-recipients/.
52. Davis, *North Carolina*, 177.
53. Lemmon and Midgette, *North Carolina*, 193-94; Davis, *North Carolina*, 105-07; Margalit Fox, "Naomi Parker Fraley, the Real Rosie the Riveter, Dies at 96," *New York Times*, January 22, 2018.
54. Davis, *North Carolina*, 189-92; Lemmon and Midgette, *North Carolina*, 162-65.
55. Billinger and Williford, "North Carolina Contributions"; Lemmon and Midgette, *North Carolina*, 158-61.
56. Billinger, Robert D., Jr. "Prisoners of War in North Carolina," NCpedia, https//www.ncpedia.org/history/20th-Century/wwii-pows.

CHAPTER FOURTEEN: FROM THE COLD WAR TO THE WAR ON TERROR

1. Stewart, *American Military History, 1917-2008*, 2:210-19.
2. David L. Cockrell, "Korean War," 2006, NCpedia, https://www.ncpedia.org/korean-war.
3. Stewart, *American Military History, 1917-2008*, 2:221-26, 231-36, 244-52.
4. Cockrell, "Korean War"; Jerry Kirt Crump, Charles George, and Bryant Homer Womack, Medal of Honor—Korean War, Home of Heroes, https://homeofheroes.com/medal-of-honor-citation/korean-war-medal-of-honor-recipients/.
5. Stewart, *American Military History, 1917-2008*, 2:257-59, 267-68.
6. Caron Myers, "The Night Hydrogen Bombs Fell over North Carolina," *Our State*, May 29, 2012, https://www.ourstate.com/hydrogen-bombs-north-carolina/; Jessica Sedgwick, "January 1961: Bombs over Goldsboro," North Carolina Miscellany (blog), UNC Library, January 1, 2008, https://blogs.lib.unc.edu/ncm/index.php/2008/01/01/this_month_jan_1961/; Joel Dobson, *The Goldsboro Broken Arrow* (n.p.: Lulu Publishing Services, 2013), 4-5.
7. "Nuclear Mishap," essay, North Carolina State Historic Marker F-70, 2011, accessed December 29, 2019, www.ncmarkers.com/Markers.aspx?Markerid=F-70; Sedgwick, "January 1961: Bombs over Goldsboro."
8. "The Full Story Behind the Goldsboro Incident," January 24, 2001, Ibiblio, www.ibiblio.org/bomb/full-story.html.
9. Stewart, *American Military History, 1917-2008*, 2:270-71; Graham Allison and Philip Zelikow, *Essence of Decision: Explaining the Cuban Missile Crisis* (New York: Addison Wesley Longman, 1999), 80; "The Cuban Missile Crisis, October 1962," Office of the Historian, Bureau of Public Affairs, US Department of State, https://history.state.gov/milestones/1961-1968/cuban-missile-crisis; President John F. Kennedy on the Cuban Missile Crisis, Great Speeches Collection, The History Place, www.historyplace.com/speeches/jfk-cuban.htm.
10. "Cuban Missile Crisis."
11. Corporal Scott L. Tomaszycki, "Cherry Point Pilots Played Pivotal Role in Cuban Missile Crisis," October 30, 2012, press release, Marine Corps Air Station Cherry Point, https://www.cherrypoint.marines.mil/News/Article/525436/cherry-point-pi-

lots-played-pivotal-role-in-cuban-missile-crisis/.

12. "Strategic Arms Limitations Talks/Treaty (SALT) I and II," Office of the Historian, Bureau of Public Affairs, US Department of State, https://www.state.gov/milestones/1969-1976/salt.

13. Stewart, *American Military History, 1917-2008*, 2:289-90.

14. Ibid., 2:306, 310-34.

15. John L. Bell, "Cherry Point Marine Corps Air Station," 2006, NCpedia, https://www.ncpedia.org/cherry-point-marine-corps-air-stati; "History, North Carolina Air National Guard," NC Air National Guard, https://www.145aw.ang.af.mil/About-Us/History/; Shelby L. Stanton, *Vietnam Order of Battle* (Washington, DC: US News Books, 1981), 217.

16. Jo Ann Williford, "Vietnam War," 2006, NCpedia, https://www.ncpedia.org/vietnam-war; Roy Parker Jr., "Fort Bragg," 2006, NCpedia, https://www.ncpedia.org/fort-bragg.

17. Stewart, *American Military History, 1917-2008*, 2:337-370.

18. Ibid., 2:368; Williford, "Vietnam War."

19. Eugene Ashley Jr., Harold Bascom Durham Jr., Lawrence Joel, Franklin Douglas Miller, Robert Martin Patterson, and Mitchell William Stout, Medal of Honor—Vietnam, Home of Heroes, https://homeofheroes.com/medal-of-honor-citation/vietnam-medal-of-honor-recipients/.

20. Edgar F. Raines and Richard W. Stewart, *Operation Urgent Fury: The Invasion of Grenada, 1983* (Washington, DC: US Army Center of Military History, 2008), 5, 7-8, 10-13, 15, 18-25, 26-29, 36.

21. Ibid., 30.

22. R. Cody Phillips, *Operation Just Cause: The Incursion into Panama* (Washington, DC: US Army Center of Military History, 2004), 8-9, 21-22, 44, 46-47, 49; US Army casualties, www.operationjustcause.us/casualties.html.

23. Frank N. Schubert and Theresa L. Kraus, eds., *The Whirlwind War: The United States Army in Operations Desert Shield and Desert Storm* (Washington, DC: US Army Center of Military History, 1995), 51-53; Alexander R. Stoesen, "Persian Gulf War," 2006, NCpedia, https://www.ncpedia.org/persian-gulf-war.

24. The Louis Berger Group, *Semper Fidelis: A Brief History of Onslow County, North Carolina, and Marine Corps Base, Camp Lejeune* (Jacksonville, NC: US Marine Corps, n.d.), 83-84.

25. Schubert and Kraus, *Whirlwind War*, 153-59, 173-205; Corporal Mike Vrabel, "Ten Years Later: Base CG Recalls Gulf War," press release, January 18, 2001, US Marine Corps, https://www.lejeune.marines.mil/News/Article/511572/ten-years-later-base-cg-recalls-gulf-war/; Stoesen, "Persian Gulf War."

26. Walter E. Kretchik, Robert F. Baumann, and John T. Fishel, *Invasion, Intervention, "Intervasion": A Concise History of the U.S. Army in Operation Uphold Democracy* (Fort Leavenworth, KS: US Army Command and General Staff College Press, 1998), 20, 27, 74-76, 166-68; Drew Brooks, "1,200 Bragg Paratroopers Deployed to Afghanistan," *Fayetteville Observer*, updated September 22, 2017, https://www.fayobserver.com/news/20170921/1200-bragg-paratroopers-deployed-to-afghanistan; Richard W. Stewart, *The United States Army in Somalia, 1992–1994* (Washington, DC: US Army Center of Military History, 2002), 5.

27. Stewart, *United States Army in Somalia*, 9-10, 19-21, 23, 25-26.

28. Mary Ellen Condon-Rall, *Disaster on Green Ramp: The Army's Response* (Washington, DC: US Army Center of Military History, 1996), 3-6.

29. Ibid., 6-17, 25-33, 127, 131-34; Drew Brooks, "The Green Ramp Disaster, 24 Years Later," *Fayetteville Observer*, March 25, 2018, www.fayobserver.com/news/20180322/green-ramp-disaster-24-years-later.

30. R. Cody Phillips, *Bosnia-Herzegovina: The U.S. Army's Role in Peace Enforcement*

Operations, 1995–2004 (Washington, DC: US Army Center of Military History, 2005), 5, 10-15.

31. On February 28, 2011, Pope Air Force Base reverted to the army and was renamed Pope Field. Paraglide, "Fort Bragg Takes Over Pope Air Force Base under BRAC," February 25, 2011, https://www.army.mil/article/52441/fort-bragg-takes-over-pope-air-force-base-under-brac; Phillips, *Bosnia-Herzegovina*, 16-23; "Bosnia Peacekeepers, 1998–1999," 1st Cavalry Division, www.first-team.us/tableaux/chapt_13/; "65th Military Police Company (Airborne)," GlobalSecurity.org, https://www. globalsecurity.org/military/agency/army/65mp-co.htm; "Week of 22–27 January 1996: Life in Tent City at Tuzla AB,", picture gallery, Operation Joint Endeavor, NATO, https://www.nato.int/ifor/pictures/i-960127.html; Major Edward B. Lescher, "How Effective Was Civil Affairs in Bosnia?" (master's thesis, Florida Atlantic University, 2001), 77-79, 84.

32. Cody R. Phillips, *Operation Joint Guardian: The U.S. Army in Kosovo* (Washington, DC: US Army Center of Military History, 2007), 15, 19, 51-57; "NATO's Role in Kosovo," updated July 15, 1999, NATO, www.nato.int/kosovo/history.htm; Drew Brooks, "Families Say Goodbye as Soldiers from the 82nd Airborne Head to Kosovo," *Fayetteville Observer*, June 22, 2017.

33. Stewart, *American Military History, 1917-2008*, 2:463-64.

34. Richard W. Stewart, *The United States Army in Afghanistan: Operation Enduring Freedom, October 2001–March 2002* (Washington, DC: US Army Center of Military History, 2005), 4-8, 30.

35. Brooks, "1,200 Bragg Paratroopers"; "Staff Sergeant Robert James Miller, Medal of Honor, Operation Enduring Freedom," Army.mil, https://www.army.mil/medalofhonor/miller/profile.html.

36. Saddam Hussein was captured in December 2003 and executed three years later. Colonel Rod Andrew Jr., "The Battle of An-Nasiriyah," US Marine Corps, https://www.marines.mil/Portals/1/Publications/U.S.%20Marines%20in%20Battle_an-Nasiriyah%20%20PCN%2010600000700_1.pdf; Stewart, *American Military History, 1917-2008*, 2:480-90.

37. Nicholas J. Schlosser, *The Surge, 2007–2008* (Washington, DC: US Army Center of Military History, 2017), 33.

38. Brooks, "1,200 Bragg Paratroopers."

Bibliography

PRIMARY SOURCES

Campbell, John. Papers, microfilm reel no.1, Tennessee State Library. http://philnorf.tripod.com/letterof.htm.

Hariot, Thomas. *A Briefe and True Report of the New Found Land of Virginia.* Frankfort, Germany: Theodore De Bry, 1590.

Johnston, Samuel. Papers, Hayes Collection, Wilson Library, University of North Carolina-Chapel Hill.

Sherman, William T. *Memoirs.* 2 vols. in 1. Reprint, New York: Da Capo Press, 1984.

Showman, Richard, Dennis M. Conrad, et al., eds. *The Papers of General Nathanael Greene.* 13 vols. Chapel Hill: University of North Carolina Press, 1976–2006.

Smith, Paul H., ed. *Letters of Delegates to Congress, 1774–1789.* 25 vols. Washington, DC: Library of Congress, 1979.

Supplement to the Official Records of the Union and Confederate Armies. 100 vols. Wilmington, NC: Broadfoot, 1997–2001.

US War Department. *Papers of the War Department, 1784–1800.* http://wardepartmentpapers.org/.

———. *The War of the Rebellion: A Compilation of the Official Records of the Union and Confederate Armies.* 128 vols. Washington, DC: Government Printing Office, 1880–1901.

Welles, Gideon. *Diary of Gideon Welles.* 3 vols. Boston and New York: Houghton Mifflin, 1911.

NEWSPAPERS

Carolina Watchman
Fayetteville Observer
New York Times
Pennsylvania Evening Post
Raleigh Confederate
Raleigh News and Observer
Washington Post

SECONDARY SOURCES

Agan, Kelly. "The *Allan Jackson*: First North Carolina Coastal Casualty in 1942 WWII U-Boat Campaign," 2014. NCpedia. https://www.ncpedia.org/allan-jackson-first-north-carolina.

———. "North Carolina's 'Last Shot' in the Civil War: Surrender of General James Green Martin at Waynesville," 2015. NCpedia.https://www.ncpedia.org/north-carolinas-last-shot-Civil-War.

Allison, Graham, and Philip Zelikow. *Essence of Decision: Explaining the Cuban Missile Crisis.* New York: Addison Wesley Longman, 1999.

Anderson, Fred. *Crucible of War: The Seven Years' War and the Fate of Empire in British North America, 1754-1766.* New York: Alfred A. Knopf, 2000.

Andrew, Colonel Rod, Jr. "The Battle of An-Nasiriyah. US Marine Corps. https://www.marines.mil/Portals/1/Publications/U.S.%20Marines%20in%20Battle_an-Nasiriyah%20%20PCN%2010600000700_1.pdf.

Andrews, Charles M., ed. *Original Narratives of Early American History: Narratives of the Insurrections, 1675–1690.* New York: Charles Scribner's Sons, 1915.

"The Atlantic Charter." North Atlantic Treaty Organization. https://www.nato.int/cps/en/natohq/official_texts_16912.htm?.

Babits, Lawrence E. *A Devil of a Whipping: The Battle of Cowpens.* Chapel Hill: University of North Carolina Press, 1998.

Babits, Lawrence E., and Joshua B. Howard. *Long, Obstinate, and Bloody: The Battle of Guilford Courthouse.* Chapel Hill: University of North Carolina Press, 2009.

Baker, Thomas E. *Another Such Victory: The Story of the American Defeat at Guilford Courthouse That Helped Win the War for Independence.* Fort Washington, PA: Eastern National, 2005.

Bandel, Jessica A. *North Carolina and the Great War, 1914–1918.* Raleigh: North Carolina Office of Archives and History, 2017.

Barbuto, Richard V. *The Canadian Theater, 1813.* Washington, DC: US Army Center of Military History, 2013.

Barratt, John. *Armada 1588: The Spanish Assault on England.* South Yorkshire, England: Penn & Sword Books, 2005.

Barrett, John G. *The Civil War in North Carolina.* Chapel Hill: University of North Carolina Press, 1963.

Barth, Jonathan. "'The Sinke of America': Society in the Albemarle Borderlands of North Carolina, 1663–1729." *North Carolina Historical Review* 87 (2010): 1-27.

Bassett, John S. "The Regulators of North Carolina, 1765-1771," *Annual Report of the American Historical Association for the Year 1894.* Washington: Government Printing Office, 1895.

Battle, Kemp P. "Otway Burns, Privateer and Legislator." *North Carolina University Magazine*, Old Series 32, no. 1 (October 1901).

Beard, Rick. "Murder in the Mountains." *New York Times*, January 19, 2013. https://opinionator.blogs.nytimes.com/2013/01/19/murder-in-the-mountains/.

Beck, Robin A., Jr. "From Joara to Chiaha: Spanish Exploration of the Appalachian Summit Area, 1540–1568," *Southeastern Archaeology* 16 (1997):162–169.

Beck, Robin A., Jr., et al. "Identifying Fort San Juan." *Southeastern Archaeology* 25, no. 1 (Summer 2006).

Bell, John L. "Cherry Point Marine Corps Air Station," 2006. NCpedia. https://www.ncpedia.org/cherry-point-marine-corps-air-stati.

Belton, Tom. "Flying the Unfriendly Skies: North Carolinians in the Two World Wars," 2003. NCpedia. https://www.ncpedia.org/history/20th-Century/two-world-wars.

Bennett, Charles E. *A Quest for Glory: Major General Robert Howe and the American Revolution*. Chapel Hill: University of North Carolina Press, 1990.

Billinger, Robert D., Jr., and Jo Ann Williford. "North Carolina Contributions in Battle and on the Home Front," 2006. NCpedia. https://www.ncpedia.org/world-war-ii-part-2-north-carolina.

———. "World War II Military Installations in the State," 2006. NCpedia. https://www.ncpedia.org/world-war-ii-part-3-world-war-ii.

Birtle, Andrew J. "The Origins of the Legion of the United States." *Journal of Military History* 67, no. 4 (October 2003): 1249-61.

Black, Jeremy. *The War of 1812 in the Age of Napoleon*. Norman: University of Oklahoma Press, 2009.

Blackmon, Richard D. *A Dark and Bloody Ground: The American Revolution along the Southern Frontier*. Yardley, PA: Westholme, 2012.

"Bosnia Peacekeepers, 1998–1999." 1st Cavalry Division. www.first-team.us/tableaux/chapt_13/.

Bradley, Mark L. *The Army and Reconstruction*. Washington, DC: US Army Center of Military History, 2015.

———. *Bluecoats and Tar Heels: Soldiers and Civilians in Reconstruction North Carolina*. Lexington: University Press of Kentucky, 2009.

———. *Last Stand in the Carolinas: The Battle of Bentonville*. Campbell, CA: Savas Woodbury, 1996.

———. *This Astounding Close: The Road to Bennett Place*. Chapel Hill: University of North Carolina Press, 2000.

Branch, Paul, and Daniel W. Barefoot. "Submarine Attacks," 2006, NCpedia. https://www.ncpedia.org/submarine-attacks.

Browning, Judkin. *Shifting Loyalties: The Union Occupation of Eastern North Carolina*. Chapel Hill: University of North Carolina Press, 2014.

Buchanan, John. *The Road to Guilford Courthouse*. New York: John Wiley and Sons, 1997.

Butler, Lindley S. "The Governors of Albemarle County, 1663–1689." *North Carolina Historical Review* 46 (1969): 281-299.

———. *North Carolina and the Coming of the Revolution, 1763–1776*. Raleigh: North Carolina Division of Archives and History, 1976.

———. *Pirates, Privateers, and Rebel Raiders of the Carolina Coast*. Chapel Hill: University of North Carolina Press, 2000.

———. "Speedwell Furnace: The Ironworks on Troublesome Creek." Rockingham County Historical Society pamphlet, 1972.

Calkins, Chris. "The Battles of Little Sailor's Creek." American Battlefield Trust. https://www.battlefields.org/learn/articles/battles-little-sailors-creek.

Calloway, Collin G. *The Revolution in Indian Country*. Cambridge: Cambridge University Press, 1995.

———. *The Scratch of a Pen: 1763 and the Transformation of North America*. New York: Oxford University Press, 2006.

Carbone, John S. *The Civil War in Coastal North Carolina*. Raleigh: North Carolina Division of Archives and History, 2001.

Carr, J. Revell. *Seeds of Discontent: The Deep Roots of the American Revolution 1650-1750*. New York: Walker Books, 2008.

Chartrand, Rene. *Colonial American Troops 1610-1774*. 3 vols. Oxford, UK: Osprey, 2002.

"The Civil War at Fort Fisher: A Joint Attack upon Wilmington." North Carolina Historic Sites. https://historicsites.nc.gov/all-sites/fort-fisher/history/civil-war-ft-fisher.

Clark, Walter, ed. *Histories of the Several Regiments and Battalions from North Carolina in the Great War, 1861–1865*. 5 vols. Goldsboro, NC: Nash Brothers, 1901.

Cockrell, David L. "Korean War," 2006. NCpedia. https://www.ncpedia.org/korean-war.

Commager, Henry Steele, and Richard B. Morris. *The Spirit of Seventy-Six*. New York: Harper & Row, 1975 reprint.

Condon-Rall, Mary Ellen. *Disaster on Green Ramp: The Army's Response*. Washington, DC: US Army Center of Military History, 1996.

Cozzens, Peter. *This Terrible Sound: The Battle of Chickamauga*. Urbana: University of Illinois Press, 1992.

Crow, Jeffery. *A Chronicle of North Carolina during the American Revolution*. Raleigh: North Carolina Division of Archives and History, 1975.

"The Cuban Missile Crisis, October 1962." Office of the Historian, Bureau of Public Affairs, US Department of State. https://history.state.gov/ milestones/1961-1968/cuban-missile-crisis.

David Duffy Barrow and Pomeroy Parker. Medal of Honor—Campaigns, Conflicts and Peacetime, Home of Heroes. https://homeofheroes.com/medal-of-honor-citation/campaigns-conflicts-peace-time/campaigns-conflicts-and-peace-time-1876-1925/.

Davies, K. G., ed. *Documents of the American Revolution (Colonial Office Series)*. 21 vols. Dublin: Irish University Press, 1976.

Davis, Anita Price. *North Carolina and World War II: A Documentary Portrait.* Jefferson, NC: McFarland, 2015.

DeMond, Robert O. The *Loyalists in North Carolina during the Revolution.* Durham, NC: Duke University Press, 1940.

DeTreville, John R. "*Shenandoah*, CSS," 2006. NCpedia. https://www.ncpedia.org/shenandoah-css.

Dobak, William A. *Freedom by the Sword: The U.S. Colored Troops, 1862–1867.* Washington, DC: US Army Center of Military History, 2011.

Dobson, Joel. *The Goldsboro Broken Arrow.* N.p.: Lulu Publishing Services, 2013.

Douglass, Elisha P. *Rebels and Democrats: The Struggle for Equal Political Rights and Majority Rule during the American Revolution.* Chapel Hill: University of North Carolina Press, 1955.

Dowd, Clement. *Life of Zebulon B. Vance.* Charlotte: Observer Printing and Publishing House, 1897.

Downey, Christopher B. *Stede Bonnet: Charleston's Gentleman Pirate.* Charleston, SC: History Press, 2012.

Drake, Francis S. *Life and Correspondence of Henry Knox: Major-general in the American Revolutionary Army.* Boston: Samuel G. Drake, 1873.

Duffus, Kevin P. "U-Boats off the Outer Banks," 2008. NCpedia. https://www.ncpedia.org/history/20th-Century/wwii-uboats.

Edwin Alexander Anderson, Rufus Zenas Johnston, and Adolphus Staton. Medal of Honor—Campaigns, Conflicts and Peacetime, Home of Heroes. https://homeofheroes.com/medal-of-honor-citation/campaigns-conflicts-peace-time/campaigns-conflicts-and-peace-time-1876-1925/.

Ekirch, Roger. "*Poor Carolina*": *Politics and Society in Colonial North Carolina, 1729-1776.* Chapel Hill: University of North Carolina Press, 1981.

Elting, John R. *Amateurs, to Arms!: A Military History of the War of 1812.* New York: Da Capo Press, 1995.

Eugene Ashley, Jr., Harold Bascom Durham, Jr., Lawrence Joel, Franklin Douglas Miller, Robert Martin Patterson, and Mitchell William Stout. Medal of Honor—Vietnam, Home of Heroes. https://homeofheroes.com/medal-of-honor-citation/vietnam-medal-of-honor-recipients/.

Farnham, Thomas J. "Camp Lejeune," 2006. NCpedia. https://www.ncpedia.org/camp-lejeune.

Fischer, Kirsten. *Suspect Relations: Sex, Race, and Resistance in Colonial North Carolina.* Ithaca, NY: Cornell University Press, 2002.

Fisher, Bernard. "Battle at Meadow Bridge: Forcing a Crossing." Virginia Civil War Trails Historical Marker, HMdb.org (Historical Marker Database). https://www.hmdb.org/marker.asp?marker=15217.

Fissel, Mark Charles. *English Warfare, 1511–1642.* London: Routledge, 2001.

Fitch, William Edward. *Some Neglected History of North Carolina; Being an Account of the Revolution of the Regulators and of the Battle of Alamance, the First Battle of the American Revolution.* New York: Neale, 1905.

Fitzpatrick, John C., ed. *The Writings of George Washington from the Original Manuscript Sources, 1745–1799.* Washington, DC: US Government Printing Office, 1931–44.

Fonvielle, Chris E., Jr. *Fort Fisher 1865: The Photographs of T. H. O'Sullivan.* Carolina Beach, NC: SlapDash, 2011.

———. *The Wilmington Campaign: Last Rays of Departing Hope.* Campbell, CA: Savas, 1997.

Fredericksen, John C. *The United States Army in the War of 1812.* Jefferson, NC: McFarland, 2009.

Frisby, Derek W. *Campaigns in Mississippi and Tennessee, February–December 1864.* Washington, DC: US Army Center of Military History, 2014.

"The Full Story Behind the Goldsboro Incident," January 24, 2001. Ibiblio. www.ibiblio.org/bomb/full-story.html.

Gabel, Christopher R. *The U.S. Army GHQ Maneuvers of 1941.* Washington, DC: US Army Center of Military History, 1992.

Gaff, Alan D. *Bayonets in the Wilderness: Anthony Wayne's Legion in the Old Northwest.* Norman: University of Oklahoma Press, 2004.

Gallay, Alan. *The Indian Slave Trade: The Rise of the English Empire in the American South, 1670–1717.* New Haven, CT: Yale University Press, 2003.

Gatewood, Willard B., Jr. "North Carolina's Negro Regiment in the Spanish-American War." *North Carolina Historical Review* 48 (October 1971): 370-87.

Gerard, Philip. *The Last Battleground: The Civil War Comes to North Carolina.* Chapel Hill: University of North Carolina Press, 2019.

Gibbes, Robert W. *Documentary History of the American Revolution.* New York: Appleton, 1855.

Gipson, Lawrence Henry. *The Great War for Empire: The Years of Defeat, 1754-1757.* New York: Alfred A. Knopf, 1946.

Gordon, William A., comp. *A Compilation of Registers of the Army of the United States, 1815–1837.* Washington, DC: James C. Dunn, 1837.

Grant, James. "Journal of Lieutenant-Colonel James Grant, Commanding an Expedition against the Cherokee Indians, June-July, 1761." *Florida Historical Society Quarterly* 12, no. 1 (July 1933).

Gruber, Ira D. "Britain's Southern Strategy." In *The Revolutionary War in the South: Power, Conflict, and Leadership,* edited by W. Robert Higgins. Durham, NC: Duke University Press, 1979.

Haarmann, Albert W. "American Uniforms during the French and Indian War." *Military Collector and Historian* 32, no. 2 (Summer 1980): 61.

Hardy, Michael C. *North Carolina in the Civil War.* Charleston, SC: History Press, 2011.

Harris, William C. *North Carolina and the Coming of the Civil War.* Raleigh: North Carolina Division of Archives and History, 1988.

Hartley, Chris J. *Stoneman's Raid 1865.* Winston-Salem, NC: John F. Blair, 2010.

Hatley, Tom. *The Dividing Paths: Cherokees and South Carolinians through the Revolutionary Era.* New York: Oxford University Press, 1995.

Henry Johnson. Medal of Honor—World War I, Home of Heroes. https://homeofheroes.com/medal-of-honor-citation/world-war-i-medal-of-honor-recipients/.

Hess, Earl J. *Kennesaw Mountain: Sherman, Johnston, and the Atlanta Campaign.* Chapel Hill: University of North Carolina Press, 2013.

———. *Pickett's Charge: The Last Attack at Gettysburg.* Chapel Hill: University of North Carolina Press, 2001.

Hickey, Donald R. *The War of 1812: A Forgotten Conflict.* Urbana and Chicago: University of Illinois Press, 1989.

Higginbotham, Don, ed. *The Papers of James Iredell.* 3 vols. Raleigh, NC: Division of Archives and History, Department of Cultural Resources, 1976.

Hinderaker, Eric, and Peter C. Mancall, *At the Edge of Empire: The Backcountry in British North America.* Baltimore: Johns Hopkins University Press, 2003.

"History, North Carolina Air National Guard." North Carolina Air National Guard. https://www.145aw.ang.af.mil/About-Us/History/.

"History, 2nd Marine Division." US Marine Corps. https://www.2ndmardiv.marines.mil/About/History/.

"History, 3rd Marine Aircraft Wing." US Marine Corps. https://3rdmaw.marines.mil/About/History.

Hitsman, J. Mackay. *The Incredible War of 1812: A Military History.* Montreal: Robin Brass Studio, updated ed., 1999.

Hoffman, Paul E. "Lucas Vazquez de Ayllon's Discovery and Colony." In *The Forgotten Centuries: Indians and Europeans in the American South, 1521–1704,* edited by Charles Hudson and Carmen Chaves Tesser. Athens: University of Georgia Press, 1994.

———. *Spain and the Roanoke Voyages.* Raleigh: North Carolina Department of Cultural Resources, 1987.

Hoffman, Williams S. *North Carolina in the Mexican War, 1846–1848.* Raleigh: North Carolina Department of Archives and History, 1959.

Hogan, David W., Jr. *The Overland Campaign, 4 May–15 June 1864.* Washington, DC: US Army Center of Military History, 2014.

Horn, James. *A Kingdom Strange: The Brief and Tragic History of the Lost Colony of Roanoke.* New York: Basic Books, 2011.

Howerton, Timothy L. "Davis, Richmond Pearson," 1986. NCpedia. https://www.ncpedia.org/biography/davis-richmond-pearson.

Hudson, Charles. "The Hernando de Soto Expedition, 1539–1543." In *The Forgotten Centuries: Indians and Europeans in the American South, 1521–1704,* edited by Charles Hudson and Carmen Chaves Tesser. Athens: University of Georgia Press, 1994.

———. *The Juan Pardo Expeditions: Exploration of the Carolinas and Tennessee, 1566–1568.* Tuscaloosa: University of Alabama Press, 2009.

Inscoe, John C., and Gordon B. McKinney. *The Heart of Confederate Appalachia: Western North Carolina in the Civil War.* Chapel Hill: University of North Carolina Press, 2000.

Jamieson, Perry D. *Spring 1865: The Closing Campaigns of the Civil War*. Lincoln: University of Nebraska Press, 2015.

———, and Bradford A. Wineman. *The Maryland and Fredericksburg Campaigns, 1862–1863*. Washington, DC: US Army Center of Military History, 2015.

Jerry Kirt Crump, Charles George, and Bryant Homer Womack. Medal of Honor—Korean War, Home of Heroes. https://homeofheroes.com/medal-of-honor-citation/korean-war-medal-of-honor-recipients/.

Johnson, Thomas H., Jr. "Watson, Cyrus Barksdale," 1996. NCpedia. https://www.ncpedia.org/biography/watson-cyrus-barksdale.

Johnson, Timothy D. *A Gallant Little Army: The Mexico City Campaign*. Lawrence: University Press of Kansas, 2007.

Johnston, W. Lee. "Lee, William Carey," 1991. NCpedia. https://www.ncpedia.org/biography/lee-william-carey.

Jones, E. Alfred. "The American Regiment in the Cartagena Expedition." *Virginia Magazine of History and Biography* 30, no.1 (January 1922): 1-20.

Jonesborough Battle Summary. American Battlefield Protection Program, National Park Service. https://www.nps.org/abpp/battles/ga022.htm.

Jordan, Weymouth T., Jr., and Gerald W. Thomas. "Massacre at Plymouth: April 20, 1864." *North Carolina Historical Review* 72 (April 1995): 125–97.

Joseph Henry Shea. Medal of Honor—Civil War, Home of Heroes. https://homeofheroes.com/medal-of-honor-citation/civil-war-medal-of-honor-recipients/.

Kars, Marjoleine. *Breaking Loose Together: The Regulator Rebellion in Pre-Revolutionary North Carolina*. Chapel Hill: University of North Carolina Press, 2002.

Keenan, Jerry. *Encyclopedia of American Indian Wars, 1492–1890*. Santa Barbara, CA: ABC-CLIO, 1997.

Kimball, Gertrude, ed. *The Correspondence of William Pitt while Secretary of State* . . . . 2 vols. New York: Macmillan, 1906.

Konstam, Angus. *Blackbeard's Last Fight: Pirate Hunting in North Carolina, 1718*. Oxford, UK: Osprey, 2013.

Kretchik, Walter E., Robert F. Baumann, and John T. Fishel. *Invasion, Intervention, "Intervasion": A Concise History of the U.S. Army in Operation Uphold Democracy*. Fort Leavenworth, KS: US Army Command and General Staff College Press, 1998.

Kupperman, Karen Ordahl. *Roanoke: The Abandoned Colony*. Lanham, MD: Rowman and Littlefield, 2007.

———. "Roanoke's Achievement." *European Visions: American Voices*. https://britishmuseum.org/pdf/1-Kupperman-Roanoke.pdf.

Lavender, David. *De Soto, Coronado, Cabrillo: Explorers of the Northern Mystery*. Washington, DC: National Park Service, 1992.

La Vere, David. *The Tuscarora War: Indians, Settlers, and the Fight for the Carolina Colonies*. Chapel Hill: University of North Carolina Press, 2013.

Leach, Douglas Edward. *Roots of Conflict: British Armed Forces and Colonial Americans, 1677-1763.* Chapel Hill: University of North Carolina Press, 1986.

Lee, Enoch L. *Indian Wars in North Carolina, 1663–1763.* Raleigh: Office of Archives and History, North Carolina Department of Cultural Resources, 2011.

Lee, Wayne. "Fortify, Fight, or Flee: Tuscarora and Cherokee Defensive Warfare and Military Culture Adaptation." *Journal of Military History* 68 (2004).

Lefler, Hugh, and Albert R. Newsome. *North Carolina: The History of a Southern State.* Chapel Hill: University of North Carolina Press, 1954.

Lefler, Hugh, and William S. Powell. *Colonial North Carolina: A History.* New York: Scribner, 1973.

Lemmon, Sarah McCulloh. *Frustrated Patriots: North Carolina and the War of 1812.* Chapel Hill: University of North Carolina Press, 1973.

———. *North Carolina and the War of 1812.* Raleigh: North Carolina Division of Archives and History, 1971.

———. and Nancy Smith Midgette. *North Carolina and the Two World Wars.* Raleigh: North Carolina Office of Archives and History, 2013.

Lengel, Edward G. "Bayonets at Midnight: The Battle of Stony Point." *Military History* (January 2010): 36-43.

———. *General George Washington: A Military Life.* New York: Random House, 2005.

Lescher, Major Edward B. "How Effective Was Civil Affairs in Bosnia?" Master's thesis, Florida Atlantic University, 2001.

Lewis, J. D. *NC Patriots, 1775-1783: Their Own Words.* 3 vols. E-book published by author, 2012.

Lichtenstein, Gaston. *Louis D. Wilson, Mexican War Martyr . . . .* Richmond, VA: H. T. Ezekiel, 1911.

"The Life of the CSS *Neuse*: 'The Ram Is No Myth.'" North Carolina Historic Sites. https://historicsites.nc.sites.gov/all-sites/css%C2%A0neuse-and-gov-caswell-memorial/history/css-neuse-history/life-css-neuse.

Lipscomb, Terry W., and George Fenwick Jones. "A Hessian Map of the Stono Battlefield." *South Carolina Historical Magazine* 82, no. 4 (Oct 1981): 371-381.

Lorenzo Dow Brown and William H. Jones. Medal of Honor—Campaigns, Conflicts and Peacetime, Home of Heroes. https://homeofheroes.com/medal-of-honor-citation/campaigns-conflicts-peace-time/campaigns-conflict-and-peace-time-1826-1875/.

The Louis Berger Group. *Semper Fidelis: A Brief History of Onslow County, North Carolina, and Marine Corps Base, Camp Lejeune.* Jacksonville, NC: US Marine Corps, n.d.

Lumpkin, Henry. *From Savannah to Yorktown: The American Revolution in the South.* New York: Paragon House, 1981.

Lytle, Richard M. *The Soldiers of the First Army, 1791.* Lanham, MD: Scarecrow Press, 2004.

Maass, John R. *Defending a New Nation, 1783–1811*. Washington, DC: Center of Military History, 2013.

———. *The French and Indian War in North Carolina: The Spreading Flames of War*. Charleston, SC: History Press, 2013.

———. *Horatio Gates and the Battle of Camden—"That Unhappy Affair," August 16, 1780*. Camden, SC: Kershaw County Historical Society, 2001.

———. "North Carolina and the Seven Years' War, 1754-1758." *Military Collector and Historian* 55, no. 3 (Fall 2003): 155-160.

———. *The Petersburg and Appomattox Campaigns, 1864–1865*. Washington, DC: US Army Center of Military History, 2015.

Mac Cuarta, Brian. *Reshaping Ireland, 1550-1700: Colonization and Its Consequences*. Dublin: Four Courts Press, 2011.

Mackesy, Piers. *The War for America, 1775-1783*. London: Longmans, 1964.

Maclay, Edgar S. *A History of American Privateers*. London: Sampson, Low, Marston, 1900.

Mahon, John K. "The Carolina Brigade Sent against the Creek Indians in 1814." *North Carolina Historical Review* 28 (1951).

McAden, John W., Jr., and Chris E. Fonvielle, Jr. *Louis Froelich, Arms-Maker to the Confederacy*. Carolina Beach, NC: NC Starburst Press, 2008.

McBarron, Charles H., et al. "The American Regiment, 1740-1746." *Military Collector and Historian* 21 (1969): 84-86.

McCarley, J. Britt. *The Atlanta and Savannah Campaigns, 1864*. Washington, DC: US Army Center of Military History, 2014.

McCrady, Edward. *The History of South Carolina in the Revolution, 1780–1783*. 2 vols. New York: Macmillan, 1902.

McGuire, Thomas J. *The Philadelphia Campaign*. Vol. 1, *Brandywine and the Fall of Philadelphia*. Mechanicsburg, PA: Stackpole Books, 2006.

McIlvenna, Noeleen. *A Very Mutinous People: The Struggle for North Carolina, 1660–1713*. Chapel Hill: University of North Carolina Press, 2009.

McKinney, Gordon B. *Zeb Vance: North Carolina's Civil War Governor and Gilded Age Political Leader*. Chapel Hill: University of North Carolina Press, 2004.

Meekins, Alex Christopher. *Elizabeth City, North Carolina and the Civil War: A History of Battle and Occupation*. Charleston, SC: History Press, 2007.

"The *Memphis Belle*: American Icon." National Museum of the United States Air Force. https://www.nationalmuseum.af.mil/Visit/Museum-Exhibits/Fact-Sheets/Display/Article/1506245/the-memphis-belle-american-icon/.

Miller, Ruth M., and Ann Taylor Andrus. *Charleston's Old Exchange Building*. Charleston, SC: History Press, 2006.

Mobley, Joe A. *"War Governor of the South": North Carolina's Zeb Vance in the Confederacy*. Gainesville: University Press of Florida, 2005.

Montaño, John Patrick. *The Roots of English Colonialism in Ireland*. New York: Cambridge University Press, 2011.

Moore, David G. "Finding a Lost Spanish Fort (North Carolina's Real First Colony)." *Tar Heel Junior Historian* 47, no. 1 (Fall 2007).

Moore, Mark Anderson, Jessica A. Bandel, and Michael Hill. *The Old North State at War: The North Carolina Civil War Atlas*. Raleigh: North Carolina Department of Cultural Resources, 2015.

Moore, R. Scott. *The Civil War on the Atlantic Coast, 1861–1865*. Washington, DC: US Army Center of Military History, 2015.

Morgan, Kenneth O., ed. *The Oxford Illustrated History of Britain*. New York: Oxford University Press, 1986.

Morris, Andrew N. *The Civil War in the West, 1863*. Washington, DC: US Army Center of Military History, 2016.

Myers, Barton A. *Executing Daniel Bright: Race, Loyalty, and Guerrilla Violence in a Coastal Carolina Community, 1861–1865*. Baton Rouge: Louisiana State University Press, 2009.

———. "'A More Rigorous Style of Warfare': Wild's Raid, Guerrilla Violence, and Negotiated Neutrality in Northeastern North Carolina." In *North Carolinians in the Era of Civil War and Reconstruction*, edited by Paul D. Escott. Chapel Hill: University of North Carolina Press, 2008, 37-67.

———. *Rebels against the Confederacy: North Carolina's Unionists*. New York: Cambridge University Press, 2014.

Myers, Caron. "The Night Hydrogen Bombs Fell over North Carolina," *Our State*, May 29, 2012. https://www.ourstate.com/hydrogen-bombs-north-carolina/.

"NATO's Role in Kosovo." Updated July 15, 1999. NATO. www.nato.int/kosovo/history.htm.

Nelson, Paul David. *William Tryon and the Course of Empire*. Chapel Hill: University of North Carolina Press, 1990.

Newlin, Algie. *The Battle of Lindley's Mill*. Burlington, NC: Alamance Historical Association, 1975.

Newsome, Hampton. *The Fight for the Old North State: The Civil War in North Carolina, January-May 1864*. Lawrence: University Press of Kansas, 2019.

"'No Man Can Take Those Colors and Live': The Epic Battle of the 24th Michigan and 26th North Carolina at Gettysburg." Civil War Trust Online. www.civilwar.org/battlefields/gettysburg/gettysburg-2011/the-battle-for-herbst-woods.html.

Norris, David A. "'The Yankees Have Been Here!': The Story of Brig. Gen. Edward E. Potter's Raid on Greenville, Tarboro, and Rocky Mount, July 19–23, 1863." *North Carolina Historical Review* 73 (1996).

The North Carolina Booklet. Vol. 12, no. 1, July. Raleigh: North Carolina Society of the Daughters of the American Revolution, 1912.

"Nuclear Mishap." Essay. North Carolina State Historic Marker F-70, 2011. www.ncmarkers.com/Markers.aspx?Markerid=F-70.

Oberg, Michael L. "Lost Colonists and Lost Tribes." In *European Visions: American Voices*, online publication of the British Museum. https://www.britishmuseum.org/pdf/4-ObergLost%20Colonists%20and%20Lost%20Tribes.pdf.

O'Donnell, James H. *The Cherokees of North Carolina in the American Revolution*. Raleigh: North Carolina Division of Archives and History, 1976.

———. *Southern Indians in the American Revolution*. Knoxville: University of Tennessee Press, 1990.

Offen, Lee. *Gooch's American Regiment, 1740-1742: America's First Marines*. Jacksonville, FL: Fortis, 2010.

Oliphant, John. *Peace and War on the Anglo-Cherokee Frontier, 1756-63*. Baton Rouge: Louisiana State University Press, 2001.

Paludan, Philip Shaw. *Victims: A True Story of the Civil War*. Knoxville: University of Tennessee Press, 1981.

Pancake, John. *This Destructive War: The British Campaign in the Carolinas, 1780–1782*. Tuscaloosa: University of Alabama Press, 1985.

Paraglide. "Fort Bragg Takes Over Pope Air Force Base under BRAC," February 25, 2011. https://www.army.mil/article/52441/fort-bragg-takes-over-pope-air-force-base-under-brac.

Pargellis, Stanley, ed. *Military Affairs in North America, 1748-1765*. New York: Appleton-Century, 1936.

Parker, Mattie Erma E. "Legal Aspects of 'Culpeper's Rebellion.'" *North Carolina Historical Review* 45, no. 2 (April 1968): 111–127.

Parker, Roy, Jr. "Fort Bragg," 2006. NCpedia. https://www.ncpedia.org/fort-bragg.

Parramore, Thomas C. "The Tuscarora Ascendancy." *North Carolina Historical Review* 59, no. 4 (October 1982): 307–326.

Patterson, Gerard A. "The Death of Iverson's Brigade." *Gettysburg Magazine* 5 (July 1, 1991), www.gdg.org/Gettysburg%20Magazine/iverson.html.

"A Pearl Harbor Fact Sheet." National World War II Museum, New Orleans. https://www.census.gov/history/pdf/pearl-harbor-fact-sheet-1.pdf.

Peckham, Howard. *The Colonial Wars, 1689–1762*. Chicago: University of Chicago Press, 1964.

Perdue, Theda, and Christopher Oakley. *Native Carolinians: The Indians of North Carolina*. Raleigh: North Carolina Department of Cultural Resources, Office of Archives and History, 2010.

Phillips, R. Cody. *Bosnia-Herzegovina: The U.S. Army's Role in Peace Enforcement Operations, 1995–2004*. Washington, DC: US Army Center of Military History, 2005.

———. *Operation Joint Guardian: The U.S. Army in Kosovo*. Washington, DC: US Army Center of Military History, 2007.

———. *Operation Just Cause: The Incursion into Panama*. Washington, DC: US Army Center of Military History, 2004.

Piecuch, Jim. *Three Peoples, One King: Loyalists, Indians, and Slaves in the Revolutionary South, 1775–1782*. Columbia: University of South Carolina Press, 2013.

Pinkerton, John. *A General Collection of the Best and Most Interesting Voyages and Travels in All Parts of the World . . . .* London: Cadell and Davies, 1812.

Powell, William S., ed. *Dictionary of North Carolina Biography*. 6 vols. Chapel Hill: University of North Carolina Press, 1979–1996.

———. *Encyclopedia of North Carolina*. Chapel Hill: University of North Carolina Press, 2006.

———. *North Carolina through Four Centuries*. Chapel Hill: University of North Carolina Press, 1989.

———. *The War of the Regulation and the Battle of Alamance, May 16, 1771*. Raleigh Division of Archives and History, North Carolina Department of Cultural Resources, 1975.

"President John F. Kennedy on the Cuban Missile Crisis," October 22, 1962. Great Speeches Collection, The History Place. www.historyplace.com/speeches/jfk-cuban.htm.

Price, Eugene. "Seymour Johnson Air Force Base," 2006. NCpedia. https://www.ncpedia.org/seymour-johnson-air-force-base.

Quinn, David Beers. *Set Fair for Roanoke: Voyages and Colonies, 1584–1606*. Chapel Hill: University of North Carolina Press, 1985.

Rable, George C. *Fredericksburg! Fredericksburg!* Chapel Hill: University of North Carolina Press, 2002.

Raines, Edgar F., and Richard W. Stewart. *Operation Urgent Fury: The Invasion of Grenada, 1983*. Washington, DC: US Army Center of Military History, 2008.

Rankin, Hugh F. *The Moore's Creek Bridge Campaign*. Conshohocken, PA: Eastern National Park and Monument Association, 1986.

———. *The North Carolina Continentals*. Chapel Hill: University of North Carolina Press, 1971.

———. *North Carolina in the American Revolution*. Raleigh: North Carolina Division of Archives and History, 1959.

———. *The Pirates of Colonial North Carolina*. Raleigh: North Carolina Division of Archives and History, 1960.

———. *Upheaval in Albemarle: The Story of Culpeper's Rebellion, 1675–1689*. Raleigh: Carolina Charter Tercentenary Commission, 1962.

Reardon, Carol, and Tom Vossler. *The Gettysburg Campaign, June–July 1863*. Washington, DC: US Army Center of Military History, 2013.

Reese, George, ed. *The Official Papers of Francis Fauquier*. 3 vols. Charlottesville: University Press of Virginia, 1981.

Reid, Richard. "Raising the African Brigade: Early Black Recruitment in Civil War North Carolina." *North Carolina Historical Review* 70 (1993): 266-301.

Rhea, Gordon C. *The Battle of the Wilderness, May 5–6, 1864*. Baton Rouge: Louisiana State University Press, 1994.

Rhodehamel, John, comp. *The American Revolution: Writings from the War of Independence*. New York: Library of America, 2001.

Richards, Constance E. "Contact and Conflict." *American Archaeology* 12, no. 1 (Spring 2008).

Rights, Douglas L. *The American Indian in North Carolina*. Winston-Salem, NC: John F. Blair, 1957.

Robinson, Blackwell P. *The Five Royal Governors of North Carolina, 1729-1775.* Raleigh: Carolina Charter Tercentenary Commission, 1963.

Roosevelt, Franklin D. "The Great Arsenal of Democracy." American Rhetoric: Top 100 Speeches. https://americanrhetoric.com/speeches/fdrarsenalofdemocracy.html.

Roster of Soldiers from North Carolina in the American Revolution. Durham: North Carolina Daughters of the American Revolution, 1932.

Rufus Geddie Herring. Medal of Honor—World War II, Home of Heroes. https://homeofheroes.com/medal-of-honor-citation/world-war-ii-medal-of-honor-recipients/.

Russell, David L. *The American Revolution in the Southern Colonies.* Jefferson, NC: McFarland, 2000.

Sauers, Richard A. *The Burnside Expedition in North Carolina: A Succession of Honorable Victories.* Dayton, OH: Morningside, 1996.

Saunders, William L., and Walter Clark, eds. *The Colonial and State Records of North Carolina.* 26 vols. Raleigh: P. M. Hale, 1886–1907.

Schlosser, Nicholas J. *The Surge, 2007–2008.* Washington, DC: US Army Center of Military History, 2017.

Schubert, Frank N., and Theresa L. Kraus, eds. *The Whirlwind War: The United States Army in Operations Desert Shield and Desert Storm.* Washington, DC: US Army Center of Military History, 1995.

Sears, Stephen W. *Chancellorsville.* Boston: Houghton Mifflin, 1996.

———. *Gettysburg.* Boston: Houghton Mifflin, 2003.

———. *To the Gates of Richmond: The Peninsula Campaign.* New York: Ticknor and Fields, 1992.

Sedgwick, Jessica. "January 1961: Bombs over Goldsboro." North Carolina Miscellany (blog), UNC Library, January 1, 2008. https://blogs.lib.unc.edu/ncm/index.php/2008/01/01/this_month_jan_1961/.

Seven Pines Battle Summary. American Battlefield Protection Program, National Park Service. https://www.nps.gov/abpp/battles/va014/htm.

Siry, Steven E. *Liberty's Fallen Generals: Leadership and Sacrifice in the American War of Independence.* Washington, DC: Potomac Books, 2012.

Sitterson, Joseph Carlyle. *The Secession Movement in North Carolina.* Chapel Hill: University of North Carolina Press, 1939.

Smith, John David, ed. *Black Soldiers in Blue: African American Troops in the Civil War Era.* Chapel Hill: University of North Carolina Press, 2002.

Smith, Mark A., and Wade Sokolosky. *"No Such Army Since the Days of Julius Caesar": Sherman's Carolinas Campaign from Fayetteville to Averasboro, March 1865.* El Dorado Hills, CA: Savas Beatie, 2017.

Smith, Williams S., Jr. "Culpeper's Rebellion," April 1990. http://www.carolana.com/Carolina/Noteworthy_Events/culpepersrebellion.html.

Sokolosky, Wade, and Mark A. Smith. *"To Prepare for Sherman's Coming": The Battle of Wise's Forks, March 1865.* El Dorado Hills, CA: Savas Beatie, 2015.

"Staff Sergeant Robert James Miller, Medal of Honor, Operation Enduring Freedom." Army.mil Features. https://www.army.mil/medalofhonor/miller/profile.html.

Stagg, John Charles Anderson. *Mr. Madison's War: Politics, Diplomacy and Warfare in the Early American Republic, 1783-1830.* Princeton, NJ: Princeton University Press, 1983.

Stanton, Shelby L. *Vietnam Order of Battle.* Washington, DC: US News Books, 1981.

Steelman, Joseph F. *North Carolina's Role in the Spanish-American War.* Raleigh: North Carolina Department of Cultural Resources, 1975.

Stevens, S. K., et al., eds. *The Papers of Henry Bouquet.* 6 vols. Harrisburg: Pennsylvania Historical and Museum Commission, 1951.

Stewart, Richard W., ed. *American Military History.* Vol. 1, *The United States Army and the Forging of a Nation, 1775–1917.* Washington, DC: US Army Center of Military History, 2004.

———. *American Military History.* Vol. 2, *The United States Army in a Global Era, 1917–2008.* Washington, DC: US Army Center of Military History, 2010.

———. *The United States Army in Afghanistan: Operation Enduring Freedom, October 2001–March 2002.* Washington, DC: US Army Center of Military History, 2005.

———. *The United States Army in Somalia, 1992–1994.* Washington, DC: US Army Center of Military History, 2002.

Stick, David. *Roanoke Island: The Beginnings of English America.* Chapel Hill: University of North Carolina Press, 1993.

Stinson, Craig M. "*North Carolina*, USS," 2006. NCpedia. https://www.ncpedia.org/north-carolina-uss.

Stoesen, Alexander R. "Persian Gulf War," 2006. NCpedia. https://www.ncpedia.org/persian-gulf-war.

"Strategic Arms Limitations Talks/Treaty (SALT) I and II." Office of the Historian, Bureau of Public Affairs, US Department of State. https://www.state.gov/milestones/1969-1976/salt.

Stumpf, Vernon O. "Josiah Martin and His Search for Success: The Road to North Carolina." *North Carolina Historical Review* 53 (1976): 55-79.

———. *Josiah Martin: The Last Royal Governor of North Carolina.* Raleigh: Carolina Academic Press, 1986.

Swisher, James. *The Revolutionary War in the Southern Backcountry.* Gretna, LA: Pelican, 2007.

Sword, Wiley. *George Washington's Indian War: The Struggle for the Old Northwest, 1790–1795.* Norman: University of Oklahoma Press, 1993.

Taaffe, Stephen. *The Philadelphia Campaign, 1777–1778.* Lawrence: University Press of Kansas, 2003.

Tagg, Larry. "The Generals of Gettysburg: The Leaders of America's Greatest Battle." Roger D. Linder. www.rocemabra.com/~roger/tagg/generals/index.html.

Tomaszycki, Corporal Scott L. "Cherry Point Pilots Played Pivotal Role in Cuban Missile Crisis," October 30, 2012. Press release, Marine Corps Air Station Cherry Point. https://www.cherrypoint.marines.mil/News/Article/525436/cherry-point-pilots-played-pivotal-role-in-cuban-missile-crisis/.

Troxler, Carole Watterson. *Farming Dissenters: The Regulator Movement in Piedmont North Carolina*. Raleigh: North Carolina Office of Archives and History, 2011.

———. *The Loyalist Experience in North Carolina*. Raleigh: North Carolina Division of Archives and History, 1975.

Tucker, Spencer. *Rise and Fight Again: The Life of Nathanael Greene*. Wilmington, DE: ISI Books, 2009.

Umfleet, LeRae Sikes. *A Day of Blood: The 1898 Wilmington Race Riot*. Raleigh: North Carolina Office of Archives and History, 2009.

Urwin, Gregory. *The United States Infantry: An Illustrated History, 1775–1918*. Norman: University of Oklahoma Press, 1988.

Vigneras, L. A. "A Spanish Discovery of North Carolina in 1655." *North Carolina Historical Review* 46 (1969).

Vrabel, Corporal Mike. "Ten Years Later: Base CG Recalls Gulf War." Press release, January 18, 2001, US Marine Corps. https://www.lejeune.marines.mil/News/Article/511572/ten-years-later-base-cg-recalls-gulf-war/.

Waddell, Alfred M. *A Colonial Officer and his Times, 1754-1773*. Raleigh, NC: Edwards & Broughton, 1890.

Walbert, David. "Ensign Worth Bagley," n.d. NCpedia. https://www.ncpedia.org/anchor/ensign-worth-bagley.

———. "The Third North Carolina Regiment," n.d. NCpedia. https://www.ncpedia.org/anchor/third-north-carolina.

Wallace, Lee A., Jr. "Raising a Volunteer Regiment for Mexico, 1846–47." *North Carolina Historical Review* 35, no. 1 (January 1958).

Ward, Harry M. *"Unite or Die": lntercolony Relations 1690–1763*. Port Washington, NY: Kennikat Press, 1971.

Weaver, Jeffrey Craig. "November 1864–January 1865—Playing Hell in Tennessee." In "58th North Carolina Infantry, Confederate States Army" (unpublished manuscript, 1997), 26th North Carolina Regiment. http://www.26nc.org/History/58th-History/58th%20history.html.

Weber, David J. *The Spanish Frontier in North America*. New Haven, CT: Yale University Press, 1994.

Wegner, Ansley Herring. *Phantom Pain: North Carolina's Artificial Limbs Program for Confederate Veterans*. Raleigh: North Carolina Department of Cultural Resources, 2004.

———. "William McBryar," 2006. NCpedia. https://www.ncpedia.org/william-mcbrayer.

Wert, Jeffrey D. "Closing the Back Door: The Shenandoah Valley Campaign of 1864." American Battlefield Trust. https://battlefields.org/learn/articles/closing-back-door.

West, Billy Kurtz, Jr. "Ector's Brigade in the Civil War." Master's thesis, Texas Tech University, 1987.

Willcox, William B. *The American Rebellion: Sir Henry Clinton's Narrative of His Campaigns, 1775–1782.* New Haven, CT: Yale University Press, 1954.

———. *Portrait of a General: Sir Henry Clinton in the War of Independence.* New York: Alfred A. Knopf, 1964.

William David Halyburton, Jr. and Jacklyn Harold Lucas. Medal of Honor—World War II, Home of Heroes. https://homeofheroes.com/medal-of-honor-citation/world-war-ii-medal-of-honor-recipients/.

"William McBryar, First Lieutenant, United States Army." Arlington National Cemetery. www.arlingtoncemetery.net/williamm.net.

William McBryar. Medal of Honor—Campaigns, Conflicts and Peacetime, Home of Heroes. https://homeofheroes.com/medal-of-honor-citation/campaigns-conflicts-peace-time/campaigns-conflict-and-peace-time-1826-1875/.

Williams, Otho Holland. "A Narrative of the Campaign of 1780." In *Sketches of the Life and Correspondence of Nathanael Greene,* vol. 1. Compiled by William Johnson. Charleston, SC: A. E. Miller, 1822.

Williford, Jo Ann. "Vietnam War," 2006. NCpedia. https://www.ncpedia.org/vietnam-war.

Wilson, David. *The Southern Strategy: Britain's Conquest of South Carolina and Georgia, 1775-1780.* Columbia: University of South Carolina Press, 2005.

Wineman, Bradford A. *The Chancellorsville Campaign, January–May 1863.* Washington, DC: US Army Center of Military History, 2013.

Winkler, John F. *Wabash 1791: St. Clair's Defeat.* Oxford, UK: Osprey, 2011.

Wise, Stephen R. *Lifeline of the Confederacy: Blockade Running during the Civil War.* Columbia: University of South Carolina Press, 1988.

Wittenberg, Eric J. *The Battle of Monroe's Crossroads and the Civil War's Final Campaign.* New York: Savas Beatie, 2006.

Wright, Robert K. *The Continental Army.* Washington, DC: US Army Center of Military History, 1989.

Acknowledgments

We'd like to thank Jessica A. Bandel, Peter Cozzens, Scott Douglas, Sherry Dowdy, Chris E. Fonvielle, Jr., Philip Gerard, Joan Halford, Michael C. Hardy, Chris J. Hartley, Michael Hill, Perry D. Jamieson, Mark A. Moore, Hampton Newsome, Mark A. Smith, Wade Sokolosky, Eric J. Wittenberg, our colleagues at the US Army Center of Military History, and the staff at Bentonville Battlefield State Historic Site: site manager Donny Taylor, assistant site manager Derrick Brown, and programs coordinator Amanda Brantley.

Index